Mastering Service Mesh

Enhance, secure, and observe cloud-native applications with Istio, Linkerd, and Consul

Anjali Khatri
Vikram Khatri

BIRMINGHAM - MUMBAI

Mastering Service Mesh

Copyright © 2020 Packt Publishing

Commissioning Editor: Vijin Boricha
Acquisition Editor: Meeta Rajani
Content Development Editor: Carlton Borges
Senior Editor: Rahul Dsouza
Technical Editor: Dinesh Pawar
Copy Editor: Safis Editing
Project Coordinator: Neil Dmello
Proofreader: Safis Editing
Indexer: Priyanka Dhadke
Production Designer: Nilesh Mohite

First published: March 2020

Production reference: 1270320

Published by Packt Publishing Ltd.
Livery Place
35 Livery Street
Birmingham
B3 2PB, UK.

ISBN 978-1-78961-579-1

www.packt.com

Packt.com

Subscribe to our online digital library for full access to over 7,000 books and videos, as well as industry leading tools to help you plan your personal development and advance your career. For more information, please visit our website.

Why subscribe?

- Spend less time learning and more time coding with practical eBooks and Videos from over 4,000 industry professionals

- Improve your learning with Skill Plans built especially for you

- Get a free eBook or video every month

- Fully searchable for easy access to vital information

- Copy and paste, print, and bookmark content

Did you know that Packt offers eBook versions of every book published, with PDF and ePub files available? You can upgrade to the eBook version at www.packt.com and as a print book customer, you are entitled to a discount on the eBook copy. Get in touch with us at customercare@packtpub.com for more details.

At www.packt.com, you can also read a collection of free technical articles, sign up for a range of free newsletters, and receive exclusive discounts and offers on Packt books and eBooks.

Foreword

This book provides an understanding of modern service mesh providers for building applications without needing to build traffic management, telemetry, and security solutions. Advanced cloud-native polyglot application developers need to focus only the business logic. The service mesh takes care of the Operations from the DevOps using automation that does not require any changes in the applications. Thanks to Anjali and Vikram for providing hands-on examples to understand these new technologies in an easy to understand fashion.

Dinesh Nirmal
Vice President
Data and AI Development
IBM Cloud and Cognitive Software
Silicon Valley Lab,
San Jose, CA, USA

The embracing of microservices by the world of business is critical as they enable significantly faster deployment of new services and quick adaption of existing services with continuous availability. Microservices platforms are going through rapid change and engineers must keep up to avoid skill obsolescence.

Capabilities such as observability and canary are key in churning applications rapidly while keeping a large microservice mesh continually available. The mesh of microservices spans businesses and their partners, where they collectively provide services to their customers, and often span multi-cloud. Common business services, such as security and single identity management have become global requirements, which has fundamentally changed the design and operation of platforms. The mesh assumes far more control as it replaces troubled microservices nodes quickly with alternatives to provide continual availability.

Keeping up with such rapid technology change at a hands-on level is a must. This book manages to cover the high-level concepts and then maps them to actual tasks that engineers need to perform to design, deploy, and operate these systems.

Hamid Pirahesh

IBM Fellow, ACM Fellow

The concepts around cloud-native development continue to mature and real use cases grow in number across a variety of industries. However, cloud native approaches are only beginning to have significant widespread impact on mission critical systems, or what some might call systems of record. This is the next big step forward for cloud-native applications.

Mission critical applications demand high levels of availability, resiliency, security, and visibility that in turn place strong demands on the underlying supporting platform. While there are many solid advantages to the cloud-native approach, the fact is that there are new and more things to be managed, and many new situations will be encountered.

A service mesh becomes a consistent and simplified way of dealing with many of those things that accompany the notion of a cloud-native mission critical system. While there are other approaches, those that are consistent with Kubernetes and based on open source will have the most significant impact and be the most easily adopted.

Mastering Service Mesh is a good book to read for an in-depth understanding of the concept of service meshes, as well as to gain detailed insights into the various service mesh offerings available today. Concrete examples throughout the book and accompanying samples help bring these topics into focus and demonstrate the concepts in action. This book is a necessary addition to the library of all those who are involved in creating, evolving, and operating cloud-native production environments that support cloud-native applications.

Eric Herness

IBM Fellow
CTO, Cloud Engagement Hub

Contributors

About the authors

Anjali Khatri is an enterprise cloud architect at DivvyCloud, advancing the cloud-native growth for the company by helping customers maintain security and compliance for resources running on AWS, Google, Azure, and other cloud providers. She is a technical leader in the adoption, scaling, and maturity of DivvyCloud's capabilities. In collaboration with product and engineering, she works with customer success around feature request architecture, case studies, account planning, and continuous solution delivery.

Prior to Divvycloud, Anjali worked at IBM and Merlin. She has 9+ years of professional experience in program management for software development, open source analytics sales, and application performance consulting.

Vikram Khatri is the chief architect of Cloud Pak for Data System at IBM. Vikram has 20 years of experience leading and mentoring high-performing, cross-functional teams to deliver high-impact, best-in-class technology solutions. Vikram is a visionary thought leader when it comes to architecting large-scale transformational solutions from monolithic to cloud-native applications that include data and AI. He is an industry-leading technical expert with a track record of leveraging deep technical expertise to develop solutions, resulting in revenues exceeding $1 billion over 14 years, and is also a technology subject matter expert in cloud-native technologies who frequently speaks at industry conferences and trade shows.

This book is written by a daughter-father team.

About the reviewers

Debasish Banerjee, Ph.D., is an executive architect who is a seasoned thought leader, hands-on architect, and practitioner of cutting-edge technologies with a proven track record of advising and working with Fortune 500 customers in the USA, Europe, and Asia with various IBM products and strategies. He is presently leading the collaborative development effort with IBM Research for Mono2Micro, an AI-based utility for transforming monoliths to microservices. Application modernization, microservice generation, and deployment are his current areas of interest. Debasish obtained his Ph.D. in combinator-based functional programming languages.

> *I fondly remember many discussions, both technical and otherwise, with Eric Herness, IBM Fellow, Danny Mace, VP, Dr. Ruchir Puri, IBM Fellow, Garth Tschetter, Director, Lorraine Johnson, Director, Mark Borowski, Directors and many others. The late Manilal Banerjee, my father, would have been very proud to see my contribution. Cheenar Banerjee and Neehar Banerjee, my daughters, as well as being my pride and joy, are sources of inspiration for me.*

Cole Calistra is an accomplished hands-on technology leader with over 20 years of diverse industry experience that includes leading fast-growing SaaS start-ups, senior architecture roles within Fortune 500 giants, and acting as a technical adviser to a mix of start-ups and established businesses. He is currently CTO at LEON Health Science. Prior to this, he served as a founding team member and CTO of the SaaS-based facial recognition and emotion analysis API provider, Kairos.

His credentials include multiple professional level certifications at both AWS and GCP, and he is currently pursuing an MS in computer science at the Georgia Institute of Technology. Cole is the proud father of two daughters, Abigail and Jill.

Jimmy Song reviewed the section on Linkerd. He is a developer advocate on cloud native and a co-founder of the ServiceMesher community. Jimmy currently works for Ant Financial.

Huabing Zhao reviewed the section on Consul. He has been involved in the information technology industry for almost 20 years, most of it at ZTE, where he works on telecommunication management systems and network function virtualization. Currently, he is a software expert at ZTE, a member of Istio, and a PTL of ONAP.

Packt is searching for authors like you

If you're interested in becoming an author for Packt, please visit `authors.packtpub.com` and apply today. We have worked with thousands of developers and tech professionals, just like you, to help them share their insight with the global tech community. You can make a general application, apply for a specific hot topic that we are recruiting an author for, or submit your own idea.

Table of Contents

Section 5: Learning about Linkerd through Examples

Preface

This book is about mastering service mesh. It assumes that you have prior knowledge of Docker and Kubernetes. As a developer, knowing **Service-Oriented Architecture (SOA)** and **Enterprise Service Bus (ESB)** patterns will be beneficial, but not mandatory.

Service mesh is the new buzzword and a relatively new concept that started in 2017, and so it does not have much history behind it. Service mesh is the evolution of already existing technologies with further improvements.

The first service mesh implementation emerged as Istio 0.1 in May 2017. Istio is a combination of different technologies from IBM, Google, and Lyft, and hence, Istio and service mesh were used interchangeably to mean the same thing.

Envoy (which originated at Lyft and is now open source) is a graduate project from the **Cloud Native Computing Foundation (CNCF)** and is a core part of Istio. Envoy, as a reverse proxy next to a microservice, forms the core of a service mesh.

William Morgan, the creator of Linkerd, which is an incubating project at CNCF, coined the term *service mesh*. The term *service mesh* was boosted when it was used prominently in KubeCon and at the CloudNativeCon 2018 conference in Copenhagen by Jason McGee, an IBM Fellow.

A service mesh is a framework on top of a cloud-native microservices application. Istio, Linkerd, and Consul are all service mesh implementations.

Linkerd is an open source network proxy and referred to as a service mesh.

Consul is another open source project backed by Hasicorp and is referred to as a service mesh, but it uses different architecture.

Who this book is for

This book covers the operation part of DevOps, and so is most suited for operational professionals who are responsible for managing microservices-based applications.

Anyone interested in starting out on a career as an operations professional (the second part of DevOps) will benefit from reading this book. This book is about managing microservices applications when in the production environment from the operations perspective.

Even if you do not have experience in developing microservices applications, you can take the role of an operations professional or become a **Site Reliability Engineer (SRE)**. A knowledge of Kubernetes and Docker is a prerequisite, but it is not necessary to know SOA and ESB in depth.

What this book covers

In this book, we are focusing on Istio, Linkerd, and Consul from the implementation perspective.

A service mesh implementation, such as Istio, takes away some of the responsibilities of developers and puts them in a dedicated layer so that they are consumable without writing any code. In other words, it frees up developers so that they can focus on business logic and places more responsibility in the hands of operational professionals.

This book is not about developing microservices, and so does not cover the persona of a developer.

Chapter 1, *Monolithic Versus Microservices*, provides a high-level overview of monolithic versus microservices-based applications. The evolution of service-oriented architecture to microservices-based architecture became possible as a result of distributed computing through Kubernetes.

Chapter 2, *Cloud-Native Applications*, provides an overview of building cloud-native applications using container-based environments to develop applications built with services that can scale independently. This chapter explains the ease of **Development (Dev)** using the polyglot app through containerization and the assumption of further responsibilities by **Operations (Ops)** due to the decoupling of services.

Chapter 3, *Service Mesh Architecture*, covers the evolution of the term *service mesh* and its origin. It provides an overview of the service mesh as a decoupling agent between Dev (provider) and Ops (consumer) and explains basic and advanced service communication through smart endpoints and trust between microservices.

Chapter 4, *Service Mesh Providers*, provides an overview of the three open source service mesh providers – Istio, Linkerd, and Consul.

Chapter 5, *Service Mesh Interface and SPIFFE*, provides an introduction to the evolving service mesh interface specification. The SPIFFE specification offers secure naming for the services running in a Kubernetes environment.

Chapter 6, *Building Your Own Kubernetes Environment*, explains how, in order to learn about service meshes with any of the three providers throughout this book, having a development environment is essential. There are choices when it comes to spinning a Kubernetes cluster in a public cloud, and that requires an upfront cost. This chapter provides a straightforward way to build your single-node Kubernetes environment so that you can practice the examples using your laptop or MacBook.

Chapter 7, *Understanding the Istio Service Mesh*, shows the architecture of the Istio control plane and its features and functions.

Chapter 8, *Installing the Demo Application*, shows how to install the demo application for Istio.

Chapter 9, *Installing Istio*, shows the different ways of installing Istio using separate profiles to suit the end goal of a service mesh.

Chapter 10, *Exploring Istio Traffic Management Capabilities*, shows Istio's features of traffic routing from the perspectives of canary testing, A/B testing, traffic splitting, shaping, and conditional routing.

Chapter 11, *Exploring Istio Security Features*, explores how to secure service-to-service communication using mTLS, securing gateways, and using Istio Citadel as a certificate authority.

Chapter 12, *Enabling Istio Policy Controls*, explores of enabling network controls, rate limits, and the enforcement of quotas without having to change the application.

Chapter 13, *Exploring Istio Telemetry Features*, looks at using observability features in Prometheus, Grafana, and Kiali to display collected metrics and service-to-service communication.

Chapter 14, *Understanding the Linkerd Service Mesh*, shows the architecture of Linkerd from the control plane perspective to demonstrate its features and functions.

Chapter 15, *Installing Linkerd*, shows how to install Linkerd in Kubernetes, how to set up a Linkerd demo emoji application, and how to inject a sidecar proxy.

Chapter 16, *Exploring the Reliability Features of Linkerd*, goes through Linkerd traffic reliability features and covers load balancing, retries, traffic splitting, timeout circuit breaking, and dynamic request routing.

Chapter 17, *Exploring the Security Features of Linkerd,* explains the process of setting up mTLS without any configuration by default and gradual installation as regards the certificate creation process.

Chapter 18, *Exploring the Observability Features of Linkerd,* details the Linkerd dashboard and CLI, which provides some insights into the service mesh for live traffic, success rates, routes, and latencies.

Chapter 19, *Understanding the Consul Service Mesh,* shows the architecture of Consul from the control plane perspective to demonstrate its features and functions.

Chapter 20, *Installing Consul,* shows how to install Consul in Kubernetes and VMs/bare-metal machines.

Chapter 21, *Exploring the Service Discovery Features of Consul,* shows a demo application explaining Consul service discovery, key/value stores, ACLs, intentions, and monitoring/metrics collection. We explain the integration process of external services running in a non-Kubernetes environment.

Chapter 22, *Exploring Traffic Management in Consul,* shows the integration of Consul using the open source project Ambassador. It shows traffic management capabilities such as rate limits, self-service routing, testing, and enabling end-to-end TLS through the use of an Envoy sidecar proxy.

Useful terms

This book contains a number of specific terms that you might not have come across before, and here is a brief glossary to help you while reading this book:

- **Ingress gateway**: In Kubernetes, an ingress is an object that allows external access to internal microservices. An ingress is a collection of rules to route external traffic to services inside the Kubernetes cluster. In Istio, the ingress gateway sits at the edge of the cluster and allows the creation of multiple ingress gateways to configure access to the cluster.
- **Egress gateway**: The egress gateway is a feature of Istio that allows external access to the microservices running inside a Kubernetes cluster. This gateway also sits on the edge of the service mesh.
- **Polyglot programming**: This is the practice of writing code in multiple languages for services. For example, we can write different microservices in different languages, such as Go, Java, Ruby, and Python, and yet they can still communicate with one another.

- **A/B testing**: This is testing between two versions (A and B) of a microservice while both are in production.
- **Canary release**: This entails moving faster for cloud-native applications. Canary release is about a new version of a microservice available to a small subset of users in a production environment along with the old version. Once the new version can be used with confidence, the old version can be taken out of service without any ensuing disruption.
- **Circuit breaker**: A failure of communication between microservices may occur due to latency or faults. The circuit breaker breaks the connection between microservices following the detection of latency/faults. The incoming traffic then reroutes to other microservices to avoid partial or cascading failures. The circuit breaker helps to attain load balancing and to prevent the continual overloading of a particular system.

To get the most out of this book

You will get the most out of this book by building an environment yourself and practicing with it using the examples provided herein.

If you have not used Kubernetes before, it is best to follow the example of building your Kubernetes environment on your Windows laptop or MacBook. This book is not about Kubernetes, but having a Kubernetes environment is a must. We explain how to build your Kubernetes environment in Chapter 6, *Building Your Own Kubernetes Environment*.

If you are comfortable with any other Kubernetes provider, you can take and test the examples in a Kubernetes environment of your choosing.

Since technology is evolving rapidly, we have a GitHub repository, which you can refer to for the latest changes.

You can practice examples given in this book either on a Windows or macOS platform. The hardware/software requirements are as under. Refer to Chapter 6, *Building Your Own Kubernetes Environment* for further details.

Software/Hardware covered in the book	OS Requirements
Workstation/Laptop or MacBook with a minimum 16 GB RAM / Intel Core i7 or higher, a minimum of 512 GB SSD	Windows 10 or macOS Pro (2015 or later)
VMware Player V15.x or VMware Fusion 11.x	Windows or macOS
7z Software for Windows or Free 7z Unarchiver for macOS	Windows or macOS

If you are using the digital version of this book, we advise you to type the code yourself or access the code via the GitHub repository (link available in the next section). Doing so will help you avoid any potential errors related to copy/pasting of code.

Download the example code files

You can download the example code files for this book from your account at `www.packt.com`. If you purchased this book elsewhere, you can visit `www.packt.com/support` and register to have the files emailed directly to you.

You can download the code files by following these steps:

1. Log in or register at `www.packt.com`.
2. Select the **Support** tab.
3. Click on **Code Downloads**.
4. Enter the name of the book in the **Search** box and follow the onscreen instructions.

Once you download the file, please make sure that you unzip or extract the folder using the latest version of:

- 7-Zip for Windows
- Free 7z Unarchiver for Mac

The code bundle for the book is on GitHub at `https://github.com/PacktPublishing/Mastering-Service-Mesh`.

Note: For the implementation chapters throughout this book, we recommend our readers to pull all the necessary source code files from `https://github.com/servicemeshbook/` for Istio, Linkerd, and Consul. We will have chapter-specific repository links, with clear instructions regarding all GitHub repository exports. Both `Mastering-Service-Mesh` and `servicemeshbook` GitHub page(s) will continue to stay active and up to date.

We also have other code bundles from our rich catalog of books and videos available at `https://github.com/PacktPublishing/`. Check them out!

Download the color images

We also provide a PDF file that has color images of the screenshots/diagrams used in this book. You can download it here: `http://www.packtpub.com/sites/default/files/ downloads/9781789615791_ColorImages.pdf`.

Conventions used

There are several text conventions used throughout this book.

`CodeInText`: Indicates code words in a text, database table names, folder names, filenames, file extensions, pathnames, dummy URLs, user input, and Twitter handles. Here is an example: "Optionally, you can configure a separate disk to mount `/var/lib/docker` and restart Docker."

A block of code is as follows:

```
apiVersion: authentication.istio.io/v1alpha1
kind: Policy
metadata:
  name: SVC-A-mTLS-disable
  namespace: ns1
spec:
  targets:
  - name: Service-A
  peers:
  - mtls:
      mode: DISABLE
```

When we wish to draw your attention to a particular part of a code block, the relevant lines shows in bold:

```
peers:
- mtls:
    mode: DISABLE
```

Any command-line input or output shows as follows:

```
$ kubectl get pods
$ istioctl proxy
```

Bold: Indicates a new term, an important word, or words that you see on screen. For example, words in menus or dialog boxes appear in the text like this. Here is an example: "On the left-hand menu under **Workloads**, click **Pods**."

 Warnings or important notes appear like this.

 Tips and tricks appear like this.

Errata

The technology landscape is evolving rapidly. When we started writing this book, the Istio release was 1.0.3, this book's current Istio release is 1.3.5. It is a similar case with Linkerd and Consul. The time to market is of the essence and these three open-source projects show a true **CICD** (short for **Continuous Improvement and Continuous Delivery**) approach using agile DevOps tools.

In order to run commands and scripts from this book, stick to the version used herein. However, we will update our GitHub repository for this book at `https://github.com/servicemeshbook` with newer versions that will be released in the future. You can switch to the newer branch in each repository for updated scripts and commands.

We were conscientious and implemented hands-on testing during development for all three service meshes and it is likely that some issues may remain. We suggest that you open issues that you encounter while going through the book. Use these links to open an issue for any errata and bugs:

- **Istio**: `https://github.com/servicemeshbook/istio/issues`
- **Linkerd**: `https://github.com/servicemeshbook/linkerd/issues`
- **Consul**: `https://github.com/servicemeshbook/consul/issues`

Your feedback is important to us and you may open an issue for suggestions and any further proposed improvements in relation to the above-mentioned service meshes.

Get in touch

Feedback from our readers is always welcome.

General feedback: If you have questions about any aspect of this book, mention the book title in the subject of your message and email us at customercare@packtpub.com.

Errata: Although we have taken every care to ensure the accuracy of our content, mistakes do happen. If you find an error in this book, we appreciate it if you report this to us. Please visit https://www.packtpub.com/support/errata, select the book, click on the Errata Submission Form link, and enter the details.

Piracy: If you come across any illegal copies of our works in any form on the internet, please report to us with the location address or website name. Please contact us at copyright@packt.com with a link to the material.

If you are interested in becoming an author: If there is a topic that you have expertise in, and you are interested in either writing or contributing to a book, please visit authors.packtpub.com.

Reviews

Please leave a review. Once you have read and used this book, please leave a review on the site you purchased from. Your comments help us to improve upon the future revisions. If you like the book, leave a positive response for other potential readers to make an informed decision. We at Packt can understand what you think about our products, and our authors can see your feedback on their book. Thank you!

For more information about Packt, please visit packt.com.

Section 1: Cloud-Native Application Management

In this section, you will look at high-level artifact of cloud-native applications in order to understand the service mesh architecture.

This section contains the following chapters:

- Chapter 1, *Monolithic Versus Microservices*
- Chapter 2, *Cloud-Native Applications*

1
Monolithic Versus Microservices

The purpose of this book is to walk you through the service mesh architecture. We will cover three main open source service mesh providers: Istio, Linkerd, and Consul. First of all, we will talk about how the evolution of technology led to Service Mesh. In this chapter, we will cover the application development journey from monolithic to microservices.

The technology landscape that fueled the growth of the monolithic framework is based on the technology stack that became available 20+ years ago. As hardware and software virtualization improved significantly, a new wave of innovation started with the adoption of microservices in 2011 by Netflix, Amazon, and other companies. This trend started by redesigning monolithic applications into small and independent microservices.

Before we get started on monolithic versus microservices, let's take a step back and review what led to where we are today before the inception of microservices. This chapter will go through the brief evolution of early computer machines, hardware virtualization, software virtualization, and transitioning from monolithic to microservices-based applications. We will try to summarize the journey from the early days to where we are today.

In this chapter, we will cover the following topics:

- Early computer machines
- Monolithic applications
- Microservices applications

Early computer machines

IBM launched its first commercial computer (`https://ibm.biz/Bd294n`), the IBM 701, in 1953, which was the most powerful high-speed electronic calculator of that time. Further progression of the technology produced mainframes, and that revolution was started in the mid-1950s (`https://ibm.biz/Bd294p`).

Even before co-founding Intel in 1968 with Robert Noyce, Gordon Moore espoused his theory of Moore's Law (`https://intel.ly/2IY5qLU`) in 1965, which states that the number of transistors incorporated in a chip will approximately double every 24 months. Exponential growth still continues to this day, though this trend may not continue for long.

IBM created its first official VM product called VM/370 in 1972 (`http://www.vm.ibm.com/history`), followed by hardware virtualization on the Intel/AMD platform in 2005 and 2006. Monolithic applications were the only choice on early computing machines.

Early machines ran only one operating system. As time passed and machines grew in size, a need to run multiple operating systems by slicing the machines into smaller virtual machines led to the virtualization of hardware.

Hardware virtualization

Hardware virtualization led to the proliferation of virtual machines in data centers. Greg Kalinsky, EVP and CIO of Geico, in his keynote address to the IBM Think 2019 conference, mentioned the use of 70,000 virtual machines. The management of virtual machines required a different set of tools. In this area, VMware was very successful in the Intel market, whereas IBM's usage of the **Hardware Management Console** (**HMC**) was prolific in POWER for creating **Logical Partitions** (**LPARs**), or the PowerVM. Hardware virtualization had its own overheads, and it has been very popular for running multiple operating systems machines on the same physical machine.

Multiple monolithic applications have different OS requirements and languages, and it was possible to run the runtime on the same hardware but using multiple virtual machines. During this period of hardware virtualization, work on enterprise applications using the **Service-Oriented Architecture** (**SOA**) and the **Enterprise Service Bus** (**ESB**) started to evolve, which led to large monolithic applications.

Software virtualization

The next wave of innovation started with software virtualization with the use of containerization technology. Though not new, software virtualization started to get serious traction when it became easier to start adopting through tools. Docker was an early pioneer in this space in order to make software virtualization available to general IT professionals.

Solomon Hykes started dotCloud in 2010 and renamed it Docker in 2013. Software virtualization became possible due to advances in technology to provide namespace, filesystem, and processes isolation while still using the same kernel running in a bare-metal environment or in a virtual machine.

Software virtualization using containers provides better resource utilization compared to running multiple virtual machines. This leads to 30% to 40% effective resource utilization. Usually, a virtual machine takes seconds to minutes to initialize, whereas containerization shares the same kernel space, so the start up time is a lot quicker than it is with a virtual machine.

As a matter of fact, Google used software virtualization at a very large scale and used containerization for close to 10 years. This revealed the existence of their project, known as Borg. When Google published a research paper in 2015 in the EuroSys conference (`https://goo.gl/Ez99hu`) about its approach in managing data centers using containerization technology, it piqued interest among many technologists and, at the very same time, Docker exploded in popularity during 2014 and 2015, which made software virtualization simple enough to use.

One of the main benefits of software virtualization (also known as containerization) was to eliminate the dependency problem for a particular piece of software. For example, the Linux glibc is the main building block library, and there are hundreds of libraries that have dependencies on a particular version of glibc. We could build a Docker container that has a particular version of glibc, and it could run on a machine that has a later version of glibc. Normally, these kinds of deep dependencies have a very complex way of maintaining two different software stacks that have been built using different versions of glibc, but containers made this very simple. Docker is credited for making a simple user interface that made software packaging easy and accessible to developers.

Software virtualization made it possible to run different monolithic applications that can run within the same hardware (bare metal) or within the same virtual machine. This also led to the birth of smaller services (a complete business function) being packaged as independent software units. This is when the era of microservices started.

Container orchestration

It is easy to manage a few containers and their deployment. When the number of containers increases, a container orchestration platform makes deployment and management simpler and easier through declarative prescriptions. As containerization proliferated in 2015, the orchestration platform for containerization also evolved. Docker came with its own open source container orchestration platform known as Docker Swarm, which was a clustering and scheduling tool for Docker containers.

Apache Mesos, though not exactly similar to Docker Swarm, was built using the same principles as the Linux kernel. It was an abstract layer between applications and the Linux kernel. It was meant for distributed computing and acts as a cluster manager with an API for resource management and scheduling.

Kubernetes was the open source evolution of Google's Borg project, and its first version was released in 2015 through the Cloud Native Computing Foundation (https://cncf.io) as its first incubator project.

Major companies such as Google, Red Hat, Huawei, ZTE, VMware, Cisco, Docker, AWS, IBM, and Microsoft are contributing to the Kubernetes open source platform, and it has become a modern cluster manager and container orchestration platform. It's not a surprise that Kubernetes has become the *de facto* platform and is now used by all major cloud providers, with 125 companies working on it and more than 2,800+ contributors adding to it (https://www.stackalytics.com/cncf?module=kubernetes).

As container orchestration began to simplify cluster management, it became easy to run microservices in a distributed environment, which made microservices-based applications loosely coupled systems with horizontal scale-out possibilities.

Horizontal scale-out distributed computing is not new, with IBM's shared-nothing architecture for the Db2 database (monolithic application) being in use since 1998. What's new is the loosely coupled microservices that can run and scale out easily using a modern cluster manager.

Monolithic applications that used a three-tier architecture, such as **Model, View, Controller (MVC)** or SOA, were one of the architectural patterns on bare metal or virtualized machines. This type of pattern was adopted well in static data center environments where machines could be identified through IP addresses, and the changes were managed through DNS. This started to change with the use of distributed applications that could run on any machine (which meant the IP address could change) in the case of failures. This shift slowly started from a static data center approach to a dynamic data center approach, where identification is now done through the name of the microservice and not the IP address of the machine or container pod where the workload runs.

This fundamental shift from static to dynamic infrastructure is the basis for the evolution from monolithic to a microservices architecture. Monolithic applications are tightly coupled and have a single code base that is released in one instance for the entire application stack. Changing a single component without affecting others is a very difficult process, but it provides simplicity. On the other hand, microservices applications are loosely coupled and multiple code bases can be released independently of each other. Changing a single component is easy, but it does not provide simplicity, as was the case with monolithic applications.

We will cover a brief history of monolithic and microservices applications in the next section in order to develop a context. This will help us transition to the specific goals of this book.

Monolithic applications

The application evolution journey from monolithic to microservices can be seen in the following diagram:

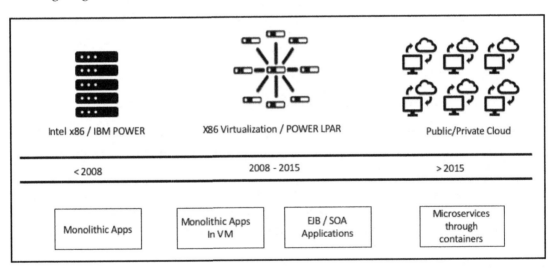

Monolithic applications were created from small applications and then built up to create a tiered architecture that separated the frontend from the backend, and the backend from the data sources. In this architecture, the frontend manages user interaction, the middle tier manages the business logic, and the backend manages data access. This can be seen in the following diagram:

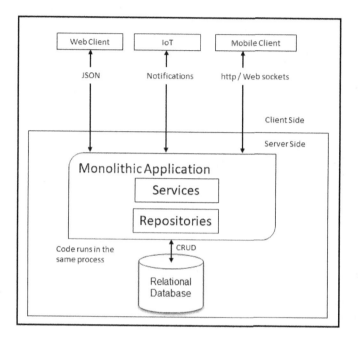

In the preceding diagram, the middle tier, also known as the business logic, is tightly bound to the frontend and the backend. This is a one-dimensional monolithic experience where all the tiers are in one straight line.

The three-tier modular architecture of the client-server, consisting of a frontend tier, an application tier, and a database tier, is almost 20+ years old now. It served its purpose of allowing people to build complex enterprise applications with known limitations regarding complexity, software upgrades, and zero downtime.

A large development team commits its code to a source code repository such as GitHub. The deployment process from code commits to production used to be manual before the CICD pipeline came into existence. The releases needed to be manually tested, although there were some automated test cases. Organizations used to declare a code freeze while moving the code into production. The application became overly large, complex, and very difficult to maintain in the long term. When the original code developers were no longer available, it became very difficult and time-consuming to add enhancements.

To overcome the aforementioned limitations, the concept of SOA started to evolve around 2002 onward and the **Enterprise Service Bus (ESB)** evolved to establish a communication link between different applications in SOA.

Brief history of SOA and ESB

The one-dimensional model of the three-tier architecture was split into a multi-dimensional SOA, where inter-service communication was enabled through ESB using the **Simple Object Access Protocol (SOAP)** and other web services standards.

SOA, along with ESB, could be used to break down a large three-tier application into services, where applications were built using these reusable services. The services could be dynamically discovered using service metadata through a metadata repository. With SOA, each functionality is built as a coarse-grained service that's often deployed inside an application server.

Multiple services need to be integrated to create composite services that are exposed through the ESB layer, which becomes a centralized bus for communication. This can be seen in the following diagram:

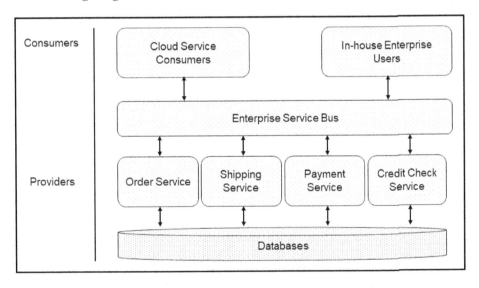

The preceding diagram shows the consumer and provider model connected through the ESB. The ESB also contains significant business logic, making it a monolithic entity where the same runtime is shared by developers in order to develop or deploy their service integrations.

In the next section, we'll talk about API gateways. The concept of the API gateway evolved around 2008 with the advent of smartphones, which provide rich client applications that need easy and secure connectivity to the backend services.

API Gateway

The SOA/web services were not ideal for exposing business functionality as APIs. This was due to the complex nature of web service-related technologies in which SOAP is used as a message format for service-to-service communication. SOAP was also used for securing web services and service-to-service communication, as well as for defining service discovery metadata. SOAP lacked a self-service model, which hindered the development of an ecosystem around it.

We use **application programming interface (API)**, as a term, to expose a service over REST (HTTP/JSON) or a web service (SOAP/HTTP). An API gateway was typically built on top of existing SOA/ESB implementations for APIs that could be used to expose business functionality securely as a managed service. This can be seen in the following diagram:

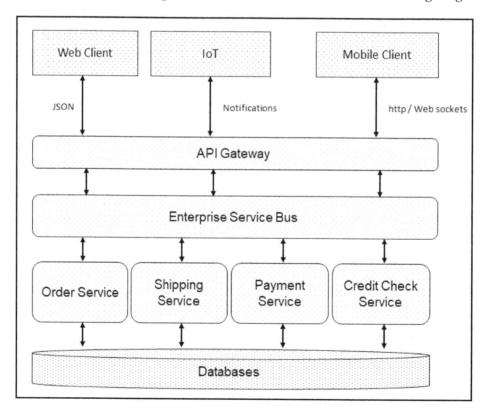

In the preceding diagram, the API gateway is used to expose the three-tier and SOA/ESB-based services in which the business logic contained in the ESB still hinders the development of the independent services.

With containerization availability, the new paradigm of microservices started to evolve from the SOA/ESB architecture in 2012 and seriously took off in 2015.

Drawbacks of monolithic applications

Monolithic applications are simple to develop, deploy, and scale as long as they are small in nature.

As the size and complexity of monoliths grow, various disadvantages arise, such as the following:

- Development is slow.
- Large monolithic code bases intimidate new developers.
- The application is difficult to understand and modify.
- Software releases are painful and occur infrequently.
- Overloaded IDE, web container.
- Continuous deployment is difficult – Code Freeze period to deploy.
- Scaling the application can be difficult due to an increase in data volume.
- Scaling development can be difficult.
- Requires long-term commitment to a technology stack.
- Lack of reliability due to difficulty in testing the application thoroughly.

Enterprise application development is coordinated among many smaller teams that can work independently of each other. As an application grows in size, the aforementioned complexities lead to them looking for better approaches, resulting in the adoption of microservices.

Microservices applications

A very small number of developers recognized the need for new thinking very early on and started working on the evolution of a new architecture, called microservices, early in 2014.

Early pioneers

A few individuals took a forward leap in moving away from monolithic to small manageable services adoption in their respective companies. Some of the most notable of these people include Jeff Bezos, Amazon's CEO, who famously implemented a mandate for Amazon (`https://bit.ly/2Hb3NI5`) in 2002. It stated that all employees have to adopt a service interface methodology where all communication calls would happen over the network. This daring initiative replaced the monolith with a collection of loosely coupled services. One nugget of wisdom from Jeff Bezos was two-pizza teams – individual teams shouldn't be larger than what two pizzas can feed. This colloquial wisdom is at the heart of shorter development cycles, increased deployment frequency, and faster time to market.

Netflix adopted microservices early on. It's important to mention Netflix's **Open Source Software Center** (**OSS**) contribution through `https://netflix.github.io`. Netflix also created a suite of automated open source tools, the Simian Army (`https://github.com/Netflix/SimianArmy`), to stress-test its massive cloud infrastructure. The rate at which Netflix has adopted new technologies and implemented them is phenomenal.

Lyft adopted microservices and created an open source distributed proxy known as Envoy (`https://www.envoyproxy.io/`) for services and applications, and would later go on to become a core part of one of the most popular service mesh implementations, such as Istio and Consul.

Though this book is not about developing microservices applications, we will briefly discuss the microservices architecture so that it is relevant from the perspective of a service mesh.

Since early 2000, when machines were still used as bare metal, three-tier monolithic applications ran on more than one machine, leading to the concept of distributed computing that was very tightly coupled. Bare metal evolved into VMs and monolithic applications into SOA/ESB with an API gateway. This trend continued until 2015 when the advent of containers disrupted the SOA/ESB way of thinking toward a self-contained, independently managed service. Due to this, the term *microservice* was coined.

The first mention of microservice as a term was used in a workshop of software architects in 2011 (`https://bit.ly/1KljYiZ`) when they used the term microservice to describe a common architectural style as a fine-grained SOA.

Chris Richardson created `https://microservices.io` in January 2014 to document architecture and design patterns.

James Lewis and Martin Fowler published their blog post (`https://martinfowler.com/articles/microservices.html`) about microservices in March 2014, and this blog post popularized the term microservices.

The microservices boom started with easy containerization that was made possible by Docker and through a *de facto* container orchestration platform known as Kubernetes, which was created for distributed computing.

What is a microservice?

The natural transition of SOA/ESB is toward microservices, in which services are decoupled from a monolithic ESB. Let's go over the core points of microservices:

- Each service is autonomous, which is developed and deployed independently.
- Each microservice can be scaled independently in relation to others if it receives more traffic without having to scale other microservices.
- Each microservice is designed based on the business capabilities at hand so that each service serves a specific business goal with a simple time principle that it does only one thing, and does it well.
- Since services do not share the same execution runtime, each microservice can be developed in different languages or in a polyglot fashion, providing agility in which developers pick the best programming language to develop their own service.
- The microservices architecture eliminated the need for a centralized ESB. The business logic, including inter-service communication, is done through smart endpoints and dumb pipes. This means that the centralized business logic of ESBs is now distributed among the microservices through smart endpoints, and a primitive messaging system or a dumb pipe is used for service-to-service communication using a lightweight protocol such as REST or gRPC.

The evolution of SOA/ESB to the microservices pattern was mainly influenced by the idea of being able to adapt to smaller teams that are independent of each other and to provide a self-service model for the consumption of services that were created by smaller teams. At the time of writing, microservices is a winning pattern that is being adopted by many enterprises to modernize their existing monolithic application stack.

Evolution of microservices

The following diagram shows the evolution of the application architecture from a three-tier architecture to SOA/ESB and then to microservices in terms of flexibility toward scalability and decoupling:

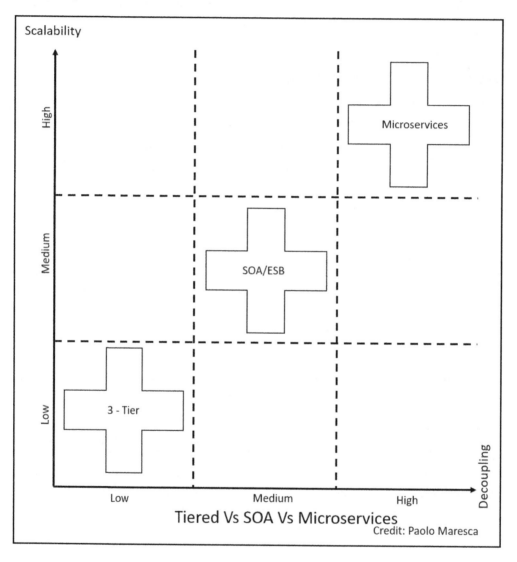

Credit: Paolo Maresca

Microservices have evolved from being tiered and the SOA architecture and are becoming the accepted pattern for building modern applications. This is due to the following reasons:

- Extreme scalability
- Extreme decoupling
- Extreme agility

These are key points regarding the design of a distributed scalable application where developers can pick the best programming language of their choice to develop their own service.

A major differentiation between monolithic and microservices is that, with microservices, the services are loosely coupled, and they communicate using dumb pipe or low-level REST or gRPC protocols. One way to achieve loose coupling is through the use of a separate data store for each service. This helps services isolate themselves from each other since a particular service is not blocked due to another service holding a data lock. Separate data stores allow the microservices to scale up and down, along with their data stores, independently of all the other services.

It is also important to point out the early pioneers in microservices, which we will discuss in the next section.

Microservices architecture

The aim of a microservice architecture is to completely decouple app components from one another so that they can be maintained, scaled, and more. It's an evolution of the app architecture, SOA, and publishing APIs:

- **SOA**: Focuses on reuse, technical integration issues, and technical APIs
- **Microservices**: Focus on functional decomposition, business capabilities, and business APIs

In Martin Fowler's paper, he states that the microservice architecture would have been better named the micro-component architecture because it is really about breaking apps up into smaller pieces (micro-components). For more information, see *Microservices*, by Martin Fowler, at https://martinfowler.com/articles/microservices.html. Also, check out Kim Clark's IBM blog post on microservices at https://developer.ibm.com/integration/blog/2017/02/09/microservices-vs-soa, where he argues microservices as micro-components.

The following diagram shows the microservice architecture in which different clients consume the same services. Each service can use the same/different language and can be deployed/scaled independently of each other:

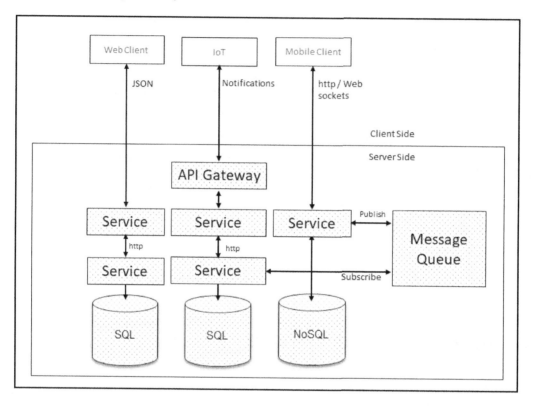

Each microservice runs its own process. Services are optimized for a single function and they must have one, and only one, reason to change. The communication between services is done through REST APIs and message brokers. The CICD is defined per service. The services evolve at a different pace. The scaling policy for each service can be different.

Benefits and drawbacks of microservices

The explosion of microservices is not an accident, and it is mainly due to rapid development and scalability:

- **Rapid development**: Develop and deploy a single service independently. Focus only on the interface and the functionality of the service and not the functionality of the entire system.

- **Scalability**: Scale a service independently without affecting others. This is simple and easy to do in a Kubernetes environment.

The other benefits of microservices are as follows:

- Each service can use a different language (better polyglot adaptability).
- Services are developed on their own timetables so that the new versions are delivered independently of other services.
- The development of microservices is suited for cross-functional teams.
- Improved fault isolation.
- Eliminates any long-term commitment to a technology stack.

However, the microservice is not a panacea and comes with drawbacks:

- The complexity of a distributed system.
- Increased resource consumption.
- Inter-service communication.
- Testing dependencies in a microservices-based application without a tool can be very cumbersome.
- When a service fails, it becomes very difficult to identify the cause of a failure.
- A microservice can't fetch data from other services through simple queries. Instead, it must implement queries using APIs.
- Microservices lead to more Ops (operations) overheads.

There is no perfect silver bullet, and technology continues to emerge and evolve. Next, we'll discuss the future of microservices.

Future of microservices

Microservices can be deployed in a distributed environment using a container orchestration platform such as Kubernetes, Docker Swarm, or an on-premises **Platform as a Service (PaaS)**, such as Pivotal Cloud Foundry or Red Hat OpenShift.

Service mesh helps reduce/overcome the aforementioned challenges and overheads on Ops, such as the operations overhead for manageability, serviceability, metering, and testing. This can be made simple by the use of service mesh providers such as Istio, Linkerd, or Consul.

As with every technology, there is no perfect solution, and each technology has its own benefits and drawbacks regarding an individual's perception and bias toward a particular technology. Sometimes, the drawbacks of a particular technology outweigh the benefits they accrue.

In the last 20 years, we have seen the evolution of monolithic applications to three-tier ones, to the adoption of the SOA/ESB architecture, and then the transition to microservices. We are already witnessing a framework evolution around microservices using service mesh, which is what this book is based on.

Summary

In this chapter, we gleaned over the evolution of computers and running multiple virtual machines on a single computer, which was possible through hardware virtualization. We learned about the tiered application journey that started 20+ years ago on bare metal machines. We witnessed the transition of three-tiered applications to the SOA/ESB architecture. The evolution of software virtualization drove the explosion of containerization, which led to the evolution of the SOA/ESB architecture to microservices. Then, we learned about the benefits and drawbacks of microservices. You can apply this knowledge of microservices to drive a business's need for rapid development and scalability to achieve time-to-market goals.

In the next chapter, we will move on to cloud-native applications and understand what is driving the motivation of various enterprises to move from monolithic to cloud-native applications. The purpose of this book is to go into the details of the service mesh architecture, and this can't be done without learning about the cloud-native architecture.

Questions

1. Microservices applications are difficult to test.

   A) True
   B) False

2. Monolithic/microservices applications are related to dynamic infrastructures.

   A) True
   B) False

3. Monolithic applications are best if they are small in size.

   A) True
   B) False

4. When a microservice fails, debugging becomes very difficult.

   A) True
   B) False

5. Large monolithic applications are very difficult to maintain and patch in the long term.

   A) True
   B) False

Further reading

- *Microservices Patterns, Richardson, Chris (2018).* Shelter Island, NY: Manning
- *Microservices Resource Guide,* Fowler, M. (2019), martinfowler.com. Available at `https://martinfowler.com/microservices`, accessed March 3, 2019
- *Microservices for the Enterprise, Indrasiri., K., and Siriwardena, P. (2018).* [S.l.]: Apress.
- *From Monolithic Three-tiers Architectures to SOA versus Microservices,* Maresca, P. (2015), TheTechSolo, available at `https://bit.ly/2GYhYk`, accessed March 3, 2019
- *Retire the Three-Tier Application Architecture to Move Toward Digital Business,* Thomas, A., and Gupta, A. (2016), Gartner.com, available at `https://gtnr.it/2F1787w`, accessed March 3, 2019
- *Microservices Lead the New Class of Performance Management Solutions,* LightStep. (2019), available at `https://lightstep.com/blog/microservices-trends-report-2018`, accessed March 3, 2019
- *What year did Bezos issue the API Mandate at Amazon?,* Schroeder, G. (2016), available at `https://bit.ly/2Hb3NI5`, accessed March 3, 2019
- *Kubernetes Components,* Kubernetes.io. (2019), available at `https://bit.ly/2JyhIGt`, accessed March 3, 2019
- *Microservices implementation – Netflix stack – Tharanga Thennakoon – Medium,* Thennakoon, T. (2017), available at `https://bit.ly/2NCDzPZ`, accessed March 3, 2019

Cloud-Native Applications 2

Cloud-Native Applications (CNAs) are systems that were *born on the cloud* and can take full advantage of the capabilities only found in cloud computing providers, such as ephemeral on-demand infrastructure and autoscaling.

This chapter provides an overview of building CNAs using container-based environments to develop services that can scale independently. Although this book is not about CNA, a service mesh is incomplete without an introduction to CNA since it is a building block to achieve service mesh capabilities.

In this chapter, we will cover the following topics:

- An introduction to CNAs
- Container runtime
- Container orchestration platforms
- Cloud-native infrastructure

An introduction to CNAs

With containerization becoming popular in 2015, the term "cloud-native" was used to describe container-based environments used to develop applications that have been built with services that can scale independently from each other and run on an infrastructure provided by a cloud provider. With DevOps processes getting automated, CNAs became part of **Continuous Integration and Continuous Delivery (CI/CD)** workflows. CNAs are related to infrastructure resources such as compute, memory, network, and storage, which are abstracted and self-provisioned as opposed to manually deployed resources.

One of the most popular cloud-native application development platforms is known as Red Hat OpenShift, a platform where we can focus on writing the business logic for the application. Containerization happens automatically, without having to write any code, while deployment (production or canary) occurs automatically through a CI/CD pipeline.

The term cloud-native has evolved organically to signify an application in which the software development process is rapid. The application's deployment and scalability are fully automatic. The time to market is the essence of making CNAs. The platform, such as OpenShift, provides a set of services north-to-south that makes it possible for an application to become cloud-native. An application by itself is not cloud-native if the supporting services are not in place. Please refer to the following architecture diagram of CNAs for a more succinct explanation:

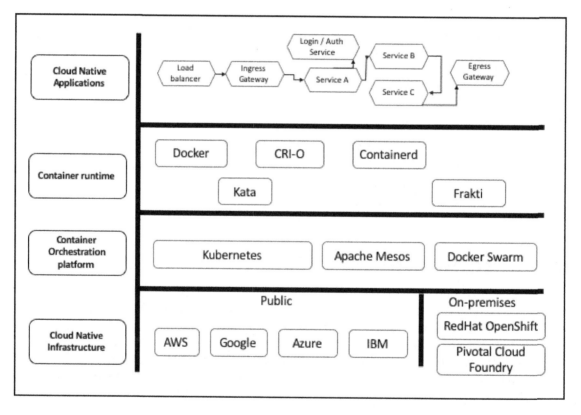

The preceding diagram shows that CNAs typically require a container runtime, which can be managed by an orchestration platform hosted on some infrastructure layer.

There must be a platform that provides integrated services, which makes microservice development easier and takes the mystery out of container image development. The platform provides a natural automatic container image development for different languages to offer a polyglot microservices environment. For example, an organization may use Python, Java, Ruby, Go, and so on, and those can be tapped into in order to quickly build small and independent microservices to market a CNA. One such open source platform is OKD (`https://okd.io`), which provides a **Source-to-Image (S2I)** capability, which allows us to build container images direct from the source code and the CI/CD pipeline built into the platform for deployment and update processes.

CNAs, which sit on the top of the aforementioned services, are collections of loosely coupled microservices. Jankiram (`https://thenewstack.io/10-key-attributes-of-cloud-native-applications`) has defined 10 critical attributes of CNAs, as follows:

- Packaged as lightweight containers
- Developed with best-of-breed languages and frameworks
- Designed as loosely coupled microservices
- Centered around APIs for interaction and collaboration
- Architected with a clean separation of stateless and stateful services
- Isolated from server and operating system dependencies
- Deployed on a self-service, elastic, cloud infrastructure
- Managed through agile DevOps processes
- Automated capabilities
- Defined, policy-driven resource allocation

The preceding vital attributes require a container runtime. These are used for runtime isolation and software virtualization. We will explore this in the next section.

Container runtime

In Chapter 1, *Monoliths Versus Microservices*, we discussed hardware (VMs) and software (containers) virtualization. Docker popularized containers, and it's led to the containerization boom since 2015. The way Docker encapsulated software and its dependencies in a single package built the base for cloud computing as we see it today.

At the time of writing, Docker as a runtime and an engine is the de facto standard for different container orchestration platforms. However, that is changing slowly since the **Container Runtime Interface (CRI)** (`https://cri-o.io`) has enabled individual providers to develop container runtimes that are compatible with the **Open Container Initiative (OCI)** (`https://www.opencontainers.org`). CRI-O is a lightweight alternative without the need to install Docker as a container runtime for Kubernetes.

Newer container runtimes such as Frakti (`https://github.com/kubernetes/frakti`) and Kata (`https://katacontainers.io`) use hardware virtualization to achieve better security and isolation. Kata containers are something between Hyper's runV and Intel's Clear Container. Another container technology is Garden and is used by Cloud Foundry systems. Finally, another widely used container runtime within Alibaba is Pouch (`https://github.com/alibaba/pouch`).

As an end user, it should not matter which container runtime is used as that choice is best left to the platform's management team. The consolidation and convergence of a container runtime should emerge in the future.

It is easy to manage containers when there are only a few running on a machine. It becomes complicated to manage a large number of containers when there's a proliferation of container-based applications in an organization. For example, a Docker container can be started using the `docker run` command to bypass network ports, a storage volume, and optionally a Docker network in order to provide an IP address to the container. The application needs to use this IP address or host port to connect to the container. So far, so good – until we have only a few containers. When proliferation starts, and the number of machines increases, the effort to manage this infrastructure to update IP addresses manually and move storage volumes between machines become time-consuming and not scalable.

This problem is solved by the container orchestration platform, which we will discuss in the next section.

Container orchestration platforms

The container revolution for software virtualization led to the development of container orchestration platforms such as Docker Swarm, Apache Mesos, Kubernetes, Cloud Foundry, and so on in order to be able to quickly deploy containers in a distributed environment.

Let's discuss a few of them:

- Since Docker was already famous, it started its own Docker Swarm (`https://docs.docker.com/engine/swarm`) as an orchestration platform. Swarm has tight integration with the main Docker API. Swarm runs an agent on each host, and a Swarm manager runs on one host. This manager is responsible for scheduling containers on a proper host when you issue the `docker run` command.
- Apache Mesos (`http://mesos.apache.org`) is a distributed cluster manager and has similar capabilities to Google Project Borg or Facebook's Tupperware. It was adopted by Twitter, Apple (Siri), Yelp, Uber, Netflix, and so on early on. It is not wise to compare Apache Mesos to Kubernetes since Mesos has many other capabilities in addition to container orchestration.
- VMware originally developed Cloud Foundry (`https://github.com/cloudfoundry`) with its container runtime garden in 2009 and then started as a joint project between EMC, VMware, and GE through Pivotal (`https://pivotal.io`).
- Kubernetes (`https://kubernetes.io`) was designed from scratch at Google in 2015 and donated to the Cloud Native Computing Foundation (`https://cncf.io`) in 2016. At the time of writing, it has become the de facto container orchestration platform.

CoreOS (`http://coreos.com`) was acquired by Red Hat/IBM in 2018 and is a lightweight open source Linux kernel for running containers for high availability. It provides automatic security updates for the operating system. The CoreOS group of servers, through its automatic leader election process, self-updates to keep Linux and its containers up and running with zero downtime. Red Hat integrated CoreOS with OpenShift starting with version 4.1 to provide a container orchestration platform for enterprises that has zero downtime. It's a self-updating operating system with Kubernetes++.

 OpenShift is a Kubernetes container orchestration platform that runs in a public or private cloud environment to provide the security that's needed by enterprise customers. OpenShift offers a catalog of applications that we can deploy in its Kubernetes cluster through a push-button approach, and it also provides an elegant development platform in which container images are created automatically from the source code of the application.

An ideal container orchestration platform provides shaded capabilities in order to eliminate any possible human intervention. This is done to provide resiliency in a dynamic infrastructure for CNAs. Let's take a look at these capabilities:

- **Speed**: Automatically deploys the container image on any machine with available resources.
- **Health**: Automatically health checks to provide self-healing systems.
- **Autoscaling**: Provides autoscaling for applications to meet increased workloads, upgrades, and rollbacks.
- **Declarative**: Achieves the desired state of the system through a declarative prescription for installs, updates, and rollbacks.
- **Efficiency**: Optimum resource utilization with fewer machines compared to the equivalent static infrastructure.
- **Decouple**: Automatically assigns the IP address to pods that link to a fixed service IP address for service discovery, load balancing, and separate configuration from application code.

Decoupling is the central theme of a container orchestration platform. For example, the container runtime is decoupled in Kubernetes so that any container runtime can be plugged in, such as Docker, CRI-O, containerd, and so on. Similarly, the network is decoupled from the container runtime using the **Container Network Interface (CNI)** to allow third-party network providers such as Calico, Flannel, Canal, or Weave. The storage is decoupled from the container runtime using the **Container Storage Interface (CSI)** so that third-party storage providers such as Portworx, Robin, Kasten, IBM, RedHat, Dell EMC, NetApp, and so on can be used.

 Note that although there are several orchestration platforms available, the focus of this book is only on the Kubernetes platform from the service mesh perspective.

The bottom-most south layer of CNAs is the cloud-native infrastructure that provides a platform runtime of the application. Next, we will go through the alternatives of cloud-native infrastructure.

Cloud-native infrastructure

When it comes to running CNAs, we don't have to run them in a public cloud. The public cloud is the manifestation of automation and easiness so that we can use a ready-made platform with all the capabilities for end user consumption. You can compare public clouds to an airport where you can buy services to go from point A to point B without buying an airplane.

The term cloud-native is not related to the public cloud as we understand it. The public cloud is one of the vehicles that's used to deploy, manage, and run CNAs.

 This book is all about the service mesh architecture, which requires a cloud-native platform. You won't need to use a paid public cloud provider to perform the exercises in this book. Instead, `Chapter 6`, *Building Your Own Kubernetes Environment*, teaches you how to build your Kubernetes platform either on Microsoft Windows, Apple macOS, or a Linux machine.

There are multiple cloud-native infrastructures available. Let's take a look at a few of them:

- **Docker**: Docker provides its own managed service for building and running containers.
- **Amazon**: Amazon use their services to provide a **Container as a Service (CaaS)** platform. These services include **Elastic Container Registry (ECR)** for Docker containers, the **Elastic Container Service (ECS)** runtime to run the containers, and CloudWatch to schedule, run, and monitor containers. After Kubernetes' success, Amazon also provided its own **Elastic Container Service for Kubernetes (EKS)**.
- **IBM**: IBM has its own cloud container service, known as **IBM Cloud Kubernetes Service (IKS)**, in addition to its own Cloud Foundry implementation for public, enterprise, and private consumption. IBM also provides many hosted services that run on its cloud platform.
- **Microsoft Azure**: Microsoft Azure adopted Apache Mesos, but it also provides **Azure Kubernetes Service (AKS)**.
- **Google**: Google provides hosted services for computing, storage, and application development, including its own **Google Kubernetes Engine (GKE)**.
- **Alibaba**: Alibaba provides its own container service for Kubernetes.

Orchestration platforms directly relate to cloud economics. This is a direct result of automation, which the orchestration platform helps with. It is worthwhile to note that AWS has the largest market share (48%) in **Infrastructure as a Service (IaaS)** as of 2019.

In addition to a public cloud, the push is now more on the hybrid cloud to seamlessly integrate the public cloud with a private cloud behind the firewall of a customer who has similar cloud agile tools with a self-service model. Red Hat OpenShift, Cloud Foundry, Apache Mesos, and others fill the hybrid cloud model.

Summary

In this chapter, we walked through the north-south infrastructure of CNAs, which require a toolchain. Then, we walked through their key essential attributes. We looked at the different container runtimes that are available, which form the basis of cloud computing. Then, we delved into the container orchestration platform. We highlighted that Kubernetes is the de facto standard and that we'll be using it in this book. Lastly, we looked at the major cloud-native infrastructures that are available so that we can deploy CNAs.

In the next chapter, we will cover the service mesh architecture, service mesh providers, the service mesh interface, and the **Secure Production Identity Framework For Everyone (SPIFFE)**. We will also look at the data plane that builds the service mesh with components that are driven through the control plane.

Questions

1. Kubernetes can use either Docker or CRI-O as a container runtime.

   A) True
   B) False

2. Cloud-native microservices are more complex than traditional monolithic applications.

   A) True
   B) False

3. CNAs are challenging to diagnose without the help of a proper toolchain.

   A) True
   B) False

4. Apache Mesos is a much broader platform than Kubernetes.

   A) True
   B) False

5. Kubernetes is now the de facto standard for container orchestration.

   A) True
   B) False

Further reading

- *The Container Landscape: Docker Alternatives, Orchestration, And Implications For Microservices*, Kai Wähner, Infoq, 2016: `https://www.infoq.com/articles/container-landscape-2016`, accessed March 11, 2019
- *10 Key Attributes Of Cloud-Native Applications*, Janakiram MSV, The New Stack, 2018: `https://thenewstack.io/10-key-attributes-of-cloud-native-applications/`, accessed March 11, 2019
- *Docker vs. Kubernetes vs. Apache Mesos: Why What You Think You Know Is Probably Wrong*, Amr Abdelrazik, Mesosphere, 2017: `https://mesosphere.com/blog/docker-vs-kubernetes-vs-apache-mesos/`, accessed March 11, 2019

Section 2: Architecture

In this section, we describe a high-level ideal service mesh architecture that most service mesh providers follow.

This section contains the following chapters:

3
Service Mesh Architecture

The service mesh architecture is an application infrastructure layer on top of cloud-native applications. Service mesh has gained popularity since 2017, and it is still a relatively young concept. A service mesh provides a layer of abstraction above your applications. For example, this could be used to decouple security from the application. The service mesh could secure communication between the microservices with TLS. The benefit here is that each developer no longer has to implement TLS encryption and decryption that's specific to the language they are writing in.

In this chapter, we will walk through a quick overview of the origin of the service and understand how it can be viewed as a decoupling agent between the provider (dev) and the consumer (ops). We will also understand basic and advanced service communication through smart endpoints and trust between microservices and then wrap this up with a quick glance at its architecture.

In a nutshell, we will cover the following topics:

- Service mesh overview
- Shifting Dev responsibilities to Ops
- Service mesh rules
- Service mesh architecture

Service mesh overview

Let's begin with the definition of the service mesh. William Morgan in 2017 defined the service mesh as follows (`https://buoyant.io/2017/04/25/whats-a-service-mesh-and-why-do-i-need-one`):

> *"A service mesh is a dedicated infrastructure layer for handling service-to-service communication. It's responsible for the reliable delivery of requests through the complex topology of services that comprise a modern, cloud-native application. In practice, the service mesh's implementation is an array of lightweight network proxies deployed alongside microservices, without the applications needing to be aware."*

We can view a service mesh as a decoupling agent between Dev (provider) and Ops (consumer). Dev does not have to write any code in the microservices to provide capabilities that Ops need. Ops does not have to recompile the system, so both can operate independently of each other. The service mesh concept is a significant shift from earlier versions of DevOps, where operations were limited to software release management.

Kubernetes orchestration provides an essential service so that we can service communication through smart endpoints and dumb pipes. Martin Fowler, in his 2014 blog article (Lewis and Fowler), provided a more advanced look at the concept of smart endpoints and dumb pipes:

> *"Smart endpoints: Service-to-service communication is done through the intelligent endpoints, which is a DNS record that resolves to a microservice. The use of DNS records facilitates one service to communicate with others, and this eliminates the load balancer between microservices.*
>
> *Dumb pipes: Service-to-service communication uses basic network traffic protocols such as HTTP, REST, gRPC, and so on. This type of connection is opposed to a centralized smart pipe using the ESB/MQ of monolithic applications."*

Christian Posta defines a service mesh as a *decentralized* application networking infrastructure between your services. This decoupling provides resiliency, security, observability, and routing control.

In Zach Jory's blog post (`https://dzone.com/articles/comparing-service-mesh-architectures`), he explains the library, node agent, and sidecar model of the service mesh architecture.

Who owns the service mesh?

So, who would take responsibility for a service mesh in a typical IT organization? The answer varies. In the legacy world, service mesh models used to belong to developers during the times of monolithic applications and SOA/ESB applications. In a cloud-native environment, the service mesh has moved from Dev to Ops, and this is a significant shift because it lets the developers focus on their specialty, developing applications, and provides important services to them without them having to think or understand how they operate.

Google started a new practice known as **Site Reliability Engineering** (**SRE**), which the service mesh may fall under.

Now, let's discuss basic and advanced service mesh capabilities.

Basic and advanced service mesh capabilities

A service mesh is a dedicated tooling or infrastructure layer for handling service-to-service communication. Let's understand this first in the context of Kubernetes:

- **Basic service mesh**: Kubernetes provides a basic service mesh out of the box, and this is the service resource. It provides a round-robin balancing for requests to the target pods. Kubernetes service is a dynamic function that manages `iptables` under the cover on each host, and this process is transparent. As a pod in Kubernetes becomes ready, or a liveliness check passes, the endpoints of the service are enabled to provide a connection from outside to the IP addresses of the pods.
- **Advanced service mesh**: Note that the service-to-service communication support from Kubernetes is a basic service mesh. Istio, Linkerd, Consul, and so on can harness some advanced capabilities such as retry logic, timeouts, fallback, circuit breaking, and distributed tracing from it.

Moving on, let's take a look at some of the emerging trends in service mesh.

Emerging trends

Integration between different service meshes is emerging. Let's take a look:

- We can extend the same service mesh control plane to multiple Kubernetes clusters, provided that each cluster has its own distinct IP address range.
- We can bring VMs, bare-metal, or other monolithic applications into the service mesh for traffic management and telemetry.
- We can have multiple Kubernetes clusters, with each having their control plane replicating the state of each group.
- We can have a federated service mesh, where each cluster runs its own control and data plane.

A service mesh provides us with a way to abstract security, traffic, monitoring, and so on outside the application code without the need for any application-specific libraries. Next, we will discuss this changing landscape.

Shifting Dev responsibilities to Ops

As soon as a developer commits the code to a source code repository, the CI/CD pipeline takes over to build the runtime, and the application gets pushed to production. Kubernetes with a container runtime (such as Docker or CRI-O) helps to automate this process without human intervention. The role of a developer ends with a commit process as they continue to focus on the implementation of business logic in the microservices.

But what happens when the runtime starts and at this juncture? The role of Ops begins. The runtime mandate is to successfully run and maintain a distributed polyglot microservice with scaling capabilities in a Kubernetes environment.

Let's look at an example. A library is used in several microservices to monitor the service and a new version of this library is available. We need to recompile, test, and deploy the microservice using this new library, even though nothing might change in the actual source code of the microservice. On the other hand, a service mesh implementation provides this capability without us having to recompile the microservice.

Monolithic and SOA/ESB applications implemented traffic routing, canary releases, A/B testing, distributed tracing, monitoring, trusts, and so on in the source code through the use of several libraries. The developers were responsible for providing additional implementation/support, which was required once runtime or production use started.

Kubernetes helps us to separate the role of Dev and Ops through loosely coupled services. The separate Ops tooling frees up developers to focus only on providing business logic in the microservices. A container runtime provides resource isolation and dependency management, and Kubernetes provides an orchestration layer, which abstracts away from the underlying hardware into a homogeneous pool (William Morgan – `https://blog.buoyant.io/2017/04/25/whats-a-service-mesh-and-why-do-i-need-one`).

It is important to note that a proper service mesh implementation frees up developers, but it adds more responsibilities to operations.

Since the service mesh concept is still new and evolving, service mesh rules can help us to separate the duties of development and operations with clear boundaries. We'll look at these next.

Service mesh rules

A perfect service mesh should establish the ORASTAR rules without having to code anything at the microservice level:

- **Observability**: The control plane provides the observability of services running in the data plane.
- **Routing**: The routing rules for traffic management can be defined either graphically or through the use of configuration files and then pushed down from the control plane to all the data planes.
- **Automatic scaling**: The control plane services automatically scale to handle the increased workload.
- **Separation of duties**: The control plane UI allows operations to manage the service mesh independent of the development team.
- **Trust**: It pushes down secure communication protocols to the data planes and provides automatic renewal and management of certificates.
- **Automatic service registration and discovery**: The control plane integrates with the Kubernetes API server and discovers the service automatically as it's registered through application deployment procedures.
- **Resilient**: Pushes resiliency rules to all of the data planes. This acts as a sidecar proxy for traffic management.

Let's understand these rules in more detail.

Observability

When we implement a service mesh, all or selected services should automatically be observable and provide the following:

- Metrics, to track such things as request rate, latency, and bandwidth usage and to help chargeback based on usage
- Distributed logging and tracing for diagnostics and fault determination
- Monitoring to observe the health and performance of microservices
- Graphical visualizations of all of the service's request flows

Routing

The routing capabilities from the service mesh traffic should provide skills such as the following:

- Shift traffic; for example, from one version of service to another version of the same service
- Split traffic; for example, smart load balancing based on weights
- Control incoming and outgoing traffic
- Service-level agreements to protect microservices from getting overloaded
- Fault and latency injection for testing
- Mirroring traffic

Automatic scaling

This refers to the ability to load balance requests and scale a service up and down based on metrics such as the following:

- Request latency
- Error rates

Separation of duties

The service mesh should establish a clear separation of duties between development and operations. The development staff should focus only on the implementation of business logic, whereas operations staff should pay attention to keeping the services up and running, in addition to other abstraction capabilities of security, routing, policies, and observability.

Trust

The service mesh should establish trust through securing communication and authentication between microservices automatically. We should always consider the network to be inherently insecure, even if it is behind a firewall.

Automatic service registration and discovery

The service mesh should work with the underlying cluster manager (such as Kubernetes) or with any external services registration tool to provide automatic registration and discovery of services.

Resiliency

The service mesh must assume that network glitches are bound to occur. It should automatically load balance the traffic and shield particular microservices from becoming overloaded while still providing access to other services of the application.

Service mesh architecture

As we discussed in the previous section, we can enforce ORASTAR rules through a control and data plane. Let's go over these concepts in a bit more detail:

- **Control plane**: You can use this to push down configurations, policies, and management services to a data plane for controlling routing, traffic, monitoring, discovery, and registration of services. The control plane is responsible for establishing communication between microservices through authentication, authorization, and securing network traffic.

- **Data plane**: All of the sidecars of the microservices form the data plane. The control and data plane, when used together, form the service mesh:

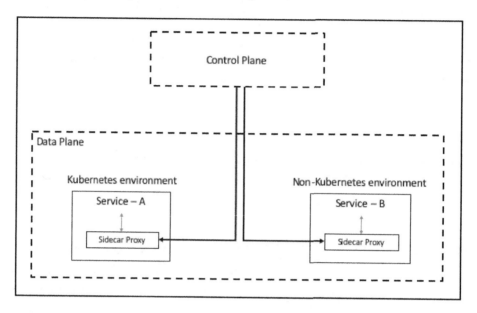

In the preceding diagram, the control plane interacts with the data plane to manage the service mesh's outcome. Its core responsibility is to translate, enforce, and forward service traffic from every service instance and analyze network traffic in parallel.

Summary

In this chapter, we learned about the abstract model of an ideal service mesh architecture, comprised of a control and data plane. A service mesh forms when each microservice has a companion proxy sidecar. We also learned that modern cloud-native applications should have a clear separation of development and operations.

In the next chapter, we will look at three popular service mesh providers: Istio, Linkerd, and Consul. We will cover each provider in a separate section through hands-on exercises for ease of learning.

Questions

1. A service mesh is an abstraction layer on top of an application.

   A) True
   B) False

2. The sidecar lives in a control plane.

   A) True
   B) False

3. A service mesh is an abstract layer on top of the application stack.

   A) True
   B) False

Further reading

- *What's a Service Mesh? And Why Do I Need One?* Morgan, William, Blog.Buoyant, 2017: https://blog.buoyant.io/2017/04/25/whats-a-service-mesh-and-why-do-i-need-one/.
- *Service-Mesh Options with Linkerd, Consul, Istio and AWS Appmesh.* Posta, Christian, Slideshare.Net, 2019: https://www.slideshare.net/ceposta/servicemesh-options-with-linkerd-consul-istio-and-aws-appmesh.
- *Microservice Principles: Smart Endpoints and Dumb Pipes.* Peck, Nathan, Medium, 2019, https://goo.gl/Lw8ffL. Accessed *March 5, 2019.*
- *What Is a Service Mesh, and Do I Need One When Developing Microservices?* Bryant, Daniel., Infoq, 2018: https://www.infoq.com/presentations/service-mesh-microservices.
- *Microservices.* Lewis, James, and Martin Fowler, Martinfowler.Com, 2019: https://martinfowler.com/articles/microservices.html.
- *Enterprise Service Bus.* Wikipedia.Org, 2019: https://en.wikipedia.org/wiki/Enterprise_service_bus
- *Google – Site Reliability Engineering.* Landing.Google.Com, 2019: https://landing.google.com/sre/
- *Comparing Service Mesh Architectures.* Jory, Zach, DZone - March 2018: https://dzone.com/articles/comparing-service-mesh-architectures.

Service Mesh Providers 4

Istio, Linkerd, and Consul are the three service mesh providers that we will cover in this book. Istio started its nascent revolution of microservices communication with an active community of contributors that have provided a very feature-rich service mesh. Linkerd, with its 2.x version, focuses on simplicity, ease of use, and performance. Finally, the Consul service mesh spans VMs, Kubernetes clusters, data centers, and regions. Each of these service mesh providers can fulfill service mesh needs based on specific requirements.

In this chapter, we will walk through a quick overview of the aforementioned open source projects, followed by a quick comparison of them. We will cover the following topics:

- Introducing service mesh providers
- A quick comparison
- Support services

Introducing service mesh providers

The service mesh revolution is very new, with just over two years to its history. It is continuously evolving, and at the time of writing, there are three leading service mesh providers known as Istio, Linkerd, and Consul. In the upcoming sections, we will introduce these three service mesh providers and look at their architecture and implementation. We will cover hands-on exercises in separate sections of this book.

Istio is covered in detail from Chapter 7, *Understanding the Istio Service Mesh*, through Chapter 13, *Exploring Istio Telemetry Features;* Linkerd from Chapter 14, *Understanding the Linkerd Service Mesh*, through Chapter 18, *Exploring the Observability Features of Linkerd;* and Consul from Chapter 19, *Understanding the Consul Service Mesh*, through Chapter 22, *Exploring Traffic Management in Consul.*

Istio

Google, IBM, and Lyft formed Istio (Jason McGee) in May 2017, and it is one of the fastest-growing service mesh projects that's been built for the Kubernetes platform. This open source project is available at `https://github.com/istio`.

Istio has a centralized control plane that manages and coordinates data collection with the data plane. Istio Pilot is a core part of the Istio control plane and can run outside the Kubernetes environment as a standalone service. It supports integration with VMs and service discovery through other third-party service catalogs such as Consul or Eureka.

Linkerd

The Buoyant founders, William Morgan and Oliver Gould, created Linkerd. William Morgan is credited for coining the term **service mesh**, which is now used by all major providers.

Linkerd, which comes from the RPC system called Finagle, was developed by Twitter to handle its extremely high volume. Linkerd 1.x turned Finagle into the first service mesh. The Conduit (`https://conduit.io`) project arose out of the desire to build a much simpler system to solve the same issues Linkerd 1.x was solving. Eventually, it was decided to rebrand Conduit as Linkerd 2.0, which is an open source service mesh for cloud-native applications. Linkerd 2.x is a graduated project from CNCF (`https://cncf.io`), and it only runs in a Kubernetes environment.

This book will only cover Linkerd 2.x, which is a service mesh for Kubernetes, and it provides runtime debugging, observability, reliability, and security for running services. Linkerd 2.x has a centralized control plane similar to Istio. This open source project is available at `https://linkerd.io`. Linkerd 1.x is a different service mesh compared to Linkerd 2.x. It runs on Kubernetes, AWS ECS, DC/OS, Docker, and locally. Linkerd uses its own sidecar, whereas all of the other service mesh providers use the Envoy sidecar proxy.

Consul

Consul is a distributed service mesh from HashiCorp. Its first release was in April 2014. Consul provides a single GO binary for server and client side service mesh capabilities that need to be managed, including services, configurations, certificate management, and many more. We can install Consul in the Kubernetes platform as well as directly on each machine. This open source project is available at `https://github.com/hashicorp/consul`.

Consul has a distributed control plane, unlike Istio and Linkerd 2.x. Consul comes with the connect feature for Kubernetes clusters. Consul is designed to work in bare-metal environments, VMs, and now with the Kubernetes environment as well. It's is an open source service discovery tool that provides service discovery APIs. The Pilot adapter in Istio can be configured to use Consul service discovery data and use a proxy to route the traffic and monitor applications. Consul 1.6 started to use the Envoy sidecar proxy for Kubernetes environments and is providing service mesh features for cloud-native applications, along with integration to monolithic applications running in legacy environments.

Other providers

We should also mention two new service meshes offered by AWS and Microsoft, which are outside the scope of this book but deserve to be mentioned here:

- **App Mesh**: In November 2018, AWS announced its own service mesh called App Mesh that went **General Availability (GA)** on March 2019. AWS manages the App Mesh control plane and is not open source. App Mesh uses an open source Envoy sidecar proxy for its data plane and is free to use on AWS.
- **Azure Service Fabric Mesh**: Microsoft announced its service mesh on September 2018. It is a fully managed service that's used to deploy microservices applications for developers by abstracting the platform layer. It uses an open source Envoy sidecar proxy for service discovery and routing.

  Azure's Service Fabric Mesh control plane is not open source. Microsoft is using the name Service Fabric Mesh, but it is not like Istio, Linkerd, Consul, or App Mesh. It is similar to Red Hat OpenShift and targeted at developers who have a service mesh's data plane to use. Since this is a managed service, developers will not have access to the control plane.

We'll learn more about Istio, Linkerd, and Consul by going through their architecture and different service mesh capabilities through a hands-on exercises in the next section.

A quick comparison

It is difficult to provide an apples-to-apples feature and function comparison of each service mesh provider. The technology landscape changes so fast that by the time you read this book, some features may be available that we mentioned as not available in a particular implementation.

The following comparison is not an exhaustive one by any means. We are comparing with Linkerd 2.x and not showing Linkerd 1.x capabilities. In this comparison, a cross mark does not necessarily mean that it is a missing feature, and at times, it could be a good thing. For example, Consul does not have a centralized control plane, and it could be a good thing for performance reasons.

Let's take a look:

Feature	Istio	Linkerd	Consul
Who coined the term service mesh?	✖	✔	✖
Pioneering of new ideas	✔	✖	✖
Official service mesh project of CNCF	✖	✔	✖
Full-featured and open source	✔	✔	✖ (1)
Feature-rich functions	✔	✖	✖
Predates Kubernetes	✖	✖	✔
Multi data center/cluster support	✔	✖	✔
Ease of use	✖	✔	✖
Service mesh GUI	✖	✔	✔
Built-in dashboard	✔	✔	✖
Single binary for the control and data planes	✖	✖	✔
Service mesh extends Kubernetes, VMs, and across data center	✖	✖	✔
Centralized control plane	✔	✔	✖
Runs on Kubernetes	✔	✔	✔
Runs on VMs without Kubernetes	✔	✔	✔
Distributed tracing	✔	✖	✖ (2)
Service discovery	✔	✔(3)	✔
Metrics collectio	✔	✔	✖
Mutual TLS	✔	✔	✔
Policy-based ACL	✔	✖	✖
Intention-based ACL	✖	✖	✔
Certificate Management	✔	✖ (4)	✔
Protocol – HTTP/1.2, HTTP/2.0, gRPC	✔	✔	✖
Protocol – TCP	✔	✔	✔
Use of CRD on Kubernetes	✔	✔	✖
Automatic sidecar injection	✔	✔	✔
Points to the exact location of the failure	✖	✔	✖
Traffic redirection (Blue/Green deployment)	✔	✖	✖
Traffic split (Canary deployment)	✔	✔	✖
Attribute-based routing	✔	✖	✖

Rate limiting	✔	✖	✖
Layer 7 support	✔	✔	✖
Layer 4 identity (SPIFFE)	✔	✖	✔
Native (legacy) app integration	✔(5)	✖	✔
Can a non-admin user install it?	✖	✔	✖
Retries	✔	✔	✖
Timeouts	✔	✔	✖
Circuit breakers	✔	✖	✖
Ingress controller	✔	✖	✖
Egress controller	✔	✖	✖

(1) – Some features that are used by the Ambassador in Consul are premium features.

(2) – It has a pluggable tracing capability.

(3) – Linkerd proxies do not integrate directly with Kubernetes but rely on Linkerd's control plane for service discovery. The control plane integrates with Kubernetes to build its service catalog. Service discovery does not integrate with Kubernetes but uses its control plane.

(4) – We can use Smallstep for certificate management.

(5) – Istio can run on VMs but at the time of writing, Consul is more popular in VMs.

Linkerd 2.x focuses mostly on performance, and it may not be as rich in functionality as Istio is. However, this won't last long since Linkerd 2.x is adding new features regularly. The performance comparisons that have been made between Istio and Linkerd by a few people are not exactly comprehensive in nature. It isn't fair to pitch one over the other since the technologies are evolving and improving continually. Consul has been around since before Kubernetes, and Hashicorp has a rich set of tools that work together very well. The adoption of Envoy as a sidecar proxy in Consul is a serious attempt to play well in the Kubernetes environment. This form of competition is due to service mesh choices that will make things better in the longer run.

Istio is a more feature-rich implementation, whereas Linkerd focuses on simplicity and performance. Istio uses a CNCF graduated project Envoy sidecar proxy, while Linkerd built its proxy from the ground-up, and claims to be highly performant but with a smaller footprint.

Injecting a sidecar into an application is an automated process in all three service mesh implementations.

It is difficult to rank the service mesh providers, and what ranks will be different for different end users. For example, the ease of use and performing service mesh winner is Linkerd. From a feature and innovation perspective, Istio is the clear winner, but it has a learning curve. To build a service mesh across data centers, including Kubernetes and traditional VM environments, Consul is the clear winner due to its distributed control plane and ease of installation. For a comprehensive service mesh solution in a large enterprise that meets a hybrid cloud, Istio is a promising winner.

Support services

Support and consulting services are available for each of the service mesh providers. Here is a list of support services for some of the leading service mesh providers:

- Linkerd services: `https://buoyant.io`
- Solo: `https://supergloo.solo.io` – A professional service mesh service provider for Istio, Linkerd, Consul, and AWS app mesh
- Teterate: `https://tetrate.io` – Istio and Envoy services
- Aspen Mesh: `https://aspenmesh.io` – Istio services
- Ambassador: `https://datawire.io` – Ambassador for Consul services
- Hashicorp: `https://www.hashicorp.com/products/consul/` – For Consul services

Istio is available as a managed service from IBM and Google:

- IBM: `https://www.ibm.com/cloud/istio`
- Google: `https://cloud.google.com/istio/`

AWS and Microsoft Azure provide a managed service mesh control plane, which is proprietary. However, they both use an open source Envoy sidecar proxy in their data plane.

Summary

In this chapter, we covered the high-level attributes of the Istio, Linkerd, and Consul service meshes and their capability matrices. We also covered managed service mesh providers and the support services that are available for each service mesh, as well as for the ones that are not included in this book.

Moving forward, you will notice that there will be three separate sections regarding the implementation details for Istio, Linkerd, and Consul. We will provide hands-on exercises that will help you to understand each service mesh implementation. To this end, the information that's present in this chapter will be of great help to you. We will go through the capabilities of each control plane for Istio, Linkerd, and Consul in their upcoming sections in this book.

In the next chapter, we will cover the **Service Mesh Interface (SMI)** specification and SPIFFE, which promises to provide interoperability between different service meshes and the concept of a strong identity.

Questions

1. Istio and Linkerd are only available in Kubernetes.

   A) True
   B) False

2. Istio and Linkerd use the same Envoy sidecar proxy.

   A) True
   B) False

3. The control plane must be running for the sidecar proxy to run appropriately in Istio as well as Linkerd.

   A) True
   B) False

Further reading

- *IBM, Google, and Lyft Give New Istio Microservices Mesh a Ride.* McGee, Jason, The Developerworks Blog, 2017: `https://developer.ibm.com/dwblog/2017/istio/`, accessed March 6, 2019

- *Service Mesh,* Acreman, Steven, Kubedex.Com,
  2018: `https://kubedex.com/istio-vs-linkerd-vs-linkerd2-vs-consul/`, accessed March 6, 2019

- *Amalgam8: An Integration Fabric For Microservices In The Cloud. IBM Cloud* Blog, Rothert, Doug, and Doug Rothert, IBM Cloud Blog, 2016: `https://www.ibm.com/blogs/bluemix/2016/06/amalgam8-integration-fabric-microservices-cloud/`, accessed March 6, 2019

- *Istio Service Mesh: The Step By Step Guide,* Irandoust, Kiarash, Medium, 2019: `https://itnext.io/istio-service-mesh-the-step-by-step-guide-adf6da18bb9a`

- *Control and Data Plane,* Network Direction. (2018), available at `https://networkdirection.net/articles/network-theory/controlanddataplane/`, accessed March 24, 2019

- *A sidecar for your service mesh,* Tiwari, A. (2017), available at `https://www.abhishek-tiwari.com/a-sidecar-for-your-service-mesh/`, accessed March 24 2019

- *What is Envoy? Envoy 1.12.0-Dev-712000 Documentation, Envoyproxy.Io, 2019:* `https://www.envoyproxy.io/docs/envoy/latest/intro/what_is_envoy`

- *Service Mesh (Envoy, Istio, Linkerd).* Mar, W. (2018), available at `https://wilsonmar.github.io/service-mesh/`, accessed March 24, 2019

- *Prana: A Sidecar for your Netflix PaaS-based Applications and Services,* Choudhury, D., Tonse, S., Spyker, A., and Uppalapati, R. (2014), available at `https://medium.com/netflix-techblog/prana-a-sidecar-for-your-netflix-paas-based-applications-and-services-258a5790a015`, accessed March 24, 2019

- *SmartStack: Service Discovery in the Cloud,* Serebryany, I. and Rhoads, M. (2013), available
  at `https://medium.com/airbnb-engineering/smartstack-service-discovery-in-the-cloud-4b8a080de619`, accessed March 24, 2019

5
Service Mesh Interface and SPIFFE

As the service mesh concept continues to evolve, a **Service Mesh Interface (SMI)** specification is emerging, which provides interoperability between different service meshes. Kubernetes has already made network and storage extensible through the **Container Network Interface (CNI)** and **Container Storage Interface (CSI)** specifications. In the same spirit, the **SMI** specification, though new, has started to gain traction from different service mesh providers.

This chapter will introduce you to the evolving SMI specification and the SPIFFE specification, which provide secure naming conventions for the services running in a Kubernetes environment.

In this chapter, we will cover the following topics:

- SMI
- SPIFFE

SMI

The SMI is a specification standard for portable APIs for interoperability between service mesh providers. Brendan Burns proposed the SMI in May 2019 for a common standard along the lines of CNI, CSI, and OCI, which are the abstraction interface standards for network, storage, and containers for Kubernetes.

As service meshes continue to gain momentum in order to provide an infrastructure layer on top of modern cloud-native applications, the need for a SMI specification is arising. Gabe Monroy announced the launch of the SMI in May 2019 with the launch of an open source project (https://smi-spec.io/) in collaboration with Istio, Linkerd, and Consul.

SMI intends to support tooling through an abstraction layer for frameworks such as Weavework's Flagger (`https://github.com/weaveworks/flagger`) and Rancher Labs' Rio (`https://rio.io` and `https://github.com/rancher/rio`). Microsoft, IBM Red Hat, VMware, Pivotal, Docker, Solo.io, Aspen Mesh, Canonical, and other service mesh consulting services providers and committers are lending their support to the SMI specification. The goal of SMI is to provide an API that can use service meshes irrespective of the provider, similar to other specifications, such as the **Open Container Initiative** (**OCI**), CNI, and CSI.

Any technology rarely starts with security in mind. Take, for example, plain HTTP and Telnet. Security was the second thought in these technologies, but not anymore. The need for firewalls around IT infrastructure and VPNs to securely connect from one endpoint to another is given much importance. Modern application and infrastructure layers are being designed with security in mind so that they can live in a zero-trust network environment. SPIFFE, the Secure Production Identity Framework for Everyone, is a specification that provides a secure identity through specially formed X.509 certificates to every microservice in order to remove the need for application-level authentication.

SMI specifications

The service mesh itself is very new (since 2016), so it does not have much history. A push for an SMI specification has been done to guide different service mesh providers to adhere to a well-defined API that will allow end users to easily change provider without being locked down to one implementation. The SMI specification fulfills the following key features:

- Provides a standard interface for meshes on Kubernetes
- Provides a basic feature set for common mesh use cases
- Provides flexibility to support new mesh capabilities
- Applies policies such as identity and transport encryption across services
- Captures key metrics such as error rate and latency between services
- Shifts and weighs traffic between different services

SMI defines a set of APIs, such as a collection of Kubernetes **Custom Resource Definitions** (**CRD**) and extension API servers, which will allow mesh providers to deliver their implementation.

Think of SMI as an abstract layer on top of different service mesh providers such as Istio, Linkerd, and Consul. The goal of using SMI APIs and seamlessly interchanging the underlying service mesh provider can happen in one of the following two ways:

- Service mesh providers start using SMI APIs and provide their implementation.
- Build Kubernetes operators to translate SMI into their native APIs.

The SMI specification is evolving and maintained at `https://github.com/deislabs/smi-spec`. At the time of writing, the specification is only 2 months old, and it is expected to gain momentum due to the participation of different service providers so that it can arrive at a set of APIs that can then be an abstract layer or a direct API call.

The specification starts with the following topics, but the list will grow in the future:

- **Traffic access control**: Configure access to routes based on the identity of a client.
- **Traffic specs**: Manage traffic at the protocol level.
- **Traffic split**: Split or mirror the traffic between two services for A/B testing or Canary rollout.
- **Traffic metrics**: Expose common traffic metrics for use by tools.

The SMI is intended to be a pluggable interface similar to other core Kubernetes APIs, such as NetworkPolicy, Ingress, and CustomMetrics.

SPIFFE

Secure Production Identity Framework for Everyone (SPIFFE – `https://spiffe.io`) was inspired by a few brilliant engineers due to their need to remove application-level authentication and network-level access control configuration. Joe Beda, one of the creators of Kubernetes, was the original author of the SPIFFE specification.

SPIFFE started as open source in 2016 for securely identifying software systems in dynamic and heterogeneous environments. It is mainly about establishing trust in a complex distributed environment where workloads are dynamically scaled and scheduled to run on any node in a cluster. The workloads using SPIFFE identify themselves with each other by looking at URIs such as `spiffe://trust-domain/path`, which are defined in a **Subject Alternative Name (SAN)** field in X.509 certificates.

SPIFFE's runtime environment is called the **SPIFFE Runtime Environment (SPIRE)** and is an implementation of the SPIFFE APIs to issue **SPIFFE Verifiable Identity Documents (SVIDs)** to workloads securely and verify SVIDs of other workloads. At its heart, SPIRE is a toolchain that automatically issues and rotates authorized credentials. The SPIRE server and agent can be available on plain Linux systems as well as in a Kubernetes cluster. A user ID in Linux is used to generate SVIDs, and similarly, a workload container in Kubernetes can be configured to access SPIRE.

Istio has implemented its own implementation of SPIRE for bootstrapping and issuing identities to services running in the data plane through its control plane. In Istio, Citadel securely provisions identities to every workload as it creates identities in SPIFFE format in the SAN field of the X.509 certificate. Pilot in Istio generates the secure naming information (SVID), and then it passes the secure naming information to the Envoy sidecar proxy.

Similarly, Consul uses the SPIFFE format for interoperability with other platforms.

Summary

In this chapter, we learned how the service mesh is evolving and that the SMI is in its infancy. It is worth mentioning that the SMI, in terms of standards and abstraction, plays an important role for different service providers so that they can use a common standard. We also covered SPIFFE as a specification, which provides a secure naming convention for the workload so that it can be run in a zero-trust network. Istio has implemented SPIFFE through its control plane to provide a security infrastructure where a certificate's time-to-live could be as small as 15 minutes and maintain the PKI as a self-service model.

From this point on, we'll look at each of the different service mesh implementations. However, before we do that, we will build a demo environment so that we can practice using each of the service meshes on our own Windows laptop or Apple MacBook.

Questions

1. SPIFFE is a specification and not a toolset.

   A) True
   B) False

## Chapter 5

2. SMI is an alternative to service mesh providers.

   A) True
   B) False

3. Only Istio and Consul use SPIFFE at the moment.

   A) True
   B) False

4. Istio does not use SPIRE, but it has its implementation.

   A) True
   B) False

Further reading

- *Hello Service Mesh Interface (SMI): A Specification For Service Mesh Interoperability*, Monroy, Gabe, Open Source Blog, 2019: `https://cloudblogs.microsoft.com/opensource/2019/05/21/service-mesh-interface-smi-release/`
- *Microsoft introduces Service Mesh Interface (SMI) for interoperability across different service mesh technologies*, Packt Hub, 2019: `https://hub.packtpub.com/microsoft-introduces-service-mesh-interface-smi-for-interoperability-across-different-service-mesh-technologies/`
- *Introduction To Service Mesh Interface (SMI)*, Brendan Burns At Qcon New York, Penchikala, Srini, Infoq, 2019: `https://www.infoq.com/news/2019/07/burns-service-mesh-interface/`
- *Weaveworks/Flagger*, GitHub, 2019: `https://github.com/weaveworks/flagger/blob/master/docs/gitbook/tutorials/flagger-smi-istio.md`
- *Introducing Rio – Containers At Their Best*, Shepherd, Darren, Rancher Labs, 2019: `https://rancher.com/blog/2019/introducing-rio/`
- *Understanding SPIRE*, 2019: `https://spiffe.io/spire/`
- *Securing The Service Mesh With SPIRE 0.3*, Jessup, Andrew, 2019: `https://blog.envoyproxy.io/securing-the-service-mesh-with-spire-0-3-abb45cd79810`
- *Istio security versus SPIFFE*, Istio, 2019: `https://archive.istio.io/v1.3/docs/concepts/security/#istio-security-vs-spiffe`

Section 3: Building a Kubernetes Environment

This book is not about Kubernetes, but it is fundamental when it comes to demonstrating the service mesh architecture. You can spin a Kubernetes environment easily in any public cloud, such as IBM Public Cloud, Google Kubernetes Engine, Amazon's Elastic Kubernetes Service, Microsoft's Azure Kubernetes Service, and Alibaba Container Service for Kubernetes. However, you may have to pay for these services.

In this section, we will show you how to build your Kubernetes environment.

This section contains the following chapter:

- Chapter 6, *Building Your Own Kubernetes Environment*

6
Building Your Own Kubernetes Environment

This book intends to implement service mesh architecture. However, to do this, we require a Kubernetes environment in order to learn and practice the examples throughout this book. Hence, in this chapter, we will be building this environment.

Using a managed Kubernetes service prebuilt by a cloud service provider of your choice is recommended. The advantage of a managed service is the operational point of view as it eliminates the need for upgrading the software, and maintaining the operating system and infrastructure. However, you have to pay for such a service.

If you want to simply learn and practice the examples in this book without paying money to any cloud provider, we suggest that you get a prebuilt **virtual machine** (**VM**) and then complete the following in this chapter:

- Downloading your base VM
- Performing prerequisite tasks
- Building Kubernetes using one VM
- Installing Helm and Tiller
- Installing the Kubernetes dashboard
- Installing metrics server, Prometheus, and Grafana
- (If needed) Uninstalling Kubernetes and Docker
- Powering down the VM

Technical requirements

To complete the exercises in this chapter, you will require the following equipment:

- A macOS or Windows computer with the following configuration:
  - **For Windows**: A minimum of 16 GB of RAM and an Intel Core i7 or higher processor with a minimum of 4 CPU cores
  - **For macOS**: A macOS Pro (2015) onwards with 16 GB of RAM, Intel Core i7 processor, with 4 cores, and preferably 512 GB SSD (minimum)
- A virtualization software to build a VM.

   As you go to through the book and example commands or script, pay attention to the commands that you need to run as root or as a user.

The username in the VM is `user`. The `root` and `user` passwords have been set to `password` for ease of memory. If the command uses # as a prefix, you should run it as `root`. Commands prefixed with $ need to be run as a regular user and not as `root`. We show the usage of `sudo` wherever it is required to use privileges.

- **Using a browser**: The VM has the Chrome browser installed and we will use it to run the demo web application. While you could use an `ssh` tunnel or run the `kubectl proxy` command to connect via a browser on your local machine, it will be a more consistent experience if you run the browser from within the VM during these hands-on examples.
- **Using a command-line shell**: You need to have command-line access to the VM. Either you can work directly from the VM by opening a **GNOME Terminal**, or you can also `ssh` to VM using a command-line shell such as *iTerm2* (`https://www.iterm2.com/downloads.html`) in macOS or Git Bash (`https://git-scm.com/downloads`) in Windows.

While you are going through the code snippets in the book, you will notice that, in some instances, a few lines from the code/output have been removed and replaced with dots (...) for brevity. The use of ellipses is only to show relevant code/output. The complete code is available on GitHub at `https://github.com/servicemeshbook`.

- **Typing commands**: After you build your VM and start going through chapters in chronological order for a particular section, you will find that you need to type commands in your shell. If it is a single-line command, it may just be more comfortable to type the command as it helps to grasp the content, and then the brain tends to retain it. However, if you are very familiar with Kubernetes, it may be just irritating to type the commands, especially if the command extends across multiple lines. If you are reading the online version, it will be just as simple to copy and paste the command into your running shell to avoid typing.

  If you are reading a hard copy, it will be easier for you to pull the command reference from GitHub so that you can copy and paste the commands easily.

For each implementation section of the book for Istio, Linkerd, and Consul, you can refer to the following links for the commands to use throughout the hands-on exercises:

- **Istio**: `https://github.com/servicemeshbook/istio`
- **Linkerd**: `https://github.com/servicemeshbook/linkerd`
- **Consul**: `https://github.com/servicemeshbook/consul`

 Be on top of the Kubernetes updates! You can visit `https://kubernetes.io/docs/setup/release/` to find out the latest release. The instructions given in this chapter can also be found at `https://github.com/servicemeshbook/byok`.

Downloading your base VM

The best software for virtualization on a Windows laptop is VMware Workstation. You can also use VMware Workstation Player for free for personal use on a Windows laptop for one VM. On the other hand, if you are using macOS, then the best virtualization software is VMware Fusion. You can download the VMware Fusion trial version for 30 days to complete the exercises presented in this book.

Whichever VM you are using—Windows or macOS—the following section will take you through the setup process for each of them.

Building an environment for Windows

In this section, we will begin by first downloading our virtualization software for Windows. Once downloaded, we will set our network address so that we have access to our internet and then power it up to check whether everything is in place. So, if you have decided to use Windows then follow along.

Downloading our virtualization software

We begin by first downloading our virtualization software. You can download either of the following:

- VMware Player
- Workstation Pro

Since we are using only one VM, you can download VMware Player—which is free and non-expiring—for personal use. Download it from `https://my.vmware.com/en/web/vmware/free#desktop_end_user_computing/vmware_workstation_player/15_0`. You can download, try and/or buy VMware Workstation Pro for Windows at `https://www.vmware.com/products/workstation-pro.html`. Note that this try and buy is only good for 30 days before you have to buy a license.

VMware Workstation allows you to run multiple VMs on the same machine, whereas you can only run one VM using VMware Player.

You may, instead, have a preference for Oracle VirtualBox, and you can use it instead of VMware Player or VMware Workstation. We have not tested the VM on VirtualBox.

Once downloaded, follow these steps:

1. Install either VMware Player or VMware Workstation on your Windows 10 machine.
2. After the installation of the VMware software, set the NAT `vmnet` subnet so that the VM can access the internet.

Now, let's set the network address.

Setting the network address

If you have downloaded VMware Workstation, follow these steps:

1. Go to **Edit | Virtual Network Editor**.
2. Select **VMnet8** and, if necessary, click on **Change Settings** to make changes. Make sure that the subnet IP for VMnet8 is set to 192.168.142.0.

 If the VMnet8 network is not set to 192.168.142.0, you will not be able to access the internet from inside the VM and, hence, the exercises will not work.

If you have downloaded VMware Player, the GUI does not give you an option to modify the VMnet8 network address:

1. After installation, open a command-line tool such as Windows CMD and type in ipconfig /all and you should see VMnet8:

```
Ethernet adapter VMware Network Adapter VMnet8:

Connection-specific DNS Suffix . :
Description . . . . . . . . . . : VMware Virtual Ethernet Adapter
for VMnet8 Physical Address. . . . . . . . . : 00-50-56-C0-00-08
DHCP Enabled. . . . . . . . . . : No
Autoconfiguration Enabled . . . . : Yes
Link-local IPv6 Address . . . . . :
fe80::1d5f:2196:60f9:6219%23(Preferred)
IPv4 Address. . . . . . . . . . : 192.168.191.1(Preferred)
Subnet Mask . . . . . . . . . . : 255.255.255.0
Default Gateway . . . . . . . . :
DHCPv6 IAID . . . . . . . . . . : 905990230
DHCPv6 Client DUID. . . . . . . : 00-01-00-01-24-7C-F2-70-98-
FA-9B-0E-0E-F3
DNS Servers . . . . . . . . . . : fec0:0:0:ffff::1%1
                                  fec0:0:0:ffff::2%1
                                  fec0:0:0:ffff::3%1
NetBIOS over Tcpip. . . . . . . : Enabled
```

In the preceding, the VMnet8 is set to 192.168.191.1. The IP address may be different for you.

2. Open Windows CMD as an administrator (important) by pressing *Win-R*. Type cmd and hit *Ctrl + Shift + Enter*.

3. Follow these commands to set the VMnet8 subnet address to 192.168.142.0:

```
C:\> cd "\Program Files (x86)\VMware\VMware Player"
C:\> vnetlib.exe -- stop dhcp
C:\> vnetlib.exe -- stop nat

C:\> cd \ProgramData\VMware
C:\> copy vmnetdhcp.conf vmnetdhcp.conf.pre
C:\> copy vmnetnat.conf vmnetnat.conf.pre

C:\> cd "\Program Files (x86)\VMware\VMware Player"
C:\> vnetlib.exe -- set vnet vmnet8 mask 255.255.255.0
C:\> vnetlib.exe -- set vnet vmnet8 addr 192.168.142.0
C:\> vnetlib.exe -- add dhcp vmnet8
C:\> vnetlib.exe -- add nat vmnet8
C:\> vnetlib.exe -- update dhcp vmnet8
C:\> vnetlib.exe -- update nat vmnet8
C:\> vnetlib.exe -- update adapter vmnet8

C:\> vnetlib.exe -- set vnet vmnet1 mask 255.255.255.0
C:\> vnetlib.exe -- set vnet vmnet1 addr 192.168.136.0
C:\> vnetlib.exe -- add dhcp vmnet1
C:\> vnetlib.exe -- add nat vmnet1
C:\> vnetlib.exe -- update dhcp vmnet1
C:\> vnetlib.exe -- update nat vmnet1
C:\> vnetlib.exe -- update adapter vmnet1

C:\> vnetlib.exe -- start dhcp
C:\> vnetlib.exe -- start nat
```

4. Check ipconfig /all and you should see that the VMnet8 IP address is set to 192.168.142.1

Next, let's perform some finalization checks.

Performing finalization checks

To make sure everything is fine and our VM is ready, follow these steps:

1. If you do not have 7z installed on your machine, download 7z from https://www.7-zip.org/download.html and install the 7z software.

2. Download the base VM image from https://7362.me/vm.tar.7z to a folder of your choice.

3. Select the folder and the `vm.tar.7z` file and click on **Extract**.

4. It's time to start the VM. Navigate to the folder where the VM was extracted. Right-click on `kube01.vmx` and then click on **Open with VMWare Player or VMWare Workstation**.

5. If VM prompts you to update your VMware software, cancel it. Alternatively, if it prompts you to update the VM tools in the VM, cancel it.

6. Now, let's perform a sanity check. Double-click on **Terminal**.

> The username is `user` and the password is `password`. The root password is `password`.

7. Test the internet connectivity from the VM:

```
$ dig +search +noall +answer google.com
```

If the VMnet8 subnet is set to `192.168.142.0` and your Windows machine has internet access, you should see the `google.com` IP addresses resolved in the preceding code block.

Now you are ready to install Kubernetes in your environment. You can skip straight to the *Performing prerequisite tasks* section. If you are using a macOS, the next section is for you.

Building an environment for macOS

Just as we did for our Windows VM, we will now download our virtualization software for macOS, set up its network address, and power it up to check whether it's running fine. So, grab your macOS and follow along.

Downloading our virtualization software

There is no VMware Player for macOS. The only option is to use VMware Fusion 11.x. You can install a trial copy of the VMware Fusion for 30 days to go through the exercises. So, let's begin:

1. Download VMware Fusion 11.x from `https://www.vmware.com/products/fusion/fusion-evaluation.html`.

You may have a preference for Oracle VirtualBox, and you can use it instead of VMware Fusion. We have not tested the VM on VirtualBox.

2. Install VMware Fusion on your macOS.
3. After the installation of VMware Fusion, set the **network address translation (NAT)** vmnet subnet so that the VM can access the internet.

It's time to set your network address. To do this, follow along in the next section.

Setting the network address

To set your network address, follow these steps:

1. Open a command-line shell in your macOS and run the following commands:

```
$ sudo -i
<type your password>

# vi /Library/Preferences/VMware\ Fusion/networking
```

2. Modify the VMNET_8_HOSTONLY_SUBNET line to match the following:

```
answer VMNET_8_HOSTONLY_SUBNET 192.168.142.0
```

3. Save the file.
4. Fix Gateway for VMnet8 by modifying the /Library/Preferences/VMware\ Fusion/vmnet8/nat.conf file:

```
# vi /Library/Preferences/VMware\ Fusion/vmnet8/nat.conf
```

5. Then, change the ip and netmask after the following comment:

```
# NAT gateway address
ip = 192.168.142.2
netmask = 255.255.255.0
```

6. Finally, restart the network:

```
# cd /Applications/VMware\ Fusion.app/Contents/Library/

# ./vmnet-cli --configure
# ./vmnet-cli --stop
# ./vmnet-cli --start
```

Next, let's perform some finalization checks.

Performing finalization checks

To make sure everything is fine and that our VM is ready, follow these steps:

1. Download the 7z software by installing the free 7z Unarchiver from Apple's App Store.
2. Now download the base VM image from `https://7362.me/vm.tar.7z` to a folder of your choice.
3. To launch the 7z software, select the folder and the `vm.tar.7z` file and double-click on it to extract the files.
4. Start the VM by navigating to the folder where VM was extracted. Right-click on `kube01.vmx` and then click on **Open with VMWare Fusion**.
5. Wait for the VM to start and then perform a sanity check. Double-click on **Terminal**.

> The username is `user` and the password is `password`. The root password is `password`.

6. Test the internet connectivity of the VM:

```
$ dig +search +noall +answer google.com
```

If the VMnet8 subnet was set to `192.168.142.0` and your macOS has internet access, you should see the `google.com` IP addresses resolved in the preceding code.

You are ready to install Kubernetes in your environment. However, before we do that, let's perform some prerequisite tasks.

Performing prerequisite tasks

Before we begin installing and setting up our Kubernetes, here are a few prerequisites tasks:

1. Install `socat`. For Helm, `socat` is used to set the port forwarding for both the Helm client and Tiller:

   ```
   # yum -y install socat
   ```

2. Set `SELINUX=disabled` in `/etc/selinux/config` and then reboot for it to take effect. After the reboot, you should get an output from `getenforce` as permissive:

   ```
   # getenforce
   Disabled
   ```

3. Add the Docker repository:

   ```
   # yum -y install yum-utils
   # yum-config-manager --add-repo
   https://download.docker.com/linux/centos/docker-ce.repo
   ```

4. Install Docker. Since we will be working with Kubernetes 1.15.6, the tested version of Docker for this release is `3:18.09.8-3.el7`.

   We will switch the Docker `cgroup` driver from `cggroupfs` to `systemd`:

   ```
   # mkdir -p /etc/docker
   # cat > /etc/docker/daemon.json <<EOF
   {
     "exec-opts": ["native.cgroupdriver=systemd"],
     "log-driver": "json-file",
     "log-opts": {
       "max-size": "100m"
     }, "storage-driver": "overlay2" }
   EOF
   ```

5. You can find an available version using `yum --showduplicates list docker-ce`:

   ```
   # yum -y install docker-ce-cli-18.09.8-3.el7.x86_64
   # yum -y install docker-ce-18.09.8-3.el7.x86_64
   # systemctl enable docker
   # systemctl start docker
   ```

6. Optionally, you can configure a separate disk to mount `/var/lib/docker` and restart Docker.

7. Now check `docker version`:

```
# docker version
Client:
 Version:           18.09.8
 API version:       1.39
 Go version:        go1.10.8
 Git commit:        0dd43dd87f
 Built:             Wed Jul 17 17:40:31 2019
 OS/Arch:           linux/amd64
 Experimental:      false

Server: Docker Engine - Community
 Engine:
  Version:          18.09.8
  API version:      1.39 (minimum version 1.12)
  Go version:       go1.10.8
  Git commit:       0dd43dd
  Built:            Wed Jul 17 17:10:42 2019
  OS/Arch:          linux/amd64
  Experimental:     false
```

Make sure that you have Docker `18.09.8` and not the higher version.

8. Check whether the storage driver is `overlay2` and the cgroup driver is `systemd`.

```
# docker info | grep -E "Cgroup|Storage Driver"
Storage Driver: overlay2
Cgroup Driver: systemd
```

That's it! Now we're ready to build our Kubernetes using our VM. So, let's dive straight in.

Building Kubernetes using one VM

This exercise uses a single VM to build a Kubernetes environment having a master node, an etcd database, and a pod network using Calico and Helm. Please refer to the "Further Reading" section if you want to build a multi-node cluster.

 You also have the option to just use `minikube` (https://kubernetes.io/docs/setup/learning-environment/minikube/), though. By going through this exercise, you will learn how to build your own Kubernetes environment.

Begin with these simple steps:

1. First, configure iptables for Kubernetes:

```
# cat <<EOF > /etc/sysctl.d/k8s.conf
net.ipv4.ip_forward = 1
net.bridge.bridge-nf-call-ip6tables = 1
net.bridge.bridge-nf-call-iptables = 1
EOF

# sysctl --system
```

2. Now add the Kubernetes repository:

```
# cat << EOF >/etc/yum.repos.d/kubernetes.repo
[kubernetes]
name=Kubernetes
baseurl=https://packages.cloud.google.com/yum/repos/kubernetes-el7-
x86_64
enabled=1
gpgcheck=1
repo_gpgcheck=1
gpgkey=https://packages.cloud.google.com/yum/doc/yum-key.gpg
https://packages.cloud.google.com/yum/doc/rpm-package-key.gpg
EOF
```

Perfect! Now it's time to install Kubernetes.

Installing Kubernetes

At the time of writing, Kubernetes 1.16.0 is the latest version, and it has a few deprecated APIs that will create issues in installing some of the Helm charts, especially for deployment and StatefulSets:

1. Check the available versions of the following packages:

```
# yum --showduplicates list kubeadm
```

For example, we will be selecting 1.15.6-0:

```
# version=1.15.6-0
# yum install -y kubelet-$version kubeadm-$version kubectl-$version
```

2. Enable kubelet:

```
# systemctl enable kubelet
```

3. Disable `firewalld`:

```
# systemctl disable firewalld
# systemctl stop firewalld
```

If you do not want to disable `firewalld`, you may need to open ports through the firewall. For Kubernetes, open the following:

```
# systemctl enable firewalld
# systemctl start firewalld
# firewall-cmd --zone=public --add-port=6443/tcp --permanent
# firewall-cmd --zone=public --add-port=10250/tcp --permanent
# firewall-cmd --zone=public --add-service=http --permanent
# firewall-cmd --zone=public --add-service=https --permanent
# firewall-cmd --reload
```

4. Disable `swap`. Note that Kuberenets does not like swap to be enabled:

```
# swapoff -a
```

5. Comment out the swap entry in `/etc/fstab`, for example:

```
#/dev/mapper/centos-swap swap      swap       defaults        0 0
```

Next, it's time to run `kubeadm`.

Running kubeadm

Before running the next steps, validate that the VM user has `sudo` authority to type root commands without requiring a password, by running `visudo`. There must be an `ALL=(ALL) NOPASSWD: ALL` entry:

1. Type `exit` to logout from root:

```
# exit
```

2. Pull the Kubernetes images—this may take a while on a slow internet connection:

```
$ sudo kubeadm config images pull
```

3. Check the images pulled by the preceding command:

```
$ sudo docker images k8s.gcr.io/*
REPOSITORY       TAG       IMAGE ID      CREATED      SIZE
kube-proxy       v1.15.6   d756327a2327  4 days ago   82.4MB
kube-apiserver   v1.15.6   9f612b9e9bbf  4 days ago   207MB
```

```
kube-controller-manager v1.15.6   83ab61bd43ad   4 days ago       159MB
kube-scheduler           v1.15.6   502e54938456   4 days ago       81.1MB
coredns                  1.3.1     eb516548c180   10 months ago 40.3MB
etcd                     3.3.10    2c4adeb21b4f   11 months ago 258MB
pause                    3.1       da86e6ba6ca1   23 months ago 742kB
```

4. Build the Kubernetes master node:

```
$ sudo kubeadm init --pod-network-cidr=10.142.0.0/16
```

The output is as follows:

```
<< removed >>
Your Kubernetes control-plane has initialized successfully!

To start using your cluster, you need to run the following as a
regular user:

  mkdir -p $HOME/.kube
  sudo cp -i /etc/kubernetes/admin.conf $HOME/.kube/config
  sudo chown $(id -u):$(id -g) $HOME/.kube/config

You should now deploy a pod network to the cluster.
Run "kubectl apply -f [podnetwork].yaml" with one of the options
listed at:
https://kubernetes.io/docs/concepts/cluster-administration/addons/

Then you can join any number of worker nodes by running the
following on each as root:
kubeadm join 192.168.142.101:6443 --token 2u0en7.g1igrb2w54g9bts7 \
--discovery-token-ca-cert-hash
sha256:cae7cae0274175d680a683e464e2b5e6e82817dab32c4b476ba9a3224342
27bb
```

You can get the preceding token by using the `kubeadm` token list command.

5. You can also generate a new token using the `kubeadm join` command:

```
# sudo su -
# kubeadm token create --print-join-command

# kubeadm join 192.168.142.101:6443 --token 1denfs.nw73pkobgksk0ej9
--discovery-token-ca-cert-hash
sha256:cae7cae0274175d680a683e464e2b5e6e82817dab32c4b476ba9a3224342
27bb
```

Since we will be using a single VM, the Kubernetes token from the preceding is for reference purposes only. You will need the preceding token command if you require a multi-node Kubernetes cluster.

Configuring kubectl

To configure kubectl, follow these steps:

1. Run the following command as a user and root to configure the kubectl CLI tool to communicate with the Kubernetes environment:

```
# exit

$ mkdir -p $HOME/.kube
$ sudo cp -i /etc/kubernetes/admin.conf $HOME/.kube/config
$ sudo chown $(id -u):$(id -g) $HOME/.kube/config
```

2. Check the version of Kubernetes:

```
$ kubectl version --short
Client Version: v1.15.6
Server Version: v1.15.6
```

3. Un-taint the node—this is required since we have only one VM in which to install objects:

```
$ kubectl taint nodes --all node-role.kubernetes.io/master-
```

4. Check the node status and note that it is not ready, since we have not yet installed a pod network:

```
$ kubectl get nodes
NAME     STATUS     ROLES     AGE     VERSION
osc01    NotReady   master    95s     v1.15.6
```

Check the pod status in kube-system and you will notice that the coredns pods are in the pending state. This is due to the fact that we have not yet installed the pod network.

5. Make sure that the `etcd`, `kube-apiserver`, `kube-controller-manager`, `kube-proxy`, and `kube-scheduler` pods are showing a `1/1` `READY` state and have a `Running` status:

```
$ kubectl get pods -A
NAME                                READY  STATUS    RESTARTS  AGE
coredns-bb49df795-lcjvx             0/1    Pending   0         119s
coredns-bb49df795-wqmzb             0/1    Pending   0         119s
etcd-osc01                          1/1    Running   0         80s
kube-apiserver-osc01                1/1    Running   0         60s
kube-controller-manager-osc01       1/1    Running   0         58s
kube-proxy-vprqc                    1/1    Running   0         119s
kube-scheduler-osc01                1/1    Running   0         81s
```

Moving forward, we will install the Calico network for pods.

Installing the Calico network for pods

It is important that we first choose a proper version of Calico. Visit `https://docs.projectcalico.org/v3.10/getting-started/kubernetes/requirements` for more information:

1. Here, we have tested Calico 3.10 with Kubernetes versions 1.14, 1.15, and 1.16, as follows:

```
$ export POD_CIDR=10.142.0.0/16
$ curl https://docs.projectcalico.org/v3.10/manifests/calico.yaml -O
$ sed -i -e "s?192.168.0.0/16?$POD_CIDR?g" calico.yaml
$ kubectl apply -f calico.yaml
```

It may take a while to pull the Calico images over a slow network.

2. Run the following and check that the Docker images are being pulled for Calico:

```
$ sudo docker images calico/*
REPOSITORY                    TAG      IMAGE ID      CREATED       SIZE
calico/node                   v3.10.1  4a88ba569c29  11 days ago   192MB
calico/cni                    v3.10.1  4f761b4ba7f5  11 days ago   163MB
calico/kube-controllers       v3.10.1  8f87d09ab811  11 days ago   50.6MB
calico/pod2daemon-flexvol     v3.10.1  5b249c03bee8  11 days ago   9.78MB
```

3. Check the status of the cluster and wait for all pods to be in the `Running` and `Ready 1/1` state:

```
$ kubectl get pods -A
NAME                                       READY  STATUS    RESTARTS  AGE
calico-kube-controllers-866db6d5f7-w9mfq   1/1    Running   0         33s
calico-node-mwgzx                          1/1    Running   0         33s
coredns-bb49df795-lcjvx                    1/1    Running   0         4m
coredns-bb49df795-wqmzb                    1/1    Running   0         4m
etcd-osc01                                 1/1    Running   0         3m21s
kube-apiserver-osc01                       1/1    Running   0         3m1s
kube-controller-manager-osc01              1/1    Running   0         2m59s
kube-proxy-vprqc                           1/1    Running   0         4m
kube-scheduler-osc01                       1/1    Running   0         3m22s
```

Our basic, single-node Kubernetes cluster is now up and running:

```
$ kubectl get nodes -o wide
NAME    STATUS  ROLES   AGE    VERSION   INTERNAL-IP      EXTERNAL-IP ---
osc01   Ready   master  5m28s  v1.15.6   192.168.142.101  <none>      ---


--- OS-IMAGE             KERNEL-VERSION            CONTAINER-RUNTIME
--- CentOS Linux 7 (Core) 3.10.0-957.21.3.el7.x86_64  docker://18.9.8
```

Now, let's create an admin account.

Creating an admin account

To create an admin account, follow these steps:

1. First, run the following command that creates the admin service account:

   ```
   $ kubectl --namespace kube-system create serviceaccount admin
   ```

2. Now, grant a cluster role binding to the `admin` service account to allow super-user priviledges.

   ```
   $ kubectl create clusterrolebinding admin --serviceaccount=kube-system:admin --clusterrole=cluster-admin
   ```

Our next step is to install `kubectl` on client machines.

Installing kubectl on client machines

For this task, we will use the existing VM—which already has `kubectl` and the GUI to run a browser.

However, you can use `kubectl` from a client machine to manage the Kubernetes environment. Follow the process at `https://kubernetes.io/docs/tasks/tools/install-kubectl/` to install `kubectl` on your choice of client machine (that is, Windows, macOS, or Linux).

Performing finalization checks

To make sure that everything is in place, let's go ahead and carry out some checks:

1. Install `busybox` to check and validate the Kubernetes deployments:

```
$ kubectl create -f https://k8s.io/examples/admin/dns/busybox.yaml
```

2. Now install the `hostname` deployment. First, create a deployment:

```
$ kubectl run hostnames --image=k8s.gcr.io/serve_hostname \
                        --labels=app=hostnames \
                        --port=9376 \
                        --replicas=3
```

3. Next, create a service:

```
$ kubectl expose deployment hostnames --port=80 --target-port=9376
```

4. Finally, perform a sanity check for the cluster. Check the pod with the following:

```
$ kubectl get pods
NAME       READY   STATUS    RESTARTS   AGE
busybox    1/1     Running   0          13s
```

 For more help regarding testing the cluster, you can visit `https://kubernetes.io/docs/tasks/debug-application-cluster/debug-service/`.

Installing Helm and Tiller

With the release of Helm v3, Tiller will not be required. We will be using Helm 2.x-related charts, so we will not be installing Helm 3.x until the charts have migrated to Helm 3.x.

We will be installing Helm v2.16.1 with Tiller. So, let's begin:

1. In principle, Tiller can be installed using `helm init`:

```
$ curl -s
https://storage.googleapis.com/kubernetes-helm/helm-v2.16.1-linux-a
md64.tar.gz | tar xz
$ cd linux-amd64
$ sudo mv helm /bin
```

2. Create the `tiller` service account and grant `cluster-admin` role to the `tiller` service account:

```
$ kubectl -n kube-system create serviceaccount tiller
$ kubectl create clusterrolebinding tiller --clusterrole cluster-
admin --serviceaccount=kube-system:tiller
```

Helm can be installed with and without security. You can choose any one of the following methods.

Installing without security

To install Helm without security (this is ideal for running in a sandbox environment), follow these steps:

1. Initialize `helm` and it will install the `tiller` server in Kubernetes:

```
$ helm init --service-account tiller
```

2. Wait for `tiller` to get deployed (you can check `kubectl get pods -A`).
3. Now, check `helm version`:

```
$ helm version --short
Client: v2.16.1+gbbdfe5e
Server: v2.16.1+gbbdfe5e
```

If you installed Helm without security, skip the next section and move straight to the *Installing the Kubernetes dashboard* section.

Installing with Transport Layer Security (TLS)

To install Helm with TLS (this is ideal for running in production), run the following commands:

```
$ curl -LOs
https://github.com/smallstep/cli/releases/download/v0.10.1/step_0.10.1_linu
x_amd64.tar.gz

$ tar xvfz step_0.10.1_linux_amd64.tar.gz

$ sudo mv step_0.10.1/bin/step /bin

$ mkdir -p ~/helm
$ cd ~/helm
$ step certificate create --profile root-ca "My iHelm Root CA" root-ca.crt
root-ca.key
$ step certificate create intermediate.io inter.crt inter.key --profile
intermediate-ca --ca ./root-ca.crt --ca-key ./root-ca.key
$ step certificate create helm.io helm.crt helm.key --profile leaf --ca
inter.crt --ca-key inter.key --no-password --insecure --not-after 17520h
$ step certificate bundle root-ca.crt inter.crt ca-chain.crt

$ helm init \
--override 'spec.template.spec.containers[0].command'='{/tiller,--
storage=secret}' \
--tiller-tls --tiller-tls-verify \
--tiller-tls-cert=./helm.crt \
--tiller-tls-key=./helm.key \
--tls-ca-cert=./ca-chain.crt \
--service-account=tiller

$ cd ~/.helm
$ cp ~/helm/helm.crt cert.pem
$ cp ~/helm/helm.key key.pem
$ rm -fr ~/helm ## Copy dir somewhere and protect it.
```

Once you have installed the Helm repository by using either of the preceding options, perform the following steps:

1. Update Helm `repo`:

   ```
   $ helm repo update
   ```

   If you are planning to use a secure helm for Kubernetes installation, use `-tls` at the end of the Helm commands to use TLS between Helm and the server.

2. List Helm `repo`:

```
$ helm repo list
NAME     URL
stable   https://kubernetes-charts.storage.googleapis.com
local    http://127.0.0.1:8879/charts
```

Congratulations! Helm is installed and ready to use. Our final step now is to install the Kubernetes dashboard, so let's jump straight into it.

Installing the Kubernetes dashboard

To install the Kubernetes dashboard, follow these simple steps:

1. Install the `kubernetes-dashboard` Helm chart:

```
$ helm install stable/kubernetes-dashboard --name k8web --namespace kube-
system --set fullnameOverride="dashboard"
```

 Add `--tls` to the preceding command if you're planning to use a secure helm for your Kubernetes installation.

2. Check Kubernetes pods:

```
$ kubectl get pods -n kube-system
```

NAME	READY	STATUS	RESTARTS	AGE
calico-kube-controllers-866db6d5f7-w9mfq	1/1	Running	0	170m
calico-node-mwgzx	1/1	Running	0	170m
coredns-bb49df795-lcjvx	1/1	Running	0	173m
coredns-bb49df795-wqmzb	1/1	Running	0	173m
etcd-osc01	1/1	Running	0	173m
k8web-kubernetes-dashboard-574d4b5798-hszh5	1/1	Running	0	44s
kube-apiserver-osc01	1/1	Running	0	172m
kube-controller-manager-osc01	1/1	Running	0	172m
kube-proxy-vprqc	1/1	Running	0	173m
kube-scheduler-osc01	1/1	Running	0	173m
tiller-deploy-66478cb847-79hmq	1/1	Running	0	2m24s

3. Check the Helm charts that we deployed:

```
$ helm list
NAME          REVISION        UPDATED                          ---
k8web         1               Mon Sep 30 22:21:01 2019         ---

--- STATUS       CHART                       APP VERSION   NAMESPACE
--- DEPLOYED     kubernetes-dashboard-1.10.0  1.10.1       kube-system
```

4. Check the service names for the dashboard:

```
$ kubectl get svc -n kube-system
NAME          TYPE        CLUSTER-IP     EXTERNAL-IP   PORT(S)         AGE
dashboard     ClusterIP   10.104.40.19   <none>        443/TCP         2m56s
kube-dns      ClusterIP   10.96.0.10     <none>        53/UDP,53/TCP   176m
tiller-deploy ClusterIP   10.98.111.98   <none>        44134/TCP       31m
```

5. We will patch the dashboard service from `CluserIP` to `NodePort` so that we can run the dashboard using the node IP address:

```
$ kubectl -n kube-system patch svc dashboard --type='json' -p
'[{"op":"replace","path":"/spec/type","value":"NodePort"}]'
```

Let's now run our Kubernetes dashboard to see if it's working.

Running the Kubernetes dashboard

In this section, we'll do a walk-through to access the recently installed Kubernetes dashboard.

1. First, check if the internal DNS server is accessible and resolves the hostname IP address:

```
$ kubectl exec -it busybox -- cat /etc/resolv.conf

nameserver 10.96.0.10
search default.svc.cluster.local svc.cluster.local cluster.local
servicemesh.local
options ndots:5
```

2. Check the internal service name resolution:

```
$ kubectl exec -it busybox -- nslookup kube-dns.kube-
system.svc.cluster.local
```

```
Server:    10.96.0.10
Address 1: 10.96.0.10 kube-dns.kube-system.svc.cluster.local

Name:      kube-dns.kube-system.svc.cluster.local
Address 1: 10.96.0.10 kube-dns.kube-system.svc.cluster.local
```

$ kubectl exec -it busybox -- nslookup
hostnames.default.svc.cluster.local
```
Server:    10.96.0.10
Address 1: 10.96.0.10 kube-dns.kube-system.svc.cluster.local

Name:      hostnames.default.svc.cluster.local
Address 1: 10.98.229.90 hostnames.default.svc.cluster.local
```

3. Edit the VM's `/etc/resolv.conf` file to add the Kubernetes DNS server:

   $ sudo vi /etc/resolv.conf

4. Add the following two lines for name resolution of the Kubernetes services and the save file:

   ```
   search cluster.local
   nameserver 10.96.0.10
   ```

Next, let's see how we can gain access to our Kubernetes environment.

Get an authentication token

If you need to access your Kubernetes environment remotely, follow these steps:

1. Create a `~/.kube` directory on your client machine and then **SCP** (short for **Secure Copy**) the `~/.kube/config` file from the Kubernetes master to your `~/.kube` directory.

2. Run this on the Kubernetes master node:

   $ kubectl -n kube-system describe secret $(kubectl -n kube-system
   get secret | grep admin | awk '{print $1}')

Here's the output:

```
Name:         admin-token-2f4z8
Namespace:    kube-system
Labels:       <none>
Annotations:  kubernetes.io/service-account.name: admin
              kubernetes.io/service-account.uid: 81b744c4-
```

```
ab0b-11e9-9823-00505632f6a0
Type:  kubernetes.io/service-account-token
Data
====
ca.crt:     1025 bytes
namespace:  11 bytes
token:
```

eyJhbGciOiJSUzI1NiIsImtpZCI6IiJ9.eyJpc3MiOiJrdWJlcm5ldGVzL3NlcnZpY2
VhY2NvdW50Iiwia3ViZXJuZXRlcy5pby9zZXJ2aWNlYWNjb3VudC9uYW1lc3BhY2UiO
iJrdWJlLXN5c3RlbSIsImt1YmVybmV0ZXMuaW8vc2VydmljZWFjY291bnQvc2VjcmV0
Lm5hbWUiOiJhZG1pbi10b2tlbi0ycjR6OCIsImt1YmVybmV0ZXMuaW8vc2VydmljZWF
jY291bnQvc2VydmljZS1hY2NvdW50Lm5hbWUiOiJhZG1pbiIsImt1YmVybmV0ZXMuaW
8vc2VydmljZWFjY291bnQvc2VydmljZS1hY2NvdW50LnVpZCI6IjgxYjc0NGM0LWFiM
GItMTFlOS05ODIzLTAwNTA1NjMyZjZhMCIsInN1YiI6InN5c3RlbTpzZXJ2aWNlYWNj
b3VudDprdWJlLXN5c3RlbTphZG1pbiJ9.iaWllI4XHQ9UQQHwXQRaafW7pSD6EpNJ_r
EaFqkd5qwedxgJodD9MJ90ujlZx4UtvUt2rTURHsJR-
qdbFoUEVbE3CcrfwGkngYFrnU6xjwO3KydndyhLb6v6DKdUH3uQdMnu4V1RVYBCq2Q1
bOsejsgNUIxJw1R8N7eUpIte64qUfGYtrFT_NBTnA9nEZPfPAiSlBBXbC0ZSBKXzqOD
4veCXsqlc0yy5oXHOoMjROm-<<REDACTED>>

3. Highlight the authentication token from your screen and right-click to copy it to the clipboard.
4. Find the node port for the dashboard service:

```
$ kubectl get svc -n kube-system
NAME           TYPE        CLUSTER-IP     EXTERNAL-IP  PORT(S)         AGE
dashboard      NodePort    10.102.12.203  <none>       443:31869/TCP   2m7s
kube-dns       ClusterIP   10.96.0.10     <none>       53/UDP,53/TCP   7m34s
tiller-deploy  ClusterIP   10.109.36.64   <none>       44134/TCP       3m13s
```

5. Double-click Google Chrome from the desktop of the VM and run `https://localhost:31869` and change the port number so it matches your output.
6. Paste the token from the clipboard.

You have a Kubernetes 1.15.6 single-node environment ready for use now.

7. Check if `kube-proxy` is OK. There must be two entries for the hostnames:

```
$ sudo iptables-save | grep hostnames
-A KUBE-SERVICES ! -s 10.142.0.0/16 -d 10.98.229.90/32 -p tcp -m comment --
comment "default/hostnames: cluster IP" -m tcp --dport 80 -j KUBE-MARK-MASQ
-A KUBE-SERVICES -d 10.98.229.90/32 -p tcp -m comment --comment
"default/hostnames: cluster IP" -m tcp --dport 80 -j KUBE-SVC-
NWV5X2332I4OT4T3
```

Congratulations! We are all set. It's time to explore our Kubernetes dashboard and navigate to objects, rather than type `kubectl` commands to see them through a command line.

Exploring the Kubernetes dashboard

The Kubernetes environment that we built in the VM is very elementary, with just a single master node, Helm, and a Kubernetes dashboard. To get hands-on experience using your Kubernetes environment, we will first launch the dashboard and then explore its various features. Follow these steps:

1. Open a command-line window in your VM and find the node port of the Kubernetes dashboard service:

   ```
   $ DASHPORT=$(kubectl -n kube-system get svc dashboard -o
   jsonpath={.spec.ports[*].nodePort}) ; echo $DASHPORT
   32296
   ```

   In this case, the node port is `32296`. The node port may be different in your case.

2. Open the Chrome browser within your VM, visit `https://localhost:32296`, and replace the node port with the value for your environment.

3. The Chrome browser will complain about the certificate. Click **Advanced** and **Proceed to localhost (unsafe)**:

4. You can either select the `kubeconfig` file or the authentication token. Select **Token**.

We can get the authentication token by looking at the **admin** service account secret. While you were building the Kubernetes environment, you might have noticed that we created an *admin* service account and granted *cluster-admin* privileges to it.

5. Run the following command to get the authentication token associated with the admin service account in the VM:

```
$ kubectl -n kube-system describe secret $(kubectl -n kube-system \
get secret | grep admin | awk '{print $1}')
```

The output from the preceding command will show the value of the token, which will be a very long string.

6. Select the string and copy it in the VM's clipboard.
7. Switch back to the web UI and paste the token in the input field. Click **SIGN IN**:

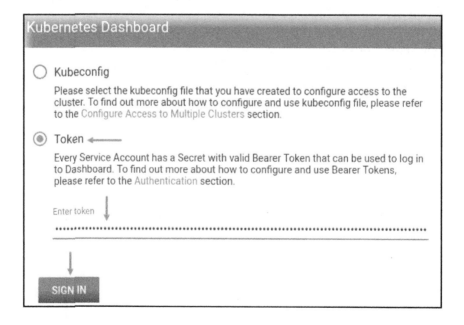

Now you can explore the Kubernetes dashboard features and navigate to the different objects, such as namespaces, workloads, discovery, load balancing, config, and storage. So let's do it!

1. Select the default namespace in the **Namespace** section.
2. On the left-hand menu under **Workloads**, click **Pods**, and you will see a `busybox` pod that you created while following the build VM instructions.
3. Click the `busybox` pod. In the top menu bar, you will see **Exec**, **Logs**, **Edit**, and **Delete** options.
4. Click **EXEC**. A command-line embedded shell will open in another browser tab. You can run commands from inside the pod.
5. Run the following command to check the DNS name resolution and the IP address of the Kubernetes DNS server:

 # nslookup kubernetes.default.svc.cluster.local

```
Server: 10.96.0.10
Address 1: 10.96.0.10 kube-dns.kube-system.svc.cluster.local
Name: kubernetes.default.svc.cluster.local
Address 1: 10.96.0.1 kubernetes.default.svc.cluster.local
```

Notice that the Kubernetes DNS server IP address is `10.96.0.10`, and the service name `kubernetes.default.svc.cluster.local` resolves to IP address `10.96.0.1`.

This was just an example of various uses of the Kubernetes dashboard. Our single-VM Kubernetes cluster is sufficient for this book. In reality, we should use a Kubernetes distribution built by a provider such as RedHat OpenShift, or use a cloud service provider such as AWS, GCP, Azure, and many others.

It is easy to build a basic Kubernetes cluster on our own, but it is very time-consuming to develop and maintain a fully functional enterprise production-ready environment. It is best in those cases to either use a public cloud or use a Red Hat OpenShift subscription for business needs. Red Hat is very developer friendly, and you can use the free Open Community distribution of Kubernetes at `https://okd.io` that powers Red Hat OpenShift.

Be on top of the Kubernetes updates! You can visit `https://kubernetes.io/docs/setup/release/` to find out the latest release.

Additional steps

The following steps are optional and are not recommended. However, if you wish, you can try them out. This section will teach you how to install the Metrics Server, VMware Octant, Prometheus, and Grafana. Then we will wind up by powering down our VM and starting it once again and thus be prepared to perform hands-on experiments in the next chapter.

Installing the Metrics Server

The Metrics Server is required if we need to run kubectl commands to show the metrics:

```
$ helm install stable/metrics-server --name metrics --namespace kube-system
--set fullnameOverride="metrics" --set args="{--logtostderr,--kubelet-
insecure-tls,--kubelet-preferred-address-
types=InternalIP\,ExternalIP\,Hostname}"
```

To install the Metrics Server, follow these steps:

1. Make sure that the v1beta1.metrics.k8s.io service is available:

```
$ kubectl get apiservice v1beta1.metrics.k8s.io
NAME                        SERVICE                AVAILABLE    AGE
v1beta1.metrics.k8s.io      kube-system/metrics    True         13m
```

   If the service shows FailedDiscoveryCheck or MissingEndpoints, it might be the firewall issue. Make sure that HTTPS is enabled through the firewall.

   If the AVAILABLE column shows False (MissingEndpoints), wait for the endpoints to become available. Try the preceding command again and make sure that the AVAILABLE column shows True for the v1beta1.metrics.k8s.io API service.

2. Run the following:

```
$ kubectl get --raw "/apis/metrics.k8s.io/v1beta1/nodes"
```

Please wait a few minutes and run the kubectl top nodes or kubectl top pods -A command to show the output.

Installing VMware Octant

VMware provides Octant, as an alternative to Kubernetes dashboard.

You can install Octant on Windows, macOS, and Linux, and it is a simple-to-use alternative to using Kubernetes dashboard. Refer to `https://github.com/vmware/octant` for the details to install Octant.

Installing Prometheus and Grafana

This is optional if we do not have enough resources in the VM to deploy additional charts.

1. Install Prometheus with the following command:

```
$ helm install stable/prometheus-operator --namespace monitoring --name mon
Note: add --tls above if using secure helm
```

2. Check the monitoring pods:

```
$ kubectl -n monitoring get pods
NAME                                         READY  STATUS    RESTARTS  AGE
alertmanager-mon-alertmanager-0              2/2    Running   0         28s
mon-grafana-75954bf666-jgnkd                 2/2    Running   0         33s
mon-kube-state-metrics-ff5d6c45b-s68np       1/1    Running   0         33s
mon-operator-6b95cf776f-tqdp8                1/1    Running   0         33s
mon-prometheus-node-exporter-9mdhr           1/1    Running   0         33s
prometheus-mon-prometheus-0                  3/3    Running   1         18s
```

3. Check the services:

```
$ kubectl -n monitoring get svc
NAME                                     TYPE        CLUSTER-IP       ---
alertmanager-operated                    ClusterIP   None             ---
mon-grafana                              ClusterIP   10.98.241.51     ---
mon-kube-state-metrics                   ClusterIP   10.111.186.181   ---
mon-prometheus-node-exporter             ClusterIP   10.108.189.227   ---
mon-prometheus-operator-alertmanager     ClusterIP   10.106.154.135   ---
mon-prometheus-operator-operator         ClusterIP   10.110.132.10    ---
mon-prometheus-operator-prometheus       ClusterIP   10.106.118.107   ---
prometheus-operated                      ClusterIP   None             ---

--- EXTERNAL-IP  PORT(S)              AGE
--- <none>       9093/TCP,6783/TCP    19s
--- <none>       80/TCP               23s
```

```
--- <none>       8080/TCP              23s
--- <none>       9100/TCP              23s
--- <none>       9093/TCP              23s
--- <none>       8080/TCP              23s
--- <none>       9090/TCP              23s
--- <none>       9090/TCP              9s
```

The Grafana UI can be opened using: `http://10.98.241.51` for the mon-grafana service. The IP address will be different in your case.

4. A node port can also be configured for `mon-grafana` to use the local IP address of the VM, instead of using the cluster IP address:

```
$ kubectl get svc -n monitoring mon-grafana
NAME           TYPE        CLUSTER-IP       EXTERNAL-IP    PORT(S)    AGE
mon-grafana  ClusterIP    10.105.49.113    <none>         80/TCP     95s
```

5. Edit the service by running `kubectl edit svc -n monitoring mon-grafana` and change the type from `ClusterIP` to `NodePort`.
6. Find out the `NodePort` for the `mon-grafana` service.

```
$ kubectl get svc -n monitoring mon-grafana
NAME           TYPE        CLUSTER-IP       EXTERNAL-IP   PORT(S)         AGE
mon-grafana  NodePort    10.105.49.113    <none>        80:32620/TCP    3m15s
```

The Grafana UI can be opened through `http://localhost:32620`, and the node port will be different in your case.

The default user ID is `admin` and the password is `prom-operator`. This can be seen through kubectl `-n` monitoring `get secret mon-grafana -o yaml`, and then run base64 `-d` against the encoded value for admin-user and admin-password secret.

You can also open the Prometheus UI either by the NodePort method described earlier or by using `kubectl port-forward`. To do this, open another command-line window to proxy the Prometheus pod's port to the original localhost terminal:

```
$ kubectl port-forward -n monitoring prometheus-mon-prometheus-operator-
prometheus-0 9090
```

Open `http://localhost:9090` to open the Prometheus UI
and `http://localhost:9090/alerts` for alerts.

If you need to free up resources from the VM, delete Prometheus using the following clean-up procedure:

```
$ helm delete mon --purge
$ helm delete ns monitoring
$ kubectl -n kube-system delete crd \
          alertmanagers.monitoring.coreos.com \
          podmonitors.monitoring.coreos.com \
          prometheuses.monitoring.coreos.com \
          prometheusrules.monitoring.coreos.com \
          servicemonitors.monitoring.coreos.com
```

Add `--tls` to the preceding command if you're using secure Helm.

Uninstalling Kubernetes and Docker

We've learned how to install and set up Kubernetes. But just if Kuberenetes needs to be uninstalled, what do you do? Follow these steps:

1. Find out the node name using `kubectl get nodes`:

```
$ kubectl drain <node name> --delete-local-data --force --ignore-daemonsets
$ kubectl delete node <node name>
```

2. Remove `kubeadm`:

```
$ sudo systemctl stop kubelet
$ sudo kubeadm reset
$ sudo iptables -F && iptables -t nat -F && iptables -t mangle -F &&
iptables -X
$ sudo yum -y remove kubeadm kubectl kubelet kubernetes-cni kube*

$ rm -fr ~/.kube
```

3. Remove Docker and the images:

```
$ sudo su -
# docker rm -f $(docker ps -qa)
# docker volume rm $(docker volume ls -q)
# docker rmi $(docker images -q)
# systemctl stop docker
# rm -fr /var/lib/docker/*
# yum -y remove docker-ce docker-ce-cli
cleanupdirs="/var/lib/etcd /etc/kubernetes /etc/cni /opt/cni /var/lib/cni
/var/run/calico /var/lib/kubelet"
for dir in $cleanupdirs; do
  echo "Removing $dir"
  rm -rf $dir
done
```

Finally, let's learn how to power up and power down the VM.

Powering the VM up and down

To **power down** the VM, follow these steps:

1. Click on **Player** | **Power** | **Shutdown Guest**.

 It is highly recommended that you take a backup of the directory after installing the Kubernetes environment. You can restore the VM from the backup to start again, should you need it.

The files in the directory may show as follows (shown using Git Bash running in Windows):

```
$ ls -lh
total 7.3G
-rw-r--r-- 1 user 197609 2.1G Jul 21 09:44 dockerbackend.vmdk
-rw-r--r-- 1 user 197609 8.5K Jul 21 09:44 kube01.nvram
-rw-r--r-- 1 user 197609    0 Jul 20 16:34 kube01.vmsd
-rw-r--r-- 1 user 197609 3.5K Jul 21 09:44 kube01.vmx
-rw-r--r-- 1 user 197609  261 Jul 21 08:58 kube01.vmxf
-rw-r--r-- 1 user 197609 5.2G Jul 21 09:44 osdisk.vmdk
-rw-r--r-- 1 user 197609 277K Jul 21 09:44 vmware.log
```

2. Copy the preceding directory to your backup drive to use later.

To **power up** the VM, follow these steps:

1. Locate `kube01.vmx` and right-click to open it either using VMware Player or VMware WorkStation.
2. Open Terminal and run `kubectl get pods -A` and wait for all pods to be ready and running.

This is a pretty basic Kubernetes cluster just using a single VM, which is good for learning purposes. Remember that, in reality, we should use a Kubernetes distribution built by a provider such as RedHat OpenShift or IBM Cloud Private, or use a public cloud provider such as AWS, Google, or Azure.

 Be on top of the Kubernetes updates! You can visit `https://kubernetes.io/docs/setup/release/` to find the latest release.

Summary

In this chapter, you have learned how to build your Kubernetes environment from the ground up using Helm and the Kubernetes dashboard. This book is not about teaching Kubernetes. However, it might be useful if you build your single VM Kubernetes environment on Windows or macOS. By doing so, you do not have to spend money to spin up compute instance(s) in a public cloud to learn the service mesh. This environment will help you to practice the hands-on experiments of different service mesh architectures in the upcoming sections.

You will now begin your journey of exploring three major service mesh architectures: Istio, Consul, and Linkerd. In the next chapter, you will learn about Istio's architecture.

Questions

1. Which of the following is not a Kubernetes platform?

   A) Apache Mesos
   B) Red Hat OpenShift
   C) Origin Community Distribution

2. Kubernetes is only available in the cloud to deploy applications.

   A) True
   B) False

3. You can deploy a legacy containerized application in a Kubernetes cluster.

   A) True
   B) False

4. You can access a monolithic application running outside the Kubernetes cluster through Kubernetes services.

   A) True
   B) False

5. Building your Kubernetes cluster on your Windows or macOS machine is very complex.

   A) True
   B) False

Further reading

- *Build Your Own Multi-Node Kubernetes Cluster With Monitoring*, Qadri, Syed Salman, 2019: https://medium.com/@salqadri/build-your-own-multi-node-kubernetes-cluster-with-monitoring-346a7e2ef6e2
- DMTN-071: *Kubernetes Installation*, Pietrowicz, Stephen, Dmtn-071.Lsst.Io, 2018, https://dmtn-071.lsst.io/
- *Kubernetes/Kubernetes*, GitHub, 2019: https://github.com/kubernetes/kubernetes

Section 4: Learning about Istio through Examples

4

Our exploration of the service mesh feature begins with Istio, which is a very popular and community-driven open source project. In this section, you will learn about the Istio service mesh through hands-on examples so that you will be able to secure, connect to, and monitor microservices.

This section contains the following chapters:

- Chapter 7, *Understanding the Istio Service Mesh*
- Chapter 8, *Installing a Demo Application*
- Chapter 9, *Installing Istio*
- Chapter 10, *Exploring Istio Traffic Management*
- Chapter 11, *Exploring Istio Security Features*
- Chapter 12, *Enabling Istio Policy Controls*
- Chapter 13, *Exploring Istio Telemetry Features*

Understanding the Istio Service Mesh

7

Istio is the first service mesh implementation that works by injecting Envoy as a sidecar proxy alongside each microservice. The sidecar intercepts all of the service's traffic and handles it more intelligently than a simple L3/L4 network does. A mesh of sidecars constitutes the data plane in which each microservice has its own sidecar as a proxy. The control plane manages and coordinates the work of the sidecars through a set of central components. Overall, the service mesh is an abstract layer on top of applications to handle service-to-service communication.

In this chapter, we will understand the architecture of Istio from the perspective of the control plane to look at its features and functions. We will see how the control plane, through policies and configurations, manages the proxies running in a data plane. By the end of this chapter, you will have a good understanding of Istio, which will be very helpful as we go about performing hands-on experiments in the upcoming chapters.

In this chapter, we will cover the following topics:

- Control plane
- Data plane
- Observability features

Technical requirements

To complete the hands-on exercises in this chapter, you need to have a Kubernetes environment up and running. For instructions on how to do this, please refer to `Chapter 6`, *Building Your Own Kubernetes Environment*.

You can find the code files for this chapter at `https://github.com/servicemeshbook/istio/`.

Introducing the Istio service mesh

Istio's journey began on May 2017 with its first alpha release of 0.1. Istio's 1.0 production-level release launched in July 2018. Since its inception, 80+ releases of Istio have been published, which shows the dynamism of this trendy open source project. At the time of writing, it is the most popular service mesh framework, with 18,000+ stars, 3,000+ forks, and 100+ companies around the world contributing to it. It has an active developer community around it.

Before the service mesh concept came to light, libraries such as Netflix's Hystrix (`https://github.com/Netflix/Hystrix`) and Twitter's Finagle (`https://github.com/twitter/finagle`) were popular for serving Java-based programs. Then came Lyft's Envoy (`https://github.com/envoyproxy/envoy`), which changed the dynamics as it could run as a sidecar proxy and hence provided a language-agnostic decoupled implementation.

The community maintains the Istio project at `http://istio.io`. Istio is a very feature-rich function framework that provides comprehensive service mesh capabilities.

Istio initially started with different technologies from IBM, Google, and Lyft (for more information, go to `https://github.com/istio/community#istio-authors`):

- **IBM**'s research project, **algam8** (Rothert), provides a programmable control plane that has unified traffic routing. This control plane helps with blue/green testing, canary releases, and testing the resilience of services against failures.
- **Google** provides a programmable control plane that has policies for rate limits, authentication, and ACLs. The control plane gathers telemetry data from various services and proxies.

- **Lyft** provided Envoy (`https://envoyproxy.io`), which is a sidecar for a microservice. Envoy is a graduated project from CNCF.

Now, let's go through Istio's architecture.

Istio's architecture

While discussing the service mesh, you will come across L4/L5 or L7 Layers. These terms originated from the **Open System Interconnect (OSI)** model (`https://tinyurl.com/y4g7zuce`), which explains that there's seven types of layers for communication, as follows:

- **Layer 1**: Physical Layer
- **Layer 2**: Data Link Layer
- **Layer 3**: Network Layer
- **Layer 4**: Transport Layer
- **Layer 5**: Session Layer
- **Layer 6**: Presentation Layer
- **Layer 7**: Application Layer

A service mesh manages traffic between microservices at Layer 7 of the OSI model.

Overall, the service mesh is an infrastructure for handling service-to-service communication. This chapter will provide a high-level overview of the control plane and the data plane.

Let's understand what the control and data planes are. The terms **control plane** and **data plane** were used initially in software-defined networks. Routers and switches use a conceptual model called **planes**. You can think of the control plane as the brain of the network (altering and filtering data) and the data plane as the device that the network traffic flows through (it forwards the traffic). For example, let's say you bought a router a few years ago that came with its own software. Later, you found that you could upgrade the software without changing the hardware. The software is the control plane, while the physical devices are the data or forwarding plane.

The same concept applies to a service mesh architecture, where a proxy handles the communication between services. The control plane manages proxies running in a data plane through policies and configurations. This can be seen in the following diagram:

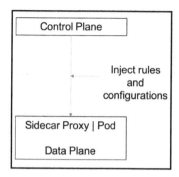

These two abstract components essentially define Istio's architecture, as shown in the following diagram:

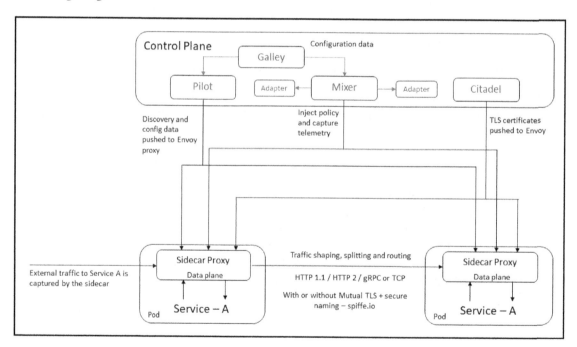

Istio uses an extended version of the Envoy proxy. Envoy is a battle-tested, highly performant, low latency, independent component. It collects shapes, shifts, and splits and routes traffic and collects telemetry for all of the service calls. It can filter L3 and L4 layers for byte-in and byte-out data through multiple protocols, such as HTTP/1.1, HTTP/2, gRPC, and TCP.

The proxy is deployed alongside all of the service pods as a sidecar proxy to intercept calls between the services and the clients. Envoy isn't a library but a separate container that can be updated independently from the microservice it is proxying.

Taking this information forward, let's go through the control and data planes to understand the concept of Istio's service mesh.

Control plane

The purpose of the control plane is to set the policies and configurations for all of the data planes running as a service mesh. As we mentioned in `Chapter 3`, *Service Mesh Architecture*, an ideal service mesh should follow the ORASTAR principle. Take a look at the following diagram:

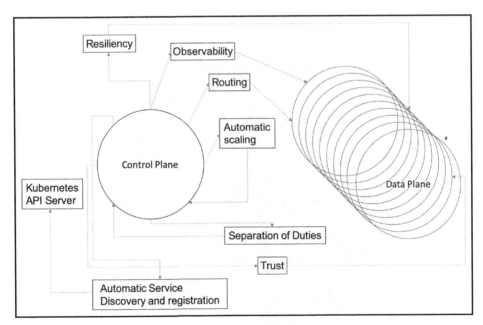

From the preceding diagram, we can see that the control plane satisfying the ORASTAR principle resides in the Kubernetes master nodes. You can run the control plane through the use of taints and tolerations to limit the control plane nodes to a set of dedicated nodes. The microservice with sidecar proxy applications running in worker nodes form a data plane. The control plane is a set of pods that communicate with the data plane's set of pods, which have a sidecar proxy.

Sometimes, the service mesh is also attributed to a mesh of a sidecar proxy, such as Envoy or Linkerd, which runs side by side with each microservice. Conceptually, this is true since a mesh is formed in the data plane. The control plane provides many more management capabilities apart from the sidecar proxy.

The Istio control plane has four main components:

- **Pilot**
- **Mixer**
- **Galley**
- **Citadel**

The control plane in Istio is like a hub and spoke architecture that manages the data plane that was created by the sidecar proxies of the application components or services:

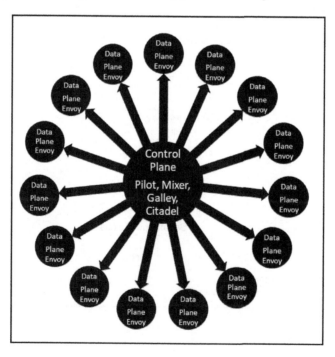

Istio extends the Kubernetes API server for configuration management and access control. It uses Kubernetes' built-in datastore, called etcd, to store its state and configuration.

Now, let's take a closer look at these components, one by one.

Galley

Galley is mostly a behind-the-scenes component for gathering and validating user configuration for the other parts of the system. It is a component of Istio's control plane and provides configuration validation, ingestion, processing, and distribution using the **Mesh Configuration Protocol** (**MCP** – `https://archive.istio.io/v1.3/docs/reference/config/istio.mesh.v1alpha1/`). An external service registry, such as Eureka Server in Spring Cloud or Zookeeper for Apache Dubbo, can integrate with the Istio control plane through Galley.

Galley works in the background by providing configuration management services to different Istio components. Galley helps to shield the rest of the Istio components from the specific details of obtaining user configuration for platforms other than Kubernetes. The Galley was initially developed to verify configuration details but was later extended to a configuration center for the entire control plane.

It contains Kubernetes **Custom Resource Definition** (**CRD**) listeners for collecting configuration using `/admitpilot` and `/admitmixer` from the Galley server, a **Mesh Configuration Protocol** (**MCP**) server implementation for distributing configuration, and a validation webhook for preingestion validation by the Kubernetes API Server:

```
$ kubectl get validatingwebhookconfiguration istio-galley
NAME            CREATED AT
istio-galley    2019-07-30T03:00:43Z
```

MCP provides a set of APIs for configuring subscriptions and distributions. Pilot and Mixer, which we will discuss in the following sections, are the consumers of the Galley. The resource is sent to the consumer. Here, it's the configuration that's applied. Pilot and Mixer connect to the Galley server as clients of the service for configuration subscription. Galley can be configured to actively connect to sinks (Pilot/Mixer) in remote Istio clusters.

For example, in a mesh of multiple Kubernetes clusters, in the primary cluster, Galley can provide configuration management for various clusters of Pilot/Mixer. Galley can initiate the connection as the client of gRPC, while Pilot/Mixer implements the ResourceSink service as the gRPC server.

There is a Galley dashboard in Grafana that we can use to view the scraped metric from Galley through Prometheus. (We will deep dive into Prometheus and Grafana in `Chapter 13`, *Exploring Istio Telemetry Features*.)

Galley sits behind the scenes performing configuration management. What pushes all of those configuration policies to the Envoy sidecar proxies? That would be Pilot. Let's learn more about it.

Pilot

Pilot is the core traffic management component of Istio's control plane for the Envoy sidecars. It pushes communication-based policies to sidecar proxies at runtime to enforce traffic management configurations for intelligent routing, such as Canary deployments, blue/green testing, and resiliency features such as timeouts, retries, and circuit breakers. These are all topics that we will look at in more detail later in this chapter.

The following diagram shows the Pilot architecture:

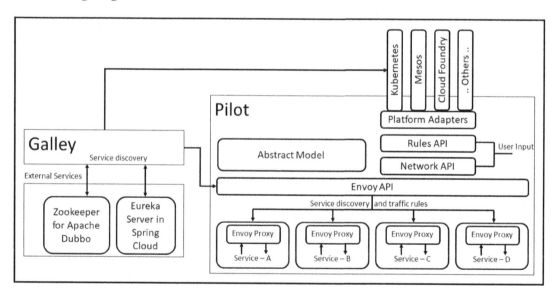

As we can see, Pilot maintains an abstract model of all of the services in the mesh that have been discovered through either Kubernetes or external services through **Galley**. The platform-specific adapters, such as Kubernetes, Mesos, Cloud Foundry, and so on, are used to populate the abstract model with the service registry and resource information. Kubernetes keeps the service discovery metadata in the etcd database when we create Kubernetes services.

The etcd database is updated when the endpoints are updated when a pod becomes healthy. The traffic management policies that are defined using Istio provide Kubernetes **Custom Resource Definitions (CRD)** and are pushed down to the Envoy sidecar for implementation.

Service discovery

Out of the box, Kubernetes has a high-level functional service mesh that provides service discovery for the necessary pods/containers and enables round-robin network requests for service versioning. There are no retries, timeouts, or any other features that the service mesh typically provides and can handle for a microservice.

The functional capability of a service registry is to keep track of all service pods and virtual machines for the designated application. With support from Istio, Kubernetes allows all new instances of a service, such as a new version, to be automatically registered within the service registry. For example, services without connections to pods are dead services and those services hide from discovery.

In Istio, the pilot consumes service configurations from the service registry and provides a platform-agnostic service discovery interface. The sidecar proxy is configured for service discovery and dynamically updates the load balancing weight pools for every service. This can be seen in the following diagram:

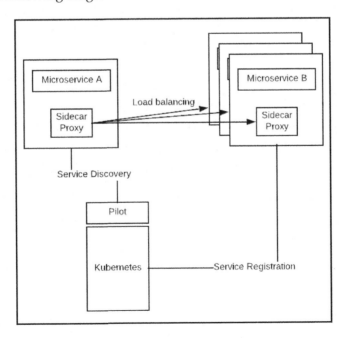

In the preceding diagram, all of the network traffic that's bound to a microservice is rerouted through the sidecar proxy. By enabling a load balancer **within the cluster**, the sidecar proxy can distribute traffic requests across any service instance. The sidecar proxy, that is, Envoy, supports a long list of load balancing algorithms. Within Istio and its latest version, Envoy is certified against three specific modules, such as weighted request, round-robin, and random percentage assignment.

Pilot has an abstract model for services that external platform services can fill to register external services. Galley can function for configuration management for external services. Pilot takes the metadata from microservices deployed in the Kubernetes API server and pushes updated pod configurations to sidecar proxies. It also abstracts service discovery so that sidecars can consume it as a standard format. Pilot receives user-defined policies, which are then pushed to the sidecar proxies to enforce policy-based rules.

Now that we understand Istio-enabled service discovery, we will learn how to implement traffic management policies using Istio-defined primitives.

Traffic management

Envoy proxies communicate directly with the application microservices. The control plane only interacts with the Envoy proxy for policy-based rules. The Envoy proxy intercepts all inbound and outbound traffic for all of the services in the mesh.

In the upcoming `Chapter 10`, *Exploring Istio Traffic Management Capabilities*, you will see the `istio-init` container at the time of its deployment. The init container sets the `iptables` rules to divert inbound and outbound traffic from the microservice to the Envoy sidecar proxy.

Pilot is easy to understand through Istio configuration primitives such as *gateways, virtual services, service entry*, and *destination rules*. The following workflow explains a gateway for a specific application that multiple virtual services can connect to. The virtual service can point to different services based upon a path, URI, headers, cookies, or subsets defined through the destination rules. Load balancing and traffic management to external services through the service entry is what happens in L7 traffic management:

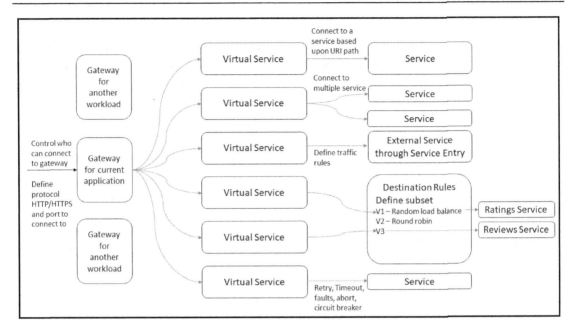

The preceding diagram is a simplified illustration of the relationship between the gateway, virtual services, destination rules, and service entry.

The Istio primitive gateway is the one that facilitates virtual service connection to external incoming and outgoing traffic. Let's explore Istio-defined gateways.

Gateway

Istio has an Ingress gateway, which is a reverse proxy that's implemented through Envoy. The purpose of Ingress is to allow access to services from outside the cluster. As shown in the following diagram, external inbound and outbound communication goes through configured Ingress and Egress gateways:

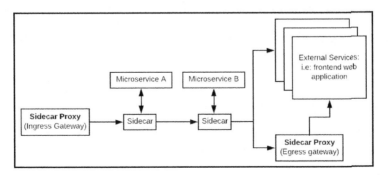

As we can see, **Microservice A** (for example, `microservice-a.mynamespace.cluster.local:9085`) is exposed to internet domain names such as `www.example.com:443` through the Istio Ingress gateway. The client **TLS** (short for **Transport Layer Security**) termination is done at the Ingress gateway.

For incoming as well as outgoing requests, the Ops can apply various failure recovery features and collect detailed telemetry data using the sidecars of the Ingress and Egress gateways. The Ingress and Egress gateways sit at the edges of the service mesh.

Gateway is an Istio primitive that's defined through custom resource definition so that it can be managed either through the `kubectl` or `istioctl` command:

```
$ kubectl get crd gateways.networking.istio.io
NAME                             CREATED AT
gateways.networking.istio.io     2019-07-21T23:09:09Z
```

 In most cases, we can use `kubectl` and `istioctl` interchangeably, but there are a few isolated instances where we have to use `istioctl`. (Also, remember that this is just sample output— we'll explain this in more detail when we dive into Chapter 9, *Installing Istio*)

The default demo profile installation of Istio provides gateways that are used to manage inbound and outbound traffic for your mesh. The Ingress gateway can be configured to provide access to microservices inside the service mesh from outside of the Kubernetes cluster. Similarly, you can configure an Egress gateway as a dedicated exit point for the traffic, leaving the mesh and configuring each Egress gateway so that it uses its policies and telemetry.

Istio provides two gateways to manage incoming (ingress) and outgoing (egress) traffic. This can be seen by using `kubectl`. This allows us to view the running pods in the Istio namespace after Istio has been installed, as follows:

```
$ kubectl get pods -n istio-system | grep gateway
NAME                                     READY   STATUS    RESTARTS  AGE
istio-egressgateway-9b7866bf5-996fc      1/1     Running   1         6d17h
istio-ingressgateway-75ddf64567-4vjqk    1/1     Running   1         6d17h
```

These gateways work seamlessly with your existing Nginx controller (or any other controller) through your Kubernetes platform provider. For the purpose of this book, we are using a bare minimum Kubernetes environment without an Nginx gateway. It is interesting to note that Istio provides these gateways out of the box to manage inbound and outbound traffic seamlessly.

We can define multiple gateways, and there can be a dedicated gateway for each application. For example, if the entry service name for an application is productpage, the sidecar proxy for this service is at the edge of the mesh receiving traffic through a user-defined virtual service referencing the user-defined gateway. This means that we are configuring an Envoy proxy for the productpage microservice to control the traffic entering the mesh.

You can use Egress gateways to limit which internal microservices can access external networks. For example, you can deny access to internal microservices from accessing any external services except whitelisted services that you trust:

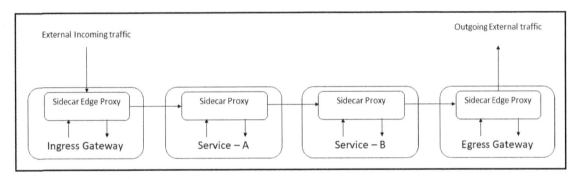

An example of a gateway is as follows:

```
apiVersion: networking.istio.io/v1alpha3
kind: Gateway
metadata:
  name: mygateway
spec:
  selector:
    istio: ingressgateway
  servers:
  - port:
      number: 80
      name: http
      protocol: HTTP
    hosts:
    - "*"
```

Istio deployments are deployed through YAML. We'll explain the Istio YAML structure in the implementation chapters of this book, that is, Chapter 10, *Exploring Istio Traffic Management Capabilities,* and Chapter 13, *Exploring Istio Telemetry Features.*

In the preceding code, we are defining that plain HTTP traffic is allowed through this gateway. The communication port can be changed so that it uses port 443 and the HTTPS protocol. The hosts defined as * means that the traffic will be allowed from any external host. This traffic can be restricted to a known external host if this application is purely a business-to-business application. Notice that no routing has been defined, which can be defined using a virtual service. The purpose of the gateway is to define ports and protocols and the proof of those names either by using a fully defined path for the server certificate and a private key bound to a particular hostname or by using the **Secret Discovery Service (SDS)** protocol to protect the certificate and keys. An example of this is as follows:

```
apiVersion: networking.istio.io/v1alpha3
kind: Gateway
metadata:
  name: httpbin-gateway
spec:
  selector:
    istio: ingressgateway # use istio default ingress gateway
  servers:
  - port:
      number: 443
      name: https
      protocol: HTTPS
    tls:
      mode: SIMPLE
      serverCertificate: /etc/istio/ingressgateway-certs/tls.crt
      privateKey: /etc/istio/ingressgateway-certs/tls.key
    hosts:
    - "httpbin.example.com"
```

The external domain name (httpbin.example.com) in the preceding gateway definition uses file mounts to present the server certificate and the private key to provide the proof of domain name to the client. SIMPLE mode means that only the server will present its identity to the client but the client will not present its identity to the server.

Note that the preceding method presents a security challenge since certificates are stored in a filesystem, so this is not recommended. Istio has a better method of using SDS to protect certificates and keys.

It is important to note here that the Istio ingress gateway operates at the Layer 4 level on top of the Layer 3 network provided by the underlying network. The connectivity between two different Ingress gateways of two different service meshes (regardless of their geographical location) can be enabled through **mutual TLS (mTLS)**, which might eliminate the need for any VPN between two locations.

Now that we've defined the Istio gateway, let's define the virtual service that uses the gateways.

Virtual service

Virtual service is an Istio configuration primitive that's created through a custom resource definition in Kubernetes. It dynamically defines how traffic destined for an internet domain name flows to a set of services inside the Kubernetes cluster, and this is all dynamic. This means that the traffic can stream to any service within the mesh based on certain rules.

The following virtual service forwards all traffic coming from the Ingress gateway to the `productpage` service in an `istio-lab` namespace. The virtual service binds to a specific gateway. Remember that the virtual service can be changed dynamically—this is the loose coupling between a gateway and a microservice:

```
apiVersion: networking.istio.io/v1alpha3
kind: VirtualService
metadata:
  name: bookinfo
spec:
  hosts:
  - "*"
  gateways:
  - mygateway
  http:
  - match:
    - uri:
        prefix: /api/v1/products
    route:
    - destination:
        host: productpage.istio-lab.svc.cluster.local
        port:
          number: 9080
```

As per the preceding definition, the `bookinfo` virtual service routes the external HTTP traffic of port `80` (which is implicit for the HTTP protocol) to the internal `productpage` microservice at port `9080`.

The virtual service is a way to create a hierarchy (top-down virtual services) to define the traffic to different services using a routing path. This allows each team to manage their own virtual service definitions instead of having one virtual service. For example, the top-level virtual service splits the traffic based upon a path to a logical set of services, and then each logical set can define a set of nested virtual services that are managed by separate teams to provide a decoupled architecture of defining virtual services.

Traffic management capabilities such as routing rules, fault injection, and abort rules are all defined through virtual services. We'll look at these in the following subsections.

Routing rules

Istio can route a service request based on HTTP headers and specific network parameters. Based on routing rules, Pilot dynamically allows the sidecar proxy to select a version of the service, defines tags based on source and destination, applies headers, assigns weights to each service, and determines the service's incremental number. Users of the microservice have no knowledge of the different versions as it doesn't disrupt their work effort. The hostname and IP address of that service will still be accessible because the sidecar proxy forwards all service requests and responses between the user and the microservice.

Istio really shines through the use of virtual services to perform traffic routing based on the following:

- Routing traffic to a specific service (one to one)
- Routing traffic to multiple services (one to many)
- Routing traffic to multiple versions of a service (one to many)
- Adding multiple match conditions to route traffic to different services
- Routing rules to rewrite a URL
- Routing rules to set a retry policy
- Routing rules based upon HTTP headers/request cookies
- Routing rules based upon the request URI

Routing is explained with a hands-on example in `Chapter 10`, *Exploring Istio Traffic Management Capabilities.*

Fault injection

The sidecar proxy provides a list of failure recovery network mechanisms for all the services being managed by Istio. As good practice, operators should not skip end-to-end service failure testing for the entire application. You may encounter restrictive timeouts of individual components when you test for overall failure recovery. Let's understand this with an example—you introduce 10 seconds of fault injection for end-to-end testing for a full life cycle of a transaction. However, you notice a particular intermediate service failure due to its own timeout of 6 seconds. You won't be able to notice the intermediate service failure without the fault injection feature.

To prevent such matters, Istio provides transparent fault injection for the service mesh. Instead of deleting service pods/containers to simulate packet loss at the TCP layer or to troubleshoot network latency, the best recommendation is to treat all observed application layers for fault tolerance, regardless of what the network failures might be. Continue to identify and isolate meaningful failures so that they can be injected at the application layer to enable application resiliency. Faults are injected into network requests that match certain conditions and enable request restrictions that might be prone to faults.

There are two types of fault injections that can be deployed:

- Delays
- Aborts

A *delay* is a *timeout* failure that can be caused by recently spiked network latency or a service overload from a downstream call. *Aborts* are service crashes that arrive from a downstream service. The majority of the time, this is either a connectivity issue or an HTTP 400 or 500 error.

Testing microservices for faults can be very challenging, but with the use of the virtual service primitive, it is possible to inject faults into the running application to test out their resiliency. This is a very important method for the **Site Reliability Engineering (SRE)** team.

By changing the definition of a service in real- time, the faults can be injected. For example, the following definition in a virtual service will introduce a delay of 2 seconds for 5% of the requests to the `ratings` service:

```
hosts:
- ratings
http:
- fault:
    delay:
      percentage:
        value: 0.05
      fixedDelay: 2s
```

Next, we'll introduce abort rules.

Abort rules

The following modification to a virtual service will inject an HTTP 400 code for 5% of the requests and abort instead of terminating to simulate a failure:

```
spec:
  hosts:
  - ratings
  http:
  - fault:
      abort:
        percentage:
          value: 0.05
        httpStatus: 400
    route:
    - destination:
        host: ratings
        subset: v1
```

Next, we'll discuss the service entry feature.

Service entry

Service entry is an Istio primitive that's created through a custom resource definition in Kubernetes. The purpose of a service entry is to add an external service entry to Istio's abstract model, as shown in the architecture diagram, to make it look as if it was a service in your mesh. Once an external service entry has been defined through service entry, it can be subjected to the same policies, such as retry, timeout, and fault injection, since they are applied to internal services.

Note that Istio configures the Envoy proxies so that they pass through requests to external unknown services by default. In such cases, Istio's features can't be used to control the traffic to destinations that are not registered in the mesh.

By adding an external service running in a **Virtual Machine** (**VM**), we can expand the mesh beyond the Kubernetes cluster. This also helps to add services from a different cluster to the mesh to configure a multi-cluster Istio mesh on Kubernetes.

Through the use of the Egress gateway and the service entry primitive, we can configure Envoy so that it performs TLS origination to secure the traffic to external endpoints.

The security posture should always begin with a deny (blacklist) and allow (whitelist) rule, for example, deny access from all and then allow access to those who have a need for it. The whitelist is a list of subjects that have a legitimate need for access, while the blacklist is a deny rule that disallows services to either all or to a list of subjects.

The following is an example of allowing access to an external endpoint as a whitelisted service for the microservices application:

```
apiVersion: networking.istio.io/v1alpha3
kind: ServiceEntry
metadata:
  name: ibm
spec:
  hosts:
  - www.ibm.com
  ports:
  - number: 443
    name: https
    protocol: HTTPS
  resolution: DNS
  location: MESH_EXTERNAL
```

Next, we'll discuss the destination rule.

Destination rule

Destination rule is an Istio primitive that's created through custom resource definition in Kubernetes. The virtual service is used to define the traffic rules. The destination rule sets policies that apply to traffic that are intended for the service after routing has occurred.

The destination rules can be used for the following reasons:

- Load balancing
- Connection pool size
- Evicting unhealthy hosts

A subset can be defined in destination rules to subdivide and label the instances of a service. This means that you can split a service into subsets based upon labels.

The load balancing feature is built-in as opposed to there being an external load balancer. The load balancer feature defines the connection pool size, while time to live or keep it live is implemented through the Istio primitive destination rule.

Load balancing

Load balancing offers traffic management for transactions at Layer 4 of the OSI model, which is the network protocol layer (TCP/UDP). Load balancing at L4 delivers traffic with limited network information. It does this with an algorithm (that is, round-robin), which calculates the best server based on the low number of connections and fast server response times.

The debate of L4/L5 versus L5/L7 is irrelevant for us if the L4 layer cannot provide load balancing for gRPC or HTTP/2 protocol, which uses a long-lived session with multiple requests.

The OSI networking model for L4-L7 is explained in more detail at https://bit.ly/2vCFLie.

HTTP/1.1 protocol load balancing works well at the connection level (L4) since one connection can have only one active request.

L7 load balancing works at the highest level of the OSI model. L7 bases its routing decisions on various characteristics of the HTTP/HTTPS header, the content of the message, the URL type, and the information in cookies.

In gRPC/HTTP/2, a connection can have multiple active requests (request multiplexing). L4 connection-level load balancing will route traffic from this one long-lived connection to just one microservice, even if we have "x" number of replicas running. This can be seen in the following diagram:

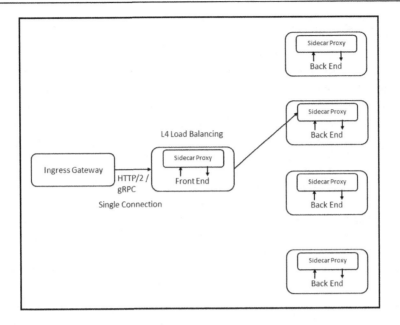

The preceding diagram shows an L4 load balancer. For gRPC, all the requests end up at one backend service, even though other replicas are available. Linkerd addresses this problem at the proxy level by resorting to request-level routing for HTTP/2 and gRPC by using L7 load balancing:

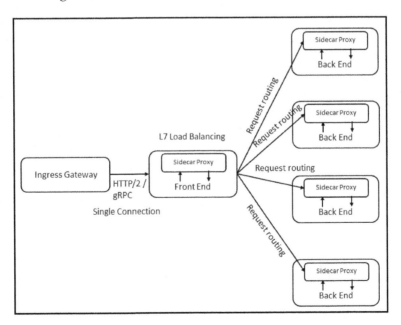

In the preceding diagram, you can see that a sidecar proxy opens connections to all of the replicas of a backend service through the L7 load balancing request for gRPC/HTTP/2.

As an add-on to load balancing, sidecar will regularly check the health of each service instance that's deployed within a platform. The sidecar proxy classifies a service instance as unhealthy or healthy based on its health checks. If a service health check has multiple failures and it surpasses the defined threshold, it will be removed from the load balancer. In parallel, when a health check runs again on that service instance and it passes the specified threshold, it will be added back into the load balancer. For example, if a service instance is a shopping application and the page unexpectedly responds with an HTTP 5xx error, the load balancer will immediately remove this service from the load balancer until the error is corrected by the operator or other sources, such as a DB.

The following are the load balancing features that can be applied through destination rules:

- Round-robin
- Random
- Weighted
- Least requests

The following is an example of load balancing three subsets. As we can see, a single destination rule is used to define multiple policies. There's a simple random load balancer for the v1 and v3 subsets and a round-robin local balancer for v2:

```
apiVersion: networking.istio.io/v1alpha3
kind: DestinationRule
metadata:
  name: my-destination-rule
spec:
  host: my-svc
  trafficPolicy:
    loadBalancer:
      simple: RANDOM
  subsets:
  - name: v1
    labels:
      version: v1
  - name: v2
    labels:
      version: v2
    trafficPolicy:
      loadBalancer:
        simple: ROUND_ROBIN
  - name: v3
    labels:
      version: v3
```

The reviews virtual service has two rules:

- All incoming requests with the Foo header that have a bar value go to the reviews service's v2 subset.
- All other requests go to the v1 subset.

This can be seen in the following code:

```
apiVersion: networking.istio.io/v1alpha3
kind: VirtualService
metadata:
  name: reviews
spec:
  hosts:
  - reviews
  http:
  - match:
    - headers:
        Foo:
          exact: bar
    route:
    - destination:
        host: reviews
        subset: v2
  - route:
    - destination:
        host: reviews
        subset: v1
```

One very important point to note about load balancing is that it occurs at the mesh level, without requiring the use of an external proxy load balancer.

Circuit breaker

The circuit breaker is an integral pattern for making microservices resilient by limiting failures, spiked latency, and other network anomalies that might disrupt a service's workflow. This capability is configured at the application layer. We should enable circuit breaker rules and then intentionally break the rules to test the resiliency of an application. The most popular tasks that enable circuit breaking are for connections, requests, and outlier detection.

Policies for circuit breaking can be defined as `DestinationRule` in the YAML configuration file for a designated service. A circuit breaker rule is defined using destination rules, which are a set of policies that are requested after a `VirtualService` routing is defined and deployed. The `DestinationRule` policy execution should be a restrictive task, and only service owners should prescribe what the load balancer, circuit breaker, and TLS settings should be.

A circuit breaker helps an application to fail fast and it prevents the application from stalling if it is waiting for an upstream service response.

We can set a limit of 100 connections for the `reviews` service's `v1` subset through the following rule:

```
apiVersion: networking.istio.io/v1alpha3
kind: DestinationRule
metadata:
  name: reviews
spec:
  host: reviews
  subsets:
  - name: v1
    labels:
      version: v1
    trafficPolicy:
      connectionPool:
        tcp:
          maxConnections: 100
```

When the `v1` subset is used in a virtual service, the circuit breaker will trip when the number of connections exceeds 100. This can happen if the `reviews:v1` service is slow and unable to handle a large number of concurrent requests. After the circuit breaker trips, `reviews:v1` will not receive any requests until the congestion clears.

Blue/green deployment

A blue/green deployment is one where old and new deployments are available, and you can flip the traffic from one set to another in the case of some issues/problems. You can perform a blue/green deployment using a destination rule with two subsets and then use a virtual service to direct the traffic to a specific subset. Then, you can switch between them by modifying the virtual service.

Canary deployment

The best way to understand the concept of a subset is to think about a canary deployment, where you split traffic into two subsets based upon labels such as **v1** and **v2** and then gradually shift the traffic to make a canary deployment production. Finally, you remove the old production deployment from service.

The term canary comes from the practice of taking a caged canary (bird) into a mine where the bird may die from carbon monoxide poisoning to ensure the miners don't die. This is because carbon monoxide is odorless. In software, the same term is used to send a small portion of the traffic to a newer service and expose it to a small set of friends, family, trusted users, and so on to gauge its worthiness. Let's think of another example. Let's say that you want to expose a brand new UI that works only on iPhone or Android to a select group of people to gather feedback. You can expose the new service with limited traffic flow to users that match the request routing (headers and so on).

Namespace isolation

Istio has a sidecar primitive that's created through custom resource definition in Kubernetes. Istio configures every sidecar proxy so that they accept traffic on all of the ports and forward traffic to any configured service.

The default behavior can be fine-tuned at the sidecar level to do the following:

- Define ports and protocols that an Envoy sidecar proxy can accept
- Limit the set of services that the Envoy proxy can reach

The sidecar primitive should be used in a large service mesh for efficiency as it reduces how much memory the sidecar uses.

The following is an example of namespace isolation being done through the sidecar resource in which all of the services in the `istio-lab` namespace can only reach services running in the same namespace through the use of the *./* value of the `hosts` field:

```
apiVersion: networking.istio.io/v1alpha3
kind: Sidecar
metadata:
  name: default
  namespace: istio-lab
spec:
  egress:
  - hosts:
    - "./*"
```

Now, let's look at Mixer, the next component in Istio's control plane.

Mixer

Mixer is a general-purpose policy and telemetry hub. It enforces access control and usage policies across the service mesh. Mixer includes a flexible plugin model that can abstract the Envoy proxy and Istio-managed services. This model allows Istio to interface with a variety of infrastructure backends.

Mixer is a platform-independent component of Istio that runs in Kubernetes or other environments.

The base model of Mixer allows it to connect to a variety of access control systems for authorization, telemetry capturing, quota enforcement, logging backend, and more. This can be seen in the following diagram:

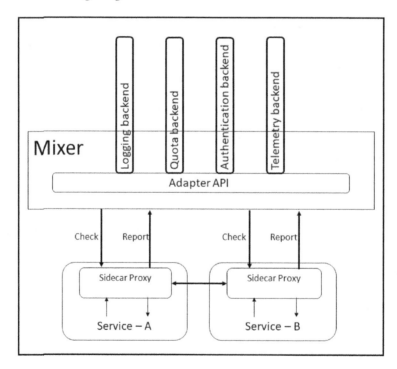

Mixer is a framework that can be seamlessly integrated with infrastructure layers to give control to operations and remove policy logic from the control plane.

The sidecar proxy function is used to call Mixer before each request to perform condition checks. This is also done after each request to report on telemetry data. This introduces Mixer as a single point of the bottleneck, and this is avoided by the proxy to keep a cache of precondition checks and to buffer telemetry data in order to avoid each hop to the Mixer.

The policy enforcement and telemetry collections are configuration-driven, which means Mixer gives us control of the operations. Mixer insulates the Istio control plane from the implementation details of individual backends.

Configuration of Mixer

The Mixer configuration is driven through Istio primitives, which are deployed in Kubernetes through custom resource definitions. The Mixer primitives are as follows:

- Handlers: `handlers.config.istio.io`
- Instances: `instances.config.istio.io`
- Rules: `rules.config.istio.io`
- Adapters: `adapters.config.istio.io`
- Templates: `templates.config.istio.io`

The adapters and templates Mixer primitives are used by vendors to integrate their products with the Istio framework. Before we understand handlers, instances, and rules, it is necessary to understand the purpose of attributes.

Attributes

Istio has a predefined dictionary of attributes that it uses. You can consider an attribute similar to a key-value pair such as `source.ip`, whose value can be `10.0.0.10`. These attributes are used to fill the configuration for a particular handler. For example, an attribute can be a label that we assign to a particular pod or service. This label could be used to trigger some rules when we map this label to an instance of a template. Another example of an attribute could be the IP address of the request, the size of the request, the response code of the operation, and so on.

The sidecar proxy invokes Mixer for every request, and it gives Mixer a set of attributes that describe the request and the environment. Mixer then processes these attributes to build an instance so that a defined handler can invoke a backend. This can be seen in the following diagram:

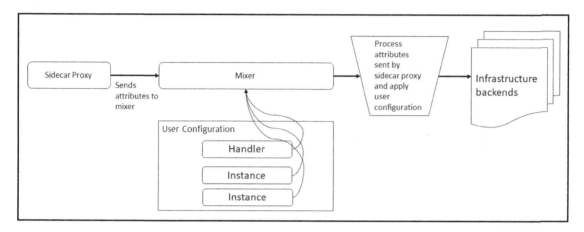

Istio has a fixed vocabulary that it understands. Refer to the following link for a list of attribute vocabulary: https://archive.istio.io/v1.3/docs/reference/config/policy-and-telemetry/attribute-vocabulary/.

Attributes expressions are used to configure instances, as follows:

```
version: destination.labels["version"] | "unknown"
```

The preceding expression will assign unknown to version (left-hand side) if destination.labels["version"] is not defined.

Handlers

A handler is a set of configurations that's needed to instantiate an external adapter. For example, a listchecker adapter needs the address of the dogstatsd server, which can be provided through a handler that's passed to the Datadog instance. The following example creates a handler for the listchecker adapter so that we can define whitelists and blacklists:

```
apiVersion: config.istio.io/v1alpha2
kind: handler
metadata:
  name: whitelist
spec:
```

```
compiledAdapter: listchecker
params:
  # providerUrl: ordinarily black and white lists are maintained
  # externally and fetched asynchronously using the providerUrl.
  overrides: ["v1", "v2"]  # overrides provide a static list
  blacklist: false
```

The `params` list attribute of the specification is specific to a given adapter. A list of all available adaptors for Mixer can be found at `https://archive.istio.io/v1.3/docs/reference/config/policy-and-telemetry/adapters/`.

Request mapping from attributes to adapter inputs is defined through instance configuration. For example, the `appversion` instance maps the source pod or service label version to the values of the `params` instances:

```
apiVersion: config.istio.io/v1alpha2
kind: instance
metadata:
  name: appversion
spec:
  compiledTemplate: listentry
  params:
    value: source.labels["version"]
```

Note that templates are used to define a mapping between attributes and `params`. In the preceding example, the `listentry` template is used to verify whether the value is present for the label-defined version or not.

Rules

When a rule is created, it specifies when a particular handler with an instance should be invoked. The following example is a rule that defines that it will invoke the `whitelist` handler with an instance of `appversion` to check its version:

```
apiVersion: config.istio.io/v1alpha2
kind: rule
metadata:
  name: checkversion
spec:
  match: destination.labels["app"] == "ratings"
  actions:
  - handler: whitelist
    instances: [ appversion ]
```

Mixer's features, such as handlers, instance, and rules, help us to perform precondition checking, quota management, and telemetry reporting. Mixer, through its plugin approach, supports integration with backend services.

As of Istio version 1.0.x and above, the Mixer in-process model has been deprecated because Mixer integrates with infrastructure backends through a set of adapters via backend protocols. This process allowed users to create custom adapter templates, such as data consumption.

The new out-of-process adapter for Mixer, currently in beta, is a similar concept but focuses on using a gRPC adapter. Mixer structures incoming attributes to backend systems through a template-based gRPC service that processes and receives data through requests. For additional information, please refer to the following URL: `https://github.com/istio/istio/wiki/Mixer-Out-Of-Process-Adapter-Dev-Guide`.

Next, we will look at Istio's security features, which are implemented through Citadel.

Citadel

Citadel provides authentication and authorization features. Its authentication feature, which has built-in identity and credential management, enables service-to-service and end user communication. Its authorization feature is used to control who can access your services. Citadel is a **Public Key Infrastructure** (**PKI**) and provides and rotates certificates for the services.

Istio really shines in service identity, RBAC, and end-to-end mTLS. Security implementation does not require making any changes to the application's code. The Istio security model is implemented through the following:

- **Citadel** is Istio's central certificate authority for issuing keys and certificates and their rotation.
- **Pilot** distributes the authentication policies and provides secure naming services using SPIFFE.
- **Mixer** is the central place that provides authorization and auditing policies.
- **Envoy** is the default proxy in Istio. Istio uses Envoy for edge proxies through Istio gateways to provide secure communication between clients and servers.

In a distributed dynamic system, managing certificates and rotation can become very time-consuming, complex, and error-prone when not all of the clients are known in advance. Citadel takes away this complexity through a self-service model to establish end-to-end encryption (mTLS) between microservices by injecting certificates into the microservices.

Citadel provides a self-signed root certificate and private key, which it uses to sign the workload certificates. Citadel can also use a customer-supplied root certificate and key.

Next, we will look at the built-in PKI generate certificates and automatically rotate keys to minimize exposure to compromised keys.

Certificate and key rotation

Istio provides us with the option of using a node agent in Kubernetes for certificate and key rotation.

If you are using a demo install profile, the node agent won't be installed by default. To install a node agent, you need to choose `values-istio-sds-auth.yaml` for the helm install. Once installed, you should see the node agent running on every node. For example, in our single VM, you will see only one node agent:

```
$ kubectl -n istio-system get pods -l app=nodeagent
NAME                    READY  STATUS    RESTARTS  AGE
istio-nodeagent-smfz7   1/1    Running   0         3m35s
```

The node agent, when deployed, will provision certificates and keys:

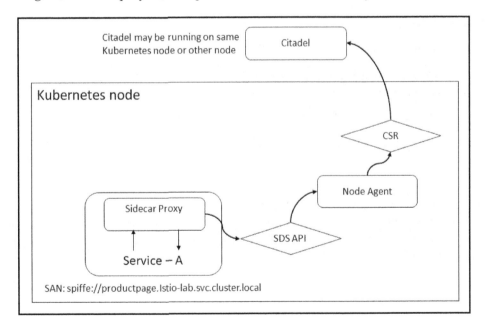

The workflow for rotating certificates and keys is as follows:

1. The Envoy proxy sends a key and certificate request through the **Secret Discovery Service (SDS)** API.
2. Then, the node's agent creates the private key and **Certificate Signing Request (CSR)** when it receives the SDS request.
3. Citadel receives the CSR through gRPC, validates it, signs the CSR, generates the certificate, and sends it to the node agent.
4. The node agent sends the key and certificate key to the proxy via the SDS API.
5. This process repeats at a certain interval for every service for certificate and key rotation.

Istio recommends that we run Citadel in the `istio-system` namespace and only protect access for administrators.

 We will cover certificate and key rotation in more detail in `Chapter 12`, *Enabling Istio Policy Controls*.

Authentication

Authenticating service-to-service communication can be done in two ways:

- **Origin**: The application is responsible for acquiring and attaching the **JSON Web Token (JWT)** credential to the request.
- **Transport**: Configuring mutual TLS between microservices.

Transport verifies and identifies the services that are trying to initiate a connection. Through mTLS, this feature can easily be turned on and off without having to change any code.

End user authentication, also known as origin authentication, validates the client, making the service request either as a user or a device. Istio allows request-level authentication through a JWT to validate and streamline developers using Auth0, Firebase, Google, or any other customer authentication mechanism:

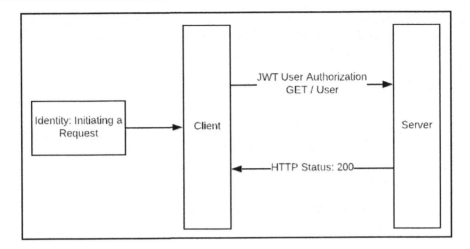

The preceding diagram shows the secure authorization steps for service requests. Let's go through them in detail:

1. First, the authenticated identity will initiate a claim where the server will successfully validate the user.
2. Next, the server will authorize JWT tokens.
3. The tokens are sent back to the client, where they will be stored after the application has confirmed an authorized identity.
4. Assuming the identity is actively making requests for the service, passed JWT tokens will continue to be processed and authorized at every request.

Both of these authentication protocols have policies that are stored within Istio's configuration store through a Kubernetes API call. Pilot maintains these policies by keeping them as the latest ones through a service sidecar proxy. Istio also allows authentication in permissive mode to help users to manage the overall security posture of their environment before it's fully enabled.

Strong identity

In a traditional monolithic environment, identity was defined mostly by hostname or IP addresses. The following are the famous Apache HTTPD server rules:

```
Deny from All
Allow from 1.2.3.4
```

In a distributed environment such as Kubernetes, due to its decoupled nature, the workload can be deployed on any machine, so IP addresses may change at any time. As we mentioned earlier, identity is either at origin or transport. At origin, we define identity as a subject (human) that is authenticated in various ways. However, at the transport layer, the old way of using IP addresses is no longer possible due to the dynamic nature of the workload.

The **Secure Production Identity Framework for Everyone (SPIFFE)** specification is used to assign an identity to a workload, and it remains the same regardless of where it runs in a distributed environment. Istio has chosen a particular naming convention to provide an identity to a workload, as follows:

```
spiffe://cluster.local/ns/istio-lab/sa/productpage
       <cluster-name><ns><name-space><sa><service-account-name>
```

As we can see, the `spiffe` prefix is mandated by the SPIFFE specification (such as HTTP). `cluster.local` is the name of a cluster—it should be different for different Kubernetes clusters if we're considering using Istio to span multiple clusters using a single control plane. `ns` is fixed, followed by `name-space`, where the workload is running. `sa` is fixed and `service-account-name` is the actual service account.

Citadel is the implementation of the SPIFFE specification and is used to build a security solution in an untrusted network. Due to this, it is sometimes referred to as security in a zero-trust network. Citadel issues SVID to the workload by signing the X.509 certificates upon a CSR being sent by a node agent running on every node on behalf of the Istio sidecar proxy running next to a workload. Once the proxy sidecar receives the certificate, it presents it to other workloads.

It is important to note the short-lived nature of the certificates, which has merits in a zero-trust network. If someone steals a certificate, the exposure is only for a short time.

Explaining the internal functionality of Citadel is beyond the scope of this book, and at a very high level, it is enough to understand that it follows the Automatic Certificate Management Environment protocol of Let's Encrypt (`https://letsencrypt.org`) to issue certificates and verify the identity of them with a set of challenges.

Once a reliable identity mechanism has been defined for use in the authentication process, the next thing we need to do is associate an identity with **Role-Based Access Control (RBAC)** to implement authorizations.

RBAC for a strong identity

RBAC works by defining a set of permissions that need to be assigned to a role that is part of service accounts or a list of users. Its main role is to authenticate services, initiate communication requests, define custom properties for user role support, and optimize performance through sidecar proxies.

Authorization

Over the years, applications have transformed and changed significantly. In parallel, application security has transformed based on user experience from client to server and vice versa. Authentication is about validating identity and verifying credentials against policies for a specific service. Authorization is about what the identity is allowed to do against what it is trying to do. Within the service mesh, authorization is inclusive to RBAC, which provides namespace, service, and method-level access for microservices.

Enabling mTLS to secure service communication

To secure service-to-service communication, it is tunneled from the client-side to the server-side via a sidecar proxy. Next, the inter-proxy communication is secured using mTLS. The benefit of mTLS is that the service identity is not expressed as a token bearer. It can't be stolen, duplicated, or replayed from a source it hasn't been authenticated with. Istio's Citadel uses the concept of secure naming and protection against attacks. The client-side verifies an authenticated service account and only allows the named service to run and traverse any network requests.

Istio's authorization feature also provides a cluster-level certificate authority with automated certificate management. Some of its key capabilities are as follows:

- For every service account, it generates a certificate and key pair.
- Using Kubernetes secrets, it distributes certificates and keys to the appropriate service pods.
- It sets up periodic certificates and key rotation.
- It sets up certificates and keys and disables policies if they're not being used or have been expired, stolen, and so on.

Whenever someone connects to any secure site, they are using TLS because this validates the server identity to the client and provides an encryption channel between the server and client. For service-to-service communication, the same concept is applied from the server to the client-side. To validate the client-side identity, a webhook application should request confirmation.

To do this, the mTLS feature can be used to validate client-level authentication by sending a certificate request message. This message will include the following:

- It includes a list of distinguished root certificates that are tested by the server.
- The client responds to the server through a certificate message stating it is a distinguished name.
- The server verifies the client certificate.
- If the verification succeeds, the server has successfully authenticated the client.

mTLS authentication is widely managed for business applications that have a limited number of homogeneous clients connecting to different web services. Overall, security requirements are a higher priority when implementing mTLS versus any other consumer.

mTLS has two modes—**permissive** and **strict**. Permissive mode allows traffic in the HTTP and HTTPS protocols, whereas strict mode only allows traffic using the HTTPS protocol.

Secure N-to-N mapping of services

Securely naming services is an N-to-N mapping listed by server identities and detailed in certificates. All of the service names are defined by service discovery or DNS files. This mapping creates a list of service communications by authenticating an identity so that they can submit a client request for any service. For instance, the *Hello* identity has permission to authorize and run the *World* service. This is monitored by the Kubernetes API server, which keeps track of all secure naming conventions and distributes this list to a service sidecar proxy.

Secure naming is critical for multiple reasons, and the following scenarios will highlight the significance of having one:

- A number of servers are running a service called **Accounts**, and only the **Payable** identity is allowed to authenticate these transactions.
- If a rogue user has access to the certificate and keys for another identity called **Finance**, their objective is to inspect all of the traversed data from the client, understand the service, and so on.
- The rogue user will set up and deploy an imposter server with the exact keys and certificates that have been detailed for **Finance**.
- If the rogue user has hacked the DNS file or service discovery and mapped **Accounts** to the imposter server.

If a new client calls the *Accounts* service, with the forged server in place, the *Finance* identity certificate is extracted. Through the secure naming information, *Finance* will be checked if it is allowed to run the *Accounts* service. The client will detect that this request is not allowed because only *Payable* has been authenticated. Through this check, authentication will fail, and the rogue user will not be able to process their transaction.

This is a very critical step to securing communication within services because only service-specific identities that have been named within secure naming are allowed to initiate and receive requests. Without this process in place, rogue identity authentications such as man-in-the-middle attacks can hack the services, which can be detrimental to the reputation of a business.

Policies

Policies in Istio are defined through Istio primitive policies that are implemented through the CRD. You can check CRD policies in your Istio cluster like so:

```
$ kubectl get crd -l app=istio-citadel
NAME                                  CREATED AT
meshpolicies.authentication.istio.io  2019-07-30T02:59:14Z
policies.authentication.istio.io      2019-07-30T02:59:14Z
```

You can configure policies in the Istio service mesh to enforce various rules at runtime, such as the following:

- Authentication
- Authorization
- Rate limiting to dynamically limit the traffic to a service
- Denials, whitelists, and blacklists, to restrict access to services
- Header rewrites and redirects

Implementing authentication

The policy scope for authentication can be for an individual service, all of the services in a namespace, or all of the services in a service mesh. Let's go through what happens:

1. The policies are defined at the Citadel level.
2. Pilot translates these policies to Envoy proxies to perform the required authentication mechanisms.

3. Pilot sends the configuration details, such as certificates and keys, to the Envoy proxy asynchronously.

4. As soon as the Proxy attached to a microservice receives the configuration, new authentication artifacts take effect.

Origin authentication is the responsibility of the client application and is used to acquire JWT and attach it to the request. You can define JWT either for any request or for all of the requests except public paths, such as /healtz or /status, to expose them without authentication. You can also only define JWT for the /admin path and expose all of the others to the public. Since this is application language-specific, we will not go into the details of this.

Transport authentication is implemented through mTLS, and the destination rules defined by Pilot determine which services in the mesh should initiate a TLS connection through the Envoy proxy:

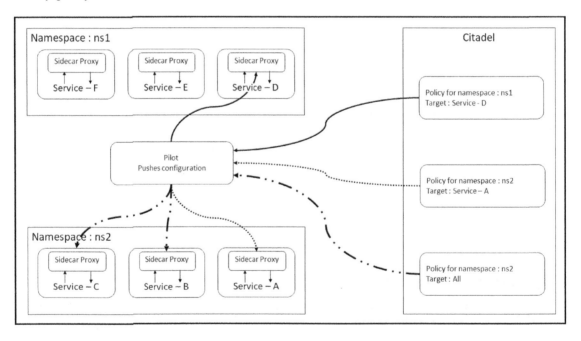

For example, let's say we define the policy for the ns1 namespace for **Service-D** in Citadel and Pilot pushes the mTLS policy to Service-D and the ns1 namespace and leaves the other services intact. Similarly, two policies are defined for the ns2 namespace. One is for **Service-A**, while the other is for all except **Service-A**. Note that the **Target: All** policy is overridden by the one defined explicitly for **Service-A**.

The preceding is known as policy enforcement at the namespace level. You could also have policy enforcement at the mesh level, where this will be applied to all the services in a mesh. In such a case, only one policy can be defined to avoid conflict precedence.

Here is an example of `MeshPolicy`:

```
apiVersion: "authentication.istio.io/v1alpha1"
kind: MeshPolicy
metadata:
  name: "default"
spec:
  peers:
  - mtls:
```

The preceding policy must have the `default` name since the scope is service mesh wide. There is no `targets:` section. If you change the kind to Policy and add a namespace to the `metadata:` section, the `targets:` section shouldn't be defined since the scope is namespace wide. The targets can be defined to limit the scope at the service level.

The `peers:` section with `mtls: {}` is equivalent to `mtls: {mode: STRICT}` for `STRICT` mTLS. You could define the `PERMISSIVE` mode for `mtls:` like so:

```
peers:
- mtls:
    mode: PERMISSIVE
```

`STRICT` mode only allows HTTPS, while `PERMISSIVE` mode allows both HTTP and HTTPS.

The following example defines two policies. The first policy, called `default`, applies mTLS for all of the services in the `ns1` namespace:

```
apiVersion: authentication.istio.io/v1alpha1
kind: Policy
metadata:
  name: default
  namespace: ns1
spec:
  peers:
  - mtls:{}
```

However, the following policy removes mTLS from `Service-A` with the use of `targets` and by specifying the mTLS mode:

```
apiVersion: authentication.istio.io/v1alpha1
kind: Policy
metadata:
  name: SVC-A-mTLS-disable
  namespace: ns1
spec:
  targets:
  - name: Service-A
  peers:
  - mtls:
      mode: DISABLE
```

Transport authentication, as we explained previously, provides granular control. Transport authentication can be implemented at the Pilot level through the use of destination rules, like so:

```
apiVersion: networking.istio.io/v1alpha3
kind: DestinationRule
metadata:
  name: productpage
spec:
  host: productpage
  trafficPolicy:
    tls:
      mode: ISTIO_MUTUAL
  subsets:
  - name: v1
    labels:
      version: v1
```

A destination rule is defined for the `productpage` service, which defines a `v1` subset with a traffic policy of `ISTIO_MUTUAL`, which is mTLS. The v1 subset we defined here will be used in a virtual service.

As you can see, there are two different implementations for mTLS. Use one for your implementation and stick to it.

Implementing authorization

Authorization is implemented through Kubernetes RBAC, which can be defined at the namespace level, service level, or method level within a service. Authorization is implemented natively at the Envoy proxy level, and it supports HTTP, HTTPS, HTTP/2, and TCP.

Istio uses Kubernetes primitives such as `Role`, `RoleBinding`, `ClusterRoles`, and `ClusterRoleBinding`. It creates its own CRD, such as `AuthorizationPolicies`, `ClusterRbacConfigs`, `RbacConfigs`, `ServiceRoleBindings`, or `ServiceRoles`, as follows:

```
$ kubectl get crd | grep -i rbac
authorizationpolicies.rbac.istio.io          2019-07-30T02:59:14Z
clusterrbacconfigs.rbac.istio.io             2019-07-30T02:59:14Z
rbacconfigs.rbac.istio.io                    2019-07-30T02:59:15Z
servicerolebindings.rbac.istio.io            2019-07-30T02:59:15Z
serviceroles.rbac.istio.io                   2019-07-30T02:59:15Z
```

Authentication is enabled through the use of `ClusterRbacConfigs`:

```
apiVersion: "rbac.istio.io/v1alpha1"
kind: ClusterRbacConfig
metadata:
  name: default
spec:
  mode: 'ON_WITH_INCLUSION'
  inclusion:
    namespaces: ["default"]
```

The preceding code creates default `ClusterRbacConfig` that grants **ON WITH INCLUSION** on the `default` namespace. `mode` can be one of the following:

- `OFF`: This mode disables authorization.
- `ON`: This mode enables authorization for all of the services in the mesh.
- `ON_WITH_INCLUSION`: With this mode, we enable authorization for the services and namespaces specified in the `inclusion` field.
- `ON_WITH_EXCLUSION`: We can enable authorization for all of the services in the mesh through this mode, except the services and namespaces defined in the `exclusion` field.

Enabling authentication does not mean that one is authorized. Istio primitives such as `ServiceRoles` and `ServiceRoleBinding` are used to define authorization policies:

- `ServiceRole` is a group through which we can set permissions to access services.
- `ServiceRoleBinding` is the link between `ServiceRole` and a user, a group, or a service.

The following is an example of `ServiceRole` in which permissions are defined for all of the methods for the services starting with a name test. However, only READ access (GET and HEAD) is defined for the path ending in `reviews` in a microservice bookstore, which resides in a default namespace:

```
apiVersion: "rbac.istio.io/v1alpha1"
kind: ServiceRole
metadata:
  name: tester
  namespace: default
spec:
  rules:
  - services: ["test-*"]
    methods: ["*"]
  - services: ["bookstore.default.svc.cluster.local"]
    paths: ["*/reviews"]
    methods: ["GET", "HEAD"]
```

Defining permissions is no good unless they are granted to a user, group, or a service account. Granting `ServiceRole` is done through `ServiceRoleBindings`.

As an example, the following grants the preceding service role (`tester`) to two subjects:

- `service-account-a`
- `istio-ingress-service-account`, were the JWT email claim is `a@foo.com`

This can be seen in the following code:

```
apiVersion: "rbac.istio.io/v1alpha1"
kind: ServiceRoleBinding
metadata:
  name: test-binding
  namespace: default
spec:
  subjects:
  - user: "service-account-a"
  - user: "istio-ingress-service-account"
    properties:
```

```
        request.auth.claims[email]: "a@foo.com"
  roleRef:
    kind: ServiceRole
    name: "tester"
```

If you want to apply a `tester` role (a set of permissions) to the public, you can use `*` in the preceding definition. Now, any authenticated or unauthenticated user will be able to access the bookstore service.

The preceding example shows authorization for HTTP/HTTPS protocols. The following is an example of authorization being used to access a service using a TCP protocol such as a database service:

```
apiVersion: "rbac.istio.io/v1alpha1"
kind: ServiceRole
metadata:
  name: mongodb-viewer
  namespace: default
spec:
  rules:
  - services: ["mongodb.istio-lab.svc.cluster.local"]
    constraints:
    - key: "destination.port"
      values: ["27017"]
---
apiVersion: "rbac.istio.io/v1alpha1"
kind: ServiceRoleBinding
metadata:
  name: bind-mongodb-viewer
  namespace: default
spec:
  subjects:
  - user: "cluster.local/ns/istio-lab/sa/bookinfo-ratings-v2"
    roleRef:
    kind: ServiceRole
    name: "mongodb-viewer"
```

As we can see, a service role creates permissions to access the MongoDB service in the `istio-lab` namespace with a constraint to access port `27017`. This permission is defined through `ServiceRole` and is granted to the `bookinfo-ratings-v2` service in the `istio-lab` namespace. This granular control ensures that the MongoDB service is only accessed from a service that has a legitimate need and blocks access to anyone who tries to access the database directly.

This authentication and authorization implementation is implemented in Istio natively. However, Mixer allows you to plug in your own or third-party authentication and authorization modules.

Policy examples can be found in `Chapter 12`, *Enabling Istio Policy Controls*, where quota enforcement, rate limits, whitelists, and blacklists are shown through hands-on exercises.

So far, we've looked at the features of Istio's control plane and its capabilities, which are used to define backend configuration (Galley), pushdown policies (Pilot), enforce quotas, collect metrics (Mixer), and implement security (Citadel). The actual implementation is done at the data plane level, where microservices-based applications will run. Next, we will deep dive into Istio's data plane capabilities.

Data plane

The data plane consists of one or more nodes running microservices containers in pods. Each pod has a sidecar that takes care of inter-service communication.

The sidecar proxy is agnostic to the language of the microservice since it works at the network layer. The proxy in a data plane intercepts inbound and outbound traffic for a microservice. With it, we can perform the following tasks:

- Traffic management
- Service-to-service user access control
- Authentication
- Communication encryption (TLS or mTLS)
- Monitoring
- Logging
- Timeouts
- Rate limits
- Retries
- Circuit breaking
- Load balancing
- Health checks

Kubernetes uses pods as single units where multiple containers within a pod share the same IP address or service name. All of the sidecar proxies conceptually form a data plane. Together, the control plane and data plane form the service mesh.

A service mesh proxy can be configured, deployed, and implemented in Kubernetes or non-Kubernetes environments.

In a Kubernetes environment, the sidecar proxy runs in the application pod, and there could be many such pods in a node. On the other hand, a sidecar proxy can run at a host level such as VM or bare metal in a non-Kubernetes environment. The next section will help us to understand sidecar proxies in more detail.

Sidecar proxy

The sidecar proxy pattern is at the heart of the data plane and provides service-to-service communication, as shown in the following diagram:

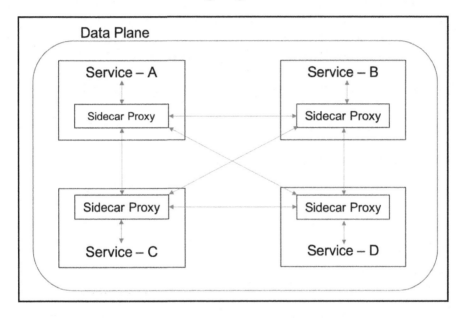

The microservices do not communicate with other microservices directly; this communication is done through the sidecar proxies. The proxy is tightly coupled with a container in a pod, and this proxy architectural pattern fits well in a Kubernetes environment.

Istio's Envoy sidecar proxy

The evolution of the sidecar has been taking place over the last couple of years. The popular among them are Lyft's Envoy and Buoyant's Linkerd.

Lyft's Envoy creator is Matt Klein. Envoy is used by Istio, AWS App Mesh, and Ambassador. Netflix has built its own proxy, called **Prana**, but it is not open source, so it is out of the scope of this book.

Nginx has been a very popular sidecar proxy that provides load balancing, rate limits, TLS offloading, traffic split, traffic distribution, and A/B testing. Modern sidecar proxies such as Envoy and Linkerd are well optimized and have a small footprint so that they work well with individual microservices as a sidecar, whereas Nginx fits well in front of the entire microservices application as it allows thousands of concurrent requests, which makes it an ideal reverse proxy and static content provider. Nginx can also run as a sidecar proxy the same way Envoy does. Envoy can also run as an edge proxy instead of running Nginx for TLS termination, and it can also replace HAProxy as a load balancer. Nginx supports HTTP/2 for downstream connections, whereas Envoy supports HTTP/2 for both upstream/downstream communications.

One of the reasons for the adoption of Envoy is how easy it is to implement fully functional traffic management, which would take a lot of work and effort to implement in Nginx.

Lyft's Envoy is a graduated open source project from the Cloud Native Computing Foundation (`https://cncf.io`) and is being used by IBM, Google, AWS, Microsoft, Salesforce, Uber, Lyft, Airbnb, and many others.

What is Envoy?

Envoy, as per its documentation (`https://www.envoyproxy.io/docs/envoy/latest/intro/what_is_envoy`), is an L7 proxy and communication bus designed for large modern service-oriented architectures.

Envoy's main goal is to make networks transparent to applications, and it attempts to do this through the following processes:

- **Out of process architecture**: This is also known as the **sidecar proxy**, which runs alongside the application and is language-agnostic.
- **Modern C++**: Envoy is written in C++ to minimize latency.

- **L3/L4 filter**: Envoy is an L3/L4 network proxy that provides a pluggable filter chain mechanism.
- **HTTP L7 filter**: There's an HTTP L7 filter layer to support buffering, rate limiting, and routing/forwarding.
- **HTTP/2 support**: Envoy supports both HTTP 1.1 and 2 can operate as a transparent HTTP/1.1 to HTTP/2 proxy in both directions. HTTP/2 allows us to create a mesh of persistent connections to multiplex requests/responses.
- **HTTP L7 routing**: It routes requests based upon a path, authority, content type, and runtime values.
- **gRPC support**: It supports routing and load balancing gRPC requests and responses.
- **Service discovery and dynamic configuration**: There's a dynamic configuration API for centralized management.
- **Health checking**: There's a active health checking for upstream services and to determine healthy load balancing targets.
- **Front/edge proxy support**: Envoy's primary use is for service-to-service communication as a front (sidecar) proxy, but it can also act like an edge proxy, similar to Nginx.
- **Best in class observability**: The statistics collection can be viewed through an admin port, and it uses `statsd` as a statistics sink.

Next, we'll learn about the Envoy architecture.

Envoy architecture

Envoy provides various service mesh capabilities such as dynamic real-time out of band configuration without the need to restart it. It also supports listeners, filters, L3/L4 filters, HTTP L7 routing, TCP proxy, support for HTTP 1.1 and HTTP/2 protocol, connection pooling, load balancing, priority request routing, observability, RBAC, rate limiting, and traffic shifting/splitting, all of which is managed through a chain of filters for Envoy connection handling.

The following diagram is of the capability/architecture matrix of Envoy:

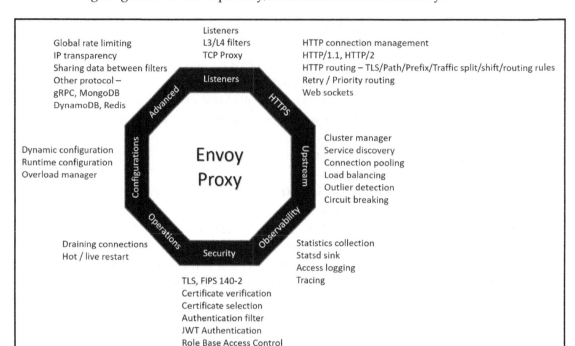

In the preceding diagram, we can see Envoy's proxy features, which are leveraged with the proper configuration in Istio. For example, Envoy is a powerful lightweight proxy engine, and Istio has more than 8,000 lines of code for its configuration. Istio hides that complexity from the end user to provide out-of-the-box solutions so that they can use a sidecar proxy with each microservice.

Deployment

Envoy comes packaged as a Docker container. If you need to run it without a container, you will need to build it from the source. Envoy is like an engine, and being familiar with it is required if you wish to configure it for serious use without using a control plane for automation. A service mesh provider such as Istio, which is in an open source space, or AWS App Mesh, which is in a closed space, takes care of the right configuration with the proper plumbing through a control plane so that it can be used out of the box.

Its ease of use is evident from the fact that once Istio has been deployed, we only have to label a namespace with `istio-injection=enabled` and the rest is taken care of automatically. If a particular pod in this namespace doesn't get its sidecar, the pod can be annotated (for example, `sidecar.istio.io/inject: False`) and that pod won't get the sidecar.

 In Kubernetes, a namespace is labeled, but the pod is annotated.

For example, let's assume that Istio has already been installed and that we label the namespace `default` with an annotation of `istio-injection=enabled` and then deploy the application. The Envoy sidecar proxy will be injected automatically. The following code shows this:

```
# Label the default name space to enable auto injection of the Envoy proxy
$ kubectl label namespace default istio-injection=enabled

# Install busybox pod
$ kubectl create -f https://k8s.io/examples/admin/dns/busybox.yaml

# Check the pod and you should see sidecar injected automatically
# With 2/2 under the READY column
$ kubectl get pods
NAME         READY    STATUS     RESTARTS    AGE
busybox      2/2      Running    0           3m55s
```

If you describe the `busybox` pod, you will be able to see details about the Envoy sidecar proxy.

Notice that the `busybox` pod has one init container, `istio-init`, that initializes the proxy. The `busybox` container is created and the `istio-proxy` sidecar proxy is also created with the proper command-line parameters:

```
$ kubectl describe pod busybox
Name:          busybox
Namespace:     default
...
Init Containers:
  istio-init:
    Image:          docker.io/istio/proxy_init:1.2.2
    Args:
      -p
      15001
      -u
```

```
            1337
            -m
            REDIRECT
            -i
            *
            -x
            -b
            -d
            15020
Containers:
  busybox:
    Image:          busybox:1.28
  . . .
```

The following code block shows the sidecar implementation of istio-proxy:

```
istio-proxy:
    Image:          docker.io/istio/proxyv2:1.2.2
    Port:           15090/TCP
    Host Port:      0/TCP
    Args:
      proxy
      sidecar
      --domain
      $(POD_NAMESPACE).svc.cluster.local
      --configPath
      /etc/istio/proxy
      --binaryPath
  . . .
```

Injecting an Envoy sidecar proxy into a deployment happens through Kubernetes mutating the admission webhook controller. The mutating controller modifies the object before it's sent to Kubernetes. In this case, the busybox deployment YAML file does not contain any information regarding deploying the sidecar proxy. However, when the deployment begins in the default namespace, which is labeled with istio-injection=enabled, the webhook admission controller is called, which modifies the busybox deployment so that it includes the sidecar proxy.

It is important to note that the deployment of the sidecar proxy is a feature of the Istio control plane, which automates the process. For example, configmap's istio-sidecar-injector contains the templates that can be used manually using istioctl or through a webhook admission controller to modify the application's deployment.

Fortunately, we don't have to worry about how a sidecar proxy deployment happens. It's part of the control plane, which makes the process easy since all we have to do is label a namespace. Everything else is taken care of automatically.

Now that we've looked at the data plane and how it's implemented, we can move on. The most essential feature of Istio is the tools it uses for its observability features, without which it is next to impossible to figure out what is going on in a distributed application. In contrast to monolithic applications, distributed microservices applications come with complex test capabilities, log collections, and knowledge of what's happening in the service mesh. Istio bundles the necessary tools to provide such capabilities. We'll explain this in more detail in the next section.

Observability

Mixer in Istio is responsible for collecting the detailed telemetry data that's generated by the service proxies on the traffic that flows through it. Three different types of telemetries — metrics, logs, and traces — are collected.

Istio offers out of the box monitoring and dashboard visualization capabilities so that we can monitor service mesh traffic. Telemetry in Istio is currently comprised of two components:

- **Prometheus** is a data store for metrics that it collects through the pull model. It has its own GUI for management purposes.
- **Grafana** is a robust graphing tool to show the data. It is pre-configured with an add-on instance for Istio and is configured to start with Prometheus, which collects data from each Istio component.

The Grafana dashboard is comprised of three main views: summary, individual services, and individual workloads. Overall, the mesh summary provides a holistic global view of the entire service mesh and shows protocol metrics for HTTP, HTTPS, and gRPC. The microservices provide metrics about individual requests and responses for all TCP workloads.

Istio has also adopted a visualization project called Kiali (`https://kiali.io`). It is installed by default using a demo profile. Kiali is a superb observability tool that helps us to find out which microservices are part of the service mesh, how they are connected with each other, and how they are contributing to network traffic.

Kiali can be used to observe external services through Istio's implementation of `ServiceEntry`. For example, you can determine how much traffic is being sent to an external service by observing it through Kiali.

To recap, Kiali provides a real-time graphical view of designated namespaces to display application and workload interactions since contextual data to be visualized with its dashboard. It provides detailed information at the application layer about the overall application health and provides a detailed list of its designated workloads. For Istio, there is a designated config menu option that lists all the available configuration objects and metrics associated with a service. It can validate YAML configurations by highlighting any errors and enabling warning and error severity flags if the YAML validation hasn't been configured correctly.

Distributed tracing through Jaeger helps us to find out what network paths are slower in the service mesh and how to identify any bottlenecks.

In the upcoming Chapter 13, *Exploring Istio Telemetry Features* of this book explains explains the telemetry functions that can be used out of the box from an observability point of view.

Summary

In this chapter, you learned that Istio is a very feature-rich open source service mesh project that uses adapters to integrate with external telemetry, authentication, authorization systems. As we have seen, the four main categories of Istio are Traffic Management, Security, Policies, and Telemetry, all of which are covered in detail in their own chapters.

Istio's architecture of Pilot, Mixer, Galley, and Citadel forms a control plane, while the proxies attached to the service pods form the data plane, which provides a complete service mesh with a separation between development and operations. The Istio service mesh is a very powerful tool in the hands of the SRE team and is used to control traffic, manage security, implement policies, and observe the service mesh.

Pilot, as its name suggests, is the main navigator for the Envoy engines and steers the application in the right direction. The Mixer plug-in model allows external telemetry, authentication, authorization, and other modules to integrate with Istio to provide extensibility. Galley is the behind the scenes configuration manager for different Istio components. Finally, Citadel is the certificate authority for Istio. It offers a self-service model so that we can implement mTLS for an entire application by abstracting all the internal details of complexities and providing the best in class security model for the application by frequently rotating certificates and keys.

The Istio service mesh architecture is evolving rapidly, and new functionality is being added constantly. When we started working on this book, Istio was at version 1.0.3, but now, it's already at version 1.5.0. Istio has evolved and has become production-ready. Any future enhancements that are made to Istio will focus on optimizing the performance of its components.

In the next chapter, to help us learn more about Istio, we will build a demo application and show you how it works without Istio at the helm. Then, in subsequent chapters, we will implement traffic management, security, policies, and telemetry to show you how to adopt Istio's service mesh features without having to modify or code anything in the existing application.

Questions

1. A service mesh works at which layer of the network?

    A) Layer 7
    B) Layer 3/4

2. Libraries such as Hystrix and Finnagle were excellent in abstracting traffic routing capabilities, but why did Envoy prove to be successful for cloud-native applications?

    A) The libraries were for Java applications, and they needed to be ported to other applications, whereas the Envoy proxy sidecar was language-agnostic and could work with polyglot applications.
    B) An update in the library will force an application to update, whereas the Envoy proxy can be upgraded independently of the application microservices.
    C) Libraries can manage traffic, but load balancing is an outside function, whereas it is integrated with the Envoy proxy with dynamic rules and configuration propagation through Istio components.
    D) All of the above.
    E) None of the above.

3. The Istio control plane is a single point of failure for microservices applications.

    A) True
    B) False

4. The true service mesh is formed through Envoy sidecar proxies.

   A) True
   B) False

5. Istio works at a single cluster level and can't span multiple clusters.

   A) True
   B) False

6. Service discovery in Istio is tightly integrated with Kubernetes, but it can also work with external service providers.

   A) True
   B) False

7. Pilot is responsible for managing traffic, whereas Envoy pushes the configuration to Pilot.

   A) True
   B) False

8. Istio primitives such as Destination Rules, Gateway, Virtual Service, and so on can only be created through `istioctl` but not using `kubectl`.

   A) True
   B) False

9. Implementing Istio transport security for mTLS is a self-service model.

   A) True
   B) False

10. You can observe the service mesh for connectivity and traffic patterns through Kiali.

    A) True
    B) False

Further reading

- *The OSI Model Explained: How To Understand (And Remember) The 7 Layer Network Model*, Shaw Keith, Network World, 2019: `https://www.networkworld.com/article/3239677/the-osi-model-explained-how-to-understand-and-remember-the-7-layer-network-model.html`

- *Amalgam8: An Integration Fabric For Microservices In The Cloud - Archive Of The IBM Cloud Blog* Rothert Doug, Archive Of The IBM Cloud Blog, 2019: `https://www.ibm.com/blogs/cloud-archive/2016/06/amalgam8-integration-fabric-microservices-cloud/`

- *Istio/Community*, GitHub, 2019: `https://github.com/istio/community#istio-authors`

- *Observability*, Istio, 2019: `https://archive.istio.io/v1.3/docs/concepts/observability/`

- *Policies and Security*, Istio, 2019: `https://archive.istio.io/v1.3/docs/concepts/security/`

- *Traffic Management*, Istio, 2019: `https://archive.istio.io/v1.3/docs/concepts/traffic-management/`

- *Envoy Proxy*, Envoyproxy.Io, 2019: `https://www.envoyproxy.io/`

- *Kiali*, Kiali.Io, 2019: `https://www.kiali.io/`

Installing a Demo Application

8

Before we go ahead and install the Istio service mesh and explore its capabilities, we will install a demo application known as BookInfo, which was created by Istio (`https://istio.io`). This demo application will help us find out about Istio's capabilities, such as traffic management, security, policies, and observability, which we'll be looking at in more detail in the upcoming chapters. This chapter will show you the basic functionality of a demo application and how it behaves without using any Istio capabilities.

In a nutshell, we will cover the following topics in this chapter:

- Overview of Istio's BookInfo application
- Deploying the BookInfo application in Kubernetes
- Enabling a DNS search for Kubernetes services in a VM
- Understanding the BookInfo application

Technical requirements

To complete the exercises in this chapter, you will need the following:

- A Windows 10 PC or laptop or an Apple MacBook, as per the minimum configuration requirements
- A Kubernetes environment
- Internet access to your host machine so that you can download applications in the VM running Kubernetes

The GitHub page for this chapter is `https://github.com/servicemeshbook/istio/` labeled `Chapter 08 - Installing a Demo Application` and will be updated as per the release schedules of Kubernetes.

> You need to have a fair understanding of Kubernetes before diving into the code exercises provided in this chapter. Please refer to the books mentioned in the *Further reading* section for more information. For detailed information regarding the installation of Kubernetes, please refer to `Chapter 6`, *Building Your Own Kubernetes Environment*.

Exploring Istio's BookInfo application

BookInfo is an open source application used by the Istio community to test and demonstrate various Istio features. A community of developers maintains it at `https://github.com/istio/istio`. The sample application represents a mix of programming languages so that we can realize the benefits of Service Mesh in later chapters.

Importantly, we don't need to make any changes in the application code to provide routing, telemetry, and policy enforcement. Think of this as a DevOps environment in which no coding is required to implement operations, which typically requires instrumentation within the application itself. Today, this is a shift in application development, and Operations can fulfill its task without making any changes to the application.

> The Istio BookInfo application is available at `https://github.com/istio/istio/tree/master/samples/bookinfo`.

BookInfo application architecture

The BookInfo microservice is a polyglot application that contains six services:

- Product Page: Programmed using Python
- Reviews (v1, v2, and v3) Pages: Programmed using Java
- Detail Page: Programmed using Ruby
- Ratings Page: Programmed using Node.js

The following diagram shows the flow of a polyglot microservice application:

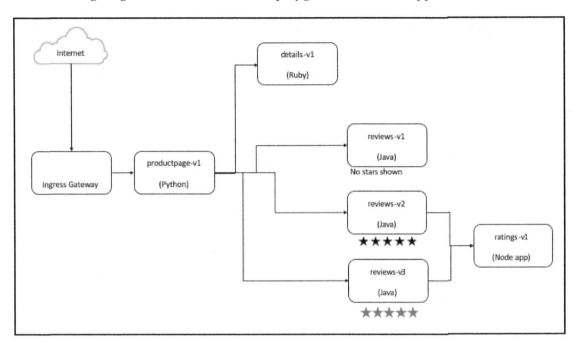

When we run the Bookinfo application, the productpage service receives traffic from the outside world through the Istio Ingress gateway. The productpage microservice calls the following:

- The details microservice, to get the details of the book
- The reviews microservice, to get the reviews of the book

As shown in the preceding diagram, the reviews microservices have three versions. By default, the requests from productpage will be round-robined to all three versions of the reviews. reviews-v1 does not call the ratings service at all, unlike reviews-v2 and reviews-v3, reviews-v1 returns immediately and shows no stars on the productpage display, and reviews-v2 displays black stars, whereas reviews-v3 shows red stars on the productpage display. Due to the absence and color of the stars, we can identify which specific version of the reviews served the request from productpage. Let's take a look at this structure:

1. First, users will log in to the main page, which is the main view. This is called the Product page.

2. Next, users can submit a book rating through the reviews microservice, which has three versions: v1 has no stars, v2 has black stars, and v3 has red stars.

3. Finally, the Details microservice provides a high-level overview of the selected book.

The following image of the BookInfo application shows the product page, which contains the details, reviews, and ratings microservices:

In the upcoming sections of this chapter, we will provide a walkthrough of how to deploy BookInfo and validating that deployment by checking its availability and overall access to an external network.

Deploying the Bookinfo application in Kubernetes

BookInfo will be deployed in our Kubernetes environment using the deployment YAML file provided by Istio's public GitHub page: `https://archive.istio.io/v1.3/docs/examples/bookinfo/`. Observe the following steps to install the BookInfo application:

1. Create a separate namespace that will be used to deploy the application:

```
$ kubectl create namespace istio-lab
namespace/istio-lab created
```

2. Now, we will grant the Cluster Admin role to the default service account in the `istio-lab` namespace to keep things simple. This approach of granting `cluster-admin` to a namespace is just for convenience, and it should not be the norm:

```
$ kubectl create clusterrolebinding istio-lab-cluster-role-binding
--clusterrole=cluster-admin --serviceaccount=istio-lab:default
clusterrolebinding.rbac.authorization.k8s.io/istio-lab-cluster-
role-binding created
```

3. Next, download the `bookinfo` demo application YAML:

```
$ mkdir -p ~/servicemesh
$ curl -L
https://raw.githubusercontent.com/istio/istio/master/samples/bookin
fo/platform/kube/bookinfo.yaml -o ~/servicemesh/bookinfo.yaml
```

4. Now, deploy the `bookinfo` application:

```
$ kubectl -n istio-lab apply -f ~/servicemesh/bookinfo.yaml
...
deployment.apps/details-v1 created
service/ratings created
serviceaccount/bookinfo-ratings created
deployment.apps/ratings-v1 created
service/reviews created
serviceaccount/bookinfo-reviews created
deployment.apps/reviews-v1 created
deployment.apps/reviews-v2 created
deployment.apps/reviews-v3 created
...
deployment.apps/productpage-v1 created
```

5. The Docker images for the `bookinfo` app will be downloaded from `docker.io/istio/*`.

6. Finally, check the progress of this BookInfo microservice application deployment by checking `kubectl -n istio-lab get all`. Note that it will take a few seconds to a few minutes for the pods to be ready and for the Kubernetes services to be enabled through the endpoints.

Now that we've gone through the scenario of deploying the BookInfo application, let's validate a fully qualified domain name for the Kubernetes service that's been deployed within the VM. This process can remove the dependency of using an IP address to access the Kubernetes service.

Enabling a DNS search for Kubernetes services in a VM

Microservices are accessed through Kubernetes services, which have a permanent name such as `kubernetes.default.svc.cluster.local` for the Kubernetes service name in the default namespace. The default domain name of the cluster is `cluster.local`. Kubernetes runs its DNS server using the `kube-dns` service in the `kube-system` namespace.

In the VM that we are using, no route has been defined for the internal Kubernetes services, so we can't access the internal service name from the VM.

In the following steps, we will validate the domain name for the Kubernetes service:

1. Run the following command:

   ```
   $ dig +search +noall +answer kubernetes.default.svc.cluster.local
   ```

   If the preceding command times out, this means it can't find a DNS server to resolve the Kubernetes service name.

    Note that this step is only needed for the purpose of following the exercises in this book. You may not have to follow these steps in a product quality Kubernetes environment, which is expected to have a DNS server.

2. Log in as root to either verify or add the following entries to your `/etc/resolv.conf` for the Kubernetes DNS server. This is done so that you have proper name resolution for the Kubernetes services:

   ```
   search cluster.local
   nameserver 10.96.0.10
   ```

3. Repeat the `dig` command. Notice that the domain name can resolve the name to the pod's IP address:

   ```
   $ dig +search +noall +answer kubernetes.default.svc.cluster.local
   kubernetes.default.svc.cluster.local. 30 IN A   10.96.0.1
   ```

Now that we've validated the domain name for the Kubernetes services in our VM environment, let's learn more about the BookInfo application we've just installed.

Understanding the BookInfo application

In a traditional environment, you cannot have multiple versions of the same service up and running at the same time unless some routing is built at the application layer.

However, in the preceding example, we have three versions of the Reviews microservice up and running at the same time. Since this application is running within a Kubernetes environment with network service definitions, it is possible to have multiple versions of the same microservice up and running. However, the traffic to each microservice is random, and we don't know which microservice will be receiving the traffic.

You can think of it this way: you have a frontend web application already running stable but not using modern web UI capabilities. You want to enable another web UI frontend with a handful of customers without affecting others. This type of selective rollout fits very well in the Continuous Improvement and Continuous Development strategy. The requirement is that we should be able to do this without having to write any piece of code.

Traditional application development requires engineers to write some form of source code because that is the *de facto* development methodology. When you're considering a cloud-native framework, things are shifting to operations staff who can manage rules and policies without any code changes.

To explore BookInfo further, let's look at the deployed pods, services, and overall availability of the different services within this application.

Exploring the BookInfo application in a Kubernetes environment

As a quick introduction, let's check the different semantics of this application from the perspective of Kubernetes.

To recap, we installed the BookInfo application in the `istio-lab` namespace. Let's get started:

1. Run the following command to check the status of this application:

```
$ kubectl -n istio-lab get pods
NAME                                 READY   STATUS    RESTARTS   AGE
details-v1-bc557b7fc-sfgcc           1/1     Running   0          90s
productpage-v1-6597cb5df9-j9wk5      1/1     Running   0          87s
ratings-v1-5c46fc6f85-vqwck          1/1     Running   0          90s
reviews-v1-69dcdb544-966tw           1/1     Running   0          90s
reviews-v2-65fbdc9f88-hvfbg          1/1     Running   0          89s
reviews-v3-bd8855bdd-d2c7p           1/1     Running   0          88s
```

   Notice that we have only one container running in each pod (1/1) and that all six microservices are in separate pods.

2. Next, let's look at the Kubernetes service description for BookInfo, which displays the internal cluster IP and the application ports of the application. Run the following command to check the `bookinfo` Kubernetes services that connect an immutable service IP address to the mutable pod's IP address:

```
$ kubectl -n istio-lab get svc
NAME          TYPE        CLUSTER-IP   EXTERNAL-IP   PORT(S)    AGE
details       ClusterIP   10.0.0.88    <none>        9080/TCP   2m3s
productpage   ClusterIP   10.0.0.33    <none>        9080/TCP   2m1s
ratings       ClusterIP   10.0.0.11    <none>        9080/TCP   2m3s
reviews       ClusterIP   10.0.0.45    <none>        9080/TCP   2m3s
```

   `productpage` is the entry point for the `bookinfo` demo application.

3. Enter `http://productpage.istio-lab.svc.cluster.local:9080` in a browser from inside the VM to open the Product page.

4. You can also use the following curl command to check whether the application response is `200 (OK)`:

```
$ curl -o /dev/null -s -w "%{http_code}\n"
http://productpage.istio-lab.svc.cluster.local:9080
200
```

   Here, we used an internal service name and IP address to check whether the Product page is giving is a proper `200 OK` response.

5. Check the service description of the Product page:

```
$ kubectl -n istio-lab describe svc productpage
Name: productpage
Namespace: istio-lab
Labels: app=productpage
        service=productpage
Annotations: kubectl.kubernetes.io/last-applied-configuration:
{"apiVersion":"v1","kind":"Service","metadata":{"annotations":{},"l
abels":{"app":"productpage","service":"productpage"},"name":"produc
tpage"
...
Selector: app=productpage
Type: ClusterIP
IP: 10.104.45.240
Port: http 9080/TCP
TargetPort: 9080/TCP
Endpoints: 192.168.230.213:9080
Session Affinity: None
Events: <none>
```

Notice that the service IP address for the Product page is `10.104.45.240`, which has an endpoint of `192.168.230.213`. This IP is the address of the running pod on a node. These IPs may be different in your case.

6. Next, expand all the running pods to get a closer look at the IP addresses and the node names:

```
$ kubectl -n istio-lab get pods -o wide
NAME                              READY  STATUS    RESTARTS  AGE  ---
details-v1-74f858558f-nv59j       1/1    Running   0         11m  ---
productpage-v1-8554d58bff-2dv6n   1/1    Running   0         11m  ---
ratings-v1-7855f5bcb9-mpzhr       1/1    Running   0         11m  ---
reviews-v1-59fd8b965b-4g22v       1/1    Running   0         11m  ---
reviews-v2-d6cfdb7d6-wfzb7        1/1    Running   0         11m  ---
reviews-v3-75699b5cfb-544c8       1/1    Running   0         11m  ---

--- IP                NODE                        NOMINATED NODE
--- 192.168.230.211   osc01.servicemesh.local     <none>
--- 192.168.230.213   osc01.servicemesh.local     <none>
--- 192.168.230.212   osc01.servicemesh.local     <none>
--- 192.168.230.216   osc01.servicemesh.local     <none>
--- 192.168.230.214   osc01.servicemesh.local     <none>
--- 192.168.230.215   osc01.servicemesh.local     <none>
```

Notice that each pod has a different IP address and that all are running under the same node. As we mentioned earlier, you can also use the curl command to check whether the application response is 200 (OK). You can also access the Product page using the IP address of the pod.

If you get an output of 000, the IP isn't correct. Make sure the IP for the Product page matches what you see in your output. In this scenario, 192.168.230.213 is the IP that we've tested.

7. (Optional) Run the following code to get the pod's IP address in a variable and then run the following curl command to make sure that the application is servicing the request:

```
$ PRODUCTPAGE_IP=$(kubectl -n istio-lab get pods -l app=productpage
-o jsonpath={.items..status.podIP}) ; echo $PRODUCTPAGE_IP
192.168.230.213

$ curl -o /dev/null -s -w "%{http_code}\n"
http://$PRODUCTPAGE_IP:9080
200
```

The HTTP response code should be 200, indicating that the request was OK. This is a sanity check to confirm that the application is working properly.

Note that the IP address of the pod can change and that when a pod is rescheduled, Kubernetes will automatically update the service endpoints with the IP address of the new pod.

These concepts are essential to understanding how Kubernetes works and will be helpful for a better understanding of it when we cover traffic routing in later chapters.

Summary

In this chapter, we understood the overall architecture of BookInfo and how to install the application through a simple deployment of its YAML file on Kubernetes. We also learned how to check BookInfo's availability for pods, services, and deployments and validated its service-based IP address for all six services. Now that we have installed the demo application, we will be able to understand Istio's different service mesh capabilities.

In the next chapter, we will jump straight into the installation of Istio's service mesh and share best practices around how each install process works. Thereafter, we will use the BookInfo application we have just installed to explain Istio's service mesh capabilities, such as traffic management, security, telemetry, and overall observability.

Questions

1. Kubernetes provides its own DNS server.

   A) True
   B) False

2. What is a polyglot application?

   A) An application that's been written using the polyglot language
   B) An application that's been written in multiple programming languages
   C) An application that can run on all platforms
   D) An application that has multiple versions of the same microservice

3. The service mesh architecture is only for microservice applications.

   A) True
   B) False

4. A pod's IP address is immutable.

   A) True
   B) False

5. A service IP address is immutable.

   A) True
   B) False

6. A Service IP address is linked to the pod's IP address through Kubernetes endpoints.

   A) True
   B) False

Further reading

- *Getting Started with Kubernetes – Third Edition*, Baier, Jonathan; and White, Jesse, Packt Publishing, October 2018, Print and Web
- *Kubernetes Cookbook*, Second Edition, Saito, Hideto, Lee, Hui-Chuan Chloe; and Hsu, Ke-Jou, Packt Publishing, May 2018, Print and Web
- *Mastering Kubernetes*, Sayfan, Gigi, Packt Publishing, April 2018, Print and Web

Installing Istio 9

So far, in this section of this book, we have learned about control and data plane concepts. We then deployed the demo application for Istio in our Kubernetes environment. In this chapter, we will go through the three installation methods of Istio and enable the demo application to use Istio through automatic sidecar injection. We will then show both the automatic and manual ways of injecting a sidecar in to each microservice for the Bookinfo demo application.

The package installation procedure in Kubernetes is going through a transformation—starting with Helm (the client) and Tiller (the server) and then the operator-based install. At the time of writing, the Istio operator based-install is evolving. We will focus on `helm install` and you will learn about the pre-packaged Istio profile-based installation.

In a nutshell, we will be carrying out the following in this chapter:

- Performing pre-installation tasks
- Installing Istio using three different methods
- Installing a load balancer
- Enabling Istio
- Setting up horizontal pod scaling

Technical requirements

To complete the exercises in this chapter, you will require the following:

- Your own working Kubernetes environment
- The Bookinfo demo application deployed in Kubernetes
- Access to the internet

 For detailed installation instructions, refer to `Chapter 6`, *Building Your Own Kubernetes*, and `Chapter 8`, *Installing a Demo Application*.

You can find the GitHub page for this chapter at: `https://github.com/servicemeshbook/istio` labeled `Chapter 09 - Installing Istio`.

The following command should show you whether the VM can resolve the name using DNS:

```
$ dig +search +noall +answer ibm.com
ibm.com.              20850   IN      A       129.42.38.10
```

We are using Istio 1.3.5 at the time of writing this book. You can get the examples used in this book for Istio 1.3.5 by switching the branch to 1.3.5.

 As technology evolves and changes quickly, the examples given here may not work with the later releases of Istio. It is recommended that you download the Istio version used in this chapter. However, we will be updating `https://github.com/servicemeshbook/istio` for the newest version of Istio and will publish any errata required for the latest release.

Getting ready

For a production environment, the recommended approach is to use a curated, validated, and tested Istio release, either by public cloud providers such as AWS, Google, IBM, and Azure or private cloud providers such as Red Hat OpenShift.

IBM maintains Helm charts for popular open source software and its own middleware. You can add the `helm` repository from `https://github.com/IBM/charts` to add IBM-curated Kubernetes packages.

However, in this chapter, we will only focus on the installation of a particular release direct from `https://github.com/istio/istio`.

 It is also important to note that you could also use managed Kubernetes services provided by public cloud providers to deploy your cloud-native microservices-based applications. In such cases, a specific setup is required before installation, depending on the Kubernetes platform. The Kubernetes managed platforms are tested as per `https://archive.istio.io/v1.3/docs/setup/platform-setup/`.

Performing pre-installation tasks

Before we move on to the installation of Istio, there are a few pre-installation tasks that we need to carry out. These include downloading the source code and validating the environment. We will learn how to carry out these tasks in this section.

Downloading the source code

We will be installing Istio in the `istio-system` namespace and will grant a cluster-admin role to it. This is just for convenience purposes and is not a requirement. The granular permissions, as per the Kubernetes administrator, can be applied to the required namespace for you to install Istio in your actual production environment.

You can download a specific version of Istio from `https://github.com/istio/istio/releases` and by switching to a specific branch. At the time of writing this book, we used branch 1.3.5, and we recommend you use the same branch as you learn Istio by following this chapter.

You can download a specific version using either the `git clone` command or direct download. For consistency, for you to be able to follow the complete hands-on exercises, we will be using the direct download method. Follow these steps:

1. Run this command to find all previous releases of Istio:

    ```
    $ curl -L -s https://api.github.com/repos/istio/istio/releases |
    grep tag_name
    ```

If you do not get any output from the preceding, remove `grep`, and you will likely see rate limits imposed on your external IP address. Use the `-u` option in `curl` to provide your user ID. You will need to generate a GitHub API password using **Settings | Developer Settings | Personal Access Token** and create a token that you can use as a password.

2. You can run the following command to find out the latest version. At the time of writing this book, we deployed and implemented Istio using version 1.3.5:

```
$ export ISTIO_VERSION=$(curl -L -s
https://api.github.com/repos/istio/istio/releases/latest | grep
tag_name | sed "s/ *\"tag_name\": *\"\\(.*\\)\",*/\\1/")

$ echo $ISTIO_VERSION
```

3. Download version 1.3.5 to stay consistent with the hands-on exercises for this book:

```
$ cd ## Switch to your home directory
$ export ISTIO_VERSION=1.3.5
$ curl -L https://git.io/getLatestIstio | sh -

$ cd istio-$ISTIO_VERSION
```

4. Edit your ~/.bashrc profile to include the following lines to add `istioctl` on the system path:

```
$ vi ~/.bashrc

export ISTIO_VERSION=1.3.5
if [ -d ~/istio-${ISTIO_VERSION}/bin ] ; then
    export PATH="~/istio-${ISTIO_VERSION}/bin:$PATH"
fi
```

5. Source `.bashrc` to make changes to the system path:

```
$ source ~/.bashrc
```

We have now downloaded the source code. Now, let's validate whether Kubernetes is ready to install Istio.

Validating the environment before installation

It will be good to check whether the current Kubernetes environment is ready for the installation of the selected Istio version. It is important to check this beforehand since a few Istio capabilities are dependent on the version of Kubernetes:

1. Run `istioctl verify-install`:

```
$ istioctl verify-install
Checking the cluster to make sure it is ready for Istio
installation...

Kubernetes-api
-----------------------
Can initialize the Kubernetes client.
Can query the Kubernetes API Server.

Kubernetes-version
-----------------------
Istio is compatible with Kubernetes: v1.15.6.Istio-existence
-----------------------
Istio will be installed in the istio-system namespace.

Kubernetes-setup
-----------------------
Can create necessary Kubernetes configurations:
Namespace,ClusterRole,ClusterRoleBinding,CustomResourceDefinition,R
ole,ServiceAccount,Service,Deployments,ConfigMap.

SideCar-Injector
-----------------------
This Kubernetes cluster supports automatic sidecar injection. To
enable automatic sidecar injection see
https://istio.io/docs/setup/kubernetes/additional-setup/sidecar-inj
ection/#deploying-an-app

-----------------------
Install Pre-Check passed! The cluster is ready for Istio
installation.
```

2. If the preceding test passes, it is good to proceed with the Istio installation.

3. Remove the Tiller pod as we will initialize `helm` again by adding a `tiller` service account:

```
$ helm reset --force
Tiller (the Helm server-side component) has been uninstalled from
your Kubernetes Cluster.
```

After making sure that the pre-installation tasks for Istio confirm that it is ready to install in our chosen Kubernetes version, we will go through the installation profiles and choose the one for our demo environment.

Choosing an installation profile

Istio has created pre-configured profiles for `helm` to install Istio with a pre-chosen set of components. A profile is nothing but a `values.yaml` file—which is an input to the `helm` command to provide installation options. The following profiles are used:

- `Default`: Enable a component that is recommended for a production install.
- `Demo`: Enable an Istio component for demo purposes with minimum resource requirements for CPU and memory. The demo profile comes with or without authentication.
- `Minimal`: This is the minimal installation that enables traffic management.
- `sds-auth`: This is similar to the default profile but enables **Secret Discovery Service (SDS)**.

 Use the `istioctl experimental profile list` command for a list of the available profiles.

The YAML for the profiles can be found in the `/install/kubernetes/helm/istio` directory. Consult https://archive.istio.io/v1.3/docs/setup/additional-setup/config-profiles/ for the features available for each of the profiles mentioned at the preceding URL. For this book, we will be using the `demo` profile for the installation.

Now that we have downloaded our source code, validated our Kubernetes environment, and selected our installation profile, we have completed all of the required pre-installation tasks and are ready to install Istio. So, let's jump straight into it.

Installing Istio

We will go through the Istio install process using three different methods:

- Install using the `helm` template to generate the YAML file
- Install using `helm` and `tiller`
- Install through a `demo` profile using the `kubectl apply` command

Installing Istio using the helm template

Helm is a package manager that gives options to install a software package using either a URI, TGZ file, or a directory. Since we downloaded Istio from GitHub, we will use the directory as an input to the `helm` command.

If using the `helm template` command, we need to make sure that we create a **Custom Resource Definition (CRD)** first:

1. Create the `istio-system` namespace, which will be used by Istio:

   ```
   $ kubectl create namespace istio-system
   namespace/istio-system created
   ```

2. Grant the `cluster-admin` role to the default service accounts for the `istio-system` namespace, which we will use for the Istio installation:

   ```
   $ kubectl create clusterrolebinding istio-system-cluster-role-
   binding --clusterrole=cluster-admin --serviceaccount=istio-
   system:default
   clusterrolebinding.rbac.authorization.k8s.io/istio-system-cluster-
   role-binding created
   ```

3. Install the Istio CRDs and re-initialize `tiller` to include the `istio-system` namespace. In the upcoming release for Helm version 3, the dependency for CRDs will be integrated as a part of the Istio installation either through `helm` or YAML directly:

   ```
   $ cd ~/istio-$ISTIO_VERSION/install/kubernetes/helm/istio-
   init/files

   $ for i in ./crd*yaml; do kubectl apply -f $i; done
   customresourcedefinition.apiextensions.k8s.io/virtualservices.netwo
   rking.istio.io created
   customresourcedefinition.apiextensions.k8s.io/destinationrules.netw
   ```

```
orking.istio.io created
customresourcedefinition.apiextensions.k8s.io/serviceentries.networ
king.istio.io created
...
customresourcedefinition.apiextensions.k8s.io/challenges.certmanage
r.k8s.io created
```

4. Change directory to the Istio helm charts, create a `tiller` service account, and re-initialize the service:

    $ cd ~/istio-$ISTIO_VERSION/install/kubernetes/helm

    $ kubectl apply -f helm-service-account.yaml
    ```
    serviceaccount/tiller created
    clusterrolebinding.rbac.authorization.k8s.io/tiller created
    ```

    $ helm init --service-account tiller
    ```
    $HELM_HOME has been configured at /home/user/.helm.
    Tiller (the Helm server-side component) has been installed into
    your Kubernetes Cluster.
    ...
    ```

 If you get a warning that `Tiller is already installed in the cluster`, ignore the warning and proceed.

5. Validate that the Tiller pod is running in the `kube-system` namespace and wait for it to become `1/1`:

    $ kubectl get pods -n kube-system | grep tiller
    ```
    NAME                                READY   STATUS    RESTARTS   AGE
    tiller-deploy-767d9b9584-bx4tf      1/1     Running   0          58s
    ```

6. Run the following `helm template` command to generate the `yaml` file using the default Istio demo configuration parameters defined in `values-istio-demo.yaml`. Next, route the generated output to the `kubectl apply` command. Helm tiller, which is a server-side component of the `helm` package manager, is not used in this case:

    $ cd ~/istio-$ISTIO_VERSION

    **$ helm template install/kubernetes/helm/istio --name istio **
    **--namespace istio-system **
    **--values install/kubernetes/helm/istio/values-istio-demo.yaml | **
    kubectl apply -f -

```
poddisruptionbudget.policy/istio-galley created
poddisruptionbudget.policy/istio-egressgateway created
...
destinationrule.networking.istio.io/istio-policy created
destinationrule.networking.istio.io/istio-telemetry created
```

7. Wait for a few minutes as it will start downloading the Docker images from the public repositories.
8. Check the status of the pods in the `istio-system` namespace.
9. When all pods are ready, press *Ctrl + C* to stop the watch:

```
$ kubectl -n istio-system get pods --watch
NAME                                      READY STATUS      RESTARTS AGE
grafana-6575997f54-tplrg                  1/1   Running     0        3m17s
istio-citadel-894d98c85-rjfqb             1/1   Running     0        3m17s
istio-cleanup-secrets-1.3.5-nzxd7         0/1   Completed   0        3m18s
istio-egressgateway-9b7866bf5-wmk55       1/1   Running     0        3m17s
istio-galley-5b984f89b-rn42f              1/1   Running     0        3m17s
istio-grafana-post-install-1.3.5-mcc92    0/1   Completed   0        3m18s
istio-ingressgateway-75ddf64567-p7h6m     1/1   Running     0        3m17s
...
```

The pods with a `Completed` status are one-time jobs. The other pods that are either 1/1 or 2/2 under the `READY` column and have a `STATUS` of `Running` are Istio's control plane pods.

Now, let's install Istio using our next method, which is by using Helm and Tiller.

Installing Istio using Helm and Tiller

Since we already installed Istio from the previous step using the `helm` template, we need to do a proper cleanup of the existing installation:

1. Begin to uninstall Istio by generating resource creation scripts and then route them with the `kubectl delete` command:

```
$ cd ~/istio-$ISTIO_VERSION

$ helm template install/kubernetes/helm/istio --name istio \
  --namespace istio-system \
  --values install/kubernetes/helm/istio/values-istio-demo.yaml |\
  kubectl delete -f -
```

The `helm` install consists of two tasks:

- Creating a CRD for Istio and cert-manager
- Installing Istio using Helm

2. First, create the custom resource definitions required by Istio:

```
$ cd ~/istio-$ISTIO_VERSION/install/kubernetes/helm

$ helm install ./istio-init --name istio-init --namespace istio-system
```

3. Next, run the `helm install` command to install `istio-demo` (permissive mutual TLS):

```
$ helm install ./istio -f istio/values-istio-demo.yaml \
--name istio --namespace istio-system
```

The output from `helm install` is long. Notice the number of resources deployed, such as Cluster Role, Cluster Role Binding, Config map, Deployment, Pod, Role, Role Binding, Secret, Service, Service Account, Attribute Manifest, Handler, Instance, Rule, Destination Rule, mutating webhook configuration, Pod Disruption Budget, and Horizontal Pod Autoscaler.

The Istio installation can also be accomplished using the `helm template` command to generate the scripts and then routing it to the `kubectl apply` command. Consult the Istio documentation at `https://archive.istio.io/v1.3/docs/setup/install/helm/` for further details.

After a successful install, you can verify the installation by running `kubectl -n istio-system get pods` and `kubectl -n istio-system get svc`.

4. Check deployment resources in `istio-system`:

```
$ kubectl -n istio-system get deployment
NAME                      READY   UP-TO-DATE   AVAILABLE   AGE
grafana                   1/1     1            1           6m18s
istio-citadel             1/1     1            1           6m18s
istio-egressgateway       1/1     1            1           6m18s
istio-galley              1/1     1            1           6m18s
istio-ingressgateway      1/1     1            1           6m18s
istio-pilot               1/1     1            1           6m18s
istio-policy              1/1     1            1           6m18s
istio-sidecar-injector    1/1     1            1           6m18s
istio-telemetry           1/1     1            1           6m18s
istio-tracing             1/1     1            1           6m18s
```

```
kiali            1/1      1        1          6m18s
prometheus       1/1      1        1          6m18s
```

Make sure that every deployment's number of pods under the UP-TO-DATE column matches with those under AVAILABLE.

Next, we will install Istio using a pre-packaged demo profile.

Installing Istio using a demo profile

The Istio install using direct YAML can be done by using the demo profile. This provides less flexibility compared to Helm, where we could override parameters using --set in the helm command line. This method is useful in a development environment.

If you installed Istio using Helm from the previous section, uninstall Istio using helm and tiller using the following commands:

```
$ helm del --purge istio
release "istio" deleted

$ helm del --purge istio-init
release "istio-init" deleted
```

We will install Istio using a demo profile:

```
$ cd ~/istio-$ISTIO_VERSION/
$ kubectl apply -f install/kubernetes/istio-demo.yaml
```

 The Istio demo profile does not include *strict* mutual TLS, and this capability is enabled and explained in further detail in Chapter 11, *Exploring Istio Security Features*.

In this section, we have seen three different methods of Istio install. Next, we want to verify whether the installation has been successful or not.

Verifying our installation

Verifying our installation is important to ensure that we have got everything right. To verify the installation of Istio, follow these steps:

1. First, check the version of `istioctl` and the different Istio modules:

```
$ istioctl version --short
client version: 1.3.5
citadel version: 1.3.5
egressgateway version: 1.3.5
galley version: 1.3.5
ingressgateway version: 1.3.5
pilot version: 1.3.5
policy version: 1.3.5
sidecar-injector version: 1.3.5
telemetry version: 1.3.5
```

2. The Istio resources are created in the `istio-system` namespace. Check the status of the Istio pods:

```
$ kubectl -n istio-system get pods
NAME                                          READY   STATUS      RESTARTS   AGE
grafana-c49f9df64-8q7gm                       1/1     Running     0          2m1s
istio-citadel-7f699dc8c8-flwc7                1/1     Running     0          113s
istio-cleanup-secrets-1.3.5-zvppz             0/1     Completed   0          2m4s
istio-egressgateway-54f556bc5c-j4rh8          1/1     Running     0          2m2s
istio-galley-687664875b-8n85n                 1/1     Running     0          2m3s
istio-grafana-post-install-1.3.5-gfsfx        0/1     Completed   0          2m4s
istio-ingressgateway-688d5886d-vsd8k          1/1     Running     0          2m2s
...
```

The pods showing the status of `Completed` are the ones that ran a job successfully. All other pods should show the `Running` status.

Note from the preceding output that the Istio control plane consists of three components. They are as follows:

- **Citadel**: `istio-citadel` provides service-to-service and end-user authentication, with built-in identity and credential management.
- **Mixer**: Mixer consists of `istio-policy`, `istio-telemetry`, and `istio-galley`.
- **Pilot**: Pilot is `istio-pilot`.

Istio-ingressgateway and istio-egressgateway are platform-independent inbound and outbound traffic gateways. Prometheus, Kiali, and Grafana are backend services for metering and monitoring.

 Installing Istio using Operator is gaining popularity but we will not be covering it since it is still in its nascent stage. To learn more about this method, visit this link: https://archive.istio.io/v1.3/docs/setup/install/operator/.

Installing a load balancer

Managed Kubernetes services such as Google or IBM Cloud will provide an external load balancer. Since our Kubernetes environment is standalone, we do not have an external load balancer; we install and use keepalived as a load balancer.

The keepalived load balancer depends on the ip_vs kernel module to be loaded. Follow these steps:

1. Make sure that the ip_vs kernel module is loaded:

```
$ sudo lsmod | grep ^ip_vs
ip_vs_wlc 12519 0
ip_vs 145497 2 ip_vs_wlc
```

2. If the preceding does not show any output, load the module:

```
$ sudo ipvsadm -ln
IP Virtual Server version 1.2.1 (size=4096)
Prot LocalAddress:Port Scheduler Flags
   -> RemoteAddress:Port            Forward Weight ActiveConn
InActConn
```

3. Run sudo lsmod | grep ^ip_vs to make sure that the module is loaded.
4. Add ip_vs to the module list so that it is loaded automatically on reboot:

```
$ echo "ip_vs" | sudo tee /etc/modules-load.d/ipvs.conf
```

5. The keepalived helm chart requires that the node be labeled as proxy=true so that it can deploy the daemon set on this master node:

```
$ kubectl label node osc01.servicemesh.local proxy=true
node/osc01.servicemesh.local labeled
```

6. Install `keepalived` through a helm chart from `https://github.com/servicemeshbook/keepalived`:

```
$ helm repo add kaal https://servicemeshbook.github.io/keepalived
"kaal" has been added to your repositories
```

```
$ helm repo update
Hang tight while we grab the latest from your chart repositories...
...Skip local chart repository
...Successfully got an update from the "kaal" chart repository
...Successfully got an update from the "stable" chart repository
Update Complete.
```

```
# Grant cluster admin to the default service account in keepalived
namespace
```

```
$ kubectl create clusterrolebinding \
keepalived-cluster-role-binding \
--clusterrole=cluster-admin --serviceaccount=keepalived:default
clusterrolebinding.rbac.authorization.k8s.io/keepalived-cluster-
role-binding created
```

```
$ helm install kaal/keepalived --name keepalived \
--namespace keepalived \
--set keepalivedCloudProvider.serviceIPRange="192.168.142.248/29" \
--set nameOverride="lb"
```

7. After creating the preceding helm chart, test the readiness and status of pods in the `keepalived` namespace:

```
$ kubectl -n keepalived get pods
NAME                                            READY    STATUS     ---
keepalived-lb-cloud-provider-c68f7b6b5-hqz2n    1/1      Running    ---
keepalived-lb-vip-manager-dlpfv                 1/1      Running    ---

--- RESTARTS    AGE
--- 0           49s
--- 0           49s
```

If you are not using the base VM (`https://github.com/servicemeshbook/byok`), you may have a different IP address for your VM or a separate node name. You may have to do customization to follow the exercises, especially if you plan to use an internal load balancer.

As a solution, you can create an alias on your default NIC adapter to use the same IP address range that we are using. For example, you could run the `IP address add 192.168.142.1/24 dev eth0` command to create another IP address on your existing NIC adapter. This will allow you to run the exercises without having to change too much.

8. Once the `keepalived` load balancer is working, check the status of the Istio services, and you should see that the Istio ingress gateway now has an external IP address assigned:

```
$ kubectl -n istio-system get services
NAME                     TYPE          CLUSTER-IP       EXTERNAL-IP
grafana                  ClusterIP     10.110.45.249    <none>
istio-citadel            ClusterIP     10.102.12.32     <none>
istio-egressgateway      ClusterIP     10.98.94.222     <none>
istio-galley             ClusterIP     10.106.47.250    <none>
istio-ingressgateway     LoadBalancer  10.108.75.6      192.168.142.249
istio-pilot              ClusterIP     10.103.70.243    <none>
istio-policy             ClusterIP     10.108.62.61     <none>
istio-sidecar-injector   ClusterIP     10.104.147.41    <none>
istio-telemetry          ClusterIP     10.107.179.4     <none>
jaeger-agent             ClusterIP     None             <none>
jaeger-collector         ClusterIP     10.105.216.0     <none>
jaeger-query             ClusterIP     10.108.215.169   <none>
kiali                    ClusterIP     10.98.39.201     <none>
prometheus               ClusterIP     10.104.175.238   <none>
tracing                  ClusterIP     10.109.27.237    <none>
zipkin                   ClusterIP     10.96.252.28     <none>
```

All services should have `cluster-ip` except `jaeger-agent` and `istio-ingressgateway`. They might show as `<pending>` initially, and `keepalivd` will provide an IP address from a subnet range that we provided to the `helm install` command. Note the external IP address assigned by the load balancer to `istio-ingressgateway` is `192.168.142.249`, but this could be different in your case.

When no external load balancer is used, the node port of the service or port forwarding can be used to run the application from outside the cluster.

Next, we enable Istio for existing applications by injecting a sidecar proxy—which may result in a very short outage of the application as pods need to restart. We will also learn how to enable new applications to get a sidecar proxy injected automatically.

Enabling Istio

In the previous chapter, we deployed the **Bookinfo** sample microservice in the `istio-lab` namespace. Run `kubectl -n istio-lab get pods` and notice that each pod is running only one container for every microservice.

Enabling Istio for an existing application

To enable Istio for an existing application, we will use `istioctl` to generate additional artifacts in `bookinfo.yaml`, so the sidecar proxy is added to every pod:

1. First, generate modified YAML with a sidecar proxy for the Bookinfo application:

```
$ cd ~/servicemesh
$ istioctl kube-inject -f bookinfo.yaml > bookinfo_proxy.yaml

$ cat bookinfo_proxy.yaml
...
  template:
    metadata:
      annotations:
        sidecar.istio.io/interceptionMode: REDIRECT
...

        traffic.sidecar.istio.io/excludeInboundPorts: "15020"
        traffic.sidecar.istio.io/includeInboundPorts: "9080"
        traffic.sidecar.istio.io/includeOutboundIPRanges: '*'
...
```

 `istioctl` in the preceding example cannot be substituted by the `kubectl` command. Notice the sidecar proxy code injected into the original YAML file.

2. Do `diff` on the original and modified file to see the additions to the YAML file by the `istioctl` command:

```
$ diff -y bookinfo.yaml bookinfo_proxy.yaml
...
  volumeMounts: volumeMounts:
  - name: tmp                              | - mountPath: /etc/istio/proxy
    mountPath: /tmp                        | name: istio-envoy
  - name: wlp-output                       | - mountPath: /etc/certs/
    mountPath: /opt/ibm/wlp/output | name: istio-certs
                                           > readOnly: true

...
```

3. The new definition of the sidecar proxy will be added to the YAML file.

4. Deploy the modified `bookinfo_proxy.yaml` file to inject a sidecar proxy into the existing `bookinfo` microservice:

```
$ kubectl -n istio-lab apply -f bookinfo_proxy.yaml
```

5. Wait a few minutes for the existing pods to terminate and for the new pods to be ready. The output should look similar to the following:

```
$ kubectl -n istio-lab get pods
NAME                            READY   STATUS    RESTARTS   AGE
details-v1-68955b8bdc-crg2s     2/2     Running   0          96s
productpage-v1-74dfdd8b47-4d2gw 2/2     Running   0          96s
ratings-v1-79b6d99979-f8mgl     2/2     Running   0          96s
reviews-v1-69b9dddccf-x8r6d     2/2     Running   0          96s
reviews-v2-84c46bf56d-q7pmr     2/2     Running   0          96s
reviews-v3-64ff5788c7-nx4jx     2/2     Running   0          96s
```

Notice that each pod has two running containers since a sidecar proxy was added through the modified YAML.

It is possible to select microservices to not have a sidecar by editing the generated YAML through the `istioctl` command.

 With Istio 1.3.5, the `istioctl add-to-mesh service` command has been added, which can be used to restart a pod to add a sidecar. For example, `istioctl experimental add-to-mesh service productpage -n istio-lab` will add a sidecar to the `productpage` service. The keyword `experimental` will be removed from future releases.

Enabling Istio for new applications

To show how to enable sidecar injection automatically, we will delete the existing `istio-lab` namespace, and we will redeploy `bookinfo` so that Istio is automatically enabled with the proxy for the new application. Follow these steps:

1. First, delete the `istio-lab` namespace:

   ```
   $ kubectl delete namespace istio-lab
   ```

   If you get namespace deletion in a perpetual terminating state, use the script to get rid of the namespace: `https://github.com/jefferyb/useful-scripts/blob/master/openshift/force-delete-openshift-project`.

2. Now, create the `istio-lab` namespace again and label it using `istio-injection=enabled`:

   ```
   $ kubectl create namespace istio-lab
   namespace/istio-lab created
   ```

   ```
   $ kubectl label namespace istio-lab istio-injection=enabled
   namespace/istio-lab labeled
   ```

   By labeling an `istio-injection=enabled` namespace, the Istio sidecar gets injected automatically when the application is deployed using `kubectl apply` or the `helm` command.

3. Deploy the application again:

   ```
   $ kubectl -n istio-lab apply -f ~/servicemesh/bookinfo.yaml
   ```

4. Run `kubectl -n istio-lab get pods` and wait for them to be ready. You will notice that each pod has two containers, and one of them is the sidecar.
5. Run `istioctl proxy-status`, which provides the sync status from pilot to each proxy in the mesh.

Now that Istio has been enabled, we are ready to learn about its capabilities using examples from `https://istio.io`. In the next section, we will set up horizontal pod scaling for Istio services.

`https://istio.io/` is the official open source site. It has in-depth examples to explain Istio. This book has leveraged many examples from the official site to explain its core capabilities to beginners and help them to grasp the fundamentals of Istio.

Setting up horizontal pod scaling

Each component of Istio has the autoscaling value set to `false` for the `demo` profile (using `install/kubernetes/istio-demo.yaml`). You can set `autoscaleEnabled` to `true` for different components in `install/kubernetes/helm/istio/values-istio-demo.yaml` to enable autoscaling. This configuration may work nicely in production environments based on deployed applications where the autoscaling of pods may help to handle increased workloads.

To get the benefits of autoscaling, we should be careful in selecting the applications since autoscaling applications in high-latency environments can make the situation go from bad to worse in handling the increased workload.

Pod scaling can be enabled at the time of the Helm installation if the following parameters are passed to the `helm install` command using the `--set` argument:

```
mixer.policy.autoscaleEnabled=true
mixer.telemetry.autoscaleEnabled=true
mixer.ingress-gateway.autoscaleEnabled=true
mixer.egress-gateway.autoscaleEnabled=true
pilot.autoscaleEnabled=true
```

 If you are deploying Istio in a multi-node Kubernetes cluster that has a minimum of three master nodes, it is recommended that you keep the horizontal pod scaling feature to absorb the increased workload.

Follow the steps given here:

1. Let's check the current autoscaling for every Istio component:

   ```
   $ kubectl -n istio-system get hpa
   No resources found.
   ```

2. If pod scaling is enabled, it can be deleted using the following command. In our case, this is not necessary:

```
$ kubectl -n istio-system delete hpa --all
horizontalpodautoscaler.autoscaling "istio-egressgateway" deleted
horizontalpodautoscaler.autoscaling "istio-ingressgateway" deleted
horizontalpodautoscaler.autoscaling "istio-pilot" deleted
horizontalpodautoscaler.autoscaling "istio-policy" deleted
horizontalpodautoscaler.autoscaling "istio-telemetry" deleted
```

3. After deleting auto pod scaling, make sure to set `replicas` to 1. In our case, it is not necessary:

```
$ kubectl -n istio-system scale deploy istio-egressgateway --replicas=1
$ kubectl -n istio-system scale deploy istio-ingressgateway --replicas=1
$ kubectl -n istio-system scale deploy istio-pilot --replicas=1
$ kubectl -n istio-system scale deploy istio-policy --replicas=1
$ kubectl -n istio-system scale deploy istio-telemetry --replicas=1
```

The promise of a service mesh architecture using a solution such as Istio is to effect changes without having to modify the existing application. This is a significant shift in which operations engineers can run modern microservices applications without having to change anything in the code.

Summary

In this chapter, you have learned how to install Istio using different methods. We discussed the different profiles that are available to install an environment that is suited to a need, such as either a production or a test environment. Installation from the GitHub repository provides options to use a particular version and customized installations. We saw that using the Helm installation is another simple choice that involves using a simple `helm install` command and override configuration parameters using `--set` variables. The third method is to do a Helm installation through a cloud provider's catalog. You can request Istio to come pre-configured with a Kubernetes cluster.

Now that we have successfully installed Istio, we will explore the various features it offers in the upcoming chapters, beginning with traffic management.

Questions

1. Istio can only be used in a Kubernetes environment.

    A) True
    B) False

2. Istio can only be enabled for a new application if the namespace is annotated with the `istio-injection=enabled` label.

    A) True
    B) False

3. Istio has extended Kubernetes via CRD.

    A) True
    B) False

4. It is mandatory to deploy CRD before Istio is installed.

    A) True
    B) False

5. Istio cannot be enabled for existing applications without deleting them first.

    A) True
    B) False

6. It is not possible to disable a sidecar for a particular microservice when a namespace is already annotated with an `istio-injection=enabled` label.

    A) True
    B) False

7. Istio custom resources can only be managed through the `istioctl` command and not through the `kubectl` command.

    A) True
    B) False

Further reading

- Istio Blog, Istio. (2019), available at `https://archive.istio.io/v1.3/blog/`, accessed 13 May 2019
- Installation Guides, Istio. (2019), available at `https://archive.istio.io/v1.3/docs/setup/install/`, accessed 13 May 2019
- The Registry For Kubernetes Operators, Operatorhub.Io, 2019, `https://operatorhub.io/contribute`

10
Exploring Istio Traffic Management Capabilities

In this chapter, we will focus on traffic management and how to split and steer network connections between different versions of microservices. We will detail the different ways this can be accomplished, identify challenges, and list the best practices.

By the end of this chapter, you will be able to create and deploy Istio-specific Kubernetes objects such as the gateway, virtual service, and destination rule, which configure incoming and outgoing requests to Istio's demo application. You will also learn how to enable and disable traffic patterns to access Istio's demo application regarding traffic routing, traffic shifting, canary deployments, fault injection, circuit breaker, ingress and egress traffic patterns, and traffic mirroring

In a nutshell, this chapter covers the following topics:

- Traffic management – gateway, virtual service, and destination rule
- Traffic shifting – identity-based traffic routing, and canary deployments
- Fault injection, and circuit breaker
- Managing ingress and egress traffic patterns
- Traffic mirroring

Technical requirements

You will get the best out of this chapter if you have the following:

- Istio and the BookInfo microservice installed within Kubernetes

    Please take note of the following regarding the Bookinfo microservice application:

- `ratings:v1` translates to no stars.
- `ratings:v2` translates to black stars.
- `ratings:v3` translates to red stars.

- Your own Kubernetes images built on a single node VM, either on a Windows laptop or MacBook prior to installing Istio—to get started, please consult `https://github.com/servicemeshbook/byok`
- OR – please refer to `Chapter 06`, *Building Your Own Kubernetes Environment*, for more information.

Once you have the preceding requirements in place, open a command-line window to follow this chapter so that you can learn about Istio through examples. Clone this book's GitHub directory, as follows:

```
$ cd # Switch to home directory
$ git clone https://github.com/servicemeshbook/istio
$ cd istio
$ git checkout $ISTIO_VERSION # Switch to branch version that we are using
```

After cloning this book's GitHub repository, go to the traffic management scripts:

```
$ cd scripts/01-traffic-management
```

Make sure that all the `istio-lab` pods show a ready 2/2 state:

```
$ kubectl -n istio-lab get pods
```

Traffic management

One of the key functionalities of microservices is their ability to decouple configurations. For instance, whenever a change happens, Kubernetes' primitive `ConfigMap` configurations are decoupled from the application and pushed down to the application by Kubernetes. Istio provides a much more powerful capability to decouple traffic routing that's independent of the application code.

Traffic management in Istio is decoupled from the application. This is possible due to the language-agnostic Envoy sidecar that sits with the microservice. The rules are defined in **Pilot**, and these are independent of the pod. This helps us to decouple traffic, independent of the replica sets' deployment. For instance, regardless of the number of replicas in a canary deployment, it is only possible to shift 10% of the live traffic to it.

Pilot plays an important role in managing and configuring all of the proxy sidecars within a service mesh. Pilot lets you define the rules that are then pushed down to the proxy sidecars to route traffic between proxies and configure various features such as timeouts, retries, and circuit breakers. Load balancing is done in an intelligent fashion based on the health of other proxies in the load balancing pool. Pilot enables service discovery, dynamic updates to load balancing pools, and routing tables.

Istio provides a gateway for managing incoming and outgoing traffic through Ingress and Egress gateways. These gateways sit on the periphery of the service mesh, which is the data plane running the microservices application:

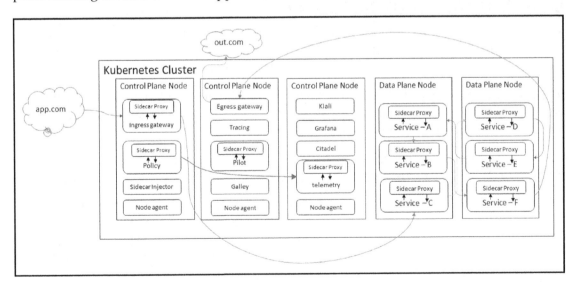

The preceding diagram shows the Istio components and the service mesh encompassing services running in the data plane. The incoming traffic arrives at the **Ingress gateway**, which has its own **sidecar proxy** that receives its configuration from **Pilot**. Through the definition of the gateway that's defined, the incoming traffic from a host can be mapped to a service running inside the Kubernetes cluster. If a microservice needs to establish a connection to the outside world, the **Egress gateway**, which sits on the edge of the proxy mesh, can be configured to originate TLS or rules and can be configured to control access.

Within Istio, there are many traffic rules that can be managed and maintained within the configuration model for controlling API calls and traffic flows across various microservices.

The configuration model allows operators to configure service-level properties such as circuit breakers, timeouts, and retries, load balancing, and many more testing and monitoring capabilities.

Istio provides three routing primitives, as follows:

- Gateway
- Virtual service
- Destination rules

Now, let's understand these routing primitives one by one.

Creating an Istio gateway

Since we are using a bare minimum Kubernetes installation, it does not have a reverse proxy running in the server. A reverse proxy, such as Nginx, provides connectivity from the outside world to the services running within the Kubernetes cluster.

If you are using a managed Kubernetes cluster in a public cloud or have built one using Red Hat OpenShift, you may have to disable the reverse proxy that comes with your Kubernetes cluster for the following exercises to work.

We are going to use Istio, which has provided a gateway controller that receives HTTP/HTTPS/TCP incoming connections:

1. First, create an Istio gateway and an Istio virtual service. This ensures that requests can be routed properly from the external world to the Kubernetes cluster.

2. Look at the `00-create-gateway.yaml` file and make sure you understand the gateway definitions:

```
# Script : 00-create-gateway.yaml

apiVersion: networking.istio.io/v1alpha3
kind: Gateway
metadata:
  name: mygateway
spec:
  selector:
    istio: ingressgateway # use istio default controller
  servers:
  - port:
      number: 80
      name: http
      protocol: HTTP
    hosts:
    - "*"
```

3. Now, let's create Istio's first primitive, that is, `Gateway`:

```
$ kubectl -n istio-system apply -f 00-create-gateway.yaml
gateway.networking.istio.io/mybookinfo created
```

The preceding code creates a gateway in the `istio-system` namespace, and it will allow traffic from all `http` external host requests on port `80`.

Finding the Ingress gateway IP address

Let's find out how to find the gateway IP addresses so that virtual services can be created later to direct traffic from outside the application to the required microservice. After doing this, we can manage the traffic based on rules that can be defined outside the application. Let's get started:

1. To find out the ingress gateway IP address, enter the following command:

```
$ kubectl -n istio-system get svc istio-ingressgateway
NAME                    TYPE           CLUSTER-IP     EXTERNAL-IP       ---
istio-ingressgateway    LoadBalancer   10.109.15.152  192.168.142.249 ---

--- PORT(S)                                                            AGE
--- 15020:30826/TCP,80:31380/TCP,443:31390/TCP,31400:31400/TCP,
    15029:31618/TCP,15030:31759/TCP,15031:31344/TCP,
    15032:30143/TCP,15443:32383/TCP                                    43m
```

The external IP address that's assigned to the Istio ingress gateway, as per the preceding output, is `192.168.142.249`. This might be different in your case.

2. Save the external IP of the ingress gateway in an environment variable that you can use later:

```
$ export INGRESS_HOST=$(kubectl -n istio-system get service istio-
ingressgateway -o jsonpath='{.status.loadBalancer.ingress..ip}') ;
echo $INGRESS_HOST
192.168.142.249
```

In reality, the external IP address will be mapped to a name using a DNS server.

3. Now, let's try to access the BookInfo application, `http://192.168.142.249`. You will notice that it can't find the page:

```
$ curl -v http://$INGRESS_HOST/productpage
* About to connect() to 192.168.142.249 port 80 (#0)
...
< HTTP/1.1 404 Not Found
...
```

We need to map the Kubernetes `productpage` service to the gateway, and we will do that by creating an Istio primitive called `Virtual Service`.

Creating a virtual service

`VirtualService` connects a Kubernetes service to the Istio gateway. It can do many things. We will look at this in detail as we go through the following code and explain the different traffic management capabilities:

1. Let's look at the `01-create-virtual-service.yaml` script:

```
# Script : 01-create-virtual-service.yaml

apiVersion: networking.istio.io/v1alpha3
kind: VirtualService
metadata:
  name: bookinfo
spec:
  hosts:
  - "*"
  gateways:
  - mygateway
  http:
```

```
    - match:
      - uri:
          exact: /productpage
      - uri:
          prefix: /static
      - uri:
          exact: /login
      - uri:
          exact: /logout
      - uri:
          prefix: /api/v1/products
      route:
      - destination:
          host: productpage.istio-lab.cluster.svc.local
          port:
            number: 9080
```

The traffic for booksinfo.istio.io, which resolves to IP address 192.168.142.249, arrives at the Istio Ingress gateway. The virtual service as per the preceding definition routes the traffic for the /productpage, /static, /login, /logout, and /api/v1/products URLs to the productpage.istio-lab.svc.cluster.local microservice at port 9080.

2. Let's create VirtualService:

```
$ kubectl -n istio-system apply -f 01-create-virtual-service.yaml
virtualservice.networking.istio.io/bookinfo created
```

The virtual service that we've created will accept traffic from all hosts coming through mygateway, which will look for a URI pattern called productpage and route the traffic to the Kubernetes productpage.istio-lab.svc.cluster.local service to port number 9080.

3. Test the return http code using the virtual service we created in the previous step to make sure that the routing from the Istio Ingress gateway to the Istio virtual service is happening properly:

```
$ curl -o /dev/null -s -w "%{http_code}\n"
http://$INGRESS_HOST/productpage
200
```

An output of 200 marks the page has loaded successfully.

Let's test http://192.168.142.249/productpage using a browser within the VM.

> **TIP**
>
> Make sure that you change your IP address with $INGRESS_HOST and that you are using the correct external IP address assigned to the Istio Ingress gateway.

4. Refresh the page several times. Under the reviews section, you will notice that the reviewer's ratings change to either **no stars**, **black stars,** or **red stars**. This is due to the fact that we have three versions of the `reviews` microservice, as shown by the output of the following command:

```
$ kubectl -n istio-lab get ep | grep reviews
NAME            ENDPOINTS                        AGE
reviews         10.142.230.236:9080,             82m
                10.142.230.238:9080,
                10.143.230.242:9080
```

5. Notice that the `reviews` microservice, which is called from `productpage`, contains three endpoints that are connected to different versions of the `reviews` pod. The three IP addresses belong to different `reviews` pods:

```
$ kubectl -n istio-lab get pods -o=custom-
columns=NAME:.metadata.name,POD_IP:.status.podIP
NAME                               POD_IP
details-v1-68955b8bdc-5bw67        10.142.230.244
productpage-v1-74dfdd8b47-xmdpn    10.142.230.241
ratings-v1-79b6d99979-k2j7t        10.142.230.239
reviews-v1-69b9dddccf-bsfps        10.142.230.238
reviews-v2-84c46bf56d-48ks9        10.142.230.236
reviews-v3-64ff5788c7-5xzbk        10.142.230.242
```

Note that the IP addresses of the pods can be different in your case.

When we refresh the `productpage`, routing is done in a round-robin fashion where all of the `reviews` microservices will show either black stars, red stars, or no stars.

6. Check the gateway and virtual service:

```
$ kubectl -n istio-system get gateway
NAME            AGE
mygateway       15m

$ kubectl -n istio-system get vs
NAME        GATEWAYS        HOSTS     AGE
bookinfo    [mygateway]     [*]       15m
```

Within the Kubernetes cluster, the sample `productpage` microservice of `bookinfo` can be called either by using the pod's IP address or the Kubernetes services that ties its IP address to the pod. The automatic coupling between the Kubernetes service and the pod makes distributed computing easy.

 You can skip the following sections and jump to the *Creating a destination rule* section if you understand the Kubernetes concepts of finding out the IP address, changing ClusterPort to NodePort, and so on.

Running using pod's transient IP address

The most basic Kubernetes concepts will be shown here since we will be using them throughout this book:

1. Find out the pod's internal IP address:

```
$ kubectl -n istio-lab get pods -o=custom-
columns=NAME:.metadata.name,POD_IP:.status.podIP
NAME                              POD_IP
details-v1-68955b8bdc-5bw67       10.142.230.244
productpage-v1-74dfdd8b47-xmdpn   10.142.230.241
ratings-v1-79b6d99979-k2j7t       10.142.230.239
reviews-v1-69b9dddccf-bsfps       10.142.230.238
reviews-v2-84c46bf56d-48ks9       10.142.230.236
reviews-v3-64ff5788c7-5xzbk       10.142.230.242
```

As we can see, the `productpage` pod IP address is `10.142.230.241`. This might be different in your output.

2. You can test the `productpage` microservice using the `curl` command. Substitute the pod's IP address as per your output:

```
$ export PRODUCTPAGE_POD=$(kubectl -n istio-lab get pods -l
app=productpage -o jsonpath='{.items..status.podIP}') ; echo
$PRODUCTPAGE_POD
10.142.230.241

$ curl -s http://$PRODUCTPAGE_POD:9080 | grep title
<title>Simple Bookstore App</title>
```

Note that the pod IP address is transient and that it will change depending on the node in which the pod is scheduled by Kubernetes.

Running using a service IP address

You can access a microservice through its dynamic IP address. This can change if the microservice is scheduled to another node:

1. The pod's IP address is linked to the service IP address, which is constant throughout its lifetime:

```
$ kubectl -n istio-lab get svc -o custom-
columns=NAME:.metadata.name,CLUSTER_IP:.spec.clusterIP
NAME           CLUSTER_IP
details        10.106.179.233
productpage    10.100.221.255
ratings        10.109.32.8
reviews        10.107.73.66
```

In the preceding code, the `productpage` service IP address is `10.100.221.255`. The IP might be different in your output.

2. You can test this `productpage` service using the `curl` command. Substitute the service IP address as per your output:

```
$ PRODUCTPAGE_IP=$(kubectl -n istio-lab get svc -l app=productpage
-o jsonpath='{.items...spec.clusterIP}') ; echo $PRODUCTPAGE_IP
10.100.221.255
$ curl -s http://$PRODUCTPAGE_IP:9080 | grep title
<title>Simple Bookstore App</title>
```

Note that the service IP address remains the same during its lifetime and may change if the service is dropped and recreated.

Accessing a service by its name is preferred as the Kubernetes DNS server will translate the name in to the proper IP address.

3. The connection between a pod's IP address and service IP address is done through endpoints:

```
$ kubectl -n istio-lab get ep productpage
NAME           ENDPOINTS              AGE
productpage    10.142.230.241:9080    89m
```

Notice that the `productpage` service endpoint is `10.142.230.241`, which is the pod's IP address. This IP address will be different in your case since it is ephemeral and may change when a service is deleted and recreated.

4. Check the IP address of the internal service name:

```
$ dig +short productpage.istio-lab.svc.cluster.local @10.96.0.10
10.100.221.255
```

This IP address, `10.100.221.255`, is the IP address of the FQDN of the service name. The IP address might be different in your case.

5. Open a browser from inside the VM and try `http://10.100.221.255:9080` to view the product page. Replace the IP address as per the output in your VM environment.

We'll learn how to run a Node Port in the next section.

Running using Node Port

You can access a microservice through the Kubernetes service name, which is a connection from a fixed service IP address to the pod IP address. In this section, you will learn how to access a service using Node Port using the node's IP address.

You can also view the service web page from outside the VM but within the firewall of an enterprise by using the server's IP address. This will require changing the service from `ClusterIP` to `NodePort`. Let's get started:

1. Edit the `productpage` service:

```
$ kubectl -n istio-lab edit svc productpage
```

2. Change the type from `ClusterIP` to `NodePort`.

You should have the following initially:

```
selector:
  app: productpage
sessionAffinity: None
  type: ClusterIP
```

Change this to the following:

```
selector:
  app: productpage
sessionAffinity: None
  type: NodePort
```

3. Save the file and check the service:

```
$ kubectl -n istio-lab get svc
NAME          TYPE        CLUSTER-IP       EXTERNAL-IP PORT(S)          AGE
details       ClusterIP   10.106.179.223   <none>      9080/TCP         103m
productpage   NodePort    10.100.221.255   <none>      9080:32384/TCP   103m
ratings       ClusterIP   10.109.32.8      <none>      9080/TCP         103m
reviews       ClusterIP   10.107.73.66     <none>      9080/TCP         103m
```

Or you can use the patch command to change the TYPE from ClusterIP to NodePort, as shown in the following command:

```
kubectl -n istio-lab patch svc productpage --type='json'
-p
'[{"op":"replace","path":"/spec/type","value":"NodePort"}
]'
```

A high port of 32384 has been assigned to the productpage service, which is mapped to port 9080. This port may be different in your case.

4. Find out the name of the VM or master node of the Kubernetes cluster:

```
# kubectl get nodes
NAME                    STATUS  ROLES   AGE     VERSION
osc01.servicemesh.local Ready   master  5h24m   v1.15.6
```

5. Access the web page from a browser on Windows or macOS using http://osc01.servicemesh.local:32384. You may need to change the port as it may be different in your case.

If you receive an err_connection_refused error, make sure that you are using the port as per your environment's output.

An external IP address is assigned to the Istio Ingress gateway, which can be used to access the application (productpage). The external IP address might be coming from an external load balancer that is on the edge of the Kubernetes cluster. In the previous chapter, we simulated an external load balancer using keepalived.

Next, we'll explore the concept of the Istio destination rule, which defines metadata for traffic shifting rules based on labels that have been defined on services.

Creating a destination rule

`DestinationRule` is just a definition that establishes a binding between a subset and the labels that are defined at the service level. A subset is a named set for one or more versions of the same service. Let's take a look:

1. Let's look at one of the destination rule `reviews` in `02-create-destination-rules.yaml`:

   ```
   # Script : 02-create-destination-rules.yaml

   apiVersion: networking.istio.io/v1alpha3
   kind: DestinationRule
   metadata:
     name: reviews
   spec:
     host: reviews
     subsets:
     - name: v1
       labels:
         version: v1
     - name: v2
       labels:
         version: v2
     - name: v3
       labels:
         version: v3
   ```

   The name of the destination rule is `reviews`, while the `host` field has the service name `reviews`. It has three subsets defined within it. The `v1` subset has an association for label `version: v1` and so on.

2. Let's look at the `reviews` pods and examine the labels assigned to these pods:

```
$ kubectl -n istio-lab get pods -l app=reviews --show-labels
NAME                          READY STATUS   RESTARTS  AGE    ---
reviews-v1-69b9dddccf-bsfps   2/2   Running  0         102m   ---
reviews-v2-84c46bf56d-48ks9   2/2   Running  0         102m   ---
reviews-v3-64ff5788c7-5xzbk   2/2   Running  0         102m   ---

--- LABELS
--- app=reviews,pod-template-hash=69b9dddccf,version=v1
--- app=reviews,pod-template-hash=84c46bf56d,version=v2
--- app=reviews,pod-template-hash=64ff5788c7,version=v3
```

Notice that the three review pods have a label of version assigned to them and that the values are set to v1, v2, and v3 for each pod.

By defining the destination rule reviews, we have defined three different subsets (v1, v2, and v3), which make a binding between the reviews service to different reviews pods.

3. Create destination rules for all of the microservices within Bookinfo:

```
$ kubectl -n istio-lab apply -f 02-create-destination-rules.yaml
destinationrule.networking.istio.io/productpage created
destinationrule.networking.istio.io/reviews created
destinationrule.networking.istio.io/ratings created
destinationrule.networking.istio.io/details created
```

Defining a subset through a destination rule does nothing except define a rule. This binding comes into force when we use the subset in the VirtualService definition.

The virtual service that we created previously defined a routing relationship between a service and the Istio gateway. We will now modify the same service to pin the routing of reviews service to version v1 of the pod.

Traffic shifting

The bookinfo application has three different versions of the reviews microservice, and all three are up and running. Earlier, we learned that traffic is sent to all three microservices in a round-robin fashion. This scenario may not be ideal in a real-world environment.

Microservices running under Kubernetes provide us with the ability to run multiple versions of the same microservice by manipulating traffic. We will show you how this is done through the use of a VirtualService using a subset. This way, we can pinpoint traffic to a particular version. Let's get started:

1. Look at the following virtual service for pinpointing all of the traffic of the reviews service only to v1 of the reviews microservice:

```
# Script : 03-create-virtual-service-for-v1.yaml

apiVersion: networking.istio.io/v1alpha3
kind: VirtualService
metadata:
  name: reviews
spec:
```

```
hosts:
- reviews
http:
- route:
  - destination:
      host: reviews
      subset: v1
```

In the preceding code, the Kubernetes `reviews` service has a routing rule that's used to define the destination to subset `v1`, which we defined through the destination rule previously.

2. Create a virtual service that uses a subset that's been defined through a destination rule:

```
$ kubectl -n istio-lab apply -f 03-create-virtual-service-for-
v1.yaml
virtualservice.networking.istio.io/productpage created
virtualservice.networking.istio.io/reviews created
virtualservice.networking.istio.io/ratings created
virtualservice.networking.istio.io/details created
```

In the preceding code, an Istio virtual service is created for the `bookinfo` Kubernetes `productpage`, `reviews`, `ratings`, and `details` services for the destination rule that was defined by subset `v1`. This only directs traffic to pods that match the label that was defined by the subsets.

3. Let's go back to the browser, run `http://192.168.142.249/productpage`, and refresh multiple times. You may need to change the IP address as per your environment.

You will notice that the black and red stars under the reviewer do not appear since the traffic is shifted to `v1` of the reviews microservice. Did you notice that, without making any changes in the application code, the traffic routing is directed only to a service that we desire? This helps operations staff to make changes without having to rely upon developers.

The change in the destination rule for the subset can be defined dynamically, and the virtual service definition can also be defined dynamically. The changes in the configuration are watched by Pilot through the Kubernetes API, and it pushes the configuration asynchronously to the Envoy sidecar proxy of the microservice without having to recycle the application.

This is a very powerful capability that is accomplished through configuration changes in a loosely coupled, distributed environment. Compare and contrast this with legacy applications where a change typically requires recycling a web server and its JVMs.

Identity-based traffic routing

Let's look at another scenario where we will route traffic to v2 of the `reviews` microservice to a named user and test the microservice. This is accomplished by making changes to the virtual service, which does not require recycling the pods or services. Let's take a look:

1. First, we will make changes to the existing reviews of the virtual service to add identity-based routing. Let's review the changes to the existing `reviews` virtual service:

```
# Script : 04-identity-based-traffic-routing.yaml

apiVersion: networking.istio.io/v1alpha3
kind: VirtualService
metadata:
  name: reviews
spec:
  hosts:
    - reviews
  http:
  - match:
    - headers:
        end-user:
          exact: jason
    route:
    - destination:
        host: reviews
        subset: v2
  - route:
    - destination:
        host: reviews
        subset: v1
```

Notice that a rule has been added to match the `http` headers. If the user is `jason`, it routes the traffic to v2 of `reviews`; otherwise, it directs all other traffic to v1, which is the default.

2. Modify the virtual service:

```
$ kubectl -n istio-lab apply -f 04-identity-based-traffic-
routing.yaml
virtualservice.networking.istio.io/reviews configured
```

It may take a few seconds for the changes to propagate to the proxy sidecar.

3. Go back to the browser and click **Sign in** (top-right corner of the screen), type in jason, and click **Sign in**.

You will notice that the review page starts to show black stars, which comes from v2 of the reviews microservice. Refresh the page a few times. You will notice that only black stars show every time. Click **Sign out** and notice that the black stars disappear and that the traffic is routed to v1 of the reviews microservice.

The preceding YAML can be updated for additional users through regex by updating the headers.

We can use regex expressions to form complex matching expressions:

```
http:
- match
  - headers:
      end-user:
        regex: (Iniesta|Don\ Andres)
  route:
  - destination:
    host: reviews
    subset: v2
```

For example, in the preceding YAML snippet, if the user is Iniesta or Don Andres, the request will be directed to the reviews:v2 microservice. This is an example of selectively directing a few users to a new version of the same microservice while retaining the original version in actual use. For example, you have created a new UI for the same service and want to get feedback from a few select users; you can accomplish the same through a set of configuration changes without having to change anything in any of the microservices.

This type of routing is sometimes referred to as *dark launches* or *friends and family testing*, as only a few select people or internal departments are chosen to test the new releases without impacting the main business before the new releases get field-tested.

The preceding code shows that the service mesh is providing an infrastructure layer for the application, which can be configured independently of the original application. Earlier, in traditional legacy applications, this capability required coding to be done at the application level to process the headers and route the traffic.

The virtual service can be configured in such a manner so that Chrome browser traffic is routed to `reviews:v3`, whereas all other browsers, traffic is shifted to `reviews:v2`.

4. Review the following script:

```
# Script : 05-chrome-browser-traffic-routing.yaml

apiVersion: networking.istio.io/v1alpha3
kind: VirtualService
metadata:
  name: reviews
spec:
  hosts:
    - reviews
  http:
  - match:
    - headers:
        user-agent:
          regex: ".*Chrome.*"
    route:
    - destination:
        host: reviews
        subset: v3
  - route:
    - destination:
        host: reviews
        subset: v2
```

5. Apply the preceding rule:

```
$ kubectl -n istio-lab apply -f 05-chrome-browser-traffic-routing.yaml
virtualservice.networking.istio.io/reviews configured
```

Refresh the `productpage` web page. Notice that if you are using the Chrome browser, `v3` of the `reviews` service will show red stars, while all other browsers (such as Firefox) will show black stars through `v2` of `reviews`.

When needed, you can easily form complex conditional matching expressions for routing traffic, like so:

```
http:
  - match:
    - headers:
        user-agent:
          regex: ".*Chrome.*"
        end-user:
          regex: (Iniesta|Don\ Andres)
    - headers:
        end-user:
          exact: Xavi
    route:
    - destination:
        host: reviews
        subset: v3
  - route:
    - destination:
        host: reviews
        subset: v1
```

In the matching expression in the preceding code, if `Iniesta` or `Don Andres` logs in from Chrome or user `Xavi` logs in from any browser, traffic will be directed to version `v3` of the `reviews` microservice. For all other login instances, traffic will be routed to `reviews:v1`.

Now that we've learned about identity-based routing, we will move on to traffic shifting concepts to show canary deployments and blue/green deployments.

Canary deployments

Kubernetes supports blue/green deployments, and they are very useful when a rollback is required. Canary deployments are referred to incremental rollouts in which the new version of the application is gradually deployed while getting a small portion of the traffic, or only a subset of live users is connected to the new version.

The previous section on identity-based routing is an example of routing only for a subset of users to the new version. It can be argued that Kubernetes already supports canary deployment, so why is there a need for Istio's canary deployment?

Let's understand this with an example.

Let's assume that we only have two versions of the `reviews` service, v1 and v2, and that the reviews service endpoints were directed toward both versions of the pods. Without an Istio virtual service in place, Kubernetes will round-robin 50% of the traffic to each of the two pods. Let's assume that v2 is the new version and that as soon as it is deployed, it is getting 50% of the traffic.

If we wanted to divert 90% of the traffic to old version v1 and allow only 10% of the traffic to v2, we could have scaled v1 to nine replicas and kept v2 to a single replica. This would have allowed Kubernetes to direct 90% of the traffic to v1 and 10% to v2.

Istio goes much further than what Kubernetes provides. Using Istio, we can separate traffic routing from replica deployment, where both are unrelated. For example, by using a single replica of v1 and v2, it is possible to divert 90% of the traffic to v1 and 10% of the traffic to v2, independent of scaling both versions. We could run four replicas of v1 and route only 20% of the traffic to it but route 80% of the traffic to a canary v2 version with just one replica.

Let's see this through an implementation example:

1. Consider that `reviews:v1` is the production version and that we are deploying `reviews:v2`, which hasn't been fully tested. We only want to route 10% of traffic to it, without increasing or decreasing the replica sets:

```
# Script: 06-canary-deployment-weight-based-routing.yaml

kind: VirtualService
metadata:
  name: reviews
spec:
  hosts:
    - reviews
  http:
  - route:
    - destination:
        host: reviews
        subset: v1
      weight: 90
    - destination:
        host: reviews
        subset: v2
      weight: 10
```

Regarding the deployment rules for the `reviews` virtual service, we have assigned 90% weight to the `v1` subset and 10% to the `v2` subset.

2. Modify the `reviews` virtual service with weight-based routing:

```
$ kubectl -n istio-lab apply -f 06-canary-deployment-weight-based-routing.yaml
virtualservice.networking.istio.io/reviews configured
```

Go back to the browser and hit refresh multiple times. You will notice that, the majority of times, it shows no stars (`reviews:v1`) and that, occasionally, it shows black stars (`reviews:v2`). If you look at the HTML source when it shows black stars, you will notice that it has two HTML comments that have the text `full stars` when the traffic is sent to `v2` of `reviews`.

3. Run the `curl` command on the `productpage` 1,000 times and count the `"full stars"` HTML comment to make an estimate of the percentage of traffic that's routed between two versions of the same reviews pod. This will take some time to complete:

```
$ echo $INGRESS_HOST
192.168.142.249

$ time curl -s http://$INGRESS_HOST/productpage?[1-1000] | grep -c "full stars"
204

real 0m42.698s
user 0m0.032s
sys 0m0.343s
```

Note: Make sure that `$INGRESS_HOST` is populated properly with the IP address of the load balancer IP address of your environment. Run the following command to find out the external IP address: `kubectl -n istio-system get svc istio-ingressgateway`.

If we divide 204 by 2 (since each output of the `curl` command from `reviews:v2` contains the string `"full stars"` twice), it is close to 10% (*102/1,000=10%* approx) of the traffic that was sent to `reviews:v2` through weight-based routing using the canary deployment capabilities of Istio.

Notice that without using a scaling of pods, we were able to divert 10% of the traffic to the canary release (`reviews:v2`). This was possible due to Pilot pushing the configuration to the Envoy sidecar proxy and because load balancing is done at Layer 7.

Let's assume that you are now satisfied with the canary deployment and want to shut down `v1` and make `v2` part of the production release.

4. Modify the `reviews` virtual service and apply the rule:

```
# Script : 07-move-canary-to-production.yaml

kind: VirtualService
metadata:
  name: reviews
spec:
  hosts:
    - reviews
  http:
  - route:
    - destination:
        host: reviews
        subset: v2
```

In the preceding code, we removed the route to the `v1` subset and removed the weight from the `v2` subset to route 100% of the traffic to `v2`, hence making it the new production release.

5. Apply the new rule by modifying the `reviews` virtual service:

```
$ kubectl -n istio-lab apply -f 07-move-canary-to-production.yaml
virtualservice.networking.istio.io/reviews configured
```

6. Now, repeat the same test again:

```
$ curl -s http://$INGRESS_HOST/productpage?[1-1000] | grep -c "full
stars"
2000
```

Since each HTML page has two occurrences of "`full stars`", we get 2000 counts from the 1,000 requests we sent using the preceding curl command. This shows that our canary deployment is now a new production. If necessary, we can take down `v1` of `reviews`.

It is important to note that the preceding capabilities are available without making changes to the application code, without taking an outage, and, more importantly, without having to change the number of replica sets.

Now that we've learned about traffic shifting features, we will explore fault injection and timeout features.

Fault injection

Fault injection is a method that's used to test the application without having to wait for an actual fault to occur. It is very likely that latency or faults will occur in a distributed environment. It is difficult to envision the effects of actual faults/latency while an application is being developed. Most of the time, it is the reaction of faults/latencies that triggers application code changes, which means new releases of the application have to be made.

While developing enterprise applications, typically, we separate small teams and make them develop microservices independent of each other. It is likely that different teams may introduce timeouts in their code, which may introduce an anomaly. For example, let's say we introduce a 7-second delay that will not affect the reviews service due to there being a 10-second hardcoded timeout between the reviews and ratings service. productpage calls the reviews service and throws an error after 6 seconds, even though our timeout was set to 7 seconds. The http delay uncovered different unexpected service behaviors. Fault injection is a method that can uncover such anomalies, which we will see with the help of an example of injecting an http delay and abort faults.

Injecting HTTP delay faults

The bookinfo application that's been built by Istio's community of developers has hardcoded timeouts at 10 seconds for calls to the ratings service from reviews:v2:

```
...
private JsonObject getRatings(String productId, HttpHeaders requestHeaders)
{
      ClientBuilder cb = ClientBuilder.newBuilder();
      Integer timeout = star_color.equals("black") ? 10000 : 2500;
...
```

Let's inject a delay of 7 seconds for the end user, `jason`, for the `ratings` service:

1. Enter the following command:

```
# Script : 08-inject-http-delay-fault.yaml

kind: VirtualService
metadata:
  name: ratings
spec:
  hosts:
  - ratings
  http:
  - match:
    - headers:
        end-user:
          exact: jason
    fault:
      delay:
        percentage:
          value: 100.0
        fixedDelay: 7s
    route:
    - destination:
        host: ratings
        subset: v1
  - route:
    - destination:
        host: ratings
        subset: v1
```

2. Now, modify the `ratings` virtual service to inject a delay for 7 seconds, but only for `jason`:

```
$ kubectl -n istio-lab apply -f 08-inject-http-delay-fault.yaml
virtualservice.networking.istio.io/ratings configured
```

3. From a browser, click **Sign In** and log in as `jason`.

4. As soon as you click **Sign in**, you will notice that the page takes a while to load. This is due to the 7-second delay we introduced for `jason`.

5. Now, you will see the message `Error fetching product reviews!`.

6. Click the three vertical bars on the top right-hand side of the Chrome address bar, click **More Tools | Developer Tools**, open the **Network** tab, and refresh `productpage` again.

7. You will notice that `productpage` timed out for 6 seconds:

Name	Status	Type	Initiator	Size	Time	Waterfall
productpage	200	docu...	Other	4.1 KB	6.03 s	
jquery.min.js	304	script	productpage	278 B	19 ms	
bootstrap.min.js	304	script	productpage	279 B	19 ms	
glyphicons-halflings-regular....	304	font	productpage	279 B	9 ms	
data:image/png;base...	200	png	onloadwff.js:71	(from ...	0 ms	
data:image/png;base...	200	png	onloadwff.js:71	(from ...	0 ms	
data:image/png;base...	200	png	onloadwff.js:71	(from ...	0 ms	

8. Close the developer tools of the Chrome browser.

Even though we had a timeout of 7 seconds injected between the `reviews` and `ratings` services, a timeout of 6 seconds (two attempts, each timing out at three seconds, as per the following code) occurred between the `productpage` and `reviews` services:

```
...
for _ in range(2):
        try:
                url = reviews['name'] + "/" + reviews['endpoint'] + "/" +
str(product_id)
                res = requests.get(url, headers=headers, timeout=3.0)
        except BaseException:
                res = None
        if res and res.status_code == 200:
                return 200, res.json()
...
```

This is due to the hardcoded timeout limit between the `productpage` and `reviews` services. This helps us to find out the effects of the timeout injection that led to the discovery of the unrelated timeout.

This demonstrates that without instrumenting anything in the original code of the application, testing the application can be done by injecting latency into the application. This is advanced testing that's done without having to wait for actual latency to occur, which can have unforeseen effects on the application. Istio's fault injection helps us to test the application without impacting other users while the application is in production. Remember that the latency rule was only injected for `jason`.

Note that injecting an `http` delay can also simulate the network latency for assigned services to test the overall application's behavior. Now, let's inject abort faults.

Injecting HTTP abort faults

Now, we will test the resiliency of the microservice by introducing the `http` abort rule for the end user, `jason`, for the `ratings` microservice:

1. View the following command:

```
# Script : 09-inject-http-abort-fault.yaml

apiVersion: networking.istio.io/v1alpha3
kind: VirtualService
metadata:
  name: ratings
spec:
  hosts:
  - ratings
  http:
  - match:
    - headers:
        end-user:
          exact: jason
    fault:
      abort:
        percentage:
          value: 100.0
        httpStatus: 500
    route:
    - destination:
        host: ratings
        subset: v1
  - route:
    - destination:
        host: ratings
        subset: v1
```

In the preceding code, we are introducing an `http` fault abort of 500 for the `jason` user for the `ratings` service.

2. Modify the `ratings` virtual service to inject an `http` abort for the test user `jason`:

```
$ kubectl -n istio-lab apply -f 09-inject-http-abort-fault.yaml
virtualservice.networking.istio.io/ratings configured
```

3. Refresh the page and make sure that you log in as `jason`.

4. You will notice the message `Ratings service is currently unavailable`, indicating that the `httpStatus` code 500 was injected when a call was made to the `ratings` service:

Book Reviews

An extremely entertaining play by Shakespeare. The slapstick humour is refreshing!

— Reviewer1

Ratings service is currently unavailable ◀————————

Absolutely fun and entertaining. The play lacks thematic depth when compared to other plays by Shakespeare.

— Reviewer2

Ratings service is currently unavailable ◀————————

---

5. Click (**sign out**) to log out as `jason`.

6. You will see that the `ratings` service works, as usual, showing v2 of `ratings`.

This type of testing is very useful for viewing the runtime behavior of the application by using the `http abort` code for different services without impacting other users. This type of proactive testing, while the application is still in production, is an example of chaos testing and continuous engineering, which is fundamental to cloud-native computing.

Request timeouts

Application timeout is disabled by default. Let's set the request timeout to 0.5 seconds for the `reviews` service:

1. Introduce a `0.5s` timeout in the `reviews` virtual service:

```
# Script : 10-set-request-timeout.yaml

apiVersion: networking.istio.io/v1alpha3
kind: VirtualService
metadata:
  name: reviews
spec:
  hosts:
  - reviews
  http:
  - route:
    - destination:
        host: reviews
        subset: v2
    timeout: 0.5s
```

2. Apply the rule:

```
$ kubectl -n istio-lab apply -f 10-set-request-timeout.yaml
virtualservice.networking.istio.io/reviews configured
```

The code snippet for `productpage` has two retires, as shown in the following code. `productpage` calls the `reviews` service, which now has a timeout of `0.5` seconds, which was defined through the virtual service. The response will take 1 second due to two retries on `productpage`:

```
...
for _ in range(2):
 try:
 url = reviews['name'] + "/" + reviews['endpoint'] + "/" +
str(product_id)
 res = requests.get(url, headers=headers, timeout=3.0)
 except BaseException:
 res = None
 if res and res.status_code == 200:
 return 200, res.json()
...
```

The timeout rule of 0.5 seconds (this is actually 1 second due to two retries) will not come into effect unless there is a latency of more than 1 second between the `reviews` and `ratings` services.

3. Now, let's introduce a 2-second latency between the `reviews` and `ratings` services:

```
# Script : 11-inject-latency.yaml

apiVersion: networking.istio.io/v1alpha3
kind: VirtualService
metadata:
  name: ratings
spec:
  hosts:
  - ratings
  http:
  - fault:
      delay:
        percent: 100
        fixedDelay: 2s
    route:
    - destination:
        host: ratings
        subset: v1
```

4. Apply the latency rule:

```
$ kubectl -n istio-lab apply -f 11-inject-latency.yaml
virtualservice.networking.istio.io/reviews configured
```

5. Go back to the browser and refresh `productpage`.

6. You will receive an error stating **Sorry, product reviews are currently unavailable for this book**.

This error is triggered due to the request timeout being set to 0.5 seconds while the `ratings` service did not respond due to the 2 seconds of latency we established between the `reviews` and `ratings` services.

We uncovered an issue with the `reviews` service by introducing a request timeout of 0.5 seconds. This is a very helpful testing effort at the application level that's done by introducing an artificial delay and timeouts by changing the configurations.

Let's remove the timeout and latency definitions from the virtual services before we begin circuit breaker testing.

7. The easiest way to do this is to delete the virtual service rules and restore the original rules from the script:

```
$ kubectl -n istio-lab delete -f 03-create-virtual-service-for-
v1.yaml
virtualservice.networking.istio.io "productpage" deleted
virtualservice.networking.istio.io "reviews" deleted
virtualservice.networking.istio.io "ratings" deleted
virtualservice.networking.istio.io "details" deleted

$ kubectl -n istio-lab apply -f 03-create-virtual-service-for-
v1.yaml
virtualservice.networking.istio.io/productpage created
virtualservice.networking.istio.io/reviews created
virtualservice.networking.istio.io/ratings created
virtualservice.networking.istio.io/details created
```

Now that we've learned about fault injection and timeouts, we will look at the circuit breaker, which helps to protect applications from undue stress or attacks.

Circuit breaker

The calls between different services in a monolithic application are in-memory only. We replace the in-memory service calls with the network calls when we move from a monolithic to a distributed microservices architecture. While we get the benefits of loose coupling and the reusability of services, the application may experience cascading failures when there is latency between the services or one or more services are not available. Application failures that occur due to the latency of network calls is one of the disadvantages of microservices compared to monolithic applications.

The circuit breaker helps to reduce the aforementioned application failures and lets us build a resilient and fault-tolerant system in the case of high latency or the unavailability of key microservices. A circuit breaker in software engineering is similar to a circuit breaker in electrical engineering, which trips the circuit if someone is drawing more current than the system can sustain to avoid a fire hazard.

The same principle applies to software engineering for detecting failures and having a mechanism to prevent failures from constantly recurring. This design pattern is encapsulated in a call to a circuit breaker object, which monitors the failures and trips the circuit once the failures reach a certain limit.

Istio provides a mechanism for testing the resiliency of microservices through circuit breakers. For example, if a microservice interacts with a backend `statefulset` database, it will wait for the response if the database query takes longer than expected. It will be very helpful to inject circuit breakers to trip a microservice due to an elongated wait. Proper design and implementation of Istio circuit breakers in an application provide resiliency to limit the impact of performance problems, latency, and other undesirable effects, such as network glitches.

Let's implement the circuit breakers for the current `bookinfo` application. The circuit breaker rules are defined using destination rules:

```
# Script : 12-modify-productpage-destination-rule-for-circuit-breaker.yaml

apiVersion: networking.istio.io/v1alpha3
kind: DestinationRule
metadata:
  name: productpage
spec:
  host: productpage
  subsets:
  - labels:
      version: v1
    name: v1
  trafficPolicy:
    connectionPool:
      tcp:
        maxConnections: 1
      http:
        http1MaxPendingRequests: 1
        maxRequestsPerConnection: 1
    outlierDetection:
      consecutiveErrors: 1
      interval: 1s
      baseEjectionTime: 3m
      maxEjectionPercent: 100
```

In the preceding code, we are defining one TCP/HTTP connection for the `productpage` service:

Parameter	Definition
`http1MaxPendingRequests`	This defines the maximum number of pending requests.
`maxRequestsPerConnection`	This defines the maximum number of requests per connection to the backend. We are setting both parameters to 1.
`consecutiveErrors`	This outlier detection parameter setting of 1 will eject the host from the connection pool if a number of 5XX error codes exceed 1.
`interval`	The interval parameter is the time interval between the ejection sweep analysis.
`baseEjectionTime`	It sets the time during which a host will remain ejected for a period equal to the product of the minimum ejection duration and the number of times the host has been ejected. This method allows Istio to increase the ejection period for unhealthy, upstream servers automatically.
`maxEjectionPercent`	This is the percentage of hosts in the load balancing pools that can be ejected. The default value is 10%, but here, we are setting this to 100%.

Now that we know about the necessary circuit breaking parameters, we will go through the implementation process:

1. Implement the circuit breaker rules using the destination rule for `productpage`:

```
$ kubectl -n istio-lab apply -f 12-modify-productpage-destination-
rule-for-circuit-breaker.yaml
destinationrule.networking.istio.io/productpage configured
```

Refresh `productpage` in the browser. You should notice the normal functionality of the web page showing no stars for `review:v1` service. The following diagram shows a closed **Circuit breaker**, in which the calls from the `productpage` go through the `details` and `reviews` services without any interruptions:

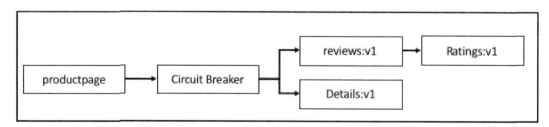

We need a testing tool to control the number of connections, concurrency, and delays for the outgoing `http` requests. The Istio developer community created its own testing tool called `Fortio`, which is available at `https://github.com/istio/fortio`. `Fortio` can run the specified number of **queries per second (qps)**, and it can record a histogram of execution time. It can run for a set duration, for a fixed number of calls, or until it's interrupted.

2. Install Istio's `Fortio` testing tool:

```
$ kubectl -n istio-lab apply -f 13-install-fortio-testing-tool.yaml
service/fortio created
deployment.apps/fortio-deploy created
```

3. Make sure that `Fortio` is deployed properly:

```
$ kubectl -n istio-lab get deploy fortio-deploy
NAME            READY   UP-TO-DATE   AVAILABLE   AGE
fortio-deploy   1/1     1            1           2m48s
```

4. Since we have already labeled the `istio-lab` namespace `istio-injection=enabled`, the Istio proxy car is automatically injected into the `Fortio` pod, as shown by `2/2` in the following output:

```
$ kubectl -n istio-lab get pods -l app=fortio
NAME                            READY   STATUS    RESTARTS   AGE
fortio-deploy-784c644f9c-v6bb8  2/2     Running   0          2m
```

5. Run a simple test that won't trigger any circuit breaker rules:

```
$ export FORTIO_POD=$(kubectl -n istio-lab get pods -l app=fortio -
-no-headers -o custom-columns=NAME:.metadata.name) ; echo
$FORTIO_POD
fortio-deploy-784c644f9c-v6bb8
```

Run `echo $FORTIO_POD` to make sure that you have the `Fortio` pod name correct.

6. Run just one iteration of the call. It should not trigger any circuit breaker rules:

```
$ kubectl -n istio-lab exec -it $FORTIO_POD -c fortio
/usr/bin/fortio -- load -c 1 -qps 0 -n 1 -loglevel Warning
http://productpage:9080
```

7. Check the output from the tool and make sure that there were no 5XX errors:

```
05:29:12 I logger.go:97> Log level is now 3 Warning (was 2 Info)
Fortio 1.3.1 running at 0 queries per second, 8->8 procs, for 1
calls: http://productpage:9080
Starting at max qps with 1 thread(s) [gomax 8] for exactly 1 calls
(1 per thread + 0)
Ended after 5.650443ms : 1 calls. qps=176.98
Aggregated Function Time : count 1 avg 0.005644373 +/- 0 min
0.005644373 max 0.005644373 sum 0.005644373
# range, mid point, percentile, count
>= 0.00564437 <= 0.00564437 , 0.00564437 , 100.00, 1
# target 50% 0.00564437
# target 75% 0.00564437
# target 90% 0.00564437
# target 99% 0.00564437
# target 99.9% 0.00564437
Sockets used: 1 (for perfect keepalive, would be 1)
Code 200 : 1 (100.0 %)
Response Header Sizes : count 1 avg 250 +/- 0 min 250 max 250 sum
250
Response Body/Total Sizes : count 1 avg 1933 +/- 0 min 1933 max
1933 sum 1933
All done 1 calls (plus 0 warmup) 5.644 ms avg, 177.0 qps
```

Notice that Code 200 is 100%, which is an indication that the circuit breaker rules were not triggered by the preceding test, where we have set only one connection.

8. Change the number of concurrent connections to three (-c 3), send 20 requests (-n 20), and run the test:

```
$ kubectl -n istio-lab exec -it $FORTIO_POD -c fortio
/usr/bin/fortio -- load -c 3 -qps 0 -n 20 -loglevel Warning
http://productpage:9080
```

9. Check the output from the testing tool:

```
05:30:24 I logger.go:97> Log level is now 3 Warning (was 2 Info)
Fortio 1.3.1 running at 0 queries per second, 8->8 procs, for 20
calls: http://productpage:9080
Starting at max qps with 3 thread(s) [gomax 8] for exactly 20 calls
(6 per thread + 2)
05:30:24 W http_client.go:679> Parsed non ok code 503 (HTTP/1.1
503)
...
> 0.009 <= 0.00999593 , 0.00949797 , 100.00, 3
# target 50% 0.00533333
# target 75% 0.007
```

```
# target 90% 0.00933198
# target 99% 0.00992954
# target 99.9% 0.00998929
Sockets used: 9 (for perfect keepalive, would be 3)
```
Code 200 : 13 (65.0 %)
Code 503 : 7 (35.0 %)
```
Response Header Sizes : count 20 avg 162.5 +/- 119.2 min 0 max 250
sum 3250
...
```

10. Notice that `Code 200` (OK) was returned from 13 requests (65%) and that `Code 503` was returned from 7 requests (35%):

```
Code 200 : 13 (65.0 %)
Code 503 : 7 (35.0 %)
```

This is an example of half-open circuit breaker rules coming into action. This can be seen in the following diagram, in which 65% of the requests go through OK and 35% of the requests fail due to the circuit breaker rule coming into action whenever the number of concurrent connections and consecutive errors is more than one. Ejecting a host from the connection pool is set dynamically by Istio using the `interval`, `baseEjectionTime`, and `maxEjectionPercent` parameters that we defined for the circuit breaker component of Istio:

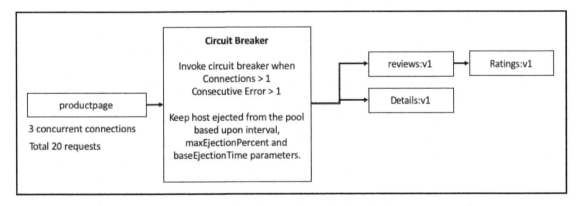

11. Revert the destination rules for all of the services to their original state so that you can test other Istio features for traffic management:

```
$ kubectl -n istio-lab apply -f 02-create-destination-rules.yaml
destinationrule.networking.istio.io/productpage configured
destinationrule.networking.istio.io/reviews unchanged
destinationrule.networking.istio.io/ratings unchanged
destinationrule.networking.istio.io/details unchanged
```

Now that we've learned about circuit breaking, we will learn how to manage ingress traffic and direct external traffic to the desired microservice.

Managing traffic

Incoming and outgoing traffic in Istio is managed through ingress and egress gateways.

The Kubernetes environment provides ingress resources for services that can be exposed for access from outside the cluster. Istio also provides its own gateway, which works seamlessly with Kubernetes, and it provides enhanced capabilities such as monitoring and route rules that can be applied to traffic entering the cluster.

Managing Ingress traffic patterns

At the beginning of this chapter, we introduced the Istio primitive gateway and created a `bookinfo-gateway`, which allowed `http` traffic from all external hosts on port 80. Let's get started:

1. Review the definition of `mygateway` that we created at the beginning of this chapter:

    ```
    $ cat 00-create-gateway.yaml
    ```

    We also created the Istio `bookinfo` virtual service, which uses `mygateway`.

2. Review the `bookinfo` virtual service:

    ```
    $ cat 01-create-virtual-service.yaml
    ```

    As shown by the output of the gateway and virtual service, we are routing any external host `http` request on route `/productpage` to the internal Kubernetes `productpage` service at port 9080.

    Let's take an example where we want to route `http://bookinfo.istio.io` to the Kubernetes `productpage` service on port 9080. For this to happen, we need to have a DNS entry for `bookinfo.istio.io` mapped to the external IP address of the Istio Ingress gateway service in our `istio-system` namespace. For example, the external IP address in our VM is mapped to `192.168.142.249`. Note that this could be a different IP address in your VM.

3. Check the external IP address of the Ingress gateway:

```
$ kubectl -n istio-system get svc istio-ingressgateway -o custom-
columns=Name:.metadata.name,EXTERNAL_IP:.status.loadBalancer.ingres
s[0].ip
Name                    EXTERNAL_IP
istio-ingressgateway    192.168.142.249
```

We will pretend that our IP address of 192.168.142.249 is mapped to bookinfo.istio.io by creating an entry in our VM's /etc/hosts file.

4. Create an entry in the /etc/hosts file:

```
$ export INGRESS_IP=$(kubectl -n istio-system get svc istio-
ingressgateway -o jsonpath='{.status.loadBalancer.ingress[0].ip}')
; echo $INGRESS_IP
192.168.142.249

$ if ! grep -q bookinfo.istio.io /etc/hosts ; then echo
"$INGRESS_IP bookinfo.istio.io" | sudo tee -a /etc/hosts; fi
```

Create a separate Istio virtual service that will use our existing bookinfo-gateway and route http://bookinfo.istio.io to our internal Kubernetes productpage service at port 9080.

5. Review the following script for the definition of the virtual service:

```
# Script : 14-create-bookinfo-virtual-service.yaml

apiVersion: networking.istio.io/v1alpha3
kind: VirtualService
metadata:
  name: bookinfo.istio.io
spec:
  hosts:
  - "bookinfo.istio.io"
  gateways:
  - mygateway
  http:
  - match:
    - uri:
        exact: /
    - uri:
        exact: /productpage
    - uri:
        prefix: /static
    - uri:
```

```
        exact: /login
  - uri:
        exact: /logout
  - uri:
        prefix: /api/v1/products
  route:
  - destination:
        host: productpage.istio-lab.svc.cluster.local
        port:
            number: 9080
```

6. Create the `bookinfo.istio.io` virtual service:

```
$ kubectl -n istio-system apply -f 14-create-bookinfo-virtual-
service.yaml
virtualservice.networking.istio.io/bookinfo.istio.io created
```

7. Test `http://bookinfo.istio.io` within the virtual machine:

```
$ curl -s http://bookinfo.istio.io | grep title
<title>Simple Bookstore App</title>
```

This demonstrates how an Istio Ingress gateway can be used using Istio's primitive of the gateway and virtual service. The advantage of using an Istio gateway is that we can leverage the routing capabilities of Istio for traffic management.

Managing Egress traffic patterns

There are three ways in which external services can be accessed from Istio:

- By configuring an Istio sidecar to allow access to any external service (not recommended for large file transfers)
- By using `ServiceEntry` to register an accessible external service from inside the service mesh
- By configuring an Istio sidecar to exclude external IPs from its remapped IP table

Using the first approach, we can't take advantage of Istio monitoring and traffic routing capabilities for external services. It is recommended to use the `ServiceEntry` primitive of Istio as that will allow us to use Istio monitoring and routing capabilities for external services. For example, using the `ServiceEntry` approach, we can set timeout rules for external services. The third approach bypasses the Istio sidecar and allows our services to access external services directly.

We will explore the second approach to control access to external services using the Istio `ServiceEntry` primitive.

We installed Istio using a `demo` profile, which allows access to any external service. Let's get started:

1. Run the following command to find out the current outbound traffic policy mode:

   ```
   $ kubectl -n istio-system get cm istio -o yaml | grep -m1 -o "mode:
   ALLOW_ANY"
   mode: ALLOW_ANY
   ```

   `ALLOW_ANY` mode permits access to external services from microservices.

2. Find out the `ratings` pod's IP address to test connectivity to an external service through our service mesh:

   ```
   $ export RATING_POD=$(kubectl -n istio-lab get pods -l app=ratings
   -o jsonpath='{.items..metadata.name}') ; echo $RATING_POD
   ratings-v1-79b6d99979-k2j7t
   ```

3. Run curl from the `ratings` pod to test `https://www.ibm.com` and check the `http` code status. If the connection is successful, we should get `200`:

   ```
   $ kubectl -n istio-lab exec -it -c ratings $RATING_POD -- curl -LI
   https://www.ibm.com | grep "HTTP/"
   HTTP/2 303 --> Note that this is the HTTP code for the redirection
   of the URL
   HTTP/2 200

   $ kubectl -n istio-lab exec -it -c ratings $RATING_POD -- curl -LI
   https://www.cnn.com | grep "HTTP/"
   HTTP/2 200
   ```

   If you receive an error stating `command terminated with exit code 6 or 35`, this is an indication that the `curl` command is unable to resolve the hostname from inside the container. This is likely due to `nameserver` not being defined properly in the VM's `/etc/resolv.conf` file. Check whether the container can get the external IP address by using the `kubectl -n istio-lab exec -it -c ratings $RATING_POD -- curl ifconfig.me` command.

If `curl` succeeds and you still get an error, you might want to recycle the `core-dns` pods by using the `kubectl -n kube-system delete pod -1 k8s-app=kube-dns` command.

Blocking access to external services

We can apply rules to outgoing services through the egress gateway to enable/disable access to external services. From a security standpoint, this is a nice capability that allows us to enforce rules outside the application framework. Let's take a look:

1. Change the config map for `mode: ALLOW_ANY` to `mode: REGISTRY_ONLY`:

```
$ kubectl -n istio-system get cm istio -o yaml | sed 's/mode:
ALLOW_ANY/mode: REGISTRY_ONLY/g' | kubectl replace -n istio-system
-f -
configmap/istio replaced
```

2. Now, double-check whether `mode: REGISTRY_ONLY` has been set:

```
$ kubectl -n istio-system get cm istio -o yaml | grep -m 1 -o
"mode: REGISTRY_ONLY"
mode: REGISTRY_ONLY
```

3. Wait a couple of seconds for the configuration to push down to the proxy sidecar.

 By doing so, we have a reverse firewall for all of our microservices for outbound access. You will need to create `ServiceEntry` for external endpoints for services to access them.

4. Repeat the `curl` test again for external services:

```
$ kubectl -n istio-lab exec -it -c ratings $RATING_POD -- curl -LI
https://www.ibm.com | grep "HTTP/"
command terminated with exit code 35

$ kubectl -n istio-lab exec -it -c ratings $RATING_POD -- curl -LI
https://www.cnn.com | grep "HTTP/"
command terminated with exit code 35
```

By using the preceding technique, it is possible to block access to external services from microservices.

Allowing access to external services

Instead of blanket denial to an external service, it is possible to allow access to certain external services using Istio's `ServiceEntry` configuration. To control access to the external services, we need to set `mode: REGISTRY_ONLY`, which we did in the previous section. Let's take a look:

1. The following is the `ServiceEntry` definition to allow `http` access to `httpbin.org`:

   ```
   # Script : 15-http-service-entry-for-httpbin.yaml

   apiVersion: networking.istio.io/v1alpha3
   kind: ServiceEntry
   metadata:
     name: httpbin
   spec:
     hosts:
     - httpbin.org
     ports:
     - number: 80
       name: http
       protocol: HTTP
     resolution: DNS
     location: MESH_EXTERNAL
   ```

2. Create `http ServiceEntry` to allow access to `http://httpbin.org`:

   ```
   $ kubectl -n istio-lab apply -f 15-http-service-entry-for-
   httpbin.yaml
   serviceentry.networking.istio.io/httpbin created
   ```

3. The following is the `ServiceEntry` definition to allow `https` access to `www.ibm.com`:

   ```
   # Script : 16-https-service-entry-for-ibm.yaml

   apiVersion: networking.istio.io/v1alpha3
   kind: ServiceEntry
   metadata:
     name: google
   spec:
     hosts:
     - www.ibm.com
     ports:
     - number: 443
       name: https
   ```

```
          protocol: HTTPS
      resolution: DNS
      location: MESH_EXTERNAL
```

4. Create `https ServiceEntry` to allow access to IBM:

```
$ kubectl -n istio-lab apply -f 16-https-service-entry-for-ibm.yaml
serviceentry.networking.istio.io/ibm created
```

5. Wait a couple of seconds and then use `curl` from the `ratings` microservice to test the external services for IBM:

```
$ kubectl -n istio-lab exec -it -c ratings $RATING_POD -- curl -LI
https://www.ibm.com | grep "HTTP/"
HTTP/2 303 --> Code due to -L switch of the curl
HTTP/2 200
```

6. Next, check for `httpbin.org`:

```
$ RATING_POD=$(kubectl -n istio-lab get pods -l app=ratings -o
jsonpath='{.items..metadata.name}') ; echo $RATING_POD
ratings-v1-79b6d99979-k2j7t
```

```
$ kubectl -n istio-lab exec -it -c ratings $RATING_POD -- curl
http://httpbin.org/headers
{
 "headers": {
 "Accept": "*/*",
 "Host": "httpbin.org",
 "User-Agent": "curl/7.52.1",
 "X-B3-Sampled": "1",
 "X-B3-Spanid": "c7d663eebf9eee7b",
 "X-B3-Traceid": "65fb4bb225147a69c7d663eebf9eee7b",
 "X-Envoy-Decorator-Operation": "httpbin.org:80/*",
 "X-Istio-Attributes":
```
"CikKGGRlc3RpbmF0aW9uLnNlcnZpY2UubmFtZRINEgtodHRwYmluLm9yZwovCh1kZX
N0aW5hdGlvbi5zZXJ2aWNlLm5hbWVzcGFjZRIOEgxpc3Rpby1zZXN0ZW0KQgoKc291c
mNlLnVpZBI0EjJrdWJlcm5ldGVzOi8vcmF0aW5jcy12MS030WI2ZDk5OTc5LWsyajd0
LmlzdGlvLWxhYgopChhkZXN0aW5hdGlvbi5zZXJ2aWNlLmhvc3QSDRILaHR0cGJpbi5
vcmc="
```
 }
}
```

Take note of the headers that were added by the Istio proxy sidecar.

7. Check the `istio-proxy` logs for the outbound traffic initiated by `curl`:

```
$ kubectl -n istio-lab logs -c istio-proxy $RATING_POD | tail |
grep curl
[2019-07-29T05:48:27.365Z] "GET /headers HTTP/1.1" 200 - "-" "-" 0
587 393 392 "-" "curl/7.52.1" "7374d794-
e724-9c90-82bc-9cd1516afd4b" "httpbin.org" "52.72.74.132:80"
outbound|80||httpbin.org - 34.202.34.10:80 192.168.230.254:59368 -
```

8. Let's test `https://www.ibm.com`:

```
$ kubectl -n istio-lab exec -it -c ratings $RATING_POD -- curl -LI
https://www.ibm.com | grep "HTTP/"
HTTP/2 303
HTTP/2 200
```

9. Check that we have access to `https://www.cnn.com`:

```
$ kubectl -n istio-lab exec -it -c ratings $RATING_POD -- curl -LI
https://www.cnn.com | grep "HTTP/"
command terminated with exit code 35
```

Notice that access to `www.cnn.com` is blocked since no `ServiceEntry` has been created for that URL.

If you require very tight access control on your microservices application, especially if you're using third-party images where you have less trust or control, you can enable `REGISTRY_ONLY` mode within Istio's service mesh. This will block all outbound access from the microservices to the external world. Consider this as a reverse firewall of the service mesh where you only allow known, external web endpoints that you require access to.

After turning on this feature, if you try to do `apt-get update` or `yum update` inside a container to install a package, you will get a bad gateway error as the Envoy proxy will block access to unknown `ServiceEntry` endpoints.

For example, try to use the `kubectl -n istio-lab exec -it -c ratings $RATING_POD -- apt-get update | grep 502` command. You will see a bad gateway error. This is also protective because it will not allow any updates to any container as a security posture. This security posture is different from traditional ways of security, where an external firewall blocks external access.

The new way of thinking is to build a software stack that works equally well in a zero-trust network.

This type of access control to external services from microservices through Istio is very useful as you can only allow access to known external services that need to be accessed from microservices. This way, we can control malicious access to external sites by third-party microservices.

Routing rules for external services

Kenneth Reitz created a popular testing tool called `http://httpbin.org`. This tool is an easy way to test HTTP code, test POST payloads, check headers, inspect requests and responses, create/read/delete cookies, and return anything that is passed to a request.

Traffic can be managed to external services if access to them is controlled through `ServiceEntry`. For example, routing rules can be applied to external services the same way we implemented them for local services.

Let's look at an example where we'll add a timeout of 3 seconds to the `httpbin.org` external site that will be accessed from our microservices:

1. Review the following script:

```
# Script : 17-add-timeout-for-httpbin-virtual-service.yaml

apiVersion: networking.istio.io/v1alpha3
kind: VirtualService
metadata:
  name: httpbin
spec:
  hosts:
    - httpbin.org
  http:
  - timeout: 3s
    route:
      - destination:
          host: httpbin.org
        weight: 100
```

2. Add a timeout rule:

```
$ kubectl -n istio-lab apply -f 17-add-timeout-for-httpbin-virtual-service.yaml
virtualservice.networking.istio.io/httpbin created
```

3. Access `httpbin.org` and introduce a delay of 5 second. Check whether a timeout occurs from our side:

```
$ time kubectl -n istio-lab exec -it -c ratings $RATING_POD -- curl
-o /dev/null -s -w "%{http_code}\n" http://httpbin.org/delay/5
504

real 0m4.820s --> Time elapsed for the command to run
user 0m0.106s --> CPU seconds in user mode
sys 0m0.021s  --> CPU seconds in kernel mode
```

Notice that `httpbin.org` was asked to wait 5 seconds by a call to `/delay/5`, but an Istio gateway timeout (`http code 504`) occurred after 3 seconds. This demonstrates that Istio can manage the same traffic/routing rules to external services, provided they are managed through `ServiceEntry`.

This feature of `ServiceEntry` allows external services to be treated as if they were part of the service mesh.

Now that we've learned how to manage incoming and outgoing traffic with the use of Ingress/Egress gateways, we will learn about traffic mirroring capabilities that can help us to feed the same incoming requests to two or more consumers. Traffic mirroring is useful to send the traffic to security and monitoring appliances that can inspect content, monitor for threats, and debug and troubleshoot.

Traffic mirroring

The live traffic mirroring capability of Istio is very useful for shadowing traffic from a production service to a mirror service. Istio allows complete mirroring from one service to another or a portion of the traffic. It is very important that mirroring should happen without impacting the critical path of the original application.

Mirroring traffic using Istio is sometimes branded as out of band since mirroring is accomplished asynchronously through Istio's sidecar proxy. The mirrored traffic should be identified distinctly. This is done by appending shadow to the Host or Authority header.

Let's understand traffic mirroring or shadowing through an example.

We will create two versions of the httpbin service and enable a logging mechanism to ensure which service is receiving or mirroring the traffic:

1. The following is a deployment example of httpbin-v1. Review the following script to deploy the sample httpbin service:

```
# Script : 18-deploy-httpbin-v1.yaml

apiVersion: extensions/v1beta1
kind: Deployment
metadata:
  name: httpbin-v1
spec:
  replicas: 1
  template:
    metadata:
      labels:
        app: httpbin
        version: v1
    spec:
      containers:
      - image: docker.io/kennethreitz/httpbin
        imagePullPolicy: IfNotPresent
        name: httpbin
        command: ["gunicorn", "--access-logfile", "-", "-b",
"0.0.0.0:80", "httpbin:app"]
        ports:
        - containerPort: 80
```

2. Deploy httpbin-v1:

```
$ kubectl -n istio-lab apply -f 18-deploy-httpbin-v1.yaml
deployment.extensions/httpbin-v1 created
```

3. The following is the deployment example for httpbin-v2:

```
# Script : 19-deploy-httpbin-v2.yaml

apiVersion: extensions/v1beta1
kind: Deployment
metadata:
  name: httpbin-v2
spec:
  replicas: 1
  template:
    metadata:
      labels:
        app: httpbin
```

```
              version: v2
        spec:
          containers:
          - image: docker.io/kennethreitz/httpbin
            imagePullPolicy: IfNotPresent
            name: httpbin
            command: ["gunicorn", "--access-logfile", "-", "-b",
    "0.0.0.0:80", "httpbin:app"]
            ports:
            - containerPort: 80
```

4. Deploy httpbin-v2:

```
$ kubectl -n istio-lab apply -f 19-deploy-httpbin-v2.yaml
deployment.extensions/httpbin-v2 created
```

Create a Kubernetes httpbin service, which will load balance the traffic between httpbin-v1 and httpbin-v2. Notice that both deployments use a label of app: httpbin, which is the same label selector that's used by the httpbin service:

```
# Script : 20-create-kubernetes-httpbin-service.yaml

apiVersion: v1
kind: Service
metadata:
  name: httpbin
  labels:
    app: httpbin
spec:
  ports:
  - name: http
    port: 8000
    targetPort: 80
  selector:
    app: httpbin
```

5. Deploy the httpbin service:

```
$ kubectl -n istio-lab apply -f 20-create-kubernetes-httpbin-
service.yaml
service/httpbin created
```

Let's disable the Kubernetes load balancing capabilities of `httpbin` for `httpbin-v1` and `httpbin-v2` through the use of an Istio destination rule. We will do this to define subsets that will be used by the Istio virtual service to direct 100% of the traffic to `httpbin-v1`. Define some destination rules to create subsets:

```
# Script : 21-create-destination-rules-subsets.yaml

apiVersion: networking.istio.io/v1alpha3
kind: DestinationRule
metadata:
  name: httpbin
spec:
  host: httpbin
  subsets:
  - name: v1
    labels:
      version: v1
  - name: v2
    labels:
      version: v2
```

6. Create the required destination rules:

```
$ kubectl -n istio-lab apply -f 21-create-destination-rules-subsets.yaml
destinationrule.networking.istio.io/httpbin created
```

7. Define a virtual service in order to direct 100% of the traffic to subset `v1`:

```
# Script : 22-create-httpbin-virtual-service.yaml

apiVersion: networking.istio.io/v1alpha3
kind: VirtualService
metadata:
  name: httpbin
spec:
  hosts:
    - httpbin
  http:
  - route:
    - destination:
        host: httpbin
        subset: v1
      weight: 100
```

8. Create a virtual service:

```
$ kubectl -n istio-lab apply -f 22-create-httpbin-virtual-
service.yaml
virtualservice.networking.istio.io/httpbin configured
```

Now, we can send some traffic to `httpbin`. However, before we do that, open two separate command-line windows to put a tail on the logs for both of the `httpbin` services.

9. Use the first command-line window for the `httpbin:v1` tail:

```
$ V1_POD=$(kubectl -n istio-lab get pod -l app=httpbin,version=v1 -
o jsonpath={.items..metadata.name}) ; echo $V1_POD
httpbin-v1-b9985cc7d-4wmcf

$ kubectl -n istio-lab -c httpbin logs -f $V1_POD
[2019-04-24 01:01:56 +0000] [1] [INFO] Starting gunicorn 19.9.0
[2019-04-24 01:01:56 +0000] [1] [INFO] Listening at:
http://0.0.0.0:80 (1)
[2019-04-24 01:01:56 +0000] [1] [INFO] Using worker: sync
[2019-04-24 01:01:56 +0000] [8] [INFO] Booting worker with pid: 8
```

10. Use the second command-line window for the `httpbin:v2` tail:

```
$ V2_POD=$(kubectl -n istio-lab get pod -l app=httpbin,version=v2 -
o jsonpath={.items..metadata.name}) ; echo $V2_POD
httpbin-v2-5cdb74d4c7-mxtfm

$ kubectl -n istio-lab -c httpbin logs -f $V2_POD
[2019-04-24 01:01:56 +0000] [1] [INFO] Starting gunicorn 19.9.0
[2019-04-24 01:01:56 +0000] [1] [INFO] Listening at:
http://0.0.0.0:80 (1)
[2019-04-24 01:01:56 +0000] [1] [INFO] Using worker: sync
[2019-04-24 01:01:56 +0000] [8] [INFO] Booting worker with pid: 8
```

11. Open one more command-line window and run the following `curl` command using the `ratings` pod to send traffic to the `httpbin` service:

```
$ RATING_POD=$(kubectl -n istio-lab get pods -l app=ratings -o
jsonpath='{.items..metadata.name}') ; echo $RATING_POD
ratings-v1-79b6d99979-k2j7t

$ kubectl -n istio-lab exec -it $RATING_POD -c ratings -- curl
http://httpbin:8000/headers | python -m json.tool
{
    "headers": {
        "Accept": "*/*",
        "Content-Length": "0",
        "Host": "httpbin:8000",
        "User-Agent": "curl/7.38.0",
        "X-B3-Parentspanid": "58e256d2258d93de",
        "X-B3-Sampled": "1",
        "X-B3-Spanid": "ad58600dc4bf258a",
        "X-B3-Traceid": "4042bd191da4131058e256d2258d93de"
    }
}
```

12. Switch back to the command-line windows that have tails for the v1 and v2 services. You will notice an additional logline in the `httpbin:v1` service; the `httpbin:v2` service does not show any additional log lines:

```
[2019-08-02 13:04:14 +0000] [1] [INFO] Using worker: sync
[2019-08-02 13:04:14 +0000] [8] [INFO] Booting worker with pid: 8
127.0.0.1 - - [24/Apr/2019:01:35:55 +0000] "GET /headers HTTP/1.1"
200 303 "-" "curl/7.38.0"
```

13. Now, let's mirror the traffic from v1 to v2. Modify the `httpbin` virtual service by adding a mirror to subset v2:

```
# Script : 23-mirror-traffic-between-v1-and-v2.yaml

apiVersion: networking.istio.io/v1alpha3
kind: VirtualService
metadata:
  name: httpbin
spec:
  hosts:
    - httpbin
  http:
  - route:
    - destination:
        host: httpbin
```

```
        subset: v1
      weight: 100
    mirror:
      host: httpbin
      subset: v2
```

14. Modify the virtual service. Run the following command from the third window and make sure that you switch to the cd ~/istio/scripts/01-traffic-management directory:

    ```
    $ kubectl -n istio-lab apply -f 23-mirror-traffic-between-v1-and-
    v2.yaml
    virtualservice.networking.istio.io/httpbin configured
    ```

15. Send the same traffic to httpbin:v1. Now, we should see log lines appear in the httpbin:v1 and httpbin:v2 pods. Just wait a few seconds for the rules to propagate:

    ```
    $ kubectl -n istio-lab exec -it $RATING_POD -c ratings -- curl
    http://httpbin:8000/headers | python -m json.tool
    ```

16. The first window, httpbin:v1, shows one more line in addition to the previous one that we had already received:

    ```
    127.0.0.1 - - [24/Apr/2019:01:46:34 +0000] "GET /headers HTTP/1.1"
    200 303 "-" "curl/7.38.0"
    127.0.0.1 - - [24/Apr/2019:01:48:30 +0000] "GET /headers HTTP/1.1"
    200 303 "-" "curl/7.38.0"
    ```

17. The second window, httpbin:v2, shows the new line:

    ```
    127.0.0.1 - - [24/Apr/2019:01:48:30 +0000] "GET /headers HTTP/1.1"
    200 343 "-" "curl/7.38.0"
    ```

While traffic is being mirrored, the response from the second `httpbin:v2` is not sent back since its purpose is to apply `httpbin` requests to and from `v1` to `v2`. The proxy sidecar of `httpbin:v2` does not return any response, as expected. This can be seen in the following diagram:

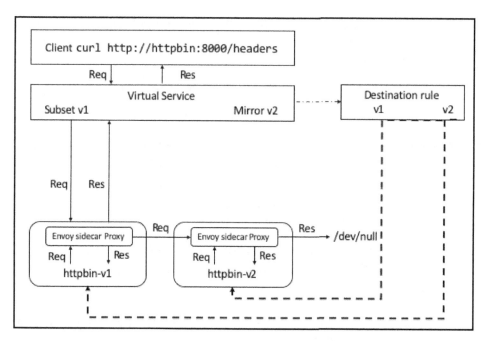

Did you notice how easy it is to mirror traffic from one microservice to another? This is a very useful case in which you can mirror the traffic from the edge service to a different namespace or another Kubernetes cluster that has the same application and do any type of testing, such as infrastructure testing, testing a different version of the complete application, and so on. There are lots of use cases, and you can enable this capability by making the necessary configuration changes.

You can press *Ctrl+C* in both command-line windows to stop the tails on the logs of both pods.

For us to be able to move on to the next chapter, we will remove the restrictions that were set on the external traffic flow.

Cleaning up

Just follow these simple steps:

1. We will change the mode from mode: REGISTRY_ONLY to mode: ALLOW_ANY for the purpose of the next chapter's lab exercises:

```
$ kubectl -n istio-system get cm istio -o yaml | sed 's/mode:
REGISTRY_ONLY/mode: ALLOW_ANY/g' | kubectl replace -n istio-system
-f -
configmap/istio replaced
```

2. Double-check whether mode: ALLOW_ANY has been set:

```
$ kubectl -n istio-system get cm istio -o yaml | grep -m 1 -o
"mode: ALLOW_ANY"
mode: ALLOW_ANY
```

3. We will delete the virtual services for httpbin as we will recreate them in the next chapter:

```
$ kubectl -n istio-lab delete -f 22-create-httpbin-virtual-
service.yaml
virtualservice.networking.istio.io "httpbin" deleted
```

With this, we have made changes in our setup so that we can show Istio's security features in the next chapter.

Summary

In this chapter, we demonstrated Istio's traffic management capabilities for traffic shifting, setting request timeouts, controlling Ingress and Egress traffic, circuit breaking to protect services from overload and attacks, and mirroring traffic from one route to another route.

These were the breakthroughs from the earlier concepts of achieving the same results either through coding in the application or by using libraries for every language. The capability to control traffic at the edge of the cluster gives operations staff ease-of-use to manage the application infrastructure dynamically and resiliently without needing intervention from developers. As an example, it is possible to completely block access to any external service from the distributed microservices application except whitelisted service entries.

It is worth noting that all of the features we learned about in this chapter did not require making any changes in the application code, which makes service mesh very attractive. Similarly, security postures are implemented in application code traditionally. In the next chapter, we will look at Istio's security features so that we can implement security without making any changes to the application code. This is possible due to the Envoy sidecar implementation.

Questions

1. Traffic routing is a feature of Envoy that receives its configuration from Pilot.
   A) True
   B) False

2. Istio can work in a zero-trust network and still provide enterprise-grade security.
   A) True
   B) False

3. You can enable a reverse firewall in Istio to block outbound access from microservices.
   A) True
   B) False

4. The concept of "Dark launches/Family and Friend Testing" is a feature that allows access to only a select group of entities to gather early feedback on a new release, which runs in the same production environment.
   A) True
   B) False

5. An Istio gateway can have multiple virtual services.
   A) True
   B) False

6. An Istio virtual service is a superset of a Kubernetes service since it provides more features and functions than a native service.
   A) True
   B) False

7. The destination rule defines the configuration, but it has no role in traffic routing since the subsets that it defines are used in virtual services.
   A) True
   B) False

8. Load balancing at the Envoy level is done at the L7 networking layer and not at L3/L4.
   A) True
   B) False

9. When you enable traffic mirroring of one service to another service, you don't get a response from the mirrored service.
   A) True
   B) False

Further reading

- *Traffic Management*, Istio. (2019), available at `https://archive.istio.io/v1.3/docs/tasks/traffic-management/`, accessed 16 May 2019

- *Incremental Istio Part 1, Traffic Management*, Parikh, S. (2019), Istio, available at `https://archive.istio.io/v1.3/blog/2018/incremental-traffic-management/`, accessed 16 May 2019

- *Deploy an Istio mesh across multiple IBM Cloud Private clusters using Istio Gateway*, Cao, M. (2019), available at `https://medium.com/ibm-cloud/deploy-an-istio-mesh-across-multiple-ibm-cloud-private-clusters-using-istio-gateway-7b33c71cb41c`, accessed 16 May 2019

11
Exploring Istio Security Features

Traditionally, the security of an application is implemented at the application level by using language-specific libraries to enable certificate-based authentication and then encryption of the network traffic. In modern cloud-native applications, these tasks are delegated to the service mesh providers to implement security so that application developers can focus on the business logic of the application.

In this chapter, we will look at service authentication and authorization using simple and mutual TLS and advanced security enhancements through examples.

In a nutshell, we will cover the following topics:

- Configuring service authentication
- Enabling and disabling service authorization

Technical requirements

You will get the best out of this chapter if you have the following:

- This chapter's exercise use dependencies from the previous chapter. Please make sure that you completed the exercises in the previous chapter before starting this one.

- Open a command-line window to follow this chapter to learn
  about `Istio` security by examples. Clone this book's GitHub directory:

  ```
  $ cd ~/istio
  $ git checkout $ISTIO_VERSION
  $ cd scripts/02-security
  ```

- Make sure that all `istio-lab` pods are in a `Ready 2/2` state:

  ```
  $ kubectl -n istio-lab get pods
  ```

Once this is done, we're ready to begin!

Overview of Istio's security

Security in Istio is very comprehensive. The high-level overview starts with Citadel, which is a key and certificate manager. It acts as a **Certificate Authority (CA)** for Istio. An additional component, `node_agent`, needs to be enabled for certificate and key rotation. The node agent runs as a daemon set on all of the nodes to take care of the certificate and key rotations. The sidecar proxies implement a secure protocol communication between microservices, and this is a self-service model that is enabled through a parameter with no changes being made to the microservices. The following control plane components are used:

- **Pilot**: Pilot in Istio distributes authentication and provides secure naming conventions for sidecar proxies. Secure naming is a new concept that is gaining traction since it identifies services securely if they are part of the trusted service mesh network. It is also referred to as Strong Identity, and it is implemented using the SPIFFE specification through the SPIRE implementation.
- **Mixer:** Mixer manages authorization and auditing.

For service meshes, it should be a strong requirement to implement an abstract layer on top of the applications being run in a Kubernetes environment. In such cases, a few guidelines can be followed for application development:

- Microservices should be designed using an HTTP protocol so that mutual TLS can be implemented through Istio in a self-service model through configuration changes.
- Microservices should not implement code for secure communication to external services as that can be implemented at the edge egress gateway for the entire service mesh.

The security implementation starts with authentication (who you are?) and authorization (what can you do?). First, we will implement an authentication infrastructure around microservices through the use of Istio.

Authentication

From the previous chapter, we configured the Istio ingress gateway to expose the `bookinfo` HTTP service's endpoints to external traffic. In this section, we will configure simple or mutual TLS to provide HTTPS access to the external traffic to access `bookinfo` services. It is our assumption that you have an understanding of simple and mutual TLS authentication. Additional information can be found here: `https://bit.ly/2voH44c`.

Simple or mutual TLS termination at the ingress gateway for incoming requests assumes that downstream services are safe and not liable to external attacks or insider threats. After the ingress gateway has been secured, downstream service communication is done using a plaintext HTTP protocol.

If access is requested to external services, TLS origination should start an egress gateway for secure communication with an external service. It is not good practice for a microservice to initiate an HTTPS session with an external service. We lose monitoring and policy enforcement because of sidecar proxies. In such cases, there are two recommended options:

- **TLS origination at the sidecar proxy level**: Communication between the sidecar and the external service is encrypted, but pod to sidecar communication is not encrypted. A simple use case could be an environment where microservices are running in a federated, multi-Kubernetes cluster, and the network is prone to internal threats and is inherently insecure.

- **TLS origination at the egress gateway**: The communication behind the egress gateway is not encrypted. A use case could be an environment where microservices are running within the same Kubernetes cluster and the internal threat is not a concern.

Modern microservices design should always be done by keeping the zero-trust network in mind without any requirement for any type of firewall. Such a requirement can be easily met by adopting Istio's service mesh architecture on top of cloud-native microservices-based applications.

We will not be covering mount-based secrets where keys and certificates from secrets are mounted within a container. This approach can cause performance regression during certificate rotation whenever a sidecar restart picks up new keys and certificates.

Since private keys are distributed through secrets, the pod owner can see the value of the secret. Through **Secret Discovery Service (SDS)**, private keys never leave the node, and it resides only at the Citadel agent and sidecar memory. The secret volumes are no longer mounted within a pod. The sidecar is able to renew keys and certificates through the SDS API; hence, there is no need to recycle the sidecar to pick up new keys and certificates.

 From a security standpoint, good application design should always run in a zero-trust network with guard rails to protect it. This is not always possible because it substantially increases the cost of development. Implementing it through an infrastructure layer of the application, such as Istio, is application security agnostic and fits well within an SRE model of operations.

Now, let's work on securing the ingress gateway with simple or mutual TLS termination using SDS by Istio.

Testing the httpbin service

In the previous chapter, we created an httpbin service that performed load balancing and traffic mirroring between the httpbin-v1 and httpbin-v2 microservices. In this chapter, we will use the same httpbin service and show you how to secure external traffic through an Istio ingress gateway using SDS.

Let's test the httpbin service internally using HTTP that outputs a teapot (/status/418) and the IP address:

```
$ curl http://httpbin.istio-lab.svc.cluster.local:8000/status/418
```

```
$ curl http://httpbin.istio-lab.svc.cluster.local:8000/ip
```

```
{
  "origin": "127.0.0.1"
}
```

Next, we'll generate some keys and certificates to enable simple or mutual TLS.

Generating keys and certificates

We need a private key, server certificate, and root certificate to enable simple or mutual TLS. Either we get them from a CA or we self-generate them. We will be generating the certificates and keys using a small-step command line. To do this, we need to install the step CLI.

 If you need a quick introduction to the **Public Key Infrastructure (PKI)**, please refer to this excellent article by Mike Malone: `https://smallstep.com/blog/everything-pki.html`.

Installing the step CLI

Smallstep is an open source piece of software that provides easy, simple to use tools to establish PKI for your applications. To install the step CLI, follow these steps:

1. Find out the latest release of the step CLI by entering the following command:

    ```
    $ curl -s
    https://api.github.com/repos/smallstep/cli/releases/latest | grep
    tag_name
    "tag_name": "v0.13.3",
    ```

2. At the time of writing this book, Step is at release version v0.13.3, so we will download this version:

    ```
    $ cd ~/
    $ curl -LOs
    https://github.com/smallstep/cli/releases/download/v0.13.3/step_0.1
    3.3_linux_amd64.tar.gz
    ```

3. Extract and copy the Step `cli` to `/bin` or copy it to your local bin:

```
$ tar xvfz step_0.13.3_linux_amd64.tar.gz
step_0.13.3/
step_0.13.3/README.md
step_0.13.3/bin/
step_0.13.3/bin/step

$ sudo mv step_0.13.3/bin/step /bin
```

Now that the step CLI has been installed, we will generate the private keys, server certificates, and root certificates for the two hosts: `httpbin.istio.io` and `bookinfo.istio.io`. Since these are not real hosts that are defined in a DNS server, we'll create local entries in `/etc/hosts` for the purpose of our tests.

Generating private key, server, and root certificates

Normally, you obtain a certificate from an established CA provider such as GeoTrust, DigiCert, GlobalSign, or GoDaddy when you want to establish that a certificate that has been issued to a computer name is legitimate to prevent a man-in-the-middle attack. The scope of issuance of the certificate is done using the name of the service using a service mesh implementation; we can either get a root certificate signed from an established provider or use our own root and intermediate certificate to issue certificates. To show this concept, we will use a simple to use open source `smallstep.com` way of using our own CA:

1. Create a directory and create a root certificate using `root --profile` by using the `step` command.
2. Specify a password to encrypt the root key. For simplicity, you may want to use the `password` string as `password`:

```
$ mkdir -p ~/step
$ cd ~/step

$ step certificate create --profile root-ca "My Root CA" root-
ca.crt root-ca.key
Please enter the password to encrypt the private key: password
# This password is used to encrypt root-ca.key

Your certificate has been saved in root-ca.crt.
Your private key has been saved in root-ca.key.
```

Now that we've created the root certificate, we need to create the intermediate certificate.

3. To establish a chain of trust, let's create an intermediate CA:

```
$ step certificate create istio.io istio.crt istio.key --profile
intermediate-ca --ca ./root-ca.crt --ca-key ./root-ca.key
Please enter the password to decrypt ./root-ca.key: password
# step asks for root-ca.key password so it can use it to sign
istio.crt
Please enter the password to encrypt the private key: password
# This password is used to encrypt istio.key

Your certificate has been saved in istio.crt.
Your private key has been saved in istio.key.
```

4. Now, we need to create an X.509 certificate.

It's fine that the `root-ca.key` and `istio.key` signing keys are encrypted. However, we need `httpbin.key` and `bookinfo.key` to be unencrypted. This is done in `step` by passing the `--no-password` and `--insecure` CLI flags. The default validity of the certificate is 24 hours, but we will use the `--not-after` flag and specify 2,160 hours (90 days) for the validity to make sure that we are able to complete the exercises in 90 days before the certificate expires. If it does, you may need to rotate the certificate by creating a new one and update the secret:

```
$ step certificate create httpbin.istio.io httpbin.crt httpbin.key
--profile leaf --ca istio.crt --ca-key istio.key --no-password --
insecure --not-after 2160h
Please enter the password to decrypt istio.key: password
# Specify password used to create intermediate CA

Your certificate has been saved in httpbin.crt.
Your private key has been saved in httpbin.key.
```

 Root and intermediate certificates are created with a password so that only authorized users with the password can create leaf certificates. The `no-password` flag is used to create a non-encrypted leaf certificate.

5. Repeat the same for `bookinfo.istio.io` using the same intermediate CA:

```
$ step certificate create bookinfo.istio.io bookinfo.crt
bookinfo.key --profile leaf --ca istio.crt --ca-key istio.key --no-
password --insecure --not-after 2160h
Please enter the password to decrypt istio.key: password
# Specify intermediate CA password

Your certificate has been saved in bookinfo.crt.
Your private key has been saved in bookinfo.key.
```

The next step is the verification step to make sure that the certificate is valid.

6. Step provides options that we can use to inspect and verify certificates and check that the validity of the certificate is 90 days (2,160 hours):

```
$ step certificate inspect bookinfo.crt --short
X.509v3 TLS Certificate (ECDSA P-256) [Serial: 1528...6042]
  Subject: bookinfo.istio.io
  Issuer: istio.io
  Valid from: 2019-08-02T13:25:47Z
          to: 2019-10-31T13:25:43Z
```

7. Check the validity of the leaf certificate by running the following command. The return code should be zero:

```
$ step certificate verify bookinfo.crt -roots istio.crt

$ echo $?
0
```

Since we are not using the real hostname and an external DNS provider to resolve these to an IP address, we will map the DNS names to internal IP addresses using a simple `/etc/hosts` file.

Mapping IP addresses to hostname

In real-world scenarios, operators use DNS to map ingress gateway IP addresses to the names that we are using.

In our case, we will define these in the `/etc/hosts` file. Let's get started:

1. Find out the external IP address and the port of the Istio ingress gateway:

```
$ export INGRESS_HOST=$(kubectl -n istio-system get service istio-
ingressgateway -o jsonpath='{.status.loadBalancer.ingress..ip}') ;
echo $INGRESS_HOST
192.168.142.249

$ export INGRESS_PORT=$(kubectl -n istio-system get service istio-
ingressgateway -o
jsonpath='{.spec.ports[?(@.name=="https")].port}') ; echo
$INGRESS_PORT
443
```

   The ingress IP address could be different in your VM.

2. Please take note of your ingress host and IP address and run the following two commands. These will create and update the `/etc/hosts` file:

```
$ if ! grep -q bookinfo.istio.io /etc/hosts ; then echo
"$INGRESS_HOST bookinfo.istio.io" | sudo tee -a /etc/hosts; fi

$ if ! grep -q httpbin.istio.io /etc/hosts ; then echo
"$INGRESS_HOST httpbin.istio.io" | sudo tee -a /etc/hosts; fi

$ cat /etc/hosts
192.168.142.249 bookinfo.istio.io
192.168.142.249 httpbin.istio.io
```

3. Ping both hosts to make sure that the IP address has been resolved:

```
$ ping -c4 bookinfo.istio.io
$ ping -c4 httpbin.istio.io
```

   If the ping does not succeed, it is likely that the `keepalived` HA proxy is not working. Check `kubectl -n keepalived get pods` and make sure that the pods are in the ready state. The most probable reason for `keepalived` not running is that the `ip_vs` module hasn't loaded. Consult `https://github.com/servicemeshbook/keepalived` or Chapter 9, *Installing Istio*, to fix it. You may load the `ip_vs` module if it hasn't already been loaded using `sudo modprobe ip_vs` and restart the failed `keepalived` pod.

Istio initially used Kubernetes secrets to mount certificates and keys inside the pod, and that posed an issue regarding security if an attacker gains access to the pod. Istio now implements the **Secret Discovery Service (SDS)** process to keep the certificates and keys in memory instead of mounting them inside the pod. Next, we will go through the process of configuring the Ingress gateway using SDS.

Configuring an Ingress gateway using SDS

The advantage of using Istio's **Secret Discovery Service (SDS)** process is that there is no need to mount Kubernetes secrets in pods. The gateway agent monitors all of the secrets that are defined in the Ingress gateway and sends them to the Ingress gateway, which can dynamically add, delete, or update key/certificate pairs and its root certificate.

The demo profile that we used during the Istio installation does not enable SDS by default. We can enable it by applying the generated YAML using the values in the `-istio-sds-auth` profile. Let's get started:

1. Apply the following command, which will add the `ingress-sds` container to the Istio Ingress gateway:

```
$ cd ~/istio-$ISTIO_VERSION

$ helm template install/kubernetes/helm/istio/ --name istio \
 --namespace istio-system \
 -x charts/gateways/templates/deployment.yaml \
 --set gateways.istio-egressgateway.enabled=false \
 --set gateways.istio-ingressgateway.sds.enabled=true \
 | kubectl apply -f -
```

Note: Since we have now enabled SDS and mTLS, you can't go back and perform the traffic management exercises since they were assumed to be done with permissive mTLS, and the destination rules we created in these exercises enforce client mTLS.

2. Check the logs in the `ingress-sds` container of the Istio Ingress gateway:

```
$ kubectl -n istio-system logs -l app=istio-ingressgateway -c ingress-sds
2019-10-16T16:45:24.721824Z   warn   Secret object: kiali has empty ---
2019-10-16T16:45:24.802527Z   info   SDS gRPC server for ingress    ---
2019-10-16T16:45:24.802745Z   info   Start SDS grpc server for       ---

--- field, skip adding secret
--- gateway controller starts, listening on "/var/run/ingress_gateway/sds"
--- ingress gateway proxy
```

3. Similarly, check the logs in `istio-proxy`, which were injected for **Secure Service Discovery (SSD)**:

```
$ kubectl -n istio-system logs -l app=istio-ingressgateway -c istio-proxy
2019-08-03T16:45:24.919109Z   info      Opening status port 15020
2019-08-03T16:45:24.919231Z   info      Received new config, resetting budget
2019-08-03T16:45:24.919316Z   info      Reconciling retry (budget 10)
2019-08-03T16:45:24.919458Z   info      watching /etc/certs for changes
...
2019-08-03T16:45:25.937318Z   info      Envoy proxy is ready
```

Now that we've made sure that SDS is enabled, we'll create the certificates and keys.

Creating secrets using key and certificate

To create certificates and keys, follow these simple steps:

1. Create secrets for the `httpbin.istio.io` and `bookinfo.istio.io` domains so that they have a certificate and key. These secrets will be watched for any changes:

```
$ kubectl -n istio-system create secret generic httpbin-keys --
from-file=key=$HOME/step/httpbin.key --from-
file=cert=$HOME/step/httpbin.crt
secret/httpbin-keys created

$ kubectl -n istio-system create secret generic bookinfo-keys --
from-file=key=$HOME/step/bookinfo.key --from-
file=cert=$HOME/step/bookinfo.crt
secret/bookinfo-keys created
```

The certificate and key will be pushed down the container memory of `ingress-sds` through the SDS, hence avoiding the need for us to mount the certificates and keys, which would make them vulnerable.

2. Add the `httpbin.istio.io` and `bookinfo.istio.io` hosts to our existing Istio `mygateway` using the `httpbin-keys` secret:

```
# Script : 01-add-bookinfo-https-to-mygateway.yaml

apiVersion: networking.istio.io/v1alpha3
kind: Gateway
metadata:
  name: mygateway
spec:
...
  servers:
  - port:
      number: 80
      protocol: HTTP
...
    tls:
      mode: SIMPLE
      credentialName: bookinfo-keys
    hosts:
    - bookinfo.istio.io
  - port:
      number: 443
      name: httpbin
      protocol: HTTPS
    tls:
      mode: SIMPLE
      credentialName: httpbin-keys
    hosts:
    - httpbin.istio.io
```

In the preceding `yaml` file, note the following:

- Plain HTTP traffic is allowed for all hosts on port 80.
- HTTPS traffic is allowed for `bookinfo.istio.io` and `httpbin.istio.io`.
- The certificate and key for each host(s) is kept in a secret in the `istio-system` namespace or other admin namespaces where an application does not have access. The certificate and key will be mounted in memory of the `istio-proxy` for the pod through SDS since we enabled it in the previous step.

- Through the definition we defined at the Istio Ingress gateway, the protocol for the hosts is defined as `SIMPLE` TLS, which means that the client establishes the authenticity of the server, but the server does not check the credentials of the client. This is something that happens a lot on the internet today.

  Apply the preceding definition to add both hosts to the existing `mygateway`. We have set TLS mode to `SIMPLE`, which is one way to authenticate, that is, the client authenticates the server.

3. Create a gateway for the `bookinfo` application:

   ```
   $ cd ~/istio/scripts/02-security

   $ kubectl -n istio-system apply -f 01-add-bookinfo-https-to-
   mygateway.yaml
   gateway.networking.istio.io/mygateway created
   ```

   As soon as the gateway definition has been defined, the secrets are mounted in-memory through SDS.

4. Check the log again in the `ingress-sds` container of the Istio Ingress gateway:

   ```
   $ kubectl -n istio-system logs -l app=istio-ingressgateway -c ingress-
   sds
   <<removed>>
   2019-08-03T17:09:08.518098Z info SDS: push key/cert pair from node
   agent to proxy: ---
   2019-08-03T17:09:08.518123Z info SDS: push key/cert pair from node
   agent to proxy: ---

   --- "router~192.168.230.230~istio-ingressgateway-7db95cf64-hb7bq. ---
   --- "router~192.168.230.230~istio-ingressgateway-7db95cf64-hb7bq. ---

   --- istio-system~istio-system.svc.cluster.local-1"
   --- istio-system~istio-system.svc.cluster.local-2"
   ```

5. [Optional: The c only do if necessary] If you do not see SDS, push the message, wait for a few seconds, and check the logs again. If it does not refresh, recycle the Istio Ingress gateway, wait for the pod to become ready, and check the logs again:

   ```
   $ export INGRESS_GW=$(kubectl -n istio-system get pods -l
   istio=ingressgateway -o jsonpath='{.items[0].metadata.name}')

   $ kubectl -n istio-system delete pod $INGRESS_GW
   ```

Now that we've SDS, we will enable our `httpbin` application so that it can use simple TLS authentication.

Enabling httpbin for simple TLS

To enable our `httpbin` application so that it can use simple TLS authentication, follow these simple steps:

1. Define a virtual service for `httpbin.istio.io` so that the gateway knows how to route the traffic for `httpbin` requests:

```
# Script : 02-create-virtual-service-for-httpbin.yaml

apiVersion: networking.istio.io/v1alpha3
kind: VirtualService
metadata:
  name: httpbin
spec:
  hosts:
  - httpbin.istio.io
  gateways:
  - mygateway
  http:
  - match:
    - uri:
        prefix: /
    - uri:
        prefix: /status
    - uri:
        prefix: /delay
    route:
    - destination:
        host: httpbin.istio-lab.svc.cluster.local
        subset: v1
        port:
          number: 8000
        weight: 100
```

2. Create the preceding virtual service in the `istio-system` namespace:

```
$ kubectl -n istio-system apply -f 02-create-virtual-service-
for-httpbin.yaml
virtualservice.networking.istio.io/httpbin created
```

3. Let's use the `curl` command to send the request. To do this, we will use the hostname by setting the header, using the resolve parameter to set the IP address, and setting the `cacert` parameter:

```
$ rm -fr ~/.pki ## Reset local NSS database

$ curl -HHost:httpbin.istio.io --resolve
httpbin.istio.io:$INGRESS_PORT:$INGRESS_HOST --cacert
$HOME/step/istio.crt https://httpbin.istio.io/status/418

    -=[ teapot ]=-

       _...._
     .'  _ _ `.
    | ."` ^ `". _,
    \_;`"---"`|//
      |       ;/
      \_     _/
        `"""`

$ curl -HHost:httpbin.istio.io --resolve
httpbin.istio.io:$INGRESS_PORT:$INGRESS_HOST --cacert
$HOME/step/istio.crt https://httpbin.istio.io/ip
{
    "origin": "192.168.142.101"
}
```

Notice that in the preceding code, we enabled edge authentication to the frontend microservice without having to make any code changes in the original application. This is because of the loosely coupled architecture of the Istio service mesh.

 An HTTP `418` status gives us the output `I'm a teapot`. `httpbin` returns a text picture of a teapot.

4. Check the TLS implementation:

```
$ HTTPBIN=$(kubectl -n istio-lab get pods -l app=httpbin -o
jsonpath={.items[0].metadata.name}) ; echo $HTTPBIN
httpbin-v1-b9985cc7d-4wmcf
```

```
$ istioctl authn tls-check $HTTPBIN.istio-lab httpbin.istio-
lab.svc.cluster.local
HOST:PORT                                    STATUS  SERVER     ---
httpbin.istio-lab.svc.cluster.local:8000  OK      HTTP/mTLS  ---

--- CLIENT      AUTHN POLICY      DESTINATION RULE
--- HTTP        default/          httpbin/istio-lab
```

TLS is permissive as it shows HTTP/mTLS at the server level. The external client protocol is HTTP. You can run `istioctl proxy-status` to check the sync status of the Envoy proxy from Pilot, which is useful if you wish to diagnose issues.

5. The PERMISSIVE policy is desired when not all services use a proxy sidecar or the process of migration is still continuing. This can be done cluster-wide by modifying the mesh policy from PERMISSIVE to STRICT, and it will enforce across all user-defined services. In such a case, the output below SERVER will only show mTLS. Note that STRICT mode can be done at a cluster level, a namespace level, or a service level:

```
$ kubectl get meshpolicies default -o yaml
```

```
apiVersion: authentication.istio.io/v1alpha1
kind: MeshPolicy
metadata:
[... removed ...]
 name: default
spec:
 peers:
 - mtls:
 mode: PERMISSIVE
```

The destination rule defines the CLIENT mode. We defined the destination rule for httpbin in the previous chapter. Run the `kubectl -n istio-lab get dr httpbin -o yaml` command to check the subsets that have been defined and then run `kubectl -n istio-lab get vs httpbin -o yaml` to find out which subset is used as a destination for the httpbin service.

Allow developers to focus only on business logic and leave security implementation to the application infrastructure team.

Next, we will enable simple TLS for the bookinfo application.

Enabling bookinfo for simple TLS

Let's define a virtual service for bookinfo.istio.io so that the gateway knows the URI matches and patterns it requires to send requests to the productpage.istio-lab.svc.cluster.local hostname on port 9080:

1. Enter the following command:

```
# Script : 03-create-virtual-service-for-bookinfo.yaml

apiVersion: networking.istio.io/v1alpha3
kind: VirtualService
metadata:
 name: bookinfo
spec:
 hosts:
 - bookinfo.istio.io
 gateways:
 - mygateway
 http:

...
 route:
 - destination:
 host: productpage.istio-lab.svc.cluster.local
 port:
 number: 9080
```

2. Create a virtual service in the istio-system namespace:

```
$ kubectl -n istio-system apply -f 03-create-virtual-service-for-bookinfo.yaml
virtualservice.networking.istio.io/bookinfo configured
```

3. From a web browser within the VM, open two more tabs:

   - Open `http://bookinfo.istio.io` from the first tab; it should load normally.
   - Open `https://bookinfo.istio.io` from the second tab.

4. You will see a notice stating that your connection is not private. This is normal as browsers don't like self-signed certificates.

5. Click **Advanced** and click **Proceed** to go to `bookinfo.istio.io` (unsafe).

   You will notice that you are able to run both protocol HTTP and HTTPS since our gateway is allowing HTTP traffic for all hosts, and the `SIMPLE tls` mode is only applicable for `httpbin.istio.io` and `bookinfo.istio.io`.

6. Open one more tab and run `http://httpbin.istio.io/headers`. Now, you should see the headers.

The internet did not provide a robust method for revoking certificates before their expiration date. A certain amount of time is lost for the revocation due to real-time distribution. Another method to check against the revocation of certificates is **Online Certificate Status Protocol** (**OCSP**—`https://tools.ietf.org/html/rfc2560`), which is also open to criticism due to latency, overhead issues, and privacy concerns regarding leaking information about websites that have been given to a central OCSP server. Until this problem is solved, another method is to rotate keys and certificates at a short interval to reduce the time window for security compromise. Next, we will look at the procedure of rotating keys and certificates.

Rotating virtual service keys and certificates

If a private key has been compromised, revoking X.509 certificates is not enough. The best option is to issue certificates that expire quickly enough so that revocation isn't necessary. In a zero-trust network, it is good practice to let certificates expire sooner, and there is an automatic way to renew certificates.

Istio Citadel and node agent provide an automatic way for us to renew a certificate when its **Time to Live (TTL)** expires for internal microservices. However, there is no automatic arrangement for renewing certificates for external hosts that are terminating at the Ingress gateway since this needs to be managed externally to Istio.

Let's take a look:

1. Let's check the certificate that we issued to `httpbin`:

   ```
   $ cd ~/step

   $ step certificate inspect httpbin.crt --short
   X.509v3 TLS Certificate (ECDSA P-256) [Serial: 2760...1376]
     Subject: httpbin.istio.io
     Issuer: istio.io
     Valid from: 2019-10-16T13:30:41Z
             to: 2020-01-14T13:30:38Z
   ```

   Notice that the certificate is only valid for 90 days since we changed the default from 1 day for the purpose of the exercises in this book. There should be an automated process to renew the certificates before they expire and recycle the secrets automatically.

   Let's do this manually.

2. Delete the `httpbin-keys` secret as we will create a new set of keys:

   ```
   $ kubectl -n istio-system delete secret httpbin-keys
   ```

3. Regenerate the key and certificate for `httpbin.istio.io` and bundle the intermediate CA. Specify a password that will be used to generate an intermediate CA private key:

   ```
   $ step certificate create httpbin.istio.io httpbin.crt httpbin.key
   --profile leaf --ca istio.crt --ca-key istio.key --no-password --
   insecure --not-after 2160h
   Please enter the password to decrypt istio.key: ☺☺☺☺☺☺☺☺
   ✔✓ Would you like to overwrite httpbin.crt [y/n]: y
   ✔ Would you like to overwrite httpbin.key [y/n]: y
   Your certificate has been saved in httpbin.crt.
   Your private key has been saved in httpbin.key.
   ```

4. Create a secret for `httpbin` using a new key and certificate:

```
$ kubectl -n istio-system create secret generic httpbin-keys --
from-file=key=$HOME/step/httpbin.key --from-
file=cert=$HOME/step/httpbin.crt
secret/httpbin-keys created
```

5. Check the SDS log entry for the certificate that we created to check the key/cert pair has been pushed to the proxy:

```
$ kubectl -n istio-system logs -l app=istio-ingressgateway -c
ingress-sds
```

6. Run the same `curl` test against `httpbin.istio.io` to make sure that the key and certificate rotation has worked. Refresh the browser tab and check the headers:

```
$ curl -HHost:httpbin.istio.io --resolve
httpbin.istio.io:$INGRESS_PORT:$INGRESS_HOST --cacert
$HOME/step/istio.crt https://httpbin.istio.io/ip
{
  "origin": "192.168.142.101"
}
```

This manual process rotates the certificate for the Ingress gateway certificate and key regeneration can be automated with the help of the `step-ca` tool. This tool runs an online CA, and the client certificates can be requested through the use of step commands. Consult `https://github.com/smallstep/certificates` for more details.

After working through the simple TLS (a client is not required to present its authenticity), we will now move toward mutual TLS in which a client is also required to present its credentials so that the server knows that the client is authentic.

Enabling an Ingress gateway for httpbin using mutual TLS

In SIMPLE TLS, the client checks the identity of the server, but in mutual TLS, the server also checks the identity of the client. The mutual TLS adds another layer in which the client sends its X.509 certificate to a server to verify the identity of the client.

Mutual TLS is useful for business-to-business applications that require strict access control. Let's get started:

1. Create a client certificate and key using RSA that will be used by the client (curl, in this case) to provide client authentication to the Istio Ingress gateway:

```
$ step certificate create httpbin.istio.io client.crt client.key --
profile leaf --ca istio.crt --ca-key istio.key --no-password --
insecure --kty RSA --size 2048
Please enter the password to decrypt istio.key: password
# Provide intermediate CA password

Your certificate has been saved in client.crt.
Your private key has been saved in client.key.
```

2. Create a chain of certificates from `root-ca` and intermediate authority:

```
$ step certificate bundle root-ca.crt istio.crt ca-chain.crt
Your certificate has been saved in ca-chain.crt.
```

3. Recreate the `httpbin-keys` secret using one additional parameter called `cacert`:

```
$ kubectl -n istio-system delete secret httpbin-keys

$ kubectl -n istio-system create secret generic httpbin-keys --
from-file=key=$HOME/step/httpbin.key --from-
file=cert=$HOME/step/httpbin.crt --from-file=cacert=$HOME/step/ca-
chain.crt
secret/httpbin-keys created
```

4. To enable mutual TLS, we need to modify our gateway definition to change TLS mode from `SIMPLE` to `MUTUAL`. We will change the definition for `httpbin.istio.io` for mutual TLS:

```
# Script : 04-add-mutual-TLS-to-bookinfo-https-to-mygateway.yaml

apiVersion: networking.istio.io/v1alpha3
kind: Gateway
metadata:
 name: mygateway
spec:
 selector:
 istio: ingressgateway
 servers:
 - port:
 number: 80
```

```
name: http
protocol: HTTP
...
tls:
mode: MUTUAL
credentialName: httpbin-keys
hosts:
- httpbin.istio.io
```

5. Modify the gateway to change `httpbin.istio.io` TLS mode from `SIMPLE` to `MUTUAL`:

```
$ cd ~/istio/scripts/02-security/

$ kubectl -n istio-system apply -f 04-add-mutual-TLS-to-bookinfo-
https-to-mygateway.yaml
gateway.networking.istio.io/mygateway configured
```

Now that we've created the gateway for `bookinfo` by implementing mutual TLS, we will verify the TLS configuration.

Verifying the TLS configuration

The `istioctl` tool can be used to check whether the TLS settings match between the authentication policy and the destination rules for a particular microservice. Let's take a look:

1. Check the TLS flow between the server and the client:

```
$ HTTPBIN=$(kubectl -n istio-lab get pods -l app=httpbin -o
jsonpath={.items[0].metadata.name}) ; echo $HTTPBIN
httpbin-v1-b9985cc7d-4wmcf

$ istioctl authn tls-check $HTTPBIN.istio-lab istio-
ingressgateway.istio-system.svc.cluster.local
HOST:PORT                                                  STATUS ---
istio-ingressgateway.istio-system.svc.cluster.local:80  OK     ---

--- SERVER    CLIENT  AUTHN POLICY  DESTINATION RULE
--- HTTP/mTLS HTTP    default/      -
```

If the status shows `Conflict`, this is an indication that the destination rules are in conflict with the protocol. In this example, the server (`httpbin` service) supports HTTP and mTLS, while the client supports HTTP, so the status is OK. If the client only supported mTLS, then the preceding status would have been in Conflict.

2. Modify the `curl` command to pass the client `cert` and `key` parameters in addition to `cacert`:

```
$ curl -HHost:httpbin.istio.io --resolve
httpbin.istio.io:$INGRESS_PORT:$INGRESS_HOST --cacert
$HOME/step/ca-chain.crt --cert $HOME/step/client.crt --key
$HOME/step/client.key https://httpbin.istio.io/status/418
```

```
    -=[ teapot ]=-

       _...._
     .'  _ _ `.
    | ."` ^ `". _,
    \_;`"---"`|//
      |       ;/
      \_     _/
        `"""`
```

This example shows how to enable mutual TLS without having to write a single line of code in the application. We have already covered terminating TLS traffic at the edge of the mesh through the Ingress gateway. The communication between microservices is still HTTP-based after the Ingress gateway.

3. Let's check the TLS settings between the `Bookinfo` productpage:

```
$ PRODUCT_PAGE=$(kubectl -n istio-lab get pods -l app=productpage -
o jsonpath={.items..metadata.name}) ; echo $PRODUCT_PAGE
productpage-v1-74dfdd8b47-xmdpn

$ istioctl authn tls-check $PRODUCT_PAGE.istio-lab istio-
ingressgateway.istio-system.svc.cluster.local
HOST:PORT                                                STATUS ---
istio-ingressgateway.istio-system.svc.cluster.local:80  OK     ---

--- SERVER     CLIENT  AUTHN POLICY  DESTINATION RULE
--- HTTP/mTLS  HTTP    default/      -
```

If you receive the message, `Error: nothing to output`, wait for a few seconds and try again.

Notice that the server supports both mTLS and HTTP (permissive TLS), but the client is only sending HTTP requests. Hence, mTLS is not enabled between the client and server. The default policy is used for authentication, and the destination rules are defined using `productpage`.

Check the default authentication policy, which is `PERMISSIVE` in this case (mTLS and HTTP). When the default mesh policy is set to `PERMISSIVE`, no authentication or authorization checks will be performed by default on plaintext HTTP traffic.

Let's go over how to secure communication between microservices using mutual TLS. This type of security is desired when processing business applications from the backend, especially when they are distributed in a zero-trust network.

Node agent to rotate certificates and keys for services

Previously, we mentioned that there is no automation for rotating certificates and keys for virtual services and suggested to use a `step-ca` tool instead. The aforementioned case was for the external service connecting to the edge microservice through the Ingress gateway. Istio is not designed to automate external services. However, Citadel and node agent are designed to automatically rotate/renew certificates and keys based on the TTL of the existing certificate, and this process is fully automatic.

In Citadel, certificate rotation is set to an interval of 90 days. The rotation window can be changed by modifying the `istio-citadel` container argument from 2,160 hours to, say, 48 hours. This allows short-lived certificates in a zero-trust network environment.

For instance, you can edit the Citadel deployment using `kubectl -n istio-system edit deploy istio-citadel` and modify the parameter from `--workload-cert-ttl=2160h` to `--workload-cert-ttl=48h`.

If the node agent is provisioned (by choosing the Helm installation option), it requests the rotation of certificates and keys based on the TTL of the certificate, while Citadel does the rotation. If the node agent is not running, the certificate and key will be in `secret-<serviceaccount>`. Citadel watches it and checks the TTL, and then it generates the certificates and pushes them to the Envoy (sidecar) proxies.

The additional significance of a node agent is for a non-Kubernetes environment where it can be deployed as a `systemd` service in a Linux machine. Here, it can request certificates and keys rotation from Citadel while it's running in the service mesh control plane.

In this section, we learned how to configure the Ingress gateway using SDS. Next, we will enable mutual TLS between microservices.

Enabling mutual TLS within the mesh

Transport Layer Security (TLS)—the successor of the Secure Sockets Layer (SSL)—provides encrypted communication by authenticating the other party in a connection (who they say they are), for example, accessing a bank site using a web browser such as Firefox, Chrome, or Safari. The TLS handshake can be seen in the following diagram:

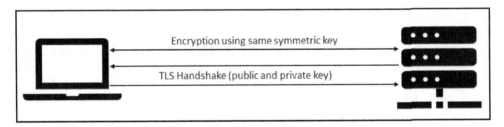

The steps for this are as follows:

1. The browser (client) sends (plaintext) a `client hello` message with the TLS version, a large random number (client_random), `session_id`, and cipher supported.

2. The website (server) replies (plaintext) with a `server hello` message with the chosen TLS version, chosen cipher, `session_id`, a large random number (`server_random`), and its certificate chain signed with its private key (issued by a trusted CA) with a `hello done` message.

3. The browser has the public keys of all the major CAs in its trust store (database). It uses the public key of the server certificate issuer to verify the chain of trust and ensure that the CA signed the server's certificate. Upon verifying the chain of trust (authentication), it sends a pre-master secret (a randomly generated sequence, as per the chosen cipher) encrypted with the server's public key to the server.

4. The server decrypts the pre-master secret and generates the encryption key (master secret). Using a client and server's random number (exchanged in the preceding steps), both the client and the server will arrive at the same key. Without making any exchanges over the network, symmetric encryption is used after a TLS handshake is complete. The server sends a change cipher spec protocol message to the client.

5. The client switches from asymmetric (public/private) encryption (computationally expensive) to symmetric encryption (client and server use the same key, which is less computational). It uses a master secret (never exchanged over a network as both the client and the server can derive it) by sending a handshake finish message.

6. The server changes the cipher and the rest of the communication starts using the symmetric key.

The following diagram shows the mTLS handshake between the client and the server (image credit: Mariano Cano):

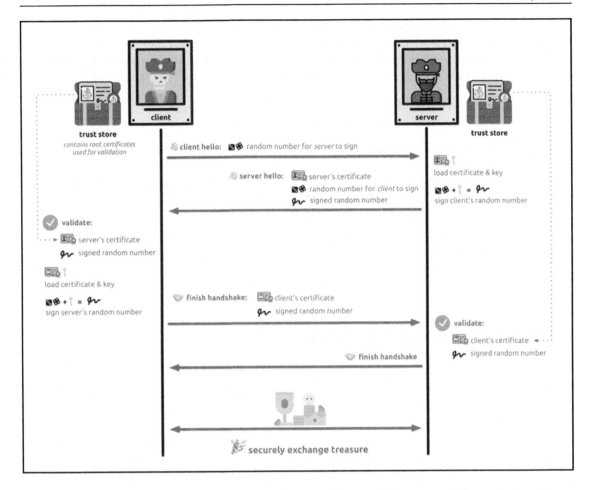

Here, the client establishes the identity of the server by verifying its certificate chain of the server. However, the bank site did not confirm the authenticity of the client. The internet has an inherent flaw where we do not establish the trust of a client. Hence, phishing attacks are prominent by tricking customers into signing in to a fraudulent site for someone to compromise their credentials.

The ideal way to establish trust is to switch to mutual TLS (also known as mTLS), in which both the client and the server authenticate each other by verifying their chain of certificates. This is like a secure line with a caller ID. The most compelling reason for using mTLS is to communicate with workloads running anywhere using a zero-trust network securely.

The other inherent flaw of the internet is its long-lived leaf certificates. The certificates eventually expire, but if a private key is compromised, a third party can impersonate the certificate owner. Revoking certificates is not trivial, and there is always a time lag (from hours to sometimes weeks) that does not prevent continued use of revoked certificates.

Now that you have a fair understanding of mTLS, let's explore how mTLS in Istio can be used to authenticate and authorize communication for microservices.

It is important to note two Istio-specific terminologies for security:

- **Authentication policies**: The authentication policies apply to requests that a microservice receives from a client who needs to specify `TLSSettings` and `DestinationRule` for upstream connections.
- **Mutual TLS authentication**: Microservice-to-microservice communication is routed through sidecar proxies, which establish mutual TLS connection. A secure naming check authenticates and verifies whether the service account in the server certificate has been authorized to run the target service.

Converting into strict mutual TLS

When we installed Istio, we used a permissive mutual TLS approach, which allows both plaintext and mutual TLS traffic. In the previous exercise, we ran `httpbin.istio.io` as plaintext, simple TLS, and mutual TLS. The permissive mutual TLS install was done using a demo profile.

In `Chapter 9`, *Installing Istio*, we used `istio-demo.yaml` to install permissive mutual TLS. Strict mutual TLS can be installed through `istio-demo-auth.yaml` if the intent is to enforce strict mutual TLS for microservice-to-microservice communication. However, it is possible to change the existing Istio install to apply a strict mutual TLS profile.

The destination rules define the traffic policies, and the default is not to use mutual TLS. Since we've already defined the destination rules, we will need to redefine them before we can enable mutual TLS globally.

Redefining destination rules

We will be using a slightly different version of the `bookinfo` application, which has a new `ratings-v2` service that calls the MongoDB service:

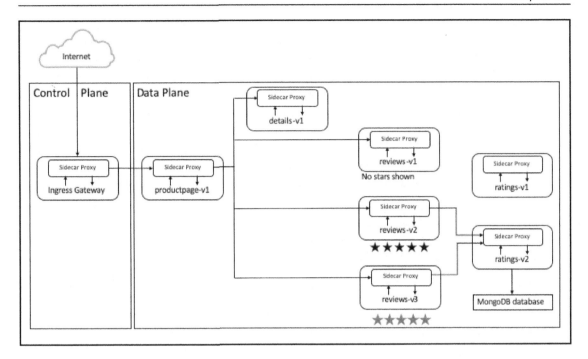

As a recap: When there are multiple versions of the same service, remember that we define subsets using the destination rules for specific service versions. Then, we create or modify the virtual services to use a specific subset to direct the traffic to the desired subset.

To redefine the destination rules, follow these steps:

1. We added the following stanza after the host for the destination rules for **productpage**, **details**, **ratings**, and **reviews**:

```
trafficPolicy:
  tls:
    mode: ISTIO_MUTUAL
```

2. Here are the modified destination rules for the `bookinfo` application. Let's take a look:

```
# Script : 05-create-mtls-bookinfo-destination-rules.yaml

apiVersion: networking.istio.io/v1alpha3
kind: DestinationRule
metadata:
  name: productpage
```

```
spec:
  host: productpage
  trafficPolicy:
    tls:
      mode: ISTIO_MUTUAL
  subsets:
  - name: v1
    labels:
      version: v1
---
```

This is the destination rule definition for the `reviews` microservice:

```
apiVersion: networking.istio.io/v1alpha3
kind: DestinationRule
metadata:
  name: reviews
spec:
  host: reviews
  trafficPolicy:
    tls:
      mode: ISTIO_MUTUAL
  subsets:
  - name: v1
    labels:
      version: v1
  - name: v2
    labels:
      version: v2
  - name: v3
    labels:
      version: v3
---
```

This is the destination rule definition for the `ratings` microservice:

```
apiVersion: networking.istio.io/v1alpha3
kind: DestinationRule
metadata:
  name: ratings
spec:
  host: ratings
  trafficPolicy:
    tls:
      mode: ISTIO_MUTUAL
  subsets:

...
```

```
    labels:
      version: v2-mysql
  - name: v2-mysql-vm
    labels:
      version: v2-mysql-vm
---
```

This is the destination rule definition for the `details` microservice:

```
apiVersion: networking.istio.io/v1alpha3
kind: DestinationRule
metadata:
  name: details
spec:
  host: details
  trafficPolicy:
    tls:
      mode: ISTIO_MUTUAL
  subsets:
  - name: v1
    labels:
      version: v1
  - name: v2
    labels:
      version: v2
---
```

3. Apply the modified destination rules for the `bookinfo` microservices:

```
$ kubectl -n istio-lab apply -f 05-create-mtls-bookinfo-
destination-rules.yaml
destinationrule.networking.istio.io/productpage configured
destinationrule.networking.istio.io/reviews configured
destinationrule.networking.istio.io/ratings configured
destinationrule.networking.istio.io/details configured
```

4. Now that we've defined the destination rule for each microservice, we can check the TLS between the `productpage` microservice and `ingress gateway`:

```
$ istioctl authn tls-check $PRODUCT_PAGE.istio-lab istio-
ingressgateway.istio-system.svc.cluster.local
HOST:PORT                                                   ---
istio-ingressgateway.istio-system.svc.cluster.local:80   ---

--- STATUS      SERVER       CLIENT
--- OK          HTTP/mTLS    HTTP

--- AUTHN POLICY      DESTINATION RULE
```

```
--- default/            -

$ istioctl authn tls-check $PRODUCT_PAGE.istio-lab
productpage.istio-lab.svc.cluster.local
HOST:PORT                                         ---
productpage.istio-lab.svc.cluster.local:9080      ---

--- STATUS       SERVER          CLIENT
--- OK           HTTP/mTLS       mTLS

--- AUTHN POLICY        DESTINATION RULE
--- default/            productpage/istio-lab
```

The preceding result shows that the traffic between the microservices is
mTLS and that the status is OK. The traffic at the Ingress gateway can be either
HTTP or HTTPS due to our definition of a simple TLS while defining the gateway
for the `bookinfo.istio.io` host.

Similarly, redefine the destination rule for `httpbin`:

```
# Script : 06-create-mtls-httpbin-destination-rules.yaml

apiVersion: networking.istio.io/v1alpha3
kind: DestinationRule
metadata:
  name: httpbin
spec:
  host: httpbin
  trafficPolicy:
    tls:
      mode: ISTIO_MUTUAL
  subsets:
  - name: v1
    labels:
      version: v1
  - name: v2
    labels:
      version: v2
```

5. Apply the destination rule for `httpbin`:

```
$ kubectl -n istio-lab apply -f 06-create-mtls-httpbin-destination-
rules.yaml
destinationrule.networking.istio.io/httpbin configured
```

After turning on mTLS (ISTIO_MUTUAL) for the httpbin microservice through the destination rule, check TLS using istioctl. The client only accepts mTLS.

From your browser window tab, refresh the third tab, that is, http://httpbin.istio.io/headers. You will notice an entry for the additional header for SECURE IDENTITY of the service through SPIFFY URI:

```
"X-Forwarded-Client-Cert": "By=spiffe://cluster.local/ns/istio-
lab/sa/default;Hash=1466acd2330485fcf8036746a6728937ea8a672bd54c5d19236
a8e8c75ad19d1;Subject=\"\";URI=spiffe://cluster.local/ns/istio-
system/sa/istio-ingressgateway-service-account"
```

We can turn on mutual TLS either globally, at the namespace level, or at the service level. The TLS policy that's defined at service level takes precedence over the namespace-level policy. In our case, we will turn on mutual TLS at the istio-lab namespace level.

The global mTLS can be enabled by editing the Istio MeshPolicy primitive and changing mtls to nil (=PERMISSIVE), as follows:

```
apiVersion: "authentication.istio.io/v1alpha1"
kind: "MeshPolicy"
metadata:
  name: "default"
spec:
  peers:
  - mtls: {}
```

We will not make any changes here at the global level.

Next, we will enable TLS at the namespace level.

Enabling mTLS at the namespace level

To enable STRICT mTLS at the namespace level, we can use Policy instead of MeshPolicy and define the namespace that it will be applied to. Let's get started:

1. Define mTLS for the istio-lab namespace:

```
# Script : 07-create-mtls-for-istio-lab-namespace.yaml

apiVersion: authentication.istio.io/v1alpha1
kind: Policy
```

```
metadata:
 name: default
 namespace: istio-lab
spec:
 peers:
 - mtls: {}
```

2. Apply the mTLS security policy at the namespace level:

```
$ kubectl -n istio-lab apply -f 07-create-mtls-for-istio-lab-
namespace.yaml
policy.authentication.istio.io/default created
```

Next, we will verify the TLS configuration.

Verifying the TLS configuration

To verify the TLS configuration, follow these steps:

1. Run the istioctl command:

```
$ export RATING_POD=$(kubectl -n istio-lab get pods -l app=ratings
-o jsonpath='{.items[0].metadata.name}') ; echo $RATING_POD
ratings-v1-79b6d99979-k2j7t

$ istioctl authn tls-check $RATING_POD.istio-lab ratings.istio-
lab.svc.cluster.local
HOST:PORT                                          STATUS    SERVER   ---
ratings.istio-lab.svc.cluster.local:9080           OK        mTLS     ---

--- CLIENT       AUTHN POLICY          DESTINATION RULE
--- mTLS         default/istio-lab     ratings/istio-lab
```

Notice that the server and client communication between microservices is mTLS and that it is protected through strong identity—a standard that is progressing. You can find out more at https://spiffe.io/.

You can use istioctl authn tls-check <istio-ingressgateway-xxx-xxx>.istio-system to check the status of each service from an mTLS perspective, as well as authentication policy and destination rule. This command is very helpful for debugging purposes to see whether there are any conflicts.

2. Run the `istioctl describe pod` command to check what type of traffic policy is being used. The output is useful for debugging/diagnostics purposes:

```
$ istioctl experimental describe pod $RATING_POD
Pod: ratings-v1-df666d977-152gh
    Pod Ports: 9080 (ratings), 15090 (istio-proxy)
--------------------
Service: ratings
    Port: http 9080/HTTP
DestinationRule: ratings for "ratings"
    Matching subsets: v1
        (Non-matching subsets v2,v2-mysql,v2-mysql-vm)
    Traffic Policy TLS Mode: ISTIO_MUTUAL
Pilot reports that pod is STRICT (enforces mTLS) and clients speak
mTLS
VirtualService: ratings
    1 HTTP route(s)
```

In the preceding section, we enabled mTLS at the `istio-lab` namespace level instead of enabling it at the global level. If we had enabled mTLS at the global level, we would have to allow the Kubernetes API server to communicate with Istio services without mTLS since there is no proxy sidecar running with the Kubernetes API server.

3. The communication with mTLS between the Istio services and the Kubernetes API server can be disabled through a destination rule:

```
# Script : 08-disable-mtls-for-kube-apiserver.yaml

apiVersion: networking.istio.io/v1alpha3
kind: DestinationRule
metadata:
 name: "api-server"
 namespace: istio-system
spec:
 host: "kubernetes.default.svc.cluster.local"
 trafficPolicy:
 tls:
 mode: DISABLE
```

4. Apply some destination rules so that communication between the Kubernetes API server and `istio-system` can happen when mTLS is set at the global level (note that we didn't set mTLS at the global level, so this step is optional and for information purposes):

```
$ kubectl -n istio-system apply -f 08-disable-mtls-for-kube-
apiserver.yaml
destinationrule.networking.istio.io/api-server created
```

To recap, we covered the following security implementation topics:

- Through the Istio Ingress gateway, we enabled simple and mutual TLS so that TLS termination can occur at the Istio Ingress gateway. We kept the TLS mode as PERMISSIVE (through the MeshPolicy definition) to enable both text and TLS communication.
- The downstream communication was still using a plaintext HTTP protocol until we enabled mTLS at the namespace level for the `bookinfo` application.
- Now that mTLS has been implemented downstream of the Ingress gateway, service-to-service communication can be done through mTLS.

 Starting with Istio 1.3.1, automatic annotations are added to a pod to exclude ports for health and liveliness checks from mTLS. This was an issue in previous versions where services status was reported unhealthy due to mTLS-enabled traffic for health and liveliness checks.

From your Chrome browser, from inside the VM, clear your local cache by pressing *Ctrl + Shift + Del*, click **Clear Data**, and close the **Settings** tab.

From your web browser within the VM, click on the second tab or go to `https://bookinfo.istio.io`. You will see a notice stating **Your connection is not private**, which is OK since our certificate is self-signed. Click **Advanced** and click to proceed with `bookinfo.istio.io`.

`https://bookinfo.istio.io` initiates a secure communication from the client (browser) to the Istio Ingress gateway. The client authenticated the server (the Istio Ingress gateway presented its X509 certificate to the browser), and downstream communication is done through mTLS. Between microservices, the client and server microservices will authenticate each other. Since the certificates are self-signed, the browser will complain about the connection being insecure, and that is OK. Normally, for the edge services (external-facing microservice), we will use a signed certificate instead of a self-generated certificate.

You will also notice that you can still run `http://bookinfo.istio.io`, where the communication between the client and the server is plaintext, but the server-side communication between microservices is using mTLS. The plain and TLS communication between the browser and Istio ingress gateway is allowed through the simple TLS mode, which is defined through the Istio primitive of a gateway. Run the `kubectl -n istio-system get gw -o yaml` command to confirm that the TLS mode for the `bookinfo.istio.io` host is SIMPLE.

5. Run `https://httpbin.istio.io/ip` from the Chrome browser. You will notice an error stating that the server could not prove that it is `httpbin.istio.io`. This is due to the fact that we had enabled TLS mode in the gateway as MUTUAL for `httpbin.istio.io`, which will require the client to present its key and certificate to the server so that a mutual authentication could occur. Previously, we used the following curl with the `cacert`, `key`, and `cert` parameters for mTLS to work for `httpbin`:

```
$ rm -fr ~/.pki

$ curl -HHost:httpbin.istio.io --resolve
httpbin.istio.io:$INGRESS_PORT:$INGRESS_HOST --cacert
$HOME/step/ca-chain.crt --cert $HOME/step/client.crt --key
$HOME/step/client.key https://httpbin.istio.io/status/418

    -=[ teapot ]=-
```

If we want to enable mTLS for the browser, additional steps need to be performed.

The example given here is only for the Chrome browser in CentOS. Chrome uses shared NSS DB stored in `$HOME/.pki/nssdb`.

Make sure you have the `certutil` and `pk12util` utilities available. On CentOS, these can be installed using `yum -y install nss-tools`.

Exit from the root in the VM to get to the default user, which was used to log in to the system and the user. This will be running the Chrome browser from the Linux CentOS VM. Also, copy the contents of `~/httpbin.istio.io` to a temporary location with proper permission for the regular user to import the root certificate and the client bundle. Let's get started:

1. Since we created a self-signed client certificate for `httpbin.istio.io`, we need to import the root certificate into the `nss` database:

   ```
   $ certutil -d sql:$HOME/.pki/nssdb -A -n httpbin.istio.io -i
   $HOME/step/root-ca.crt -t "TC,,"
   ```

2. Create a client bundle using the client's key and a certificate in `pk12` format:

   ```
   $ openssl pkcs12 -export -clcerts  -inkey $HOME/step/client.key -in
   $HOME/step/client.crt -out httpbin.istio.io.p12 -passout
   pass:password -name "Key pair for httpbin.istio.io"
   ```

3. The password to create the client bundle is `password`, and the same must be used to import the client key bundle into the `nss` database using `pk12util`. You can choose a password of your choice:

   ```
   $ pk12util -i httpbin.istio.io.p12 -d sql:$HOME/.pki/nssdb -W
   password
   pk12util: PKCS12 IMPORT SUCCESSFUL
   ```

4. List the certificates in the `nss` database:

   ```
   $ certutil -d sql:$HOME/.pki/nssdb -L
   Certificate Nickname                      Trust Attributes
                                             SSL,S/MIME,JAR/XPI

   httpbin.istio.io                          CT,,
   Key pair for httpbin.istio.io             u,u,u
   ```

Run `https://httpbin.istio.io/ip` from the Chrome browser. A popup will appear where you can choose the certificate to authenticate to `httpbin.istio.io` and select `httpbin.istio.io`. Now, you'll be able to see the output.

This is an example of a secured authenticated communication in which both the client and the server authenticate each other. This is why this is known as mutual TLS as opposed to simple TLS. Mutual TLS is preferred for internal business applications such as `bookinfo`, where microservice-to-microservice communication is through mTLS. It shields the microservices, even in a zero-trust environment. It will be interesting to see the decline of VPN and firewall and the rise of secure authenticated communication in a zero-trust network.

The web client and server's mutual authentication is not typical in the internet world where a client (me) needs to validate whether the bank site that they are visiting is genuine, but the bank does not verify the authenticity of the client. This is how the internet works, and in one sense, it fails to establish the trust between a bank and its customer. The preceding example shows mutual TLS between the client and the server, and the same is common for a business-to-business application.

With this, we have covered the first step of security authentication (who you are?). Next, we will cover the second step of security authorization (what can you do?).

Authorization

Once someone has been authenticated, what they can or cannot do depends upon authorization. Mixer plays an important role in authorization enablement in Istio. Let's learn about authorization through some examples:

1. First, let's switch to subset `v2` of the `reviews` virtual service so that it shows black stars in the ratings (remember: review-1: no star, review-2: black stars, review-3: red stars(:

   ```
   $ kubectl -n istio-lab patch vs reviews --type json -p
   '[{"op":"replace","path":"/spec/http/0/route/0/destination/subset",
   "value": "v2"}]'
   virtualservice.networking.istio.io/ratings patched

   $ kubectl -n istio-lab get vs reviews -o yaml | grep -B1 subset:
           host: reviews
           subset: v2
   ```

2. Refresh `https://bookinfo.istio.io/productpage`. You should see **black stars** in the ratings.

   Authorization can be enabled by defining the `ClusterRbacConfig` object. The name of the object must be a default, and there can only be one instance of `ClusterRbacConfig`.

3. Define `ClusterRbacConfig` for the `istio-lab` namespace:

   ```
   # Script : 09-create-clusterrbac-config.yaml

   apiVersion: "rbac.istio.io/v1alpha1"
   kind: ClusterRbacConfig
   metadata:
     name: default
   spec:
     mode: 'ON_WITH_INCLUSION'
     inclusion:
       namespaces: ["istio-lab"]
   ```

4. Create default `ClusterRbacConfig` for enabling Istio authorization for services defined in an `istio-lab` namespace:

   ```
   $ kubectl -n istio-lab apply -f 09-create-clusterrbac-config.yaml
   clusterrbacconfig.rbac.istio.io/default created
   ```

5. Wait for a few seconds for the rule to propagate. Point your browser to `https://bookinfo.istio.io/productpage`. You should see a message stating `RBAC: access denied`.

If necessary, clear your cache if the page doesn't load.

With this, deny access to all and then only allow access to users, groups, or roles to edge services and to service accounts for internal services.

Next, we will go through authorization at the namespace level so that each microservice that's defined in that namespace inherits the same authorization.

Namespace-level authorization

After Istio authorization has been enabled, the authorization policy is defined using `ServiceRole` and `ServiceRoleBinding`. `ServiceRole` is used to define a group of permissions to access services, while `ServiceRoleBinding` grants `ServiceRole` to a user, group, or service.

The rules that are defined through `ServiceRole` have three fields: services, methods, and paths. The services define a list of services that the rules have been defined for. The methods are a list of HTTP method names. The paths are HTTP paths. Let's take a look:

1. The following `ServiceRole` defines all of the services (*) that the viewer has access to (GET) on all services where the `app` label is set to `productpage`, `details`, `ratings`, or `reviews`:

   ```
   # Script : 10-create-service-role.yaml

   apiVersion: "rbac.istio.io/v1alpha1"
   kind: ServiceRole
   metadata:
     name: service-viewer
   spec:
     rules:
     - services: ["*"]
       methods: ["GET"]
       constraints:
       - key: "destination.labels[app]"
         values: ["productpage", "details", "reviews", "ratings"]
   ```

2. Create the `ServiceRole` definition to GET access to the `bookinfo` services so that they're available to all services:

   ```
   $ kubectl -n istio-lab apply -f 10-create-service-role.yaml
   servicerole.rbac.istio.io/service-viewer created
   ```

   Now that the preceding rules (permissions) have been defined, they need to be granted to either user, group, or services.

3. Define `ServiceRoleBinding`:

```
# Script : 11-create-service-role-binding.yaml

apiVersion: "rbac.istio.io/v1alpha1"
kind: ServiceRoleBinding
metadata:
 name: bind-service-viewer
spec:
 subjects:
 - properties:
 source.namespace: "istio-system"
 - properties:
 source.namespace: "istio-lab"
 roleRef:
 kind: ServiceRole
 name: "service-viewer"
```

4. Create `ServiceRoleBinding` that grants `service-viewer ServiceRole` to all of the services in the `istio-system` and `istio-lab` namespaces:

```
$ kubectl -n istio-lab apply -f 11-create-service-role-binding.yaml
servicerolebinding.rbac.istio.io/bind-service-viewer created
```

Run `https://bookinfo.istio.io`. You should be able to see the page. Wait a few seconds for the rule to propagate.

If you try to log in as any user, you will receive an *RBAC: Access denied* error. This is due to the fact that we granted GET (read-only) permission to all of the services to access all of the services in the `istio-system` and `istio-lab` namespaces, but we did not grant any permission for any logged-in user.

Service-level authorization at the individual level

So far, we've looked at an example of namespace-level abstraction for granting authorizations. Now, let's provide granular access control to define authorizations at the individual service level. Refer to the following diagram for implementing authorizations through service accounts:

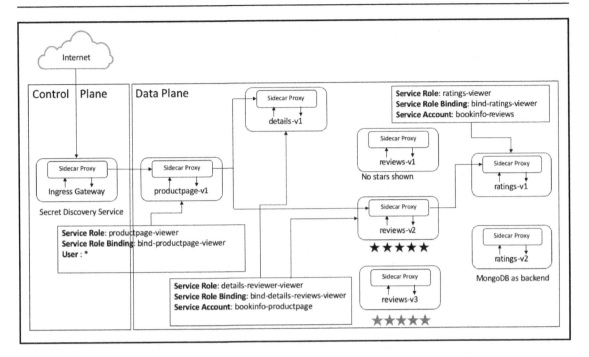

As shown in the preceding diagram, the granular access control on each microservice is as follows:

- Define a service role for the **productpage** service for the GET permission only. For example, the **productpage** service is available for GET, but only for the users connecting through the ingress gateway. Grant the service role (permissions) to the **productpage** service.

- Create a service role for details and the reviews services for GET permissions. Grant the service role to the service account **bookinfo-productpage** of the **productpage** microservice. The **productpage** service can have GET access to details and reviews services. Note that **productpage** does not have access to the ratings service.

- Create a service role for the ratings service for the GET permission. Grant a service role to the **bookinfo-reviews** service account of the reviews service. This allows the reviews service to access the ratings service. Note that the **productpage** service has no need to access the ratings service. This eliminates a security breach that might occur if a hacker gets access to the **productpage** service.

1. First, let's delete `ServiceRole` and `ServiceRoleBinding` that we created in the previous section:

    ```
    $ kubectl -n istio-lab delete -f 11-create-service-role-
    binding.yaml
    servicerolebinding.rbac.istio.io "bind-service-viewer" deleted

    $ kubectl -n istio-lab delete -f 10-create-service-role.yaml
    servicerole.rbac.istio.io "service-viewer" deleted
    ```

2. Define `ServiceRole` to create an access rule for the GET method for the `productpage` service:

    ```
    # Script : 12-create-service-role-productpage.yaml

    apiVersion: "rbac.istio.io/v1alpha1"
    kind: ServiceRole
    metadata:
      name: productpage-viewer
    spec:
      rules:
      - services: [productpage.istio-lab.svc.cluster.local]
        methods: ["GET"]
    ```

3. Create `ServiceRole` for external GET access:

    ```
    $ kubectl -n istio-lab apply -f 12-create-service-role-
    productpage.yaml
    servicerole.rbac.istio.io/productpage-viewer created
    ```

4. Define `ServiceRoleBinding` that allows access to all users through `ServiceRole` `productpage-viewer` authorization:

    ```
    # Script : 13-create-service-role-binding-productpage.yaml

    apiVersion: "rbac.istio.io/v1alpha1"
    kind: ServiceRoleBinding
    metadata:
      name: bind-productpage-viewer
    spec:
      subjects:
      - user: "*"
      roleRef:
        kind: ServiceRole
        name: "productpage-viewer"
    ```

5. Create `ServiceRoleBinding` using `productpage_viewer` for all users:

    $ kubectl -n istio-lab apply -f 13-create-service-role-binding-productpage.yaml
    servicerolebinding.rbac.istio.io/bind-productpage-viewer created

Browse to `https://bookinfo.istio.io/productpage` without logging in as a user. You will notice that the page loads since we granted `GET` access to all of the users on our `productpage` edge service. The other internal microservices fail with `Error fetching product details!` and `Error fetching product reviews!` messages. These errors are fine since we have not granted access from the `productpage` to the `details` and `reviews` services.

6. To grant such access, define `ServiceRole` rules for `details` and `reviews`:

    # Script : 14-create-service-role-details-reviews.yaml

    ```
    apiVersion: "rbac.istio.io/v1alpha1"
    kind: ServiceRole
    metadata:
      name: details-reviews-viewer
    spec:
      rules:
      - services: ["details.istio-
    lab.svc.cluster.local","reviews.istio-lab.svc.cluster.local"]
        methods: ["GET"]
    ```

7. Create `ServiceRole`:

    $ kubectl -n istio-lab apply -f 14-create-service-role-details-reviews.yaml
    servicerole.rbac.istio.io/details-reviews-viewer created

8. The service accounts for each microservice were created at the time we installed the `bookinfo` application:

    ```
    $ kubectl -n istio-lab get sa
    NAME                   SECRETS   AGE
    bookinfo-details       1         100m
    bookinfo-productpage   1         22m
    bookinfo-ratings       1         100m
    bookinfo-reviews       1         22m
    default                1         108m
    ```

9. Define `ServiceRoleBinding` by granting the `details-reviews-viewer` service role to the `bookinfo-productpage` service account of the `istio-lab` namespace, which is defined by the user through the syntax of `cluster.local/ns/istio-lab/sa/bookinfo-productpage`:

```
# Script : 16-apply-service-role-binding-details-reviews.yaml

apiVersion: "rbac.istio.io/v1alpha1"
kind: ServiceRoleBinding
metadata:
  name: bind-details-reviews-viewer
spec:
  subjects:
  - user: "cluster.local/ns/istio-lab/sa/bookinfo-productpage"
  - properties:
      source.namespace: "istio-lab"
    roleRef:
      kind: ServiceRole
      name: "details-reviews-viewer"
```

10. Grant `ServiceRoleBinding` to a service account of `productpage`:

```
$ kubectl -n istio-lab apply -f 16-apply-service-role-binding-details-reviews.yaml
servicerolebinding.rbac.istio.io/bind-details-reviews-viewer
created
```

Wait a few seconds for the rules to propagate. Point your browser to `https://bookinfo.istio.io/productpage`. You should see the **Book Details** and **Book Reviews** sections being populated. The ratings service shows a currently unavailable message, which is natural since we have not defined the access control for the ratings service.

11. The Fix Ratings service is currently unavailable. We can make it available by creating a service role for the `ratings` service using `GET`:

```
# Script : 17-create-service-role-ratings.yaml

apiVersion: "rbac.istio.io/v1alpha1"
kind: ServiceRole
metadata:
  name: ratings-viewer
spec:
  rules:
  - services: ["ratings.istio-lab.svc.cluster.local"]
    methods: ["GET"]
```

12. Create `ServiceRole ratings-viewer`:

```
$ kubectl -n istio-lab apply -f 17-create-service-role-ratings.yaml
servicerole.rbac.istio.io/ratings-viewer created
```

13. Define `ServiceRoleBinding` to grant the `ratings-viewer` service role to the `bookinfo-reviews` service account:

```
# Script : 18-create-service-role-binding-ratings.yaml

apiVersion: "rbac.istio.io/v1alpha1"
kind: ServiceRoleBinding
metadata:
  name: bind-ratings-viewer
spec:
  subjects:
  - user: "cluster.local/ns/istio-lab/sa/bookinfo-reviews"
  roleRef:
    kind: ServiceRole
    name: "ratings-viewer"
```

14. Create `ServiceRoleBinding bind-ratings-viewer`:

```
$ kubectl -n istio-lab apply -f 18-create-service-role-binding-
ratings.yaml
servicerolebinding.rbac.istio.io/bind-ratings-viewer created
```

Refresh your web page. You will see the `ratings` service working and showing black stars. Note that it may take a few seconds for the authorizations to propagate.

 Use the `istioctl auth validate` command to check whether a service role or service role bindings are valid or not, as in the example:

```
istioctl experimental auth validate -f 17-create-service-
role-ratings.yaml,18-create-service-role-binding-
ratings.yaml
```

To protect databases from unauthorized access, we need to implement service-level authorization for databases.

Service-level authorization for databases

To protect TCP connection-based services such as databases, only a legitimate service should be able to connect.

In this section, we will create a new `ratings-v2` version and connect it to a MongoDB database service. Our aim is for only the `ratings-v2` service to be able to access the MongoDB database:

1. Review `19-create-sa-ratings-v2.yaml`. Notice the `bookinfo-ratings-v2` service account, which we will use to create a `ratings-v2` deployment that will use MongoDB:

```
# Script : 19-create-sa-ratings-v2.yaml

apiVersion: v1
kind: ServiceAccount
metadata:
  name: bookinfo-ratings-v2
---
apiVersion: extensions/v1beta1
kind: Deployment
metadata:
  name: ratings-v2
...
        version: v2
    spec:
      serviceAccountName: bookinfo-ratings-v2
      containers:
      - name: ratings
        image: istio/examples-bookinfo-ratings-v2:1.10.0
        imagePullPolicy: IfNotPresent
        env:
          # ratings-v2 will use mongodb as the default db backend.
          - name: MONGO_DB_URL
            value: mongodb://mongodb:27017/test
        ports:
        - containerPort: 9080
...
```

2. Create a service account called `bookinfo-ratings-v2` and a `ratings-v2` deployment:

```
$ kubectl -n istio-lab apply -f 19-create-sa-ratings-v2.yaml
serviceaccount/bookinfo-ratings-v2 created
deployment.extensions/ratings-v2 created
```

3. Next, we need to define a destination rule for the `ratings` service so that we can use v2. We created the destination rule while enabling mTLS for services. Verify it using the following command:

```
$  kubectl -n istio-lab get dr ratings -o yaml | grep -A6 subsets:
---
  subsets:
  - labels:
      version: v1
    name: v1
  - labels:
      version: v2
    name: v2
```

4. The `ratings` virtual service is tagged to subset v1. Let's check this:

```
$ kubectl -n istio-lab get vs ratings -o yaml | grep -B1 subset:
host: ratings
subset: v1
```

5. To route traffic to version v2 of the ratings service, we will update (patch) the existing `ratings` virtual service so that it uses subset v2 of the `ratings` service:

```
$ kubectl -n istio-lab patch vs ratings --type json -p
'[{"op":"replace","path":"/spec/http/0/route/0/destination/subset",
"value": "v2"}]'
virtualservice.networking.istio.io/ratings patched
```

6. Confirm this was set properly. With this, the `ratings` service will direct its traffic to the `ratings-v2` microservice:

```
$ kubectl -n istio-lab get vs ratings -o yaml | grep -B1 subset:
host: ratings
subset: v2
```

7. The `ratings-v2` microservice calls MongoDB. Define `mongodb service` and deploy it for MongoDB:

```
# Script : 20-deploy-mongodb-service.yaml

apiVersion: v1
kind: Service
metadata:
  name: mongodb
  labels:
    app: mongodb
spec:
  ports:
  - port: 27017
    name: mongo
  selector:
    app: mongodb
...
```

8. The following is the deployment definition for MongoDB:

```
apiVersion: extensions/v1beta1
kind: Deployment
metadata:
  name: mongodb-v1
spec:
  replicas: 1
  template:
    metadata:
      labels:
        app: mongodb
        version: v1
    spec:
      containers:
      - name: mongodb
        image: istio/examples-bookinfo-mongodb:1.10.1
        imagePullPolicy: IfNotPresent
        ports:
        - containerPort: 27017
...
```

9. Create a `mongodb` service and a `mongodb-v1` deployment:

```
$ kubectl -n istio-lab apply -f 20-deploy-mongodb-service.yaml
service/mongodb created
deployment.extensions/mongodb-v1 created
```

10. Wait for the `mongodb` pods to be ready and check them:

```
$ kubectl -n istio-lab get pods -l app=mongodb
NAME                          READY   STATUS    RESTARTS   AGE
mongodb-v1-787688669c-1qcbq   2/2     Running   0          45s
```

Run `https://bookinfo.istio.io/productpage`. Note that the `Ratings` `service` is currently unavailable. This is expected since we pointed the `ratings` virtual service to v2, which we haven't defined `ServiceRole` (permission) and `ServiceRoleBinding` (grant) for yet.

11. Define `ServiceRole` for MongoDB:

```
# Script : 21-create-service-role-mongodb.yaml

apiVersion: "rbac.istio.io/v1alpha1"
kind: ServiceRole
metadata:
  name: mongodb-viewer
spec:
  rules:
  - services: ["mongodb.istio-lab.svc.cluster.local"]
    constraints:
    - key: "destination.port"
      values: ["27017"]
```

Note that the permission is created through the `ServiceRole` primitive, which is for the `mongodb` service so that it allows a connection to port `27017`. This is an example of a firewall rule being defined at the service level.

12. Create `ServiceRole` for MongoDB:

```
$ kubectl -n istio-lab apply -f 21-create-service-role-mongodb.yaml
servicerole.rbac.istio.io/mongodb-viewer created
```

13. Define `ServiceRoleBinding` to authorize the `bookinfo-ratings-v2` service account so that it can use the rule (permission) we defined through `ServiceRole mongodb-viewer`:

```
# Script : 22-create-service-role-binding-mongodb.yaml

apiVersion: "rbac.istio.io/v1alpha1"
kind: ServiceRoleBinding
metadata:
  name: bind-mongodb-viewer
spec:
```

```
subjects:
- user: "cluster.local/ns/istio-lab/sa/bookinfo-ratings-v2"
roleRef:
kind: ServiceRole
name: "mongodb-viewer"
```

14. Create `ServiceRoleBinding bind-mongodb-viewer`:

```
$ kubectl -n istio-lab apply -f 22-create-service-role-binding-
mongodb.yaml
servicerolebinding.rbac.istio.io/bind-mongodb-viewer created
```

Wait for a few seconds and refresh `https://bookinfo.istio.io`. The `rating` service should be available now. Unfortunately, it isn't, and the `ratings` service is still showing up as currently unavailable. Let's debug this.

First, let's check whether we have any conflicts in our destination rules between the `ratings` pod and the `mongodb` service:

1. Find out the `ratings v2` pod name:

```
$ export RATINGS_POD=$(kubectl -n istio-lab get pods -l app=ratings
-o jsonpath='{.items[0].metadata.name}') ; echo $RATINGS_POD
ratings-v1-79b6d99979-k2j7t
```

2. Check for mTLS conflicts between the `ratings-v2` pod and the `mongodb` service. You may either see a `CONFLICT` status or an output stating `Error: Nothing to output`:

```
$ istioctl authn tls-check $RATINGS_POD.istio-lab mongodb.istio-
lab.svc.cluster.local
HOST:PORT                                          STATUS     SERVER ---
mongodb.istio-lab.svc.cluster.local:27017          CONFLICT   mTLS   ---

--- CLIENT    AUTHN POLICY         DESTINATION RULE
--- HTTP      default/istio-lab    mongodb/istio-lab

OR

Error: nothing to output
```

Notice that there is a conflict between the `ratings-v2` pod and the `mongodb` service. This is due to the fact that we didn't create a destination rule for the `mongodb` mTLS traffic, which will enforce mutual TLS for the client (`ratings:v2`).

3. Define `DestinationRule` for the MongoDB service:

```
# Script : 23-create-mongodb-destination-rule.yaml

apiVersion: networking.istio.io/v1alpha3
kind: DestinationRule
metadata:
  name: mongodb
spec:
  host: mongodb.istio-lab.svc.cluster.local
  trafficPolicy:
    tls:
      mode: ISTIO_MUTUAL
```

4. Create `DestinationRule` and wait for a few seconds for the rule to propagate:

```
$ kubectl -n istio-lab apply -f 23-create-mongodb-destination-
rule.yaml
destinationrule.networking.istio.io/mongodb created
```

5. Check for any mTLS conflicts:

```
$ istioctl authn tls-check $RATINGS_POD.istio-lab mongodb.istio-
lab.svc.cluster.local
HOST:PORT                                      STATUS SERVER CLIENT ---
mongodb.istio-lab.svc.cluster.local:27017  OK     mTLS   mTLS   ---

--- AUTHN POLICY          DESTINATION RULE
--- default/istio-lab     mongodb/istio-lab
```

If the status shows OK, try refreshing `https://bookinfo.istio.io/productpage`. The `rating` service should work now.

Let's do one more simple test to change `ratings` in the MongoDB database:

1. Run the following command to change `ratings` from 5 to 1 and 4 to 3, respectively:

```
$ export MONGO_POD=$(kubectl -n istio-lab get pod -l app=mongodb -o
jsonpath='{.items..metadata.name}') ; echo $MONGO_POD
mongodb-v1-787688669c-1qcbq

$ cat << EOF | kubectl -n istio-lab exec -i -c mongodb $MONGO_POD -
- mongo
use test
db.ratings.find().pretty()
db.ratings.update({"rating": 5},{\$set:{"rating":1}})
db.ratings.update({"rating": 4},{\$set:{"rating":3}})
db.ratings.find().pretty()
exit
EOF

MongoDB shell version v4.0.6
connecting to: mongodb://127.0.0.1:27017/?gssapiServiceName=mongodb
Implicit session: session { "id" : UUID("22ba0a3d-d2d4-480e-
bac5-359d74912beb") }
MongoDB server version: 4.0.6
switched to db test
{ "_id" : ObjectId("5d42d77d07ec5966640aea1b"), "rating" : 4 }
{ "_id" : ObjectId("5d42d77d07ec5966640aea1c"), "rating" : 5 }
WriteResult({ "nMatched" : 1, "nUpserted" : 0, "nModified" : 1 })
WriteResult({ "nMatched" : 1, "nUpserted" : 0, "nModified" : 1 })
{ "_id" : ObjectId("5d42d77d07ec5966640aea1b"), "rating" : 3 }
{ "_id" : ObjectId("5d42d77d07ec5966640aea1c"), "rating" : 1 }
bye
```

Refresh the page to see the ratings change from 4 to 3 and 5 to 1.

We need to create `ServiceRole` and `ServiceRoleBinding` for the `httpbin` service so that we can use the same service in later chapters.

2. Run the `24-create-service-role-binding-httpbin.yaml` script:

```
$ kubectl -n istio-lab apply -f 24-create-service-role-binding-
httpbin.yaml
servicerole.rbac.istio.io/httpbin created
servicerolebinding.rbac.istio.io/bind-httpbin created
```

3. Delete role-based access control for the next chapter and patch the `ratings` service so that it goes back to `v1`:

```
$ kubectl -n istio-lab delete -f 09-create-clusterrbac-config.yaml

$ kubectl -n istio-lab patch vs ratings --type json -p
'[{"op":"replace","path":"/spec/http/0/route/0/destination/subset",
"value": "v1"}]'
```

This concludes security implementation in Istio. Istio is dynamic, and new security capabilities are being continuously added to allow integration with various services. We haven't covered all of the advanced capabilities here. Next, we'll mention some of these advanced capabilities. It's recommended that you read up on these to find out more.

Advanced capabilities

Some of the advanced topics of Istio authentication and authorization are beyond the scope of this book. The following is a brief description of a few important ones:

- Istio authorization allows us to work with **JSON Web Tokens (JWTs)** and open source OpenID connect providers such as Google Auth, Auth0, and ORY Hydra. Refer to `https://archive.istio.io/v1.3/docs/concepts/security/` for how to apply authentication policies for JWT and OpenID.
- Istio can integrate with Hashicorp's Vault CA to secure, store, and tightly control access to tokens, passwords, certificates, encryption keys for protecting secrets, and other sensitive data.
- Istio multi-cluster installation, control plane replication, and creating shared control planes using single or multi-networks are not explored in this book. Refer to `https://archive.istio.io/v1.3/docs/setup/install/multicluster/` for more information.

This concludes Istio's security authentication and authorization capabilities, all of which can be implemented in an existing microservices-based application without having to modify or write a single line of application code. This capability gives Operations (SRE team) the ability to manage changes in realtime without having to approach developers.

Summary

Security sometimes creates **Fear, Uncertainty, and Doubt** (FUD), and many times, it results in unnecessary controls that hamper productivity. Sadly, breaches do still occur. Major corporations have a chief information security officer, but often, the focus is on putting locks and controls in the wrong places and not knowing which backdoors are wide open. Security breaches can harm the reputation of a company and can cause huge financial damage. A recent example is a fine of $148 million that was imposed on a ride-sharing company, which failed to report the security breach to the Federal Trade Commission. The hackers, in this case, found AWS credentials in their GitHub repository and stole the data of millions of people from an AWS S3 bucket.

The security in Istio is enterprise-grade. You must have noticed the granular nature of security at the namespace level. You have also used a service account to implement authorizations as if security was built through coding at the service level. The good news is that security through Istio can be implemented without having to change any coding. This task is now in the domain of Operations staff when using a service mesh architecture. The backend service contains sensitive data and can be locked down to the frontend service, which has legitimate access needs, and block access to all other services. The short-lived certificates that are used in mutual TLS and their automatic renewal through Citadel provides us with a high-security layer. If access to the AWS S3 bucket is only limited to the microservice that has a legitimate need, security breaches can be avoided.

In the next chapter, we will go through policy enforcement to implement quotes and rate limits, build white/blacklists, and perform routing using policy adapters though modifying request headers. It will be interesting to note that policy enforcement is also configuration-driven and can be done without the need to modify any application source code.

Questions

1. Istio will not rotate certificates and keys that have been defined for the services through an Ingress gateway to secure traffic from external clients to the edge microservice.
   A) True
   B) False

2. There can only be one MeshPolicy with name as default that will apply mTLS mesh-wide.
   A) True
   B) False

3. Mutual TLS can be as granular as possible from the namespace level to the service level by defining a policy.
   A) True
   B) False

4. Mutual TLS can also be defined through destination rules for the subsets, which can be used to define virtual services.
   A) True
   B) False

5. Istio is capable of shielding modern microservices applications so that they can run in a zero-trust network without the need to make any changes to the application code.
   A) True
   B) False

6. Istio makes VPN and firewalls redundant if security is implemented properly.
   A) True
   B) False

7. It is the responsibility of the edge microservice to manage JWT for authorizations. Istio does not have native automation support yet.
   A) True
   B) False

8. Istio's Secret Discovery Service mounts secrets in pods automatically.
   A) True
   B) False

9. Istio's Citadel will rotate certificates and keys by default every 90 days. However, this can be changed by editing Citadel's `workload-cert-ttl` to `1h` deployment argument in a zero-trust network. This change can be done without restarting Citadel.
   A) True
   B) False

10. The Envoy sidecar checks the TTL of the certificates. The Istio node agent, if enabled, can request a new certificate for Citadel. It is Citadel that pushes the certificates to Envoy, not the node agent.
    A) True
    B) False

Further reading

- *Securing Gateways with HTTPS Using Secret Discovery Service,* Istio (2019), available at `https://archive.istio.io/v1.3/docs/tasks/traffic-management/ingress/secure-ingress-sds/`, accessed 16 May 2019
- *Everything you should know about certificates and PKI but are too afraid to ask,* Malone, M. (2019), Smallstep, available at `https://smallstep.com/blog/everything-pki.html#intermediates-chains-and-bundling`, accessed 18 May 2019

Enabling Istio Policy Controls

In a traditional environment, a centralized proxy receives all traffic, and that traffic is routed to the services that do the actual work. As workloads grow, scalability issues can arise. However, Istio solves this and other similar problems with the use of a lean and thin proxy, which we will learn about in this chapter. We will discuss in detail the enablement of policies related to rate limits, service denials, and the enforcement of quotas without having to change any application source code.

By the end of this chapter, you will learn how to enable network-based policies for resource quotas and quota limits, as well as learning about how quota rules are assigned to a demo microservice. Besides this, we will set up a white/blacklist of services (based on IP) within the demo application for service denials.

In a nutshell, we will cover the following topics in this chapter:

- An introduction to rate limits
- Enabling rate limits
- Controlling access to a service

Technical requirements

This chapter's scripts have dependencies from the previous chapter. Make sure that you complete the exercises in `Chapter 11`, *Exploring Istio Security Features*, before starting here.

Let's change the directory for scripts that we will be using in this chapter:

```
$ cd ~/istio
$ cd scripts/03-policies
```

Make sure that all istio-lab pods show a Ready 2/2 state:

```
$ kubectl -n istio-lab get pods
```

Once that's done, we're ready to begin!

Introduction to policy controls

To tackle scalability issues, Istio uses a proxy that runs alongside any service, and this model fits well within a distributed environment. The distributed proxy (sidecar) caches the first level of information for the services, hence making distributed scaling easier. Each proxy calls a central control plane service (Mixer) to make precondition checks that contain the second layer of shared cache before and after every request.

Most of these operations can be performed from the local cache of proxy and hence considerably reduce the number of calls to Mixer. Each of the precondition check requests is synchronous and performed from the local cache. The sidecar buffers telemetry information and sends it asynchronously to Mixer, which can then send it to the backend services through the use of adapters. Hence, we can say that Mixer is a component for providing policy controls and telemetry collection.

Before we carry out any hands-on experiments and enable policy controls, let's first check whether the current Istio environment is enabled for policy controls or not. Run the following command:

```
$ kubectl -n istio-system get cm istio -o jsonpath="{@.data.mesh}" | grep
disablePolicyChecks
disablePolicyChecks: false
```

If disablePolicyCheck is true, the policy controls can be enabled. If disablePolicyChecks is set to true, you may need to edit ConfigMap istio using kubectl -n istio-system edit cm istio and modify the value of disablePolicyChecks from true to false in the data section and save the config map.

Now that we've enabled policy control in our Istio, we will now see the procedure of implementing rate limits. Notice that there is no need to change the application code.

Enabling rate limits

Through Mixer, we can rate limit a service dynamically. If you are providing software as a service through a REST API for some business function, rate limits can be handy to prevent abuse of the system by users. Rules can be set to identify a user, count the number of requests, and reject requests after a limit. Rate limits allow a fair share of the system for the users.

In this example, we configure rate-limit traffic to `productpage` originating from the local IP address to showcase this feature. We use the `x-forwarded-for` request header as the client IP address and use a conditional rate limit that exempts logged-in users.

We can accomplish rate limit enforcement through the following scheme:

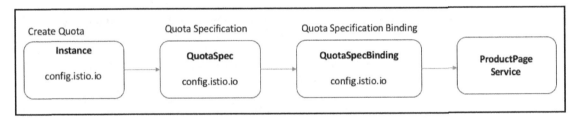

It creates a quota, then defines the quota specification and quota specification binding. Finally, the quota specification is bound to the `productpage` microservice.

Defining quota and assigning to services

Define an instance of quota with the name `requestcountquota` using a template, `quota`. The source for enabling this quota will be applicable for IP address defined in `x-forwarded-for`. The `destination` dimension is for microservices that have `apps` labels or the service's name.

The `label` version assigned to the microservice determines the destination version:

1. The definition of the request quota count is as follows:

   # Script : 01-create-quota-instance.yaml

   ```
   apiVersion: config.istio.io/v1alpha2
   kind: instance
   metadata:
     name: requestcountquota
   spec:
     compiledTemplate: quota
     params:
       dimensions:
         source: request.headers["x-forwarded-for"] | "unknown"
         destination: destination.labels["app"] |
   destination.service.name | "unknown"
         destinationVersion: destination.labels["version"] | "unknown"
   ```

2. Create a quota:

   $ kubectl -n istio-system apply -f 01-create-quota-instance.yaml
   ```
   instance.config.istio.io/requestcountquota created
   ```

3. Once we create an instance of quota, associate this with a quota specification. Define `QuotaSpec` for the quota instance, `requestcountquota`:

   # Script : 02-create-quotaspec.yaml

   ```
   apiVersion: config.istio.io/v1alpha2
   kind: QuotaSpec
   metadata:
    name: requestcount
   spec:
    rules:
    - quotas:
    - charge: 1
    quota: requestcountquota
   ```

4. Create `QuotaSpec` `requestcount` for the `requestcountquota` instance:

   $ kubectl -n istio-system apply -f 02-create-quotaspec.yaml
   ```
   quotaspec.config.istio.io/requestcount created
   ```

5. Define QuotaSpecBinding for requestcount to the productpage service:

```
# Script : 03-create-quotaspecbinding.yaml

apiVersion: config.istio.io/v1alpha2
kind: QuotaSpecBinding
metadata:
  name: requestcount
spec:
  quotaSpecs:
  - name: requestcount
    namespace: istio-system
  services:
  - name: productpage
    namespace: istio-lab
```

6. Create QuotaSpecBinding using the requestcount quota specification for the productpage service:

```
$ kubectl -n istio-system apply -f 03-create-quotaspecbinding.yaml
quotaspecbinding.config.istio.io/requestcount created
```

Next is the procedure to define the quota limits, which is essential in modern-day applications to restrict the over-usage of services and set limits to protect the use of resources.

Defining rate limits

Follow these steps to define the rate limits:

1. After we identify and assign a quota instance to a service or a set of services, a handler manages the quota limits:

```
# Script : 04-create-memquota-handler.yaml

apiVersion: config.istio.io/v1alpha2
kind: handler
metadata:
  name: quotahandler
spec:
  compiledAdapter: memquota
  params:
    quotas:
    - name: requestcountquota.instance.istio-system
      maxAmount: 500
      validDuration: 1s
```

```
        overrides:
        - dimensions:
             destination: reviews
          maxAmount: 1
          validDuration: 5s
        - dimensions:
             destination: productpage
          maxAmount: 5
          validDuration: 1s
```

The rate limits (quotas) are processed from top to bottom. The values defined before overrides are default values. The default rate limit is 500 requests in 1 second. The default rate limit comes into effect when there is no match in the requests for the overrides. The requests are matched based upon source and destination service names. The first override is for the destination `reviews` service, regardless of the source, for which a rate limit of one request every five seconds will be applied to the incoming requests. The second override is for the destination `productpage` service, regardless of the source, for which a rate limit of five requests every second is applied to the incoming requests.

2. Create the `memquota` handler that defines the quota limits:

```
$ kubectl -n istio-system apply -f 04-create-memquota-handler.yaml
handler.config.istio.io/quotahandler created
```

Note that we are only discussing the `memquota` handler here for our test environment. In a production environment, an appropriate in-memory grid should be used to set the `memquota` limits. Istio documentation uses the `redisquota` handler.

After a quota has been defined, we have to define the quota rule to use a quota handler.

Defining quota rules

To define a quota rule, follow these steps:

1. Define a quota rule that uses `quotahandler` defined in the previous step and applies the rule only to users who are not logged in to the system:

```
# Script : 05-create-quota-rule.yaml

apiVersion: config.istio.io/v1alpha2
kind: rule
metadata:
  name: quota
```

```
spec:
  # quota only applies if you are not logged in.
  match: match(request.headers["cookie"], "session=*") == false
  actions:
  - handler: quotahandler
    instances:
    - requestcountquota
```

2. Create the rule:

```
$ kubectl -n istio-system apply -f 05-create-quota-rule.yaml
rule.config.istio.io/quota created
```

The rule quota created in the preceding, tells Istio Mixer to invoke the `memquota` handler and pass the quota instance object, `requestcountquota`. This maps the dimensions from the quota template to `memquota`.

Browse to `https://bookinfo.istio.io/productpage` and refresh the page several times and you will receive the message `RESOURCE_EXHAUSTED:Quota is exhausted for requestcountquota` intermittently.

Click **Sign-in** to log in as any user. A session request cookie is set for the logged-in user. Refresh the `https://bookinfo.istio.io/productpage` page several times, and you will not see any quota exhausted messages as the logged-in user is not subjected to the rate limits. In real life, we would use a JWT for authenticated users instead of a session request cookie, since we have logged-in user information.

We will now remove the override for `productpage` to limit five requests per second for the next exercise.

3. Define `quotahandler` by removing the override for `productpage`—compare with the `04-create-memquota-handler.yaml` script:

```
# Script : 06-modify-memquota-handler.yaml

apiVersion: config.istio.io/v1alpha2
kind: handler
metadata:
  name: quotahandler
spec:
  compiledAdapter: memquota
  params:
    quotas:
    - name: requestcountquota.instance.istio-system
      maxAmount: 500
```

```
        validDuration: 1s
        overrides:
        - dimensions:
            destination: reviews
          maxAmount: 1
          validDuration: 5s
```

4. Modify `quotahandler` and remove the second override:

$ kubectl -n istio-system apply -f 06-modify-memquota-handler.yaml
handler.config.istio.io/quotahandler configured

After learning the three-step process of quota implementation (instance definition, `QuotaSpec`, `QuotaSpecBinding`), we will go through the process of controlling access to a service.

Controlling access to a service

We will see how to control access to a service using denials, attribute or IP-based white/blacklisting:

1. Let's test this out first by modifying the reviews virtual service to add a default route to `reviews:v3` for all users except for the user `jason`, who will be directed to `review:v2`:

```
# Script : 07-modify-reviews-virtual-service.yaml

apiVersion: networking.istio.io/v1alpha3
kind: VirtualService
metadata:
  name: reviews
spec:
  hosts:
  - reviews
  http:
  - match:
    - headers:
        end-user:
          exact: jason
    route:
    - destination:
        host: reviews
        subset: v2
  - route:
    - destination:
```

```
host: reviews
subset: v3
```

2. Modify the `reviews` virtual service:

```
$ kubectl -n istio-lab apply -f 07-modify-reviews-virtual-
service.yaml
virtualservice.networking.istio.io/reviews configured
```

If the logged-in user is `jason`, the ratings service will show `reviews:v2`, which will show black stars. If you log out as `jason`, you should see red stars—an indication that the routing rules based upon virtual service subsets are working and `reviews:v3` is being called.

Denying access

Now, we will create a rule to deny access to `reviews:v3`. To do this, follow these steps:

1. Define a `denier` handler that will return status code seven and the message `not allowed`:

```
# Script : 08-create-denier-handler.yaml

apiVersion: "config.istio.io/v1alpha2"
kind: handler
metadata:
  name: denyreviewsv3handler
spec:
  compiledAdapter: denier
  params:
    status:
      code: 7
      message: Not allowed
```

2. Now, create the `denier` handler:

```
$ kubectl -n istio-system apply -f 08-create-denier-handler.yaml
handler.config.istio.io/denyreviewsv3handler created
```

3. Next, review the `checknothing` instance:

```
# Script : 09-create-check-nothing-instance.yaml

apiVersion: "config.istio.io/v1alpha2"
kind: instance
metadata:
  name: denyreviewsv3request
spec:
  compiledTemplate: checknothing
```

4. Create a `checknothing` instance, which is nothing but a bridge between a handler and the rule:

```
$ kubectl -n istio-system apply -f 09-create-check-nothing-
instance.yaml
instance.config.istio.io/denyreviewsv3request created
```

5. Define a deny rule that denies the services where applicable and implement it using a `checknothing` instance (`denyreviewsv3request`) through a deny handler (`denyreviewsv3handler`):

```
# Script : 10-create-denier-rule.yaml

apiVersion: "config.istio.io/v1alpha2"
kind: rule
metadata:
  name: denyreviewsv3
spec:
  match: destination.labels["app"] == "ratings" &&
source.labels["app"]=="reviews" && source.labels["version"] == "v3"
  actions:
  - handler: denyreviewsv3handler
    instances: [ denyreviewsv3request ]
```

In the preceding, pay attention to the match expression—which defines that if the source service is `reviews:v3`, then deny access to the destination, `ratings`.

6. Create the deny rule for source services that match the `app=reviews` label and the destination service labeled as `app=ratings` with a subset set to `v3`:

```
$ kubectl -n istio-system apply -f 10-create-denier-rule.yaml
rule.config.istio.io/denyreviewsv3 created
```

7. Refresh `https://bookinfo.istio.io/productpage`.

Notice the message: `Ratings service is currently not available.` On the contrary, if you log in as the user `jason`, you will continue to see black stars as that is not coming under the denier rule. Note that if you log in as any user other than `jason`, you will encounter `Ratings service is currently not available.`

8. Finally, let's delete the denier rule for the next exercise for creating a white/blacklist:

```
$ kubectl -n istio-system delete -f 10-create-denier-rule.yaml
rule.config.istio.io "denyreviewsv3" deleted

$ kubectl -n istio-system delete -f 09-create-check-nothing-instance.yaml
instance.config.istio.io "denyreviewsv3request" deleted

$ kubectl -n istio-system delete -f 08-create-denier-handler.yaml
handler.config.istio.io "denyreviewsv3handler" deleted
```

After learning about denier rule implementation for all except the logged-in user, `jason`, we will see the process of implementing white/blacklists to enforce deny rules based upon attributes as opposed to matching labels to identify source and destination service names.

Creating attribute-based white/blacklists

The white/blacklist is also a type of denier, but instead of service names, this is based upon any attribute available in the Istio Mixer vocabulary: `https://archive.istio.io/v1.3/docs/reference/config/policy-and-telemetry/attribute-vocabulary/`. This method is conditional denial based on Mixer selectors.

We will build a denier rule based upon the Mixer vocabulary instead of labels.

Make sure that you log out as the `jason` user and refresh `https://bookinfo.istio.io/productpage`, and you should see red stars as we removed the denier rule created in the previous section:

1. First, define a handler using `listchecker`:

```
# Script : 11-create-listchecker-handler.yaml

apiVersion: config.istio.io/v1alpha2
kind: handler
```

```
metadata:
  name: whitelist
spec:
  compiledAdapter: listchecker
  params:
    # providerUrl: ordinarily black and white lists are maintained
    # externally and fetched asynchronously using the providerUrl.
    overrides: ["v1", "v2"]  # overrides provide a static list
    blacklist: false
```

2. Then, create the `listchecker` handler:

```
$ kubectl -n istio-system apply -f 11-create-listchecker-
handler.yaml
handler.config.istio.io/whitelist created
```

3. Now, define an instance of `listentry` that will match the label's version:

```
# Script : 12-create-listentry-instance.yaml

apiVersion: config.istio.io/v1alpha2
kind: instance
metadata:
  name: appversion
spec:
  compiledTemplate: listentry
  params:
    value: source.labels["version"]
```

4. Create a `listentry` instance:

```
$ kubectl -n istio-system apply -f 12-create-listentry-
instance.yaml
instance.config.istio.io/appversion created
```

5. Define a rule using the `whitelist` handler through an instance of `listentry`:

```
# Script : 13-create-whitelist-rule.yaml

apiVersion: config.istio.io/v1alpha2
kind: rule
metadata:
  name: checkversion
spec:
  match: destination.labels["app"] == "ratings"
  actions:
  - handler: whitelist
    instances: [ appversion ]
```

6. Create a `whitelist` rule:

```
$ kubectl -n istio-system apply -f 13-create-whitelist-rule.yaml
rule.config.istio.io/checkversion created
```

Refresh `https://bookinfo.istio.io/productpage`, and you should see `Ratings unavailable without a user login`. This whitelist is equivalent to the denier request that we created in the previous section to reject the requests from `reviews:v3`.

Creating an IP-based white/blacklist

The `source.ip` Mixer attribute can be used to define a list checker of `IP_ADDRESSES`, list IP addresses to block, and then apply the rule to the ingress gateway.

We will now configure Istio to accept or reject requests from a specific IP address or a subnet:

1. The following Istio example is shown for a handler defining `entryType` of `IP_ADDRESSES` for a subnet, `10.57.0.0`:

   ```
   # Script : 14-create-listchecker-handler.yaml

   apiVersion: config.istio.io/v1alpha2
   kind: handler
   metadata:
     name: whitelistip
   spec:
     compiledAdapter: listchecker
     params:
       # providerUrl: ordinarily black and white lists are maintained
       # externally and fetched asynchronously using the providerUrl.
       overrides: ["10.57.0.0/16"]  # overrides provide a static list
       blacklist: false
       entryType: IP_ADDRESSES
   ```

2. Create a handler:

   ```
   $ kubectl -n istio-system apply -f 14-create-listchecker-
   handler.yaml
   handler.config.istio.io/whitelistip created
   ```

3. A `sourceip` instance is created for the Mixer attribute of `source.ip` of the request, and if that is not present, then access is allowed for all:

```
# Script : 15-create-listentry-instance.yaml

apiVersion: config.istio.io/v1alpha2
kind: instance
metadata:
  name: sourceip
spec:
  compiledTemplate: listentry
  params:
    value: source.ip | ip("0.0.0.0")
```

4. Create an instance:

```
$ kubectl -n istio-system apply -f 15-create-listentry-instance.yaml
instance.config.istio.io/sourceip created
```

5. Create a `checkip` rule that will use the `whitelistip` handler to check the source IP for an incoming request at the ingress gateway. If the source IP is not from `10.57.0.0/16`, the request will be denied:

```
# Script : 16-create-whitelist-rule.yaml

apiVersion: config.istio.io/v1alpha2
kind: rule
metadata:
  name: checkip
spec:
  match: source.labels["istio"] == "ingressgateway"
  actions:
  - handler: whitelistip
    instances: [ sourceip ]
```

6. Create a rule:

```
$ kubectl -n istio-system apply -f 16-create-whitelist-rule.yaml
rule.config.istio.io/checkip created
```

Refresh `https://bookinfo.istio.io/productpage`, and you will see the message `PERMISSION_DENIED:whitelistip.istio-system:192.168.230.224 is not whitelisted`. The IP address may be different in your case.

This was an example of creating a whitelist of IP addresses that will be allowed. We have completed this exercise to implement a denial of service. We will delete the rule, instance, and handler for attribute- and IP-based whitelists for the next lab exercise:

```
$ kubectl -n istio-system delete -f 16-create-whitelist-rule.yaml
rule.config.istio.io "checkip" deleted

$ kubectl -n istio-system delete -f 15-create-listentry-instance.yaml
instance.config.istio.io "sourceip" deleted

$ kubectl -n istio-system delete -f 14-create-listchecker-handler.yaml
handler.config.istio.io "whitelistip" deleted

$ kubectl -n istio-system delete -f 13-create-whitelist-rule.yaml
rule.config.istio.io "checkversion" deleted

$ kubectl -n istio-system delete -f 12-create-listentry-instance.yaml
instance.config.istio.io "appversion" deleted

$ kubectl -n istio-system delete -f 11-create-listchecker-handler.yaml
handler.config.istio.io "whitelist" deleted
```

The Istio component of Mixer is used to push down policies to Envoy. In this section, we learned how to enforce rules through Envoy at runtime to dynamically apply rate limits to incoming traffic and to apply service denial rules.

Press *Ctrl + Shift + Del* and clear the browser cache so that it does not interfere with the next exercises.

Summary

In this chapter, you have seen that a thin proxy is helpful to scale microservices. A proxy caches requests to avoid multiple trips to the control plane, and it sends asynchronous requests to Istio's Mixer, which can communicate to the backend services.

We've shown scenarios using the `Bookinfo` microservice where policy controls can be enabled in Istio through a simple edit to its config map. You can enable rate limits to prevent rogue users from abusing the system. This process defines rules where we identify a user, count their requests, and reject the requests after a rate limit. Finally, if there is a rogue user, control access to enable service denial can be configured through an IP-based whitelist or blacklist. This process defines a deny rule for services where we can deny access through instances and denier handlers.

In the next chapter, we will cover Istio telemetry and the visualization of metrics collected by Istio through Prometheus, Grafana, and Kiali.

Questions

1. Quota assignment to services is enforced through Pilot.

   A) True
   B) False

2. Rate limits to services are pushed down to the Envoy proxy through Mixer.

   A) True
   B) False

3. A list checker handler is assigned a list of source IPs to create a list. A source IP instance list entry is created to check against the IP address found at the ingress gateway. The rule can be created to enforce a blacklist or whitelist of the IP addresses that can connect to the service.

   A) True
   B) False

4. To enable policy enforcement, you could edit the Istio config map to set `disablePolicyChecks=true`.

   A) True
   B) False

Further reading

- Policies, Istio, 2019, `https://archive.istio.io/v1.3/docs/tasks/policy-enforcement/`
- *Policy Enforcement in Service Mesh – Istio/Envoy*, Iturria, Carlos Rodriguez, Redthunder, Blog, 2019, `https://redthunder.blog/2018/07/30/policy-enforcement-in-service-mesh-istio-envoy/`

13
Exploring Istio Telemetry Features

Distributed microservices-based applications have many advantages and disadvantages, as we discussed in Chapter 1, *Monoliths Versus Microservices*. It is very difficult to test, debug, and monitor microservice applications without the proper tools. Istio makes these tasks much easier by providing proper utilities to visualize metrics, logs, traces, runtime component dependencies, traffic flow, and so on from a central place.

In this chapter, we will cover the telemetry and observability features that are available in Istio. We will enable these features for a demo application through Istio's metrics collectors and visualization tools, that is, *Prometheus*, *Grafana*, and *Kiali*.

In a nutshell, we will cover the following topics:

- Built-in metrics collection
- Distributed tracing
- Exploring Prometheus
- Visualization and observability

Technical requirements

This chapter is dependent on the previous chapter. If you haven't already done so, complete the exercises in Chapter 12, *Enabling Istio's Policy Controls*.

Let's change the directory for the scripts that we will be using in this chapter:

```
$ cd ~/istio
$ cd scripts/04-telemetry
```

Make sure that all `istio-lab` pods show `Ready state 2/2`:

```
$ kubectl -n istio-lab get pods
```

Once done, we're ready to begin!

Telemetry and observability

The promise of observability in a complex distributed environment is much more important to the Site Reliability Engineering team or IT Operations. Without the use of proper tools, it can be tough to maintain such a system for the long term, especially when we are using an *abstraction layer* such as Istio on top of the application.

Traditionally, monitoring stacks, such as events, stack traces, log4j, ELK, Fluentd, Splunk, and so on for collecting metrics, incrementing counters, preparing histograms, and so on need to be embedded or instrumented in the application code. Some frameworks provide integration with the metrics system. This issue becomes complicated when *polyglot* applications are used and different sets of APIs need to be used to instrument and collect metrics.

In Istio, sidecar proxies have full control over the network traffic, and they automatically send telemetry data asynchronously to the Mixer, which can then send it to the backend services for storage. The Istio-enabled applications can be traced, metered, and monitored without additional code.

The focus of this chapter is on *telemetry, monitoring,* and *observability*. There are differences between a system that provides monitoring capabilities versus a system that includes observability. The Istio community is striving to put more emphasis on observability features in addition to collecting events, metrics, and logs, which are essential to get to the root of a problem.

The role of standard telemetry is vital in *microservices*. *Prometheus* is a monitoring and alerting toolkit that was initially developed at https://SoundCloud.com and made open source at https://prometheus.io. *Prometheus* is a graduated project from https://cncf.io, and it has become a de facto standard for telemetry. We will learn how the pull model of *Prometheus* works and the different dashboards for *Grafana* that have been built by Istio for monitoring purposes.

From an observability standpoint, we will see how *Kiali* can show the real-time flow of the traffic on an entire service mesh through visualization with a focus on active services in a mesh. We are also going to see how metrics are collected for HTTP and **Transmission Control Protocol (TCP)** packets are sent to the backend.

It is not necessary to access the web UIs for monitoring tools of Istio from outside the Kubernetes cluster. We will provide examples of accessing the web UIs of *Grafana*, *Prometheus*, *Kiali*, and *Jaeger* through an Ingress gateway using a domain name.

Configuring UI access

Configuring web UI access to *Grafana*, *Prometheus*, *Kiali*, and *Jaeger* can be done in various ways, as follows:

- Using `port-forward` while using the `kubectl` command for the pod's port number.
- Configuring a node port and accessing the UI through `hostIP:NodePort` and by configuring an Istio virtual service.
- Using the `istioctl` dashboard command to open the Web UI.

The first two approaches are well documented and refer to the Kubernetes documentation. In this section, we will show Istio's approach to defining a virtual service to access the UI. In a real-world situation, you would use a DNS server to resolve the names, but, in our case, we are going to use the `/etc/hosts` file to resolve the names. Let's get started:

1. Edit the `/etc/hosts` file and add entries for the following additional hosts:

```
$ cat /etc/hosts
127.0.0.1 localhost localhost.localdomain localhost4
localhost4.localdomain4
192.168.142.101 osc01.servicemesh.local osc01
192.168.142.249 bookinfo.istio.io bookinfo
192.168.142.249 httpbin.istio.io httpbin
192.168.142.249 grafana.istio.io grafana
192.168.142.249 prometheus.istio.io prometheus
192.168.142.249 kiali.istio.io kiali
192.168.142.249 jaeger.istio.io jaeger
```

Here, we've added four additional hosts using the same IP address for *Grafana*, *Prometheus*, *Kiali*, and *Jaeger*.

In an actual example, you will use a domain name that can be resolved through a DNS server, which can point to the IP address of the Ingress gateway. In the preceding code, we are using /etc/hosts to resolve our made-up hostnames to the IP address of our Ingress gateway.

Now, let's create and define some virtual hosts. We will point these to the respective service using a particular port.

2. Check the services and note the port numbers that these web UI services for telemetry are running on:

```
$ kubectl -n istio-system get svc | grep -E
"grafana|prometheus|kiali|jaeger"
grafana              ClusterIP    10.99.238.230     <none>    ---
jaeger-agent         ClusterIP    None              <none>    ---
jaeger-collector     ClusterIP    10.105.138.178    <none>    ---
jaeger-query         ClusterIP    10.104.117.150    <none>    ---
kiali                ClusterIP    10.104.122.142    <none>    ---
prometheus           ClusterIP    10.108.236.193    <none>    ---

---   3000/TCP                                        45h
---   5775/UDP,6831/UDP,6832/UDP                      45h
---   14267/TCP,14268/TCP                             45h
---   16686/TCP                                       45h
---   20001/TCP                                       45h
---   9090/TCP                                        45h
```

We need port numbers for *Grafana*, *Jaeger*, *Kiali*, and *Prometheus*. These will be 3000, 16686, 20001, and 9090, respectively.

3. Define the virtual service for *Grafana*:

```
# Script : 01-create-vs-grafana-jaeger-prometheus.yaml

apiVersion: networking.istio.io/v1alpha3
kind: VirtualService
metadata:
  name: grafana
spec:
  hosts:
  - grafana.istio.io
  gateways:
  - mygateway
  http:
  - match:
    - uri:
        prefix: /
```

```
      route:
    - destination:
        host: grafana.istio-system.svc.cluster.local
        port:
          number: 3000
    ...
```

4. The definition of the virtual services for *Prometheus, Jaeger,* and *Kiali* can be seen in the `01-create-vs-grafana-jaeger-prometheus.yaml` script.

5. Create all the necessary virtual services:

```
$ kubectl -n istio-system apply -f 01-create-vs-grafana-jaeger-
prometheus.yaml
virtualservice.networking.istio.io/grafana created
virtualservice.networking.istio.io/prometheus created
virtualservice.networking.istio.io/jaeger created
virtualservice.networking.istio.io/kiali created
```

6. The virtual service route information is pushed to each sidecar proxy in the mesh. First, let's check the `istioctl` command and then use the sidecar proxy that's internal to the web UI:

```
$ export INGRESS_HOST=$(kubectl -n istio-system get pods -l
app=istio-ingressgateway -o jsonpath='{.items..metadata.name}') ;
echo $INGRESS_HOST
istio-ingressgateway-688d5886d-vsd8k

$ istioctl proxy-config route $INGRESS_HOST.istio-system -o json
...
"name": "prometheus.istio.io:80",
...
"routes": [
    {
  "match": {
            "prefix": "/"
        },
        "route": {
            "cluster": "outbound|9090||prometheus.istio-
system.svc.cluster.local",
    ...
```

7. In the output of the `istioctl` command, scroll up and locate the entry labeled `"name": "prometheus.istio.io:80"`. Check and validate that the route rules for the virtual host labeled `"cluster"` have been pushed to the sidecar proxy.

8. Let's check the same through the sidecar proxy's internal web UI. Note that port `15000` is the management port for the sidecar proxy:

```
$ kubectl -n istio-system port-forward $INGRESS_HOST 15000
```

From inside the VM, open a browser, open `http://localhost:15000`, and click on **config_dump**. Scroll all the way down to view the route information that was pushed to the sidecar proxy.

9. Press *Ctrl* + *C* from the command-line window to stop port forwarding. The same routing rule is pushed to all the sidecars in the `istio-lab` namespace. The following code shows the routing rules from the sidecar of the `ratings` service:

```
$ RATING_POD=$(kubectl -n istio-lab get pods -l app=ratings -o
jsonpath='{.items[0].metadata.name}') ; echo $RATING_POD
ratings-v1-79b6d99979-k2j7t
```

```
$ kubectl -n istio-lab port-forward $RATING_POD 15000
```

Browse to `http://localhost:15000/config_dump` and scroll down to check the pushed routing rule virtual service telemetry.

10. Press *Ctrl* + *C* to stop port forwarding from the command-line window.

The sidecar proxy web UIs are local to the cluster. Configuring external web UI access, as shown here, is appropriate when you need to expose the web UI to users who may not have access to *Kubectl*. If you have access to a Kubernetes cluster through your Windows or Mac machine, you can use the `kubectl port-forward` command and use `localhost:<portNumer>` to access the web UI. *Istioctl* provides a dashboard command that you can use to run the web UI. Let's take a look at two examples.

11. Show the web UI for any control plane pod:

```
$ INGRESS_HOST=$(kubectl -n istio-system get pods -l app=istio-
ingressgateway -o jsonpath='{.items[0].metadata.name}') ; echo
$INGRESS_HOST
istio-ingressgateway-688d5886d-vsd8k
```

```
$ istioctl dashboard controlz $INGRESS_HOST.istio-system
http://localhost:39284
```

12. Now, you can open the web UI using `http://localhost:39284`. Here, you will see the web UI's ControlZ pod:

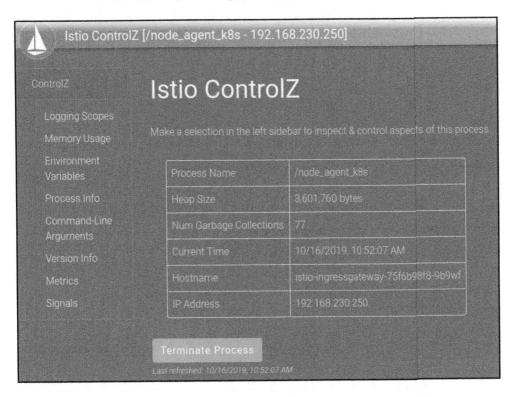

13. Open Envoy's admin dashboard for a *microservice:*

```
$ RATING_POD=$(kubectl -n istio-lab get pods -l app=ratings -o
jsonpath='{.items[0].metadata.name}') ; echo $RATING_POD
ratings-v1-79b6d99979-k2j7t

$ istioctl dashboard envoy $RATING_POD.istio-lab
http://localhost:41010
```

The dashboard looks as follows:

Command	Description
certs	print certs on machine
clusters	upstream cluster status
config_dump	dump current Envoy configs (experimental)
contention	dump current Envoy mutex contention stats (if enabled)
cpuprofiler	enable/disable the CPU profiler
healthcheck/fail	cause the server to fail health checks
healthcheck/ok	cause the server to pass health checks
heapprofiler	enable/disable the heap profiler
help	print out list of admin commands
hot_restart_version	print the hot restart compatibility version
listeners	print listener info
logging	query/change logging levels
memory	print current allocation/heap usage
quitquitquit	exit the server
ready	print server state, return 200 if LIVE, otherwise return 503
reset_counters	reset all counters to zero
runtime	print runtime values
runtime_modify	modify runtime values
server_info	print server version/status information
stats	print server stats
stats/prometheus	print server stats in prometheus format

Dashboard

14. Similarly, you can open a dashboard for *Grafana, Jaeger, Kiali,* and *Prometheus* like so:

```
$ istioctl dashboard grafana

$ istioctl dashboard jaeger

$ istioctl dashboard prometheus

$ istioctl dashboard kiali
```

Now that we've gained web access to the tools, we will look at Prometheus's in-built metrics collection. Istio has been coded with built-in Prometheus APIs to allow for data scrapping from different components.

Collecting built-in metrics

Istio collects a number of metrics automatically by default. Metrics can be added or removed by changing the configuration at any time. Let's take a look:

1. Let's check out `attributemanifest`, which is a list of attributes for Kubernetes and Istio:

    ```
    $ kubectl -n istio-system get attributemanifest
    NAME           AGE
    istioproxy     5d
    kubernetes     5d
    ```

    As we can see, Kubernetes has its own set of `manifest` attributes. Istio also provides a set of `manifest` attributes.

2. Check the attribute list for `istioproxy` and notice the list of predefined matrices:

    ```
    $ kubectl -n istio-system get attributemanifest istioproxy -o yaml
    ...
    spec:
     attributes:
       check.error_code:
    ...
        check.error_code:
    valueType: INT64
    check.error_message:
    valueType: STRING
    connection.duration:
        valueType: DURATION
    ...
    ```

Here, we can see various attributes, such as `errorcode`, `error_message`, and `connection.duration`. These attributes are generated and consumed by different services. Istio uses shared attributes that can be used across various components. For example, the authenticated user information that's generated by a certain function can be used by the Envoy proxy to store that information in the logging backend.

 The preceding attribute vocabulary list for Istio is maintained at `https://archive.istio.io/v1.3/docs/reference/config/policy-and-telemetry/attribute-vocabulary/`.

Next, we will implement a new metrics collection that can be pushed down to Mixer. Then, Mixer pushes those down to the Envoy proxy level.

Collecting new metrics

Istio provides a simple mechanism for collecting metrics for the microservices that we developed without adding any instrumentation to them. In the following example, we will use Mixer's attribute vocabulary to define an instance of Mixer metrics that can be applied to the `bookinfo` microservices to generate metrics. Then, we'll collect them without having to make any code changes to the application. Let's get started:

1. Define the configuration for the metric instance to double the request count:

```
# Script : 02-create-metric-instance.yaml

apiVersion: config.istio.io/v1alpha2
kind: instance
metadata:
  name: doublerequestcount
spec:
  compiledTemplate: metric
  params:
    value: "2" # count each request twice
    dimensions:
      reporter: conditional((context.reporter.kind | "inbound") ==
"outbound", "client", "server")
      source: source.workload.name | "unknown"
      destination: destination.workload.name | "unknown"
      message: '"twice the fun!"'
    monitored_resource_type: '"UNSPECIFIED"'
```

In the preceding example, any request originating from the source attribute (`source.workload.name`) to the destination attribute (`destination.workload.name`) or the context attribute (`context.reporter.kind` can be either outbound, client, or server) will be counted as 2.

2. Create a metric instance:

```
$ kubectl -n istio-system apply -f 02-create-metric-instance.yaml
instance.config.istio.io/doublerequestcount created
```

3. Define the configuration for a Prometheus handler:

```
# Script : 03-create-prometheus-handler.yaml

apiVersion: config.istio.io/v1alpha2
kind: handler
metadata:
  name: doublehandler
spec:
  compiledAdapter: prometheus
  params:
    metrics:
    - name: double_request_count # Prometheus metric name
        instance_name: doublerequestcount.instance.istio-system #
Mixer instance name (fully-qualified)
        kind: COUNTER
        label_names:
        - reporter
        - source
        - destination
        - message
```

4. Create a Prometheus handler using the double request counter we created previously:

```
$ kubectl -n istio-system apply -f 03-create-prometheus-
handler.yaml
handler.config.istio.io/doublehandler create
```

5. Define a rule to send metric data to the Prometheus handler:

```
# Script : 04-create-rule-to-send-metric-to-prometheus.yaml

apiVersion: config.istio.io/v1alpha2
kind: rule
metadata:
  name: doubleprom
spec:
  actions:
  - handler: doublehandler
    instances: [ doublerequestcount ]
```

6. Create the rule:

```
$ kubectl -n istio-system apply -f 04-create-rule-to-send-metric-
to-prometheus.yaml
rule.config.istio.io/doubleprom created
```

7. Let's launch the Prometheus UI. From the browser within the VM, launch `http:/`
   `/prometheus.istio.io`. The GUI should open.
8. Refresh `http://bookinfo.istio.io` in your browser a few times to generate the
   required metrics.
9. Switch to the Prometheus Web UI at `http://prometheus.istio.io`.

In the **Expression** input box at the top of the web page,
enter `istio_double_request_count` and click the **Execute** button.

In the **Console** tab, you will see the entries that were logged after we refreshed
the `productpage`:

```
istio_double_request_count{destination="details-
v1",instance="10.1.230.250:42422",job="istio-mesh",message="twice the
fun!",reporter="client",source="productpage-v1"} 2
istio_double_request_count{destination="details-
v1",instance="10.1.230.250:42422",job="istio-mesh",message="twice the
fun!",reporter="server",source="productpage-v1"} 2
istio_double_request_count{destination="istio-
policy",instance="10.1.230.250:42422",job="istio-mesh",message="twice the
fun!",reporter="server",source="details-v1"} 2
```

The same metric collection logs can be seen through the Prometheus web UI:

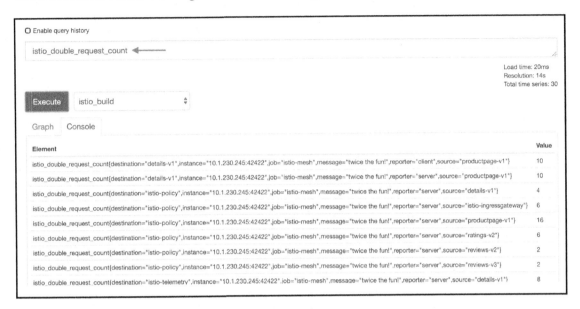

This exercise demonstrates that Istio allows us to add our metrics with the use of *instance*, *handler*, and *rule*. These metrics are scrapped by Prometheus for analysis. We didn't have to add any code to the applications.

Database metrics

We can collect TCP metrics after we run the `MongoDB` database for `ratings:v2`. As we did in the previous section, here, we'll create an *instance, handler,* and a *rule* to collect metrics. Let's get started:

1. Define a configuration for the *sent* and *receive* bytes from a server to a client:

```
# Script : 05-create-metric-instance.yaml

apiVersion: config.istio.io/v1alpha2
kind: instance
metadata:
  name: mongosentbytes
...
  params:
    value: connection.sent.bytes | 0 # uses a TCP-specific
attribute
```

```
      dimensions:
        source_service: source.workload.name | "unknown"
        source_version: source.labels["version"] | "unknown"
        destination_version: destination.labels["version"] |
"unknown"
...
metadata:
  name: mongoreceivedbytes
...
```

2. Create a *handler* for bytes sent and received for the `MongoDb` database service:

```
$ kubectl -n istio-system apply -f 05-create-metric-instance.yaml
instance.config.istio.io/mongosentbytes created
instance.config.istio.io/mongoreceivedbytes created
```

3. Configure a Prometheus *handler* in order to generate `MongoDB` *sent* and *received* byte instances:

```
# Script : 06-create-prometheus-handler.yaml
```

```
apiVersion: config.istio.io/v1alpha2
kind: handler
metadata:
  name: mongohandler
spec:
  compiledAdapter: prometheus
  params:
    metrics:
    - name: mongo_sent_bytes # Prometheus metric name
      # Mixer instance name (fully-qualified)
      instance_name: mongosentbytes.instance.istio-system
      kind: COUNTER
      label_names:
      - source_service
      - source_version
      - destination_version
      # Prometheus metric name
    - name: mongo_received_bytes
      # Mixer instance name (fully-qualified)
      instance_name: mongoreceivedbytes.instance.istio-system
      kind: COUNTER
label_names:
- source_service
- source_version
    - destination_version
```

4. Create a Prometheus *handler*:

```
$ kubectl -n istio-system apply -f 06-create-prometheus-
handler.yaml
handler.config.istio.io/mongohandler created
```

5. Define a rule to send the sent and received metrics instances to the Prometheus handler:

```
# Script : 07-create-rule-to-send-metric-to-prometheus.yaml

apiVersion: config.istio.io/v1alpha2
kind: rule
metadata:
  name: mongoprom
spec:
  match: context.protocol == "tcp"
         && destination.service.host == "mongodb.istio-
lab.svc.cluster.local"
  actions:
    - handler: mongohandler
      instances:
      - mongoreceivedbytes
      - mongosentbytes
```

6. Create a rule:

```
$ kubectl -n istio-system apply -f 07-create-rule-to-send-metric-
to-prometheus.yaml
rule.config.istio.io/mongoprom created
```

7. Switch back to your Prometheus UI (http://prometheus.istio.io), type istio_mongo_received_bytes, and click **Execute**. You will see the value of the received bytes from the MongoDB service:

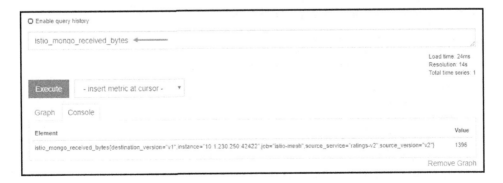

8. Repeat the same for `istio_mongo_sent_bytes`. Note that these metrics collections were defined outside the application through the pushdown configuration of the Istio *instance, handler,* and *rule* primitives.

If a database provides Prometheus-enabled metric collection, it is easier to integrate with Istio using a *Prometheus handler*. This was just an example of TCP metrics that are available through connection metrics.

The purpose of this exercise was to show you that Istio has a built-in mechanism that we can use to collect data using predefined attributes. We can use them to create an instance, allow that instance to be handled through a predefined handler, and generate a rule to execute the handler to generate and collect metrics. This is done at the Mixer level.

Next, we will explore distributed tracing and the different backend adapters that are available.

Distributed tracing

At the heart of distributed tracing are the sidecar proxies, which intercept the network traffic going in and out of each microservice. These sidecar proxies can trace any network request, such as HTTP/1.1, HTTP/2.0, and gRPC.

If the incoming request doesn't have tracing headers, then the sidecar proxy adds a root span before passing the request to the application container in the same pod. Let's look at an example using `curl -s` (`http://httpbin.istio.io/headers`):

 Refer to `https://zipkin.io/zipkin/2.11.3/zipkin/zipkin2/Span.html` for a definition of span.

```
$ curl -s http://httpbin.istio.io/headers
{
  "headers": {
    "Accept": "*/*",
    "Content-Length": "0",
    "Host": "httpbin.istio.io",
    "User-Agent": "curl/7.29.0",
    "X-B3-Parentspanid": "b8679a57978531d7",
    "X-B3-Sampled": "1",
    "X-B3-Spanid": "3ac636cd58f4fc88",
    "X-B3-Traceid": "ec017991cd822f03b8679a57978531d7",
    "X-Envoy-Internal": "true",
```

```
    "X-Forwarded-Client-Cert": "By=spiffe://cluster.local/ns/istio-
lab/sa/default;Hash=63c3fac8c0da77b4ab0fb2a9c5f26b9559f994c0c84895302030ae5
e387516f1;Subject=\"\";URI=spiffe://cluster.local/ns/istio-system/sa/istio-
ingressgateway-service-account"
  }
}
```

In the preceding headers information, the trace span is X-B3-Traceid, the parent span ID
is X-B3-Parentspanid, and the span ID is X-B3-Spanid. If all of these are the same, then
this is known as a root span. If the incoming headers have tracing elements present, the
sidecar proxy extracts the span's context and creates a child span. This new context is
propagated as a tracing header in the request to the application service. Keep in mind that,
in order to entirely benefit from Istio's distributed tracing, the application should propagate
tracing headers from incoming requests to outgoing requests.

 As an exception to the "no additional code" rule of Istio, we may need to
add a bit of application code in order to propagate headers down the call
chain for distributed traces.

For instance, if you look at the sample Python productpage service (https://git.io/
JeC2z), you'll see that the application extracts the required headers from an HTTP request
using OpenTracing libraries:

```
def getForwardHeaders(request):
    headers = {}

    # x-b3-*** headers can be populated using the opentracing span
    span = get_current_span()
    carrier = {}
    tracer.inject(
        span_context=span.context,
        format=Format.HTTP_HEADERS,
        carrier=carrier)

    headers.update(carrier)

    # ...

    incoming_headers = ['x-request-id']

    # ...

    for ihdr in incoming_headers:
  val = request.headers.get(ihdr)
  if val is not None:
```

```
headers[ihdr] = val

    return headers
```

Istio will report two spans from every hop in the microservice chain: one from the source sidecar and another from the destination sidecar.

In Istio, distributed tracing through trace span requires applications to write code to make sure that the tracing headers are collected and propagated and that the span headers aren't truncated. If we follow this best practice of header propagation, we can get an end-to-end timeline of distributed tracing.

Next, we will look at the trace sampling rate and learn how to change it.

Trace sampling

When we installed Istio using a demo profile, the sampling rate was set to 100%.

1. Let's confirm this:

```
# kubectl -n istio-system get deploy istio-pilot -o yaml | grep
"name: PILOT_TRACE_SAMPLING" -A1
        - name: PILOT_TRACE_SAMPLING
          value: "100"
```

When we access the `productpage`, we will see a corresponding trace in the dashboard. The 100% sample is OK for a test or low traffic environment. For performance reasons, we can lower the sampling rate in a high traffic mesh by editing the `istio-pilot` deployment to change the value of `PILOT_TRACING_SAMPLING` to a lower number, say, 1%.

2. As an example, let's modify the sampling rate to 99%:

```
$ kubectl -n istio-system patch deployment istio-pilot --type json
-p '[{"op": "replace","path":
"/spec/template/spec/containers/0/env/4/value","value": "99"}]'
deployment.extensions/istio-pilot patched
```

An easier way to do this is to simply edit the deployment, that is, `kubectl -n istio-system edit deployment istio-pilot`, and change the value of `PILOT_TRACING_SAMPLING` manually.

Trace sampling has an impact on the performance of the application as each Envoy will send tracing information directly to the tracing backends. For example, if you choose the aforementioned value of 1, only one out of every 100 trace spans will be sent to the tracing backend.

Next, we will look at an example of additional backend adapters that can be added to Mixer in order to send traces to backends.

Tracing backends

Istio comes with backends for tracing, such as *Jaeger*, *LightStep*, and *Zipkin*. We installed Istio using a demo profile, which has *Jaeger* as its backend. If *Zipkin* needs to be used as a backend, this can be done while installing Istio by adding the `--set` `tracing.provider=zipkin` Helm option.

Istio supports a variety of backends, all of which can be enabled through the use of adapters.

Adapters for the backend

One of the features of Mixer is that it can interface with a variety of infrastructure backends and send its metrics and logs over them. A list of all the available adapters can be found at `https://archive.istio.io/v1.3/docs/reference/config/policy-and-telemetry/adapters`.

Next, we will explore Prometheus.

Exploring prometheus

Prometheus is a data collection toolset that has its own basic web UI for visualizing and allowing the usage of the Prometheus Query Language to test and see the aggregation of scrapped data.

Istio's Mixer has built-in scraps for the following endpoints:

1. Mixer has an endpoint for ports `42422` and `15014`. Use endpoint `15014` to monitor Mixer itself:

```
$ curl
http://istio-telemetry.istio-system.svc.cluster.local:42422/metrics

$ curl
http://istio-telemetry.istio-system.svc.cluster.local:15014/metrics
```

2. The metrics that are generated by *Pilot*, *Policy*, and *Galley* are visible on port `15014`:

```
$ curl http://istio-pilot.istio-system.svc.cluster.local:15014/metrics

$ curl http://istio-policy.istio-system.svc.cluster.local:15014/metrics

$ curl http://istio-galley.istio-system.svc.cluster.local:15014/metrics
```

The preceding endpoints show Prometheus data for the `Istio Telemetry`, `Pilot`, `Policy`, and `Galley` components of the Istio control plane.

Next, we will see how data is collected from Envoy sidecar proxies.

Sidecar proxy metrics

Pilot generates dynamic configuration for the sidecar based upon the startup parameters and configuration information that's saved in the Kubernetes API server. Let's take a look:

1. We can get this configuration by using the following code for the `productpage`:

```
$ PRODUCTPAGE_POD=$(kubectl -n istio-lab get pod -l app=productpage -o jsonpath='{.items[0].metadata.name}')

$ kubectl -n istio-lab exec -i $PRODUCTPAGE_POD -c istio-proxy -- cat /etc/istio/proxy/envoy-rev0.json
```

2. If you scroll through the preceding JSON output, you will notice that the listener port `15090` has a route called `/stats/prometheus` that Prometheus will scrape to gather data:

```
...
    "listeners":[
        {
            "address": {
                "socket_address": {
                    "protocol": "TCP",
                    "address": "0.0.0.0",
                    "port_value": 15090
                }
            },
            "filter_chains": [
                {
                    "filters": [
                        {
                            "name": "envoy.http_connection_manager",

...

                            "routes": [
                                {
                                    "match": {
                                        "prefix": "/stats/prometheus"

...
```

3. Run the `curl` command to scrape the Prometheus metrics:

```
$ kubectl -n istio-lab exec -i $PRODUCTPAGE_POD -c istio-proxy --
curl http://localhost:15090/stats/prometheus
```

Each sidecar proxy has a management port of `15000`, which is bound to the local loopback adapter of the pod and hence can only be accessed within the pod.

4. The sidecar proxy stats can be seen by running the following command:

```
$ kubectl -n istio-lab exec -i $PRODUCTPAGE_POD \
-c istio-proxy -- curl http://localhost:15000/stats
```

5. Let's look at an example for all the pods in `istio-lab` to check how many days are left until the certificates expire:

```
$ ALL_PODS=$(kubectl -n istio-lab get pods -o
jsonpath='{.items..metadata.name}')

$ for pod in $ALL_PODS; do echo For pod $pod; kubectl -n istio-lab
exec -i $pod -c istio-proxy -- curl -s http://localhost:15000/stats
| grep server.days_until_first_cert_expiring; done
```

6. The output will look similar to the following:

```
...
For pod details-v1-6886b56dc8-ksmrh
server.days_until_first_cert_expiring: 82
...
```

7. The configuration for the proxy can be seen through proxy management port `15000` using the `config_dump` route:

```
$ kubectl -n istio-lab exec -i $PRODUCTPAGE_POD -c istio-proxy --
curl http://localhost:15000/config_dump
```

The preceding output can be used to confirm route propagation from Mixer to the sidecar proxy when Istio virtual services are created.

Now, we know how each Istio component publishes its Prometheus metrics through different endpoints. The Prometheus collector then scraps such metrics and puts in its own backend system.

Let's use the Prometheus UI to query some of the metrics that were collected. These values can be in the console or in the form of a graph. Prometheus is not a frontend web UI tool for visualizing such data, but it provides a basic UI. We will use *Grafana* as a UI frontend to show how data is collected from Istio's various components.

First, let's take a look at a basic Prometheus query through its UI. Later, we will switch to the *Grafana* UI.

Prometheus query

The power of *Prometheus* is its query language, through which we can use expressions, aggregations, and so on to collect data from data, which can then be used by different graphing tools such as *Kibana* to show valuable derived data.

In the **Expression** input box at the top of the web page, enter `istio_requests_total` . Then, click the **Execute** button.

Let's try out some different queries:

1. Let's get the total count of all the requests to the `productpage` service:

    ```
    istio_requests_total{destination_service="productpage.istio-
    lab.svc.cluster.local"}
    ```

    The preceding Prometheus query language expression gives us the total request count, as shown in the following screenshot:

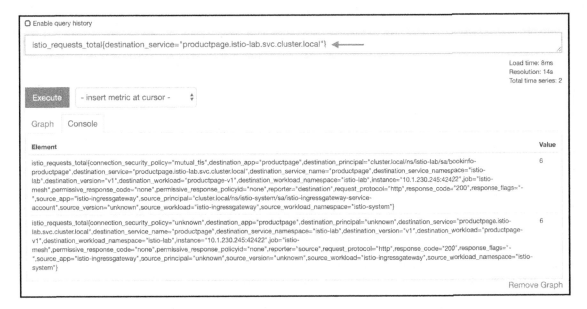

2. To get the total count of all requests to `v2` of the `reviews` service, use the following code:

    ```
    istio_requests_total{destination_service="reviews.istio-
    lab.svc.cluster.local", destination_version="v2"}
    ```

3. To get the rate of requests over the past 5 minutes to all the instances of the `productpage` service, use the following code:

```
rate(istio_requests_total{destination_service=~"productpage.*",
response_code="200"}[5m])
```

The preceding query expression builds the rate of requests over a period of 5 minutes, as shown in the following screenshot:

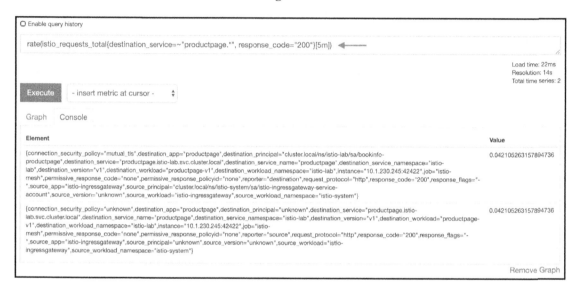

Here, we have seen that it is possible to build any custom data preparation from raw data so that it can be used in a dashboard. Grafana's dashboard in Istio can display time-series data and the aggregations that have been derived from the data.

Next, we will explore the state of Prometheus data collection and the list of targets that it collects data from.

Prometheus target collection health

We've already looked at the `istio-proxy` container inside each pod and looked at port `15090`, which uses the `/stats/prometheus` route to scrape metrics. How do we know if the route is healthy or not? Let's take a look.

Go to `http://prometheus.istio.io/targets`, as follows:

The preceding screenshot shows that all the data scraping endpoints are available and healthy. If you don't see the data for a particular endpoint, such as Mixer or Pilot, simply click on the target.

Now that we know how to check the health status of Prometheus's data collection endpoints, we will take a look at Prometheus's configuration parameters.

Prometheus configuration

Prometheus's configuration can be seen through the `/config` route for the Prometheus web UI. In our case, this will be `http://prometheus.istio.io/config`.

For example, you can verify the interval and route it uses to scrape the data like so:

```
...
- job_name: envoy-stats
    scrape_interval: 15s
    scrape_timeout: 10s
    metrics_path: /stats/prometheus
    scheme: http
...
```

Now that we've learned about Prometheus data collection, scrapping targets, and query expressions, we will delve into the visualization tools that we can use to observe data from Grafana.

Visualizing metrics through Grafana

Let's take a look at some of the open source visualization tools that can be used for distributed tracing, dependency visualization between services, and monitoring dashboards with the data we've collected through Prometheus. First, let's take a look at the *Grafana* dashboard, which has been built by the Istio community to show monitoring features:

1. Launch the *Grafana* dashboard by going to `http://grafana.istio.io`.
2. From the left-hand navigation panel, click on the **Configuration** (gear) and click on **Data Sources:**

Notice that the backend data source is configured using Prometheus.

3. Go back to the navigation panel, click on **Dashboard**, and navigate to **Manage**.
4. Next, go to the **search bar** and type Istio. The search output shows **Galley, Mesh, Mixer, Performance, Pilot, Service**, and **Workload dashboard**.
5. Click on **Istio Mesh Dashboard:**

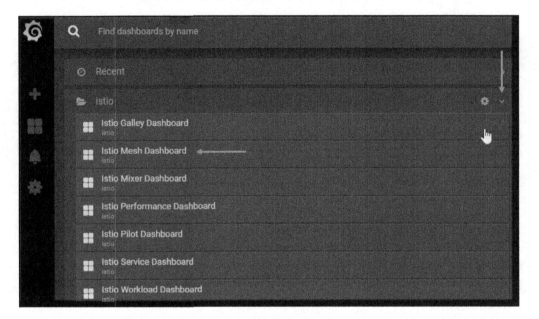

6. Switch to the command-line window and run a curl command to fetch the productpage 10,000 times:

```
$ curl -k -s -o /dev/null -w "time=%{time_total} http code=
%{http_code}\n" https://bookinfo.istio.io/productpage?[1-10000]
```

The preceding curl command will call
https://bookinfo.istio.io/productpage 10,000 times and emit the
timestamp with an http return code after each request.

We are using `?[1-10000]` at the end of the curl command to repeat the command 10,000 times.

The Mesh dashboard shows the statistics that were captured through Prometheus scraping data from various endpoints. The following dashboard shows the results:

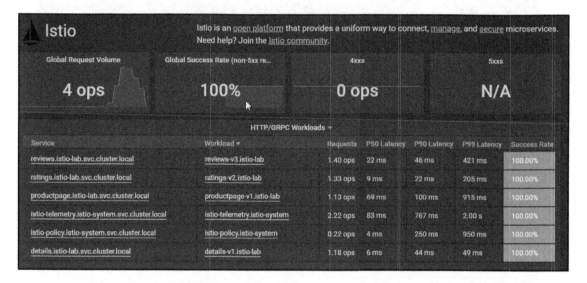

The **Key Performance Indicators (KPI)** metrics for the 50, 90, and 99 percentile latency, success rate, number of *4xx*, and *5xx* errors, global request volume, and global success rate give us a brief glimpse at the overall performance of the *microservices* application.

7. Switch to the **Istio Performance dashboard**:

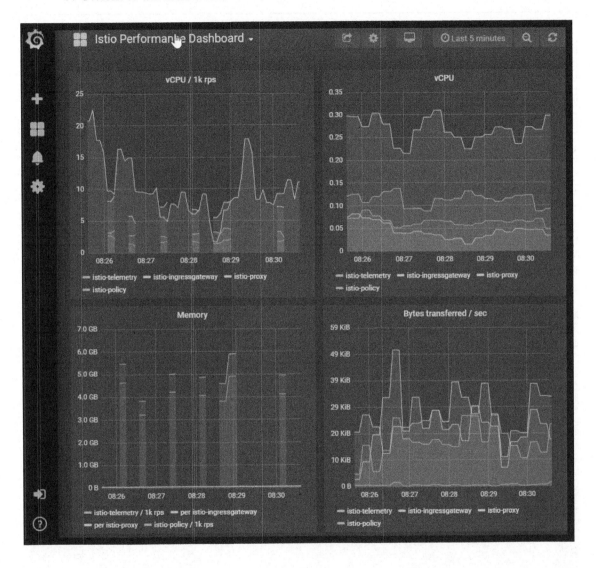

The following table shows what the various dashboard components represent:

Component	Representation
vCPU/1k rps	Shows vCPU utilization through the main Istio components normalized by 1,000 requests/second.
vCPU	Shows vCPU usage by Istio components, not normalized.
Memory	Shows a memory footprint for the components. Telemetry and policy are normalized by 1k rps.
Bytes transferred/sec	Shows the number of bytes flowing through each Istio component.

Notice the spikes in memory that are required per 1,000 requests/second for `istio-telemetry` and `istio-policy`. This is understandable since Mixer (telemetry and policy) is pushing monitoring data to the backend (Prometheus, in this case) since we ran 10,000 refreshes of `productpage` continuously.

One of the useful features of the *Grafana* dashboard is that we can slide the observability window to check on performance. You can choose from 5 mins, 15 mins, 30 mins, 1 hour, and 3 hours, all the way to five years. For example, the following screenshot shows the performance that was observed from the past **3 hours**:

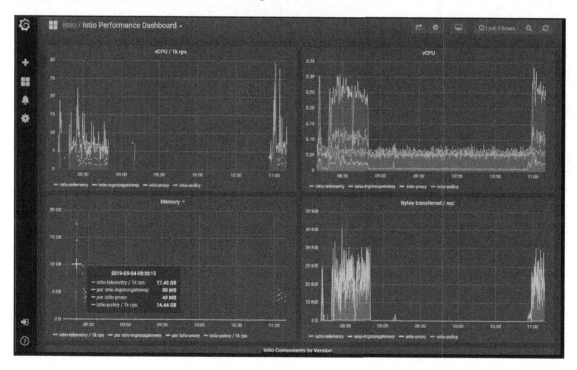

Go to the **Istio Service Dashboard**. Here, you can view metrics details about microservices such as **client request volume, client success rate**, and **client request duration** for clients coming through the **Istio Ingress gateway**. Client workloads are microservices that service client requests:

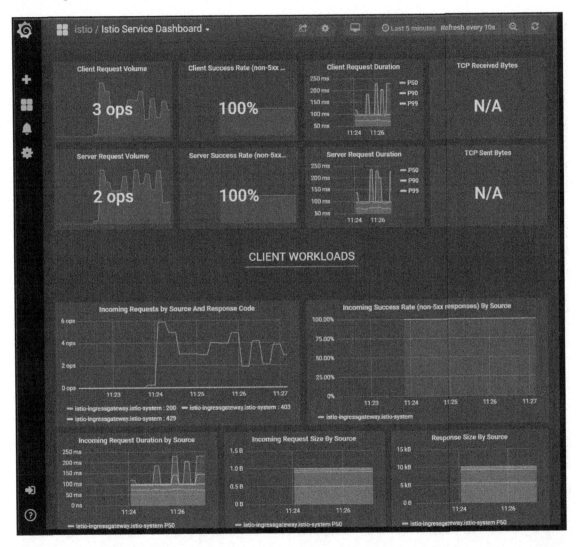

On the **Istio Workload Dashboard**, you can view metrics details for individual microservices behind the Istio Ingress gateway, which shows metrics such as **request duration**, **request size**, **response duration**, and **response size for HTTP**, as well as **TCP traffic**:

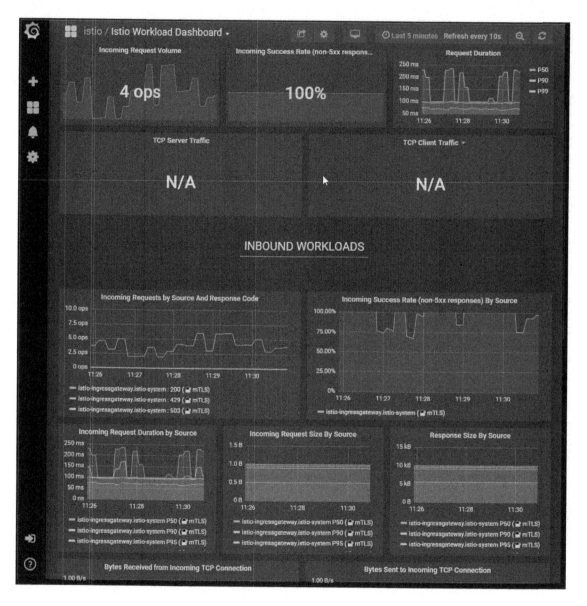

The preceding dashboard also shows us that it has been confirmed that all the service traffic has been secured through mTLS. It also allows us to make visual comparisons of individual microservices and the incoming client workload being received at the Ingress gateway for monitoring purposes. It is easier to find out which microservices are resource-hungry by looking at the metrics of the individual workloads. You can improve their overall performance by focusing incrementally on the optimization of specific microservices.

In the next section, we will look at service observability through *Kiali*.

Service mesh observability through Kiali

Kiali is a service mesh observability utility that was originally developed at Red Hat and now is an open- source project. *Kiali* provides a visual network flow/dependency diagram between different microservices behind the Ingress gateway. Let's take a look:

1. Open `http://kiali.istio.io/kiali/console` and use admin/admin as the user ID and password.

2. If the previous `curl` command to drive the traffic has stopped in the command-line window, start it again to keep sending the traffic to the `productpage`.

3. Navigate to the **menu** icon from the top left of the page and click on **Graph**. Select the `istio-lab` namespace:

   - Toggle the **Display** drop-down and check **Node Names**, **Service Nodes**, **Traffic animation**, **Virtual Services**, and **Security**.
   - Select **Requests per second** from **Edge Labels**.
   - Select **App** from **Graph Type**, as follows:

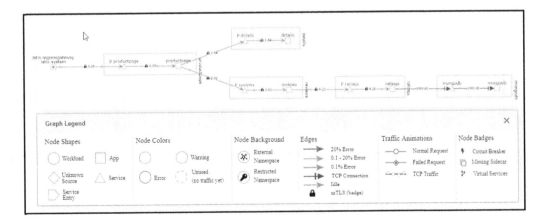

The animation shows how traffic flows from service to service. The lock icon shows the **mTLS**-enabled services. The traffic rate/seconds is also between services. The blue line between **ratings** and **mongodb** shows the TCP connection. The right-hand sidebar shows HTTP requests/second and TCP traffic bytes sent and received per second. These are useful metrics to gain insight into the application and, more importantly, to see if services are throwing *5XX* or *4XX* errors.

Next, we'll explore the real-time animation of the network flow between services:

1. Select the `istio-system` namespace, inclusive of `istio-lab`, and notice the animation and flow of metrics from the different services to the Istio components:

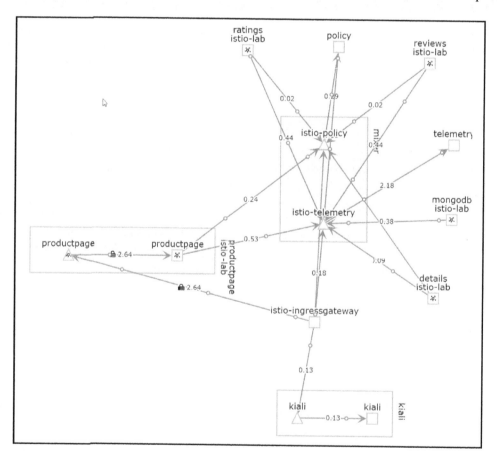

Network flow between services

The live animation shows how each service is sending metrics to Istio Mixer.

2. Select **istio-lab** from the namespace drop-down and click **Applications**. The health of the applications will appear:

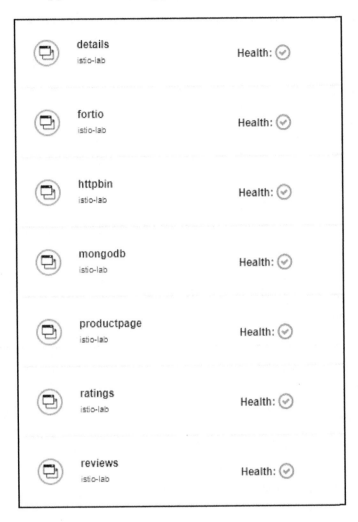

details
istio-lab

Health: ✓

fortio
istio-lab

Health: ✓

httpbin
istio-lab

Health: ✓

mongodb
istio-lab

Health: ✓

productpage
istio-lab

Health: ✓

ratings
istio-lab

Health: ✓

reviews
istio-lab

Health: ✓

Health of the application

3. Click **Service details** and click **Destination Rules** (notice the red cross sign, indicating that we have an issue):

4. Click **View YAML**:

```
 1 ▾ metadata:
 2     name: details
 3     namespace: istio-lab
 4 ▾   selfLink: >-
 5       /apis/networking.istio.io/v1alpha3/namespaces/istio-lab/destinationrules/details
 6     uid: c4e6693d-6afc-11e9-8752-00505632f6a0
 7     resourceVersion: '986875'
 8     generation: 1
 9     creationTimestamp: '2019-04-30T04:02:27Z'
10 ▾   annotations:
11 ▾     kubectl.kubernetes.io/last-applied-configuration: >
12         {"apiVersion":"networking.istio.io/v1alpha3","kind":"DestinationRule","metadata'
13 ▾ spec:
14     host: details
15 ▾   trafficPolicy:
16 ▾     tls:
17         mode: ISTIO_MUTUAL
18 ▾   subsets:
19 ▾     - labels:
20           version: v1
21         name: v1
22 ▾     - labels:
23           version: v2
24         name: v2
25
```

5. Notice that **subset v2** is shown in red. This is happening because there is no details service that has a label of **v2**.

6. Navigate to **Services** (left navigation bar) and click **productpage**. Click **Inbound Metrics**, which can be found in the middle of the tab:

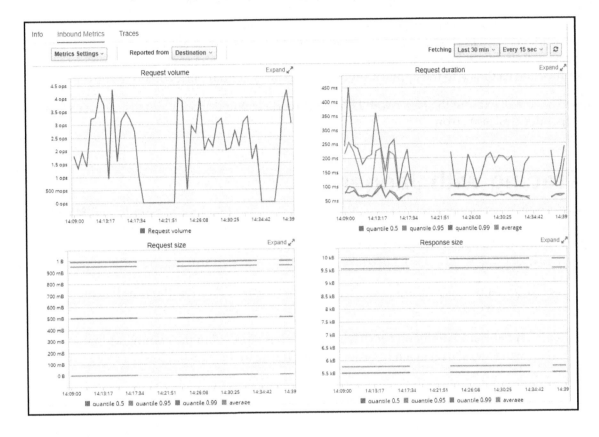

The **50**, **95**, and **99** percentiles for the request and response sizes show the network traffic that was generated by a particular service.

Istio Config open (left nav bar) shows the configuration for the destination rules, virtual services, and service entries. These can be modified using the web UI.

Kiali is one of the most useful tools in Istio for gaining immediate insight into a service's dependencies. *Kiali* shows real-time animated traffic of the application. This tool helps **Service Reliability Engineering** (**SRE**) or application infrastructure teams to provide immediate feedback to the application owners about potential performance issues.

Next, we will explore the *Jaeger* web UI regarding distributed tracing details, service mesh dependencies, and so on.

Tracing with Jaeger

Jaeger is an open source tool (`https://jaegertracing.io`) that recently graduated from the CNCF project. It provides distributed transaction monitoring, service dependency information, and span tracing using an open standard specification (`https://github.com/opentracing/specification`). Let's take a look at how to perform tracing with Jaeger:

1. Open `http://jaeger.istio.io` and use `admin/admin` as the user ID and password.

   If the `curl` command for driving traffic has stopped in the command-line window, start it again in order to send traffic to the `productpage`.

2. Select the **productpage.istio-lab** service from the drop-down and click **Find Traces**:

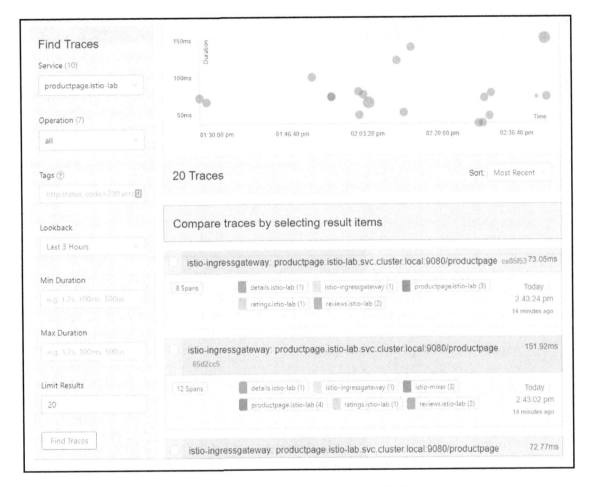

The graph shows the duration, while the bottom section shows the data that has been collected from productpage tracings

3. Click on the **productpage.istio-lab.svc.cluster.local** service and visualize the distributed trace:

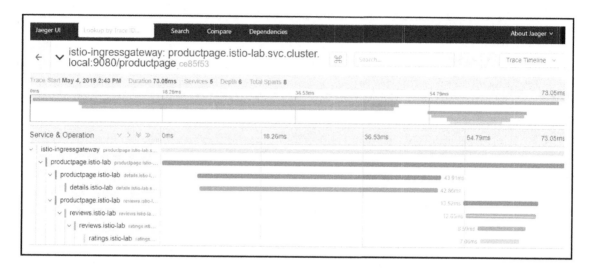

Notice the **73 ms** end-to-end response time of the request (see the top bar of the **Service & Operation** panel), which arrived at **istio-ingressgateway**. The **staggered bars** and **labels** on the left-hand side of the panel show the elapsed time in each microservice. This helps us clearly see the amount of time that was spent in each dependent microservice.

From this, it is evident that if we optimize the *details* microservice, it will reduce the overall end-to-end response time. This is an example of important observation derived through *Jaeger*. Note that the sample *BookInfo* application propagates the span headers from the sidecar proxy. Subsequently, the next upstream sidecar creates a child span. If the application does not propagate headers, all the spans that are built will be root spans, and they will be aligned to the left.

Click on any service and expand the **Tag section**. Notice the value of **span.kind**. It should be a **client** if header propagation is allowed through the application; otherwise, each **span.kind** will show up as a **server**.

4. Click **Dependencies** and then **DAG** (short for **Directed Acyclic Graph**) to see the dependencies among services. Note that, as expected, the number of invocations from the `productpage` to the `details` and `reviews` microservices is identical (**46046**):

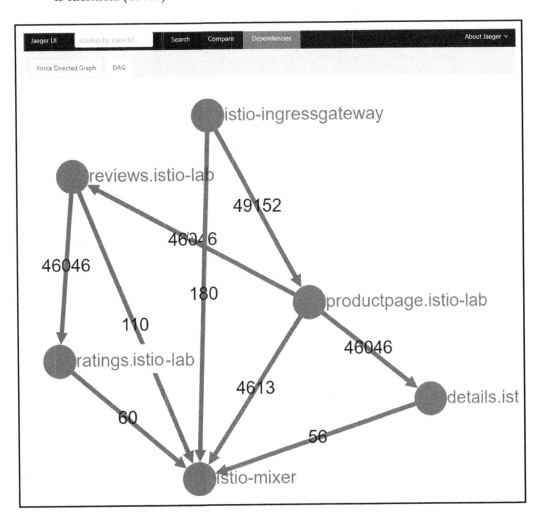

5. Go to **Search** again, select the **istio-mixer** service, and click **Find Traces**. Select the latest trace (**showing 12 spans**):

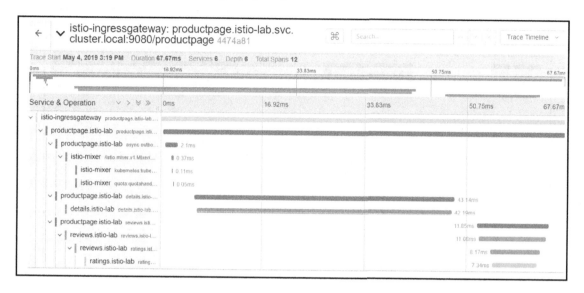

Notice the elapsed time that was spent on the **istio-mixer** level, which is negligible compared to the end-to-end time for the `productpage`.

Cleaning up

This concludes the Istio hands-on-exercises in this chapter. Now, it's time to clean up before we finish. Run the following commands:

```
$ cd istio-$ISTIO_VERSION/install/kubernetes
$ kubectl -n istio-system delete -f istio-demo.yaml
$ kubectl delete ns istio-lab

# Delete the keepalived pod security policy
$ kubectl delete psp kube-keepalived-vip
```

The preceding commands will uninstall Istio and *bookinfo* to free up resources in the VM.

 By the time you read this book, new versions of Istio will be available with new features and functions. You can visit `https://github.com/servicemeshbook/istio` for updated Istio scripts for the new version.

Summary

In this chapter, you have learned how to configure new metrics collection using Mixer's attribute vocabulary for microservices. You have gone through the Prometheus pull model for data scrapping from the Istio control plane, as well as from Envoy sidecar proxies. You have also explored Grafana for visualizing collected and aggregated data and service mesh observability, looked at animation through *Kiali*, and looked at distributed tracing using *Jaeger*.

In this section of the book, we've covered traffic management, security, policy, and telemetry features of Istio in detail. In the next section of this book, we will cover the Linkerd service mesh.

Questions

1. A sidecar proxy sends asynchronous telemetry data to backend services.

    A) True
    B) False

2. Observability and monitoring of a system are the same things.

    A) True
    B) False

3. The recommended web UI for Istio's monitoring and observability are *Grafana, Prometheus, Kiali,* and *Jaegar*.

    A) True
    B) False

4. Port forwarding is the only way to access different web UI components.

    A) True
    B) False

5. Istio reports multiple spans within a microservices chain.

    A) True
    B) False

6. Prometheus can be used as a web UI tool to visualize collected data or metrics.

    A) True
    B) False

7. Custom dashboards in *Grafana* provide details for inbound and outbound workloads.

    A) True
    B) False

8. In *Kiali's* YAML view, all mis-configurations will be highlighted in red.

    A) True
    B) False

Further reading

- *Overview*, Istio. (2019) available at https://istio.io/docs/tasks/telemetry/distributed-tracing/overview/, accessed 3 May 2019
- *Distributed Tracing, Istio, and Your Applications - The New Stack*, Poddar, N. (2018), The New Stack, available at https://thenewstack.io/distributed-tracing-istio-and-your-applications/, accessed 3 May 2019
- *Distributed tracing for cloud-native applications in the Istio service mesh* - The developerWorks Blog, Oliveira, F. (2017), The developerWorks Blog, available at https://developer.ibm.com/dwblog/2017/istio-service-mesh-distributed-tracing-zipkin/, accessed 3 May 2019

Section 5: Learning about Linkerd through Examples

Linkerd's journey as an open source project started in February 2016. Linkerd was accepted as an incubating project of the Cloud Native Computing Foundation in January 2017. In this section, you will learn about Linkerd through the use of hands-on exercises.

This section contains the following chapters:

- Chapter 14, *Understanding the Linkerd Service Mesh*
- Chapter 15, *Installing Linkerd*
- Chapter 16, *Exploring Linkerd's Reliability Features*
- Chapter 17, *Exploring Linkerd's Security Features*
- Chapter 18, *Exploring Linkerd's Observability Features*

14
Understanding the Linkerd Service Mesh

In the previous section, we delved into the Istio architecture, how to install it, and hands-on exercises regarding traffic management, security, policies, and observability. Istio is a highly configurable feature-rich service mesh. However, some may find that Istio is a bit difficult to start with. In this chapter, we will discuss another open source service mesh called Linkerd (pronounced *Linker-Dee*).

The architecture of Linkerd can alleviate some complexities of Istio's deployment, proxy injection, traffic management, observability, and basic security practices. Linkerd is an incubating project of CNCF with many contributors. In this section of the book, we will perform a deep dive and explain significant Linkerd capabilities that are run and managed on a Kubernetes environment. By the end of this chapter, you will have a strong sense of Linkerd and its capabilities, which will prove to be very useful as we move on.

In a nutshell, we will be covering the following topics in this chapter:

- Linkerd architecture for the control plane and the data plane
- Control plane installation overview
- Data plane overview
- Linkerd proxy for service configuration and Ingress rules
- Observability using Linkerd's dashboard, Grafana, and Prometheus
- Distributed tracing and exporting metrics
- Debugging sidecar proxies
- Traffic reliability and its many capabilities
- Securing Linkerd's service mesh

Technical requirements

You will need to continue using the VM that we used to learn about Istio. Make sure that you have performed the cleanup procedure that was demonstrated at the end of the previous chapter to free up resources so that you can use the same VM and the Kubernetes environment to explore the Linkerd service mesh.

You can find the code files for Linkerd here: `https://github.com/servicemeshbook/linkerd`.

Introducing the Linkerd Service Mesh

Istio is feature-rich, but it may take a while to get a good grasp of its core functionalities. Linkerd is designed to keep the service mesh simple, efficient, and easy to work with. Out-of-the-box, Linkerd works with a bare minimum configuration in comparison to Istio.

Linkerd is an open source project and is backed by a startup, Buoyant (`https://buoyant.io`). Buoyant was started by William Morgan and Oliver Gould, both formerly from Twitter. William Morgan, as we mentioned earlier in this book, is credited with coining the phrase service mesh. He describes it as a dedicated infrastructure layer built directly into the application for an SRE. In 2016, Linkerd 1.x was the first service mesh to be created.

It has two flavors: version 1.x and 2.x. Both are very different technologies:

- **Linkerd 1.x**: Built on top of Netty (`https://github.com/netty/netty`), which is written in Java, and Finagle (`https://twitter.github.io/finagle/`), which is written in Scala. Linkerd 1.x is still supported, but we are not covering it in this book. Linkerd 1.x runs in Kubernetes, Apache Mesos's DC/OS, Consul, and Zookeeper-based environments.
- **Linkerd 2.0**: Built from scratch using Rust (proxy) and Go (Control plane components), it claims to be significantly faster than Linkerd 1.x. It is open source and is maintained by Buoyant and many contributors at `https://github.com/linkerd`.

At the time of writing, Linkerd 2.0 is only available on the Kubernetes platform, which may change in the future.

Istio and Consul Connect use the Envoy sidecar proxy, which is also used by AWS's App Mesh and Microsoft's Azure Service Fabric Mesh. Linkerd has developed its sidecar proxy from the ground-up, which makes it different from other service mesh implementations.

Regarding its installation and overall maintenance, Istio is more challenging to operate than Linkerd. This is mainly because of its interaction between services, which could be ideal for engineering but tricky for operators and administrators. Linkerd is very easy to configure because of its simpler architecture and due to the fact that it only requires a single process per node. Istio requires several processes because it has a complex control plane.

For traffic management, Istio offers more features than Linkerd, such as circuit breaking, timeouts, routing rules, subset load balancing, fault injection, and so on. However, this may change in the future based on what's on their roadmap. For security, Linkerd and Istio offer support for certificate rotation, external root certificate assignment, and features such as mTLS, but Linkerd doesn't support automatic mTLS for non-HTTP traffic. This request is on their roadmap for future support. For monitoring, both Linkerd and Istio leverage open source tools to provide insights via dashboards provided by Grafana for querying (used by Linkerd and Istio), as well as Kiali (used by Istio).

Finally, regarding performance, Linkerd is better because its processing load is 3x better than Istio's. The reason for this is that Istio has a complex networking architecture around integration, traffic management, and overall policy management.

Linkerd also has a participating service mesh interface specification, which you can find at https://smi-spec.io/.

 In this chapter, we'll focus on the Linkerd 2.x architecture. The term Linkerd henceforth refers exclusively to Linkerd 2.x and not to Linkerd 1.x.

Linkerd architecture

Linkerd has a dedicated layer 7 proxy that deals with HTTP and HTTP/2 for requests and responses. It can use a filter chain for these requests for success, failure, latency, and responses. A service mesh implies that you deploy one Linkerd proxy alongside a microservice. When you initiate a service call, instead of it being direct, that request is received by the Linkerd proxy and then sent to the microservice. Next, the microservice response is routed through the Linkerd proxy, which again sends that response to another microservice. The proxy sitting next to each microservice wraps the network call and collects the metrics. Service-to-service communication is secured through TLS, and all the traffic on the wire is encrypted.

Linkerd provides an abstract layer so you can manage, control, and monitor microservices. Linkerd facilitates a service-oriented infrastructure through load balancers, TLS, request routing, and service scalability to make applications resilient. Linkerd Proxy allows application owners to develop microservices in the programming language of their choice.

There are two primary architecture components to Linkerd for deploying and running standalone proxies:

- Control plane
- Data plane

Linkerd's control and data plane architecture can be seen in the following diagram:

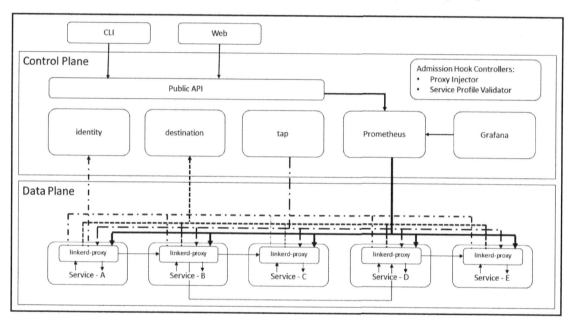

In this chapter, we will understand this architecture. Let's begin with the control plane.

Control plane

Linkerd's control plane can be deployed in a Kubernetes environment. Its primary functionality is around telemetry data aggregation, service API calls, and enabling data access between the control plane and service proxy. It is made up of four major components:

- **Controller**: Deploys four containers called `public-api`, `identity`, `destination`, and `tap` to manage traffic between the application proxy.
- **Web**: Once Linkerd has been installed and deployed, this is the frontend dashboard.
- **Prometheus**: This is an open source component that's used to store metrics, telemetry, and monitoring data that's been captured by Linkerd proxies and metrics that have been generated by other Linkerd components.
- **Grafana**: This is an out-of-the-box open source component that's integrated with Prometheus to visualize metrics that have been captured by Prometheus.

Istio and Linkerd's service mesh patterns are similar to a hub and spoke architecture, except for Consul, which is a peer-to-peer architecture pattern based upon the gossip protocol.

As shown in the preceding diagram, the control plane has the following step-by-step configuration:

1. Prometheus scraps data that Linkerd's proxies generate.
2. Next, Grafana takes data from Prometheus to provide monitoring and observability features.
3. Tap is a unique concept native to getting requests and responses in real-time from a Linkerd sidecar proxy.
4. Linkerd Identity is the PKI that provisions certificates and keys for sidecar proxies to enable mutual TLS.

The Public API and destination is the heart of the control plane. It provides various functionality and pushes down configuration to the data plane's Linkerd proxies. The CLI and web are frontends of the control plane and are used to get input from the user to either configure, monitor, or observe.

The control plane also has Kubernetes admission webhook controllers for automatic sidecar injection and a validator to validate a new service profile.

One of the features of Linkerd is its web-based dashboard. This dashboard provides a high-level view of applications using its unique *tap* feature, which provides live traffic analysis. It is used to view metrics such as success rate, **requests per second** (**RPS**), visualize microservices dependencies, and more.

Once we've installed Linkerd, we can run the Linkerd dashboard by typing the `linkerd dashboard` command from a Terminal window. The output will be a URL that you can point to your browser. The dashboard UI will run in your local machine through port forwarding to the Linkerd web port:

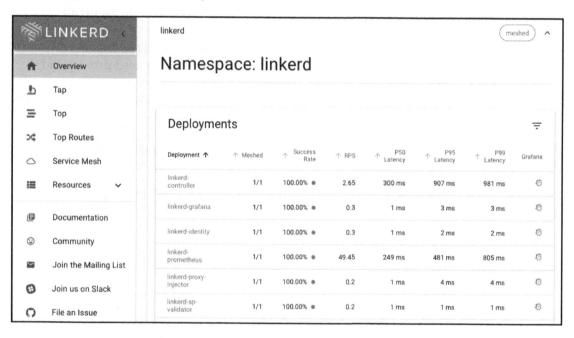

Note that running a dashboard through Linkerd's dashboard is easy. You could expose the dashboard through your Ingress controller to provide access through an external web address. You can also use NodePort to gain access, which requires access to the Kubernetes cluster's master node IP address.

Using the command-line interface (CLI)

The command-line interface of Linkerd's control plane is a Linkerd tool that helps users accomplish various tasks when it comes to installing Linkerd's control plane.

The following steps are at a conceptual level and point out the operational simplicity of Linkerd. Don't try out these commands yet. In the next chapter, we will walk through Linkerd's installation in more detail:

1. Check if Linkerd's prerequisites have been met or not. This checker will validate your current virtual machine and provide an output of all the passed or failed checks. Then, deploy the service mesh:

```
$ linkerd check --pre
```

```
$ linkerd install | kubectl apply -f -
```

2. Launch the Linkerd dashboard locally through your client machine:

```
$ linkerd dashboard
```

Alternatively, you can also apply Ingress rules to your Linkerd dashboard to access it remotely. We will explain this capability in the following chapters.

3. Enable injecting a sidecar proxy automatically through a webhook admission controller. This process can also be done for existing applications by routing YAML files to the `linkerd inject` command:

```
$ kubectl get deploy -o yaml | linkerd inject - | kubectl apply -f -
```

4. Carry out real-time live traffic analysis through a Kubernetes deployment known as the web:

```
$ linkerd tap deploy/web
```

5. Carry out command-line monitoring of the Linkerd service mesh by using the `top` command. The following example shows how to monitor a Kubernetes deployment known as the web:

```
$ linkerd top deploy/web
```

6. Finally (this is optional), users can upgrade the existing Linkerd control plane by using the `upgrade` command. This will generate the YAML configuration files that can be routed to Kubernetes:

```
$ linkerd upgrade | kubectl apply -f -
```

As you can see, it is rather easy to install Linkerd and its control plane components. These steps have provided you with a high-level overview of the following:

- Pre-checking the environment for Linkerd's installation
- Installing Linkerd
- Accessing the dashboard
- Visibility into live traffic metrics
- Easily upgrading the control plane

Next, let's dive into Linkerd's data plane capabilities.

Data plane

Let's take a closer look at the data plane architecture:

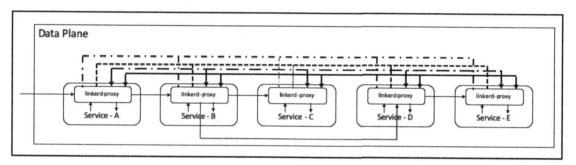

From the preceding diagram, we can see the following:

- **Service-A** is the edge service that receives traffic from an external network.
- **Service-A** calls **Service-B**, which calls two other services, such as **Service-C** and **Service-D**.
- Finally, **Service-D** calls **Service-E**.

A mesh of the Linkerd proxy at the application level forms the data plane, which can be configured, monitored, and observed through the control plane.

By now, you should have a good understanding of Linkerd's control plane and data plane regarding services that are deployed and how they're managed through the UI dashboard or CLI. The next section will take you through Linkerd's sidecar proxy architecture.

Linkerd proxy

In Linkerd, the sidecar proxy is written in the Rust programming language, which was designed by Graydon Hoare from Mozilla Research. Rust is similar in syntax to C and C++, and it offers better performance and strong typing. There are no **Garbage Collection (GC)** related constraints, as Rust performs resource utilization in the constructor, and, when an object goes out of scope, the owned resources are freed.

The choice of Rust by Linkerd developers was to attain performance, reliability, and productivity (https://rust-lang.org). The Linkerd proxy is lightweight and efficient, since it has a small footprint.

Some of the features of the Linkerd proxy are as follows:

- **Out of process architecture**: The Linkerd proxy runs alongside the application and is language-agnostic.
- **Rust**: The Linkerd proxy is written in Rust for performance and to minimize latency.
- **Protocol**: It has zero-config and supports HTTP/1.2, HTTP/2.0, and arbitrary TPC. It also has a web socket proxy.
- **HTTP L7 routing**: Latency-aware automatic load balancing.
- **L4 routing**: Load balancing for non-HTTP traffic.
- **TLS**: Automatic TLS.
- **On-demand diagnostics**: Uses the Tap API.
- **Service discovery**: Through DNS and the destination gRPC API.

With this information in hand, let's move on to understanding its architecture.

Architecture

The architecture of the Linkerd proxy is very similar to that of Envoy. Linkerd proxies intercept traffic to and from application containers in pods. It has a `linkerd-init` container that runs before starting the proxy and an application container that's used to set the rules in `iptables` so that it can configure the incoming and outgoing flow of traffic, as shown in the following diagram:

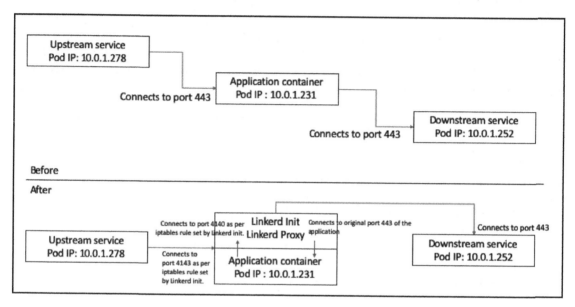

In the preceding diagram, we can see the following steps being carried out:

1. The Linkerd sidecar proxy is injected into an application pod.
2. The Linkerd Init container sets the rules in iptables to forward incoming traffic on IP `10.0.1.231` to port `4143` and outgoing traffic to port `4140`.
3. The Linkerd proxy gathers the incoming traffic and applies the rules that it receives from the control plane.
4. Then, it forwards traffic to the application container at its original port of `443`. The outgoing traffic is sent to port `4140`.
5. After applying any rules, the Linkerd proxy will send that traffic to the downstream application designated port.

Next, we will explain how to configure a microservice with a sidecar proxy.

Configuring a service

To deploy Linkerd's sidecar proxy for a running microservice, the proxy definition needs to be applied to the pod's resource definition. This configuration setup can be done through the Linkerd CLI (`https://linkerd.io/2/architecture/#cli`). The CLI is the recommended tool for installing the Linkerd control plane. Once the control plane has been deployed, deploying the Linkerd sidecar proxy to an application is simple, as is the case with Istio. Follow these steps:

1. Annotate the namespace, pod, or deployment with `linkerd.io/inject: enabled`.
2. The Linkerd sidecar will be injected automatically through the Kubernetes admission webhook controller.
3. If a particular pod doesn't need a sidecar, that pod can be annotated as `linkerd.io/inject: disabled`.
4. To add Linkerd to a running microservice service, run the `linkerd inject` command.
5. This will add a `linkerd-init` and provision a sidecar proxy for every service pod that has been defined in the deployment YAML.
6. Deploying this configuration file through `kubectl` will trigger rolling updates and replace old pods with new ones.
7. The newly added pods can be viewed on the Linkerd dashboard.

In the next chapter, we will show you a step-by-step deployment of the Linkerd control and data plane.

For now, let's assume that Linkerd is already installed and that we've annotated the default namespace with `linkerd.io/inject: enabled`. Next, we need to deploy the application. During deployment, the Linkerd sidecar proxy will be injected automatically. Here is the code example:

```
$ kubectl annotate namespace default linkerd.io/inject=enabled

$ kubectl create -f https://k8s.io/examples/admin/dns/busybox.yaml
```

If you check the pod, you should see that the sidecar is injected automatically with 2/2 under the READY column:

```
$ kubectl get pods
NAME       READY   STATUS     RESTARTS   AGE
busybox    2/2     Running    0          9s
```

If you describe the busybox pod, you will see details about the Linkerd sidecar proxy.

Notice that the busybox pod has one init container called linkerd-init that puts entries in the iptables to route the traffic to the proxy. The busybox container and the sidecar proxy's linkerd-proxy containers are created with a distinction of (2/2) with proper command-line parameters.

Let's look at what's within the busybox containers:

```
$ kubectl describe pod busybox
Name: busybox
Namespace: default
...
Containers:
 busybox:
 Container ID: docker://...
 Image: busybox:1.28
...
 linkerd-proxy:
 Container ID: docker://...
 Image: gcr.io/linkerd-io/proxy:stable-2.6.0
...
 LINKERD2_PROXY_CONTROL_LISTEN_ADDR: 0.0.0.0:4190
 LINKERD2_PROXY_ADMIN_LISTEN_ADDR: 0.0.0.0:4191
 LINKERD2_PROXY_OUTBOUND_LISTEN_ADDR: 127.0.0.1:4140
 LINKERD2_PROXY_INBOUND_LISTEN_ADDR: 0.0.0.0:4143
 LINKERD2_PROXY_DESTINATION_PROFILE_SUFFIXES: svc.cluster.local.
 LINKERD2_PROXY_INBOUND_ACCEPT_KEEPALIVE: 10000ms
 LINKERD2_PROXY_OUTBOUND_CONNECT_KEEPALIVE: 10000ms
 LINKERD2_PROXY_DESTINATION_CONTEXT: ns:$(_pod_ns)
...
```

Injecting a Linkerd sidecar proxy is enabled by default. Any changes that are made to the existing deployment are done through mutating the admission controller using linkerd.io/inject: disabled. Such calls to the admission controller will modify the busybox deployment to enable/disable the Linkerd sidecar proxy.

Injecting a Linkerd sidecar proxy is part of the control plane, which makes the process easy since all we have to do is annotate the namespace and automate proxy injections.

Moving forward, let's explore how Linkerd enables incoming traffic through the Kubernetes Ingress controller.

Ingress controller

Kubernetes' Ingress controller is an edge infrastructure that transmits all external web traffic and forwards it to the designated microservice running inside the cluster. You configure access by creating a collection of rules that define which inbound connections reach which services.

Unlike Istio, Linkerd does not provide an Ingress controller. Instead, it piggybacks on an existing Ingress controller that comes with your Kubernetes providers, such as public cloud (Google, AWS, Azure, IBM, and so on) or on-premises implementations such as RedHat OpenShift or the Pivotal Container Service. In this book, we will build our own Nginx Ingress Controller in the next chapter.

Linkerd discovers services based on the authority (HTTP/2) or host (HTTP 1.1) headers of the incoming requests. The incoming request for a host, such as example.com, needs to be translated to an internal service name, for example, `example.linkerd-lab.svc.cluster.local` at the Ingress controller. This translation requires rewriting the request header so that the Linkerd proxy can route the traffic properly.

For example, the following annotation (in bold) needs to be added to the Ingress definition of the Nginx controller:

```
apiVersion: extensions/v1beta1
kind: Ingress
metadata:
  name: web-ingress
  namespace: emojivoto
  annotations:
    kubernetes.io/ingress.class: "nginx"
    nginx.ingress.kubernetes.io/configuration-snippet: |
      proxy_set_header l5d-dst-override
$service_name.$namespace.svc.cluster.local:80;
      proxy_hide_header l5d-remote-ip;
      proxy_hide_header l5d-server-id;
spec:
  rules:
  - host: emojivoto.linkerd.io
    http:
      paths:
      - backend:
          serviceName: web-svc
          servicePort: 80
```

From the preceding Linkerd YAML, we can see that the Ingress controller will be using the `nginx` adapter through the `kubernetes.io/ingress.class: "nginx"` annotation. The following annotation is the configuration snippet that's meant for the Linkerd proxy:

```
nginx.ingress.kubernetes.io/configuration-snippet: |
    proxy_set_header l5d-dst-override
$service_name.$namespace.svc.cluster.local:80;
    proxy_hide_header l5d-remote-ip;
    proxy_hide_header l5d-server-id;
```

Through the preceding annotation, the headers starting with `l5d-*` are added to the incoming request's headers. These `l5d-*` headers are only meaningful to the Linkerd proxy and inbound and outbound proxies strip these headers away as they are not meant for either internal microservices or the external outbound destinations. With the help of these `l5d-*` headers, the Linkerd proxy can now route the traffic appropriately.

If you are using the Traefik (pronounced like traffic) HTTP reverse proxy and load balancer (`https://github.com/containous/traefik`), you may need to define the Ingress controller with the appropriate headers, like so:

```
apiVersion: extensions/v1beta1
kind: Ingress
metadata:
  name: web-ingress
  namespace: emojivoto
  annotations:
    kubernetes.io/ingress.class: "traefik"
    ingress.kubernetes.io/custom-request-headers: l5d-dst-override: web-
svc.emojivoto.svc.cluster.local:80
    ingress.kubernetes.io/custom-response-headers: "l5d-remote-ip: || l5d-
server-id:"
spec:
  rules:
  - host: emojivoto.linkerd.io
    http:
      paths:
      - backend:
          serviceName: web-svc
          servicePort: 80
```

From the preceding Linkerd Ingress YAML, we can see that Ingress will be using the `kubernetes.io/ingress.class: "traefik"` traefik adapter. The following annotation is a configuration snippet that's meant for the Linkerd proxy:

```
ingress.kubernetes.io/custom-request-headers: l5d-dst-override: web-
svc.emojivoto.svc.cluster.local:80
ingress.kubernetes.io/custom-response-headers: "l5d-remote-ip: || l5d-
server-id:"
```

Through this annotation, the Linkerd proxy knows how to process these requests due to the presence of `l5d-*` headers.

Other Ingress controllers, such as Gloo (`https://github.com/solo-io/gloo`), have native integration with Linkerd, in which it adds Linkerd specific headers automatically to the incoming requests. This feature is enabled by modifying settings and adding a route:

```
$ kubectl patch settings -n gloo-system default -p
'{"spec":{"linkerd":true}}' --type=merge

$ glooctl add route --path-prefix=/ --dest-name booksapp-webapp-7000
```

Now that we've learned how to enable Ingress rules for Linkerd, let's explore the observability capabilities and metrics that can be visualized through Linkerd's dashboard.

Observability

Linkerd provides out-of-the-box observability functionality through its interactive dashboard. It can instrument critical metrics such as service request volume, success rates, and network latency. In addition to these metrics, Linkerd can enable real-time data streams of network requests for all incoming and outgoing traffic for all the running services being monitored by Linkerd.

The Linkerd dashboard provides a high-level, robust view of the services being monitored in real-time. There is a term called **golden metrics** that can offer perspective to the overall service details, such as success rate, network requests, network latency, service dependency visualization, and view service route health checks.

This can be seen in the following screenshot:

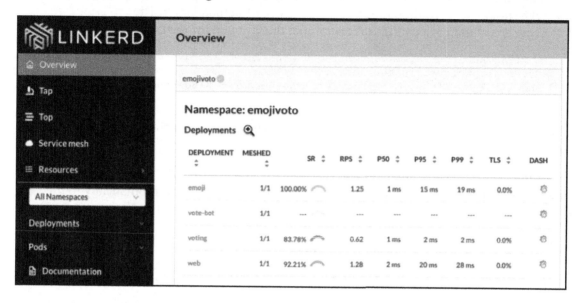

To recap from earlier in this chapter, the dashboard can be enabled by running the `linkerd dashboard` command from the CLI.

Outside of the dashboard, there are two other open source visualization tools called Grafana and Prometheus. They are both supported by Linkerd and Kubernetes.

Grafana and Prometheus

As an out-of-the-box component of the control plane, Grafana provides dashboard insights for registered running services. Grafana enables drilling down to the service-level pods and container details. Some of those metrics are top-line, deployment, pod, and Linkerd health.

Prometheus is the backend monitoring solution that collects and stores all Linkerd telemetry metrics for services that are enabled for monitoring. It is also part of the control plane and collects data that's used by the CLI, the Linkerd dashboard, and Grafana.

The proxy exposes a `/metrics` endpoint for Prometheus to scrape on port `4191`. This is scraped every 10 seconds. These metrics are then available to all the other Linkerd components, such as the CLI and dashboard.

Distributed tracing

Distributed tracing in Linkerd is automated and does not require any special configuration. The data that's collected from the Linkerd proxy is aggregated to show health, latencies, and request volumes at the service level and path/route level.

The dashboard also shows a live dependency graph and the topology of the services. There are four golden metrics for monitoring distributed systems; that is, Latency, Traffic (RPS), Errors, and Saturation, which an SRE team will be very interested in getting a report on. The Linkerd dashboard shows these golden metrics through its dashboard. The following screenshot shows five metrics for a web app:

deployment/webapp

Route ↑	Service ↑	↑ Success Rate	↑ RPS	↑ P50 Latency	↑ P95 Latency	↑ P99 Latency
GET /	webapp	100.00% ●	0.47	50 ms	95 ms	99 ms
GET /authors/{id}	webapp	100.00% ●	0.47	30 ms	85 ms	97 ms
GET /books/{id}	webapp	100.00% ●	0.93	25 ms	72 ms	94 ms
POST /authors	webapp	100.00% ●	0.48	37 ms	85 ms	97 ms
POST /authors/{id}/delete	webapp	100.00% ●	0.47	75 ms	188 ms	198 ms
POST /authors/{id}/edit	webapp	---	---	0 s	0 s	0 s
POST /books	webapp	46.28% ●	2.02	43 ms	89 ms	98 ms
POST /books/{id}/delete	webapp	100.00% ●	0.47	27 ms	39 ms	40 ms
POST /books/{id}/edit	webapp	50.00% ●	0.97	86 ms	183 ms	197 ms
[DEFAULT]	webapp	---	0	0 s	0 s	0 s

Distributed tracing requires applications to preserve request headers if they are set by the proxy. Future releases of Linkerd may use distributed tracing through span headers. Istio supports application tracing through span headers already, but it lacks in showing the golden metrics, as shown by Linkerd.

P50, P95, and P99 are percentile metrics. For example, P50 with a value of 27 ms signifies that 50% of the time, you will notice a latency of 27 ms or lower.

The P50, P95, and P99 latency metrics can help application developers identify application bottlenecks. This aggregated latency information is a very useful feature of Linkerd.

Exporting metrics

Prometheus, which runs as part of Linkerd's control plane, retains data for approximately 6 hours. If further data retention is required, the metrics can be exported to a data store such as the **Elasticsearch, Logstash, and Kibana (ELK)** stack or to a dedicated Prometheus instance.

The Prometheus federation API or ServiceMonitors can be used to copy data using the /federate path from Linkerd Prometheus to the dedicated Prometheus store.

Alternatively, you can call the federation API directly, and then it can be ingested by a Kafka stream, which can then dump it to an ELK stack, like so:

```
$ curl -G \
--data-urlencode 'match[]={job="linkerd-proxy"}' \
--data-urlencode 'match[]={job="linkerd-controller"}' \
http://linkerd-prometheus.linkerd.svc.cluster.local:9090/federate
```

From the preceding curl command, you can use an external name through Ingress to route traffic to the linkerd-prometheus microservice if the /federate path needs to be scraped external to the cluster.

There can be multiple Linkerd proxies running within a data plane and a control plane. You can scrape metrics directly from a Linkerd proxy like so:

```
$ kubectl -n linkerd port-forward \
  (kubectl -n linkerd get pods \
 -l linkerd.io/control-plane-ns=linkerd \
 -o jsonpath='{.items[0].metadata.name}') \
 4191:4191
```

From your local machine, after you run the preceding kubectl command, you can run the following curl command and access the Prometheus federated metrics datastore:

```
$ curl localhost:4191/metrics
```

Next, let's dive into the Linkerd sidecar proxy and how to enable the debugging flag. This will provide detailed views into the microservice it's attached to.

Injecting the debugging sidecar

In addition to the Linkerd proxy, you can also add a debugging sidecar automatically by setting up the `config.linkerd.io/enable-debug-sidecar: true` pod annotation or using the `linkerd inject` command with `--enable-debug-sidecar`. The debugging sidecar provides the `tshark`, `tcpdump`, `lsof`, and `iproute2` tools, which we can use for low-level system monitoring.

In this section, we had a quick overview of Linkerd's observability. We will explore this in more detail in `Chapter 18`, *Exploring the Observability Features of Linkerd*. Now, let's move on to Linkerd's traffic managing features for reliability and microservice resiliency.

Reliability

Linkerd addresses traffic management features as reliabilities due to some of the capabilities around auto-pilot to provide resiliency from inherent application failures. We will have a quick overview of all these traffic patterns in this section. Let's start with traffic splitting.

Traffic split

Traffic split is a key concept that has recently gained popularity. It abstracts networking functions through a proxy without having to change the application. Traffic split allows dark launches of applications to select groups of users such as co-workers, friends, and family. Canary deployments (progressive traffic shift), A/B testing (HTTP header and cookie traffic routing), and blue/green deployments (traffic switch) are all examples of dark launches for testing applications in production environments by routing a percentage of the live traffic to selected groups of users without their knowledge. These capabilities do not exist out of the box in a traditional monolithic environment.

Linkerd works with Flagger (`https://flagger.app`), which is an open source Kubernetes operator for canary deployment that uses Linkerd. Flagger can be used with Linkerd to provide canary and blue-green deployments.

Linkerd recently announced the service mesh interface specification for traffic split.

Fault injection

Chaos testing is gaining importance when it comes to distributed applications discovering issues early on rather than waiting for them to appear. If faults can be injected into services to induce artificial latencies and errors, it might help uncover unpredictable behavior or timeouts from downstream services. SREs or Operations need tooling to inject faults to gauge the resiliency of the application proactively. Linkerd allows fault injection through the traffic split API of service mesh interface specification.

```
apiVersion: split.smi-spec.io/v1alpha1
kind: TrafficSplit
metadata:
  name: error-split
  namespace: booksapp
spec:
  service: books
  backends:
  - service: books
    weight: 900m
  - service: error-injector
    weight: 100m
```

In the preceding traffic split specification, 10% of traffic is shifted to an error-injector pod, which is nothing but an nginx pod that returns error 500 through its proxy configuration:

```
apiVersion: v1
kind: ConfigMap
metadata:
  name: error-injector
  namespace: booksapp
data:
 nginx.conf: |-
    http {
        server {
          listen 8080;
            location / {
                return 500;
            }
        }
    }
```

The preceding is a smart way to induce faults through traffic split. Introducing a fixed delay and a percentage of error code can be quickly done at the proxy level, and the future releases of Linkerd may provide a more straightforward approach through Linkerd service profiles. We'll look at these in the next section.

Service profiles

A service profile is implemented as a **Custom Resource Definition (CRD)** in Kubernetes and is used to define a list of routes for a service that can then be used by the Linkerd proxy to report per-route metrics and configure retries and timeouts.

Service profiles can be generated automatically if you have `swagger` or `protobuf` specifications for your services. For example, the following code will create a service profile from a `webapp.swagger` or `web.proto` file for the `webapp` service. This is then fed to `kubectl` to generate the service profile:

```
$ linkerd profile --open-api webapp.swagger webapp | kubectl apply -f -

$ linkerd profile --proto webapp.proto webapp | kubectl apply -f -
```

If no service profile specifications exist, Linkerd can also automatically generate a service profile by watching live traffic. The following example shows that `tap` is used to get the live feed for the `emojivoto` service for 10 seconds. The output is fed to `kubectl` to create the service profile:

```
$ linkerd profile -n emojivoto web-svc --tap deploy/web --tap-duration 10s
| kubectl apply -f -
```

Linkerd also allows you to generate a template, as follows:

```
$ linkerd profile -n emjoivoto web-svc --template
```

Make changes to the `emojivoto` microservice template and then apply it using `kubectl` to create the service profile.

Retries and timeouts

Linkerd implements intelligent retries automatically to handle application failures gracefully. However, incorrect automatic retries can also aggravate the problem due to a retry storm (amplifying the retry to a service that is already either overloaded, experiencing backpressure, or sending a negative acknowledgment).

Linkerd solves this by limiting risks by using retry budgets rather than a fixed number of retries. If the retry budget is defined at 10%, only 10% more requests may be added to avoid an indefinite retry amount, which can lead to a retry storm. The retry budget and timeouts can be specified through a service profile that's been created for specific routes.

A service profile for a service/specific path can be defined for retries as follows for
`/api/annotations`, which has a configuration to turn on retries
through `isRetryable: true`:

```
...
spec:
  routes:
  - name: GET /api/annotations
    condition:
      method: GET
      pathRegex: /api/annotations
    isRetryable: true
...
```

The retry budget can be defined in the service profile by using the ratio as a percentage and
by setting the **time-to-live (ttl)** parameter. The following specification is for a retry budget
of 20% retries with a minimum of 10 retries per second. This retry attempt will not last for
more than 15 seconds:

```
spec:
  retryBudget:
    retryRatio: 0.2
    minRetriesPerSecond: 10
    ttl: 15s
```

Timeouts can be configured through the service profile, as shown in the following example:

```
...
spec:
  routes:
  - condition:
      method: HEAD
      pathRegex: /authors/[^/]*\.json
    name: HEAD /authors/{id}.json
    timeout: 300ms
...
```

The preceding specification defines a maximum of 300 milliseconds of wait time before the
Linkerd proxy cancels the request and returns a 504 code for paths starting
with `/authors` and ending with `.json`.

Load balancing

Linkerd automatically load balances requests (not connections) across all destination services without any special configuration for HTTP/1.1, HTTP/2, and gRPC connections. For TCP, it does load balancing at the connection level.

Protocols and the TCP proxy

The Linkerd proxy will detect protocols (HTTP/1.1, HTTP/2, or gRPC) automatically and provide HTTP-level metrics, load balancing, and routing without any user-defined configuration. If the Linkerd proxy cannot detect the protocol, it will simply direct the connection to the edge microservices without injecting any quality of service. Linkerd is capable of proxying all TCP traffic, including TLS connections, WebSockets, and HTTP tunneling.

In this section, we had a quick overview of Linkerd's reliability. We will explore this in more detail in `Chapter 16`, *Exploring the Reliability Features of Linkerd*. Now, let's move on to Linkerd's service mesh security based-on entity management.

Security

Security involves authentication and authorization. Linkerd leaves the task of authentication to third parties, such as TLS termination at Ingress, TLS origination at Egress, time-bound **JSON Web Tokens (JWTs)**, and so on. Authorization can be implemented at the proxy level.

Automatic mTLS

The implementation of mTLS between microservices is out-of-the-box in Linkerd and doesn't need any special configuration. The Linkerd Identity component of the control plane acts as a PKI for signing certificates and renews them every 24 hours automatically.

Summary

Linkerd is simple to install, easy to use, and works out of the box as there are very few knobs that we have to tune. Istio is feature-rich, but some may encounter a bit of a learning curve to be able to use it effectively. Istio and Linkerd have their pros and cons, as we discussed in Chapter 4, *Service Mesh Providers*. Linkerd is heavily focussed on ease of use and performance. For example, Linkerd's 2.x proxy is developed in the Rust language to mitigate the performance problems of Linkerd 1.x, which was a very heavy-duty JVM-based implementation.

In this chapter, we explained Linkerd's architecture around control and data planes, installation, proxy configuration, ingress rules, observability, reliability, and security.

In the next chapter, we will delve into Linkerd's installation process and provide step-by-step instructions through live examples.

Questions

1. Linkerd has automatic protocol and TCP connection detection.

   A) True
   B) False

2. Linkerd uses its own Ingress controller.

   A) True
   B) False

3. The Linkerd proxy is written in *GO*, while the control plane components are written in Rust.

   A) True
   B) False

4. The control and data plane can be in a single namespace if so desired.

   A) True
   B) False

5. When a Linkerd proxy is injected using the `linkerd inject` command to a running pod, pods are restarted automatically.

   A) True
   B) False

6. You can add a debug sidecar to a microservice without having to restart the pod.

   A) True
   B) False

7. The retry budget helps us avoid a retry storm, and we don't need to do any configuration in Linkerd to achieve this.

   A) True
   B) False

8. For automatic sidecar injection, Istio needs a labeled namespace with `istio-injection=enabled`, while Linkerd needs a namespace annotated with `linkerd.io/inject: Enabled`.

   A) True
   B) False

9. `istio-init` and `linkerd-init` are run before the sidecar proxy to set the entries in `iptables` to route the application pod traffic through the sidecar proxy.

   A) True
   B) False

10. We can use the Istio and Linkerd sidecars as an edge proxy.

    A) True
    B) False

11. Horizontal pod autoscaling for the control plane for Istio and Linkerd is automatic.

    A) True
    B) False

Further reading

- *Architecture,* Linkerd.Io, 2019: `https://linkerd.io/2/reference/architecture/`
- *Using Ingress,* Linkerd.Io, 2019: `https://linkerd.io/2/tasks/using-ingress/#nginx`
- *Service Discovery On Header Other Than Authority,* Issue #1998, Linkerd/Linkerd2, GitHub, 2019: `https://github.com/linkerd/linkerd2/issues/1998`
- *Containous/Traefik,* GitHub, 2019: `https://github.com/containous/traefik/`
- *Solo-Io/Gloo,* GitHub, 2019: `https://github.com/solo-io/gloo/`
- *The Four Golden Signals For Monitoring Distributed Systems,* Skowronski, Jason, Appoptics Blog, 2019: `https://blog.appoptics.com/the-four-golden-signals-for-monitoring-distributed-systems/`
- *Linkerd Canary Deployments,* Docs.Flagger.App, 2019: `https://docs.flagger.app/usage/linkerd-progressive-delivery`
- *Deislabs/Smi-Spec,* GitHub, 2019: `https://github.com/deislabs/smi-spec/blob/master/traffic-split.md`
- *Retries And Timeouts,* Linkerd.Io, 2019: `https://linkerd.io/2/features/retries-and-timeouts/`

15
Installing Linkerd

In this chapter, we will install the Linkerd **command-line interface (CLI)** and then install the control plane. We will install a demo application and inject a Linkerd sidecar proxy after it is connected to show you how to enable a sidecar proxy for existing applications. Then, we will install the `nginx` ingress controller and create an Ingress route to access this microservice from outside the Kubernetes cluster. We will install Buoyant's `booksapp` microservice and enable automatic sidecar injection so that proxies get injected while a new application is being installed. Then, we'll create an Ingress rule to route the traffic to the `booksapp` microservice.

In a nutshell, we will cover the following topics in this chapter:

- Installing Linkerd's CLI using the latest version
- Installing the control plane
- Defining cluster-wide roles and permissions
- Validating Linkerd's installation by checking services, deployments, and pods
- Downloading and deploying the Emojivoto and BooksApp microservices
- Installing and configuring an Ingress controller
- Defining the Ingress rules for a microservice

Technical requirements

To complete the exercises in this chapter, you will need the following:

- A Windows 10/Apple MacBook, as per the minimum configurations requirement
- A Kubernetes environment
- Internet access to your host machine in order to download applications in the VM running Kubernetes

For detailed information regarding the installation of Kubernetes, please refer to `Chapter 6`, *Building Your Own Kubernetes Environment*. The scripts that are used for the Linkerd section of this book are managed at `https://github.com/servicemeshbook/linkerd`.

Check if the `keepalived` pods are showing a `READY 1/1` state and that the `STATUS` is `Running`:

```
$ kubectl -n keepalived get pods
```

 The `keepalived` load balancer was installed in `Chapter 9`, *Installing Istio*.

The scripts that are used for Linkerd are available at `https://github.com/servicemeshbook/linkerd`. Let's clone the git repository to get the scripts as it relates to Linkerd for our lab exercises:

```
$ cd ~/ # Switch to home directory
$ git clone https://github.com/servicemeshbook/linkerd.git
$ cd linkerd
$ git checkout stable-2.6.0
$ cd scripts
```

Now that we have the source code, we will install the Linkerd CLI.

Installing the Linkerd CLI

Installing Linkerd is simple and easy to do in a Kubernetes cluster. It begins with the installation of the Linkerd CLI, which is used to install Linkerd in a Kubernetes environment. At the time of writing, Linkerd 2.6.0 is the latest stable version, and we will use this version so that we're consistent with the exercises that we will be performing to understand and learn about Linkerd. Follow these steps to install Linkerd:

1. Visit `https://github.com/linkerd/linkerd2/releases` to check the latest releases of Linkerd.
2. Run the following command to list the Linkerd releases:

   ```
   $ curl -Ls https://api.github.com/repos/linkerd/linkerd2/releases |
   grep tag_name
   ```

   You will see `stable-2.6.0` release in the list, and that is what we will use in this chapter to install Linkerd.

3. Run the following command to install the Linkerd CLI in the VM environment:

```
$ cd ## Switch to the home directory
$ export LINKERD2_VERSION=stable-2.6.0
$ curl -s -L https://run.linkerd.io/install | sh -
```

4. The preceding `curl` command will download the specific version defined by `LINKERD2_VERSION` environment variable:

```
Download complete!, validating checksum...
Checksum valid.

Linkerd was successfully installed

Add the linkerd CLI to your path with:

  export PATH=$PATH:$HOME/.linkerd2/bin

Now run:

  linkerd check --pre                    # validate that Linkerd can --
  -- be installed
  linkerd install | kubectl apply -f - # install the control plane --
  -- into the 'linkerd' namespace
  linkerd check                          # validate everything worked!
  linkerd dashboard                      # launch the dashboard

Looking for more? Visit https://linkerd.io/2/next-steps
```

5. Before running any of the pre-checks, edit and source your local `.bashrc` file and add `linkerd2` to the path:

```
$ vi ~/.bashrc

## Add these two lines
export LINKERD2_VERSION=stable-2.6.0
export PATH=$PATH:$HOME/.linkerd2/bin

$ source ~/.bashrc
```

6. Validate Linkerd's client version:

```
$ linkerd version
Client version: stable-2.6.0
Server version: unavailable
```

You will notice that the server version is unavailable. This is because the control plane hasn't been installed yet. Now that we have installed the CLI, let's go ahead and install Linkerd.

Installing Linkerd

The service mesh technology is evolving fast, and Linkerd has an aggressive release schedule for rolling out new changes. Linkerd has two channels for their releases: stable releases for production, and edge releases. Edge releases have new features and functions, and they roll up in a stable release on maturity.

We will only use stable releases in this book. By the time you read this book, there may be a new stable release already out there. The scripts that will be used in this section of this book will be regularly updated so that they correspond to the new releases of Linkerd. Please refer to `https://github.com/servicemeshbook/linkerd` for the updated scripts. However, we suggest that you select the version of Linkerd that's being used in this chapter so that everything's consistent with the hands-on exercises.

Now, we will install the Linkerd control plane using the Linkerd CLI. But first, let's check the prerequisites.

Validating the prerequisites

To check if we have all the prerequisites required for installing Linkerd, run the following command:

```
$ linkerd check --pre
```

The preceding command will check all the prerequisites that are necessary for Linkerd's installation:

```
kubernetes-api
--------------
√ can initialize the client
√ can query the Kubernetes API

kubernetes-version
------------------
√ is running the minimum Kubernetes API version
√ is running the minimum kubectl version

pre-kubernetes-setup
```

```
--------------------
√ control plane namespace does not already exist
...
√ can create ConfigMaps
√ no clock skew detected

pre-kubernetes-capability
-------------------------
√ has NET_ADMIN capability
√ has NET_RAW capability

pre-linkerd-global-resources
----------------------------
√ no ClusterRoles exist
√ no ClusterRoleBindings exist
...
√ no PodSecurityPolicies exist

linkerd-version
---------------
√ can determine the latest version
√ cli is up-to-date

Status check results are √
```

You may see the following warning while running the pre-check under the NET_ADMIN capability:

```
found 1 PodSecurityPolicies, but none provide NET_ADMIN, proxy injection
will fail if the PSP admission controller is running
```

If you receive this warning, delete the PSP (kubectl get psp and then remove the policy) and rerun the check. If the status check results are fine, we can proceed and install the Linkerd control plane.

Installing the Linkerd control plane

To install the Linkerd control plane, follow these steps:

1. Grant the cluster_admin privilege to the service account default for the linkerd namespace, as follows:

    ```
    $ kubectl create clusterrolebinding linkerd-cluster-role-binding \
    --clusterrole=cluster-admin --group=system:serviceaccounts:linkerd
    clusterrolebinding.rbac.authorization.k8s.io/linkerd-cluster-role-
    binding created
    ```

2. Next, run the `linkerd install` command to generate all the necessary Kubernetes resources and route them through the `kubectl apply` command:

```
$ linkerd install | kubectl apply -f -
```

By default, the Linkerd control plane will be installed in the `linkerd` namespace. For this walkthrough, we will keep the default namespace, but it can be changed by passing `--linkerd-namespace`. Check Linkerd's `install --help` command for other parameters that you can change the default behavior of.

3. Run `linkerd check` to ensure that the installation succeeded:

```
$ linkerd check
```

The preceding command will also check for any mismatch in the Kubernetes version, the ability to connect to the API server, and so on. It will wait for the Linkerd control plane pods to be available. This is an excellent tool for pinpointing issues that might hinder the Linkerd installation.

Note that `linkerd check` may take a long time to complete. This may happen due to a slow internet speed while downloading the required Linkerd docker images. At any point after the install, you can run `linkerd check config` to ensure that all the necessary resources of the control plane are available.

4. Run `linkerd version` to check the client and the server version:

```
$ linkerd version
Client version: stable-2.6.0
Server version: stable-2.6.0
```

5. After the Linkerd check has finished running the checklists, verify the Linkerd deployments:

```
$ kubectl -n linkerd get deployments
NAME                      READY   UP-TO-DATE   AVAILABLE   AGE
linkerd-controller        1/1     1            1           3m35s
linkerd-grafana           1/1     1            1           3m34s
linkerd-identity          1/1     1            1           3m35s
linkerd-prometheus        1/1     1            1           3m34s
linkerd-proxy-injector    1/1     1            1           3m34s
linkerd-sp-validator      1/1     1            1           3m34s
linkerd-tap               1/1     1            1           3m34s
linkerd-web               1/1     1            1           3m34s
```

6. Next, verify the Linkerd services:

```
$ kubectl -n linkerd get services
NAME                       TYPE        CLUSTER-IP        ---
linkerd-controller-api     ClusterIP   10.100.102.213    ---
linkerd-destination        ClusterIP   10.101.233.105    ---
linkerd-grafana            ClusterIP   10.103.68.173     ---
linkerd-identity           ClusterIP   10.98.215.247     ---
linkerd-prometheus         ClusterIP   10.107.100.107    ---
linkerd-proxy-injector     ClusterIP   10.97.254.11      ---
linkerd-sp-validator       ClusterIP   10.106.158.157    ---
linkerd-tap                ClusterIP   10.103.252.102    ---
linkerd-web                ClusterIP   10.108.113.87     ---


---  EXTERNAL-IP    PORT(S)              AGE
---  <none>         8085/TCP             4m14s
---  <none>         8086/TCP             4m14s
---  <none>         3000/TCP             4m13s
---  <none>         8080/TCP             4m14s
---  <none>         9090/TCP             4m13s
---  <none>         443/TCP              4m13s
---  <none>         443/TCP              4m13s
---  <none>         8088/TCP,443/TCP     4m13s
---  <none>         8084/TCP,9994/TCP    4m13s
```

7. Finally, verify the Linkerd pods:

```
$ kubectl -n linkerd get pods
NAME                                        READY  STATUS   RESTARTS  AGE
linkerd-controller-84b76f8f8d-9mjn9         3/3    Running  0         30m
linkerd-grafana-65d9998cd5-zv5cl            2/2    Running  0         30m
linkerd-identity-864b86546d-qknjb           2/2    Running  0         30m
linkerd-prometheus-988bcc5cc-nqqsw          2/2    Running  0         30m
linkerd-proxy-injector-7f74699c95-bgtwz     2/2    Running  0         30m
linkerd-sp-validator-74ff8bb46-nwnc9        2/2    Running  0         30m
linkerd-tap-7cdbfb7cff-lvw77                2/2    Running  0         30m
linkerd-web-5b59d96cc6-2xczd                2/2    Running  0         30m
```

Next, let's separate roles and responsibilities.

Separating roles and responsibilities

In some organizations, there is a separation of roles and responsibilities in which the cluster-admin role will not be available to the application administrator. In such a case, the installation can be separated into two different steps that different people can perform.

The following steps are for reference purposes only. Don't run these commands as we've already installed the Linkerd control plane.

Cluster administrator

We need to create the necessary objects that require the cluster-admin role. Let's see how to do this:

1. To create objects that require the cluster-admin role, run the following command:

   ```
   $ linkerd install config | kubectl apply -f -
   ```

   These objects include ClusterRole, ClusterRoleBinding, CustomResourceDefinition, MutatingWebhookConfiguration, Secret, ServiceAccount, and so on.

2. To validate the objects, run the following command:

   ```
   $ linkerd check config
   ```

Now that the necessary objects have been created, we can install the control plane.

Application administrator

The application administrator, who doesn't have the cluster-admin role available, can install a control plane after the necessary objects requiring cluster-admin in the previous steps have been created. Let's take a look:

1. To install the control plane, run the following command:

   ```
   $ linkerd install control-plane | kubectl apply -f -
   ```

   The preceding command will install Linkerd control plane objects such as ConfigMap, Deployment, Secret, Service, and so on using the less privileged account credentials.

2. To validate the installation of control-plane, run the following command:

   ```
   $ linkerd check
   ```

This overview was done to provide reasoning for using `cluster-role` and other user-based roles. Next, we'll explain the steps for setting up the Ingress controller, which is required to enable Linkerd dashboard access from outside the Kubernetes cluster.

Ingress gateway

Linkerd relies on the Ingress controller through your Kubernetes provider. In our case, we are using the bare-minimum Kubernetes cluster to keep resource consumption at a minimum so that we can perform the hands-on exercises. Let's get started:

1. Now, we can install the `nginx` Ingress controller in our cluster using Helm chart at `https://github.com/nginxinc/kubernetes-ingress/tree/v1.5.3/deployments/helm-chart`:

   ```
   $ helm repo add nginx-stable https://helm.nginx.com/stable
   "nginx-stable" has been added to your repositories

   $ helm repo update

   $ helm install nginx-stable/nginx-ingress --name nginx --namespace
   kube-system \
   --set fullnameOverride=nginx \
   --set controller.name=nginx-controller \
   --set controller.config.name=nginx-config \
   --set controller.service.name=nginx-controller \
   --set controller.serviceAccount.name=nginx
   <<removed>>
   NOTES:
   The NGINX Ingress Controller has been installed.
   ```

> This step will not be necessary if you are using a managed Kubernetes service from a cloud provider.

2. Check the Ingress controller service:

   ```
   $ kubectl -n kube-system get services -o wide -l
   app.kubernetes.io/instance=nginx
   NAME                TYPE           CLUSTER-IP     EXTERNAL-IP       ---
   nginx-controller    LoadBalancer   10.97.158.221  192.168.142.249 ---

   --- PORT(S)                        AGE   SELECTOR
   --- 80:32383/TCP,443:31466/TCP     3m9s  app=nginx-controller
   ```

Note that the external IP address is assigned to `nginx-controller` from the running `keepalived` load balancer. If there is no load balancer, the external IP will show as pending.

We create an Ingress to access the Linkerd dashboard from outside. In real situations, we would use an external load balancer, through which we can use an external hostname to access the Linkerd dashboard microservice running in the Kubernetes cluster.

To simulate a real domain name, we create a hostname called `dashboard.linkerd.local` in our VM's `/etc/hosts` file, pretending that this is an actual hostname with an external IP address that terminates at the Ingress gateway.

3. Create an entry in `/etc/hosts` for the following host:

```
$ export INGRESS_HOST=$(kubectl -n kube-system get service nginx-
controller -o jsonpath='{.status.loadBalancer.ingress..ip}') ; echo
$INGRESS_HOST
192.168.142.249

$ sudo sed -i '/dashboard.linkerd.local/d' /etc/hosts

$ echo "$INGRESS_HOST dashboard.linkerd.local" | sudo tee -a
/etc/hosts
```

4. Define an Ingress rule to route traffic from `dashboard.linkerd.local` to Linkerd's internal dashboard service, called `linkerd-web`, at port `8084`:

```
# Script : 01-create-linkerd-ingress.yaml

apiVersion: extensions/v1beta1
kind: Ingress
metadata:
  name: linkerd
  annotations:
    nginx.org/websocket-services: "linkerd-web"
    ingress.kubernetes.io/rewrite-target: /
    nginx.ingress.kubernetes.io/configuration-snippet: |
      proxy_set_header l5d-dst-override
$service_name.$namespace.svc.cluster.local:80;
      proxy_hide_header l5d-remote-ip;
      proxy_hide_header l5d-server-id;
spec:
  rules:
```

```
- host: dashboard.linkerd.local
  http:
    paths:
    - backend:
        serviceName: linkerd-web
        servicePort: 8084
      path: /
```

We used specific annotations while defining the Ingress rule. We set the `proxy_set_header` annotation for Linkerd traffic management. If the microservice is using a web socket, as is the case with `dashboard` and `booksapp`, we need to set the `nginx.org/websocket-services` annotation so that it's pointing to the service name.

5. Now, we can create the Ingress rule:

```
$ kubectl -n linkerd apply -f 01-create-linkerd-ingress.yaml
ingress.extensions/linkerd created
```

After creating the Ingress controller, it's time to gain some hands-on experience using the Linkerd dashboard.

Accessing the Linkerd dashboard

There are multiple ways to access the management UI. The preferred method is to use the Linkerd dashboard. This will open a tunnel between the localhost and the Kubernetes cluster. You can access the Linkerd dashboard using a port. Let's take a look:

1. Access the dashboard by running the following command:

```
$ linkerd dashboard
Linkerd dashboard available at:
http://localhost:50750
Grafana dashboard available at:
http://localhost:50750/grafana
Opening Linkerd dashboard in the default browser
START /usr/bin/google-chrome-stable "http://localhost:50750"

Visit http://localhost:50750 in your browser to view the dashboard
```

The Linkerd dashboard will open in the browser using `http://localhost:50750`. We will learn how to access this dashboard later. Now, press *Ctrl+ C* to stop this proxy.

2. Check if the Ingress is working:

```
$ curl -s -H "Host: dashboard.linkerd.local" http://$INGRESS_HOST |
grep -i title
  <title>Linkerd</title>
```

 You can access `http://dashboard.linkerd.local` from your localhost machine (outside of a VM) if you create an entry in your Windows/MacBook hosts file as you did in the VM.

3. Launch the Linkerd dashboard. Open `http://dashboard.linkerd.local` from your local browser or a browser in the VM:

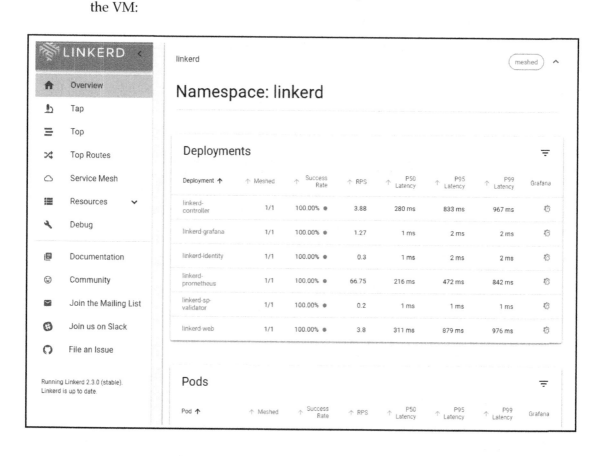

Now, let's explore microservices by using the Linkerd dashboard. We will do this to explain the various capabilities of Linkerd's service mesh.

Deploying the Linkerd demo emoji app

Linkerd provides a demo `emojivoto` application that can be used to explore the capabilities of Linkerd. This app is installed in the `emojivoto` namespace. We will grant the `cluster_admin` role to it, like so:

```
$ kubectl create clusterrolebinding emojivoto-cluster-role-binding \
--clusterrole=cluster-admin --group=system:serviceaccounts:emojivoto
clusterrolebinding.rbac.authorization.k8s.io/emojivoto-cluster-role-binding
created
```

In the following subsection, we will install this demo `emojivoto` application.

Installing a demo application

To install the demo `emojivoto` application, follow these steps:

1. Deploy the `emojivoto` application through its YAML file:

```
$ curl -Ls https://run.linkerd.io/emojivoto.yml | kubectl apply -f -
```

2. Check the application's status:

```
$ kubectl -n emojivoto get deployments,services,pods
NAME        READY   UP-TO-DATE   AVAILABLE   AGE ---
emoji       1/1     1            1           64s ---
vote-bot    1/1     1            1           63s ---
voting      1/1     1            1           64s ---
web         1/1     1            1           64s ---

NAME         TYPE           CLUSTER-IP     EXTERNAL-IP       ---
emoji-svc    ClusterIP      None           <none>            ---
voting-svc   ClusterIP      None           <none>            ---
web-svc      LoadBalancer   10.109.50.125  192.168.142.251   ---

--- PORT(S)        AGE
--- 8080/TCP       64s
--- 8080/TCP       64s
--- 80:30593/TCP   63s
```

```
NAME                          READY   STATUS    RESTARTS   AGE
emoji-58c9579849-ql2z9        1/1     Running   0          64s
vote-bot-774764fd7f-rcd47     1/1     Running   0          63s
voting-66d5cdc46d-mrmb7       1/1     Running   0          64s
web-7f8455487f-p8tvf          1/1     Running   0          64s
```

The `emojivoto` app web UI can be accessed in multiple ways. We will create a hostname and an Ingress rule to route the traffic.

3. Create the `emojivoto.linked.local` entry in `/etc/hosts`:

```
$ export INGRESS_HOST=$(kubectl -n kube-system get service nginx-controller -o jsonpath='{.status.loadBalancer.ingress..ip}') ; echo $INGRESS_HOST
192.168.142.249

$ sudo sed -i '/emojivoto.linkerd.local/d' /etc/hosts

$ echo "$INGRESS_HOST emojivoto.linkerd.local" | sudo tee -a /etc/hosts
```

4. Define the `emojivoto` Ingress routing rule to route traffic from the `emojivoto.linkerd.local` external host to the `web-svc` internal microservice at port 80:

```yaml
# Script : 02-create-emojivoto-ingress.yaml

apiVersion: extensions/v1beta1
kind: Ingress
metadata:
  name: emojivoto
  annotations:
    nginx.org/websocket-services: "web-svc"
    ingress.kubernetes.io/rewrite-target: /
    nginx.ingress.kubernetes.io/configuration-snippet: |
      proxy_set_header l5d-dst-override
$service_name.$namespace.svc.cluster.local:80;
      proxy_hide_header l5d-remote-ip;
      proxy_hide_header l5d-server-id;
spec:
  rules:
  - host: emojivoto.linkerd.local
    http:
      paths:
      - backend:
          serviceName: web-svc
          servicePort: 80
```

```
path: /
```

 You can access `http://emojivoto.linkerd.local` from your localhost virtual machine. To access `emojivoto` from your local browser, create an entry in your Windows/MacBook hosts file.

5. Create an `emojivoto` Ingress rule:

```
$ kubectl -n emojivoto apply -f 02-create-emojivoto-ingress.yaml
ingress.extensions/emojivoto created
```

You can check Ingress access through using the `curl -s -H "Host: emojivoto.linkerd.local" http://$INGRESS_HOST | grep -i title` command.

6. Access the `emojivoto` web UI by launching `http://emojivoto.linkerd.local` from your browser in the VM:

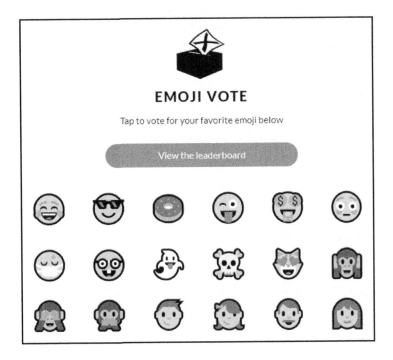

Explore the app by clicking on an emoji. By doing this, you will vote for it. If you click on the doughnut emoji (third on the top row), you will get a 404 error. This is intentional and will cause the success rate to be less than 100%. We will refer to this error again in next chapter, when we deal with Linkerd's reliability features.

7. Now let's inject the Linkerd sidecar proxy into the emoji application:

```
$ kubectl get -n emojivoto deploy -o yaml | linkerd inject - |
kubectl apply -f -
deployment "emoji" injected
deployment "vote-bot" injected
deployment "voting" injected
deployment "web" injected

deployment.extensions/emoji configured
deployment.extensions/vote-bot configured
deployment.extensions/voting configured
deployment.extensions/web configured
```

Using the preceding command, we generate the emojivoto application deployment artifacts and pipe them through linkerd inject to generate a Linkerd sidecar proxy for each pod. The complete YAML is then fed to the kubectl apply command.

8. Now, let's check the deployment, services, and pods. Run the following command to check the deployments:

```
$ kubectl -n emojivoto get deployments
NAME       READY   UP-TO-DATE   AVAILABLE   AGE
emoji      1       1            1           64s
vote-bot   1       1            1           63s
voting     1       1            1           64s
web        1       1            1           64s
```

9. Next, we will check the pods:

```
$ kubectl -n emojivoto get pods
NAME                        READY   STATUS    RESTARTS   AGE
emoji-58c9579849-ql2z9      2/2     Running   0          64s
vote-bot-774764fd7f-rcd47   2/2     Running   0          63s
voting-66d5cdc46d-mrmb7     2/2     Running   0          64s
web-7f8455487f-p8tvf        2/2     Running   0          64s
```

10. Finally, we will check the services:

```
$ kubectl -n emojivoto get services
NAME          TYPE           CLUSTER-IP    EXTERNAL-IP        ---
emoji-svc     ClusterIP      None          <none>             ---
voting-svc    ClusterIP      None          <none>             ---
web-svc       LoadBalancer   10.0.0.132    192.168.142.251 ---

--- PORT(S)       AGE
--- 8080/TCP      64s
--- 8080/TCP      64s
--- 80:31443/TCP  63s
```

Notice the difference between the previous deployment and the sidecar proxies. Each pod has an additional container, which is a Linkerd proxy.

Now, let's deploy the `booksapp` application to explore the features of Linkerd's service mesh.

Deploying the booksapp application

Buoyant maintains the `booksapp` microservice application for the Linkerd open source project. We will be using this application to show service mesh features such as debugging, observability, and monitoring, which are provided by Linkerd. This application is maintained at `https://github.com/BuoyantIO/booksapp`.

This application is comprised of four microservices:

- A Go program that's used to generate traffic
- The main web application – `webapp.rb`
- Authors – `authors.rb`
- Books – `books.rb`

These can be seen in the following diagram:

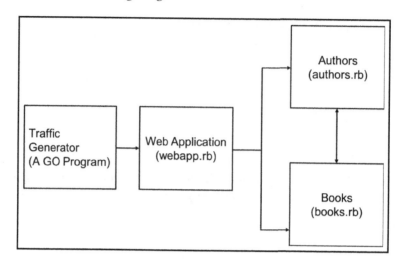

In the previous step, we injected Linkerd sidecar proxies into all the pods for an already deployed `emojivoto` application. Now, we'll deploy a new `booksapp` app in the `linkerd-lab` namespace and enable auto-injection for the Linkerd sidecar proxy. Let's get started:

1. The admission webhook is enabled automatically when we install a Linkerd control plane:

    ```
    $ kubectl -n linkerd get deploy -l linkerd.io/control-plane-
    component=proxy-injector
    NAME                        READY    UP-TO-DATE    AVAILABLE    AGE
    linkerd-proxy-injector      1/1      1             1            110m
    ```

2. When `linkerd-proxy-injector` is running, do the following to ensure that injecting the Linkerd sidecar is automatic:

    *   Annotate the namespace with `linkerd.io/inject:` `enabled`. Any pod that is created in the namespace will have the sidecar proxy injected automatically.
    *   If a namespace is not annotated or annotated as `linkerd.io/inject:` `disabled`, annotate a pod's deployment specification with `linkerd.io/inject:` `enabled`. The sidecar proxy will be injected automatically for the pods that have been deployed.

- If a namespace is annotated with `linkerd.io/inject:`
  `enabled` and the pod's deployed annotation
  is `linkerd.io/inject: disabled`, the sidecar proxy will not be
  injected.

3. Grant the `cluster-admin` role to the `linkerd-lab` namespace:

```
$ kubectl create clusterrolebinding linkerd-lab-cluster-role-
binding \
--clusterrole=cluster-admin --serviceaccount=linkerd:default
clusterrolebinding.rbac.authorization.k8s.io/linkerd-lab-cluster-
role-binding created
```

4. Define the `linkerd-lab` namespace with the `linkerd.io/inject:`
   `enabled` annotation:

```
# Script : 03-create-namespace-sidecar-enabled-annotation.yaml

apiVersion: v1
kind: Namespace
metadata:
  name: linkerd-lab
  annotations:
    linkerd.io/inject: enabled
```

5. Create a namespace called `linkerd-lab`:

```
$ kubectl apply -f 03-create-namespace-sidecar-enabled-
annotation.yaml
namespace/linkerd-lab created
```

6. Install the `booksapp` microservice application from `linkerd.io`:

```
$ curl -Ls https://run.linkerd.io/booksapp.yml | kubectl -n
linkerd-lab apply -f -
service/webapp created
deployment.extensions/webapp created
service/authors created
deployment.extensions/authors created
service/books created
deployment.extensions/books created
deployment.extensions/traffic created
```

7. Check the network services:

```
$ kubectl -n linkerd-lab get svc
NAME       TYPE          CLUSTER-IP    EXTERNAL-IP       PORT(S)          AGE
authors    ClusterIP     None          <none>            7001/TCP         10s
books      ClusterIP     None          <none>            7002/TCP         10s
webapp     LoadBalancer  10.98.66.99   192.168.142.251   7000:31004/TCP   10s
```

The load balancer web app is running on internal port `7000`. You may have noticed that the external IP is fetched from `keepalived`, which we used in the Istio section of this book. The external IP address may be different in your case.

The application can be accessed using a local service name and a port; for example, open `http://webapp.linkerd-lab.svc.cluster.local:7000` from inside the VM:

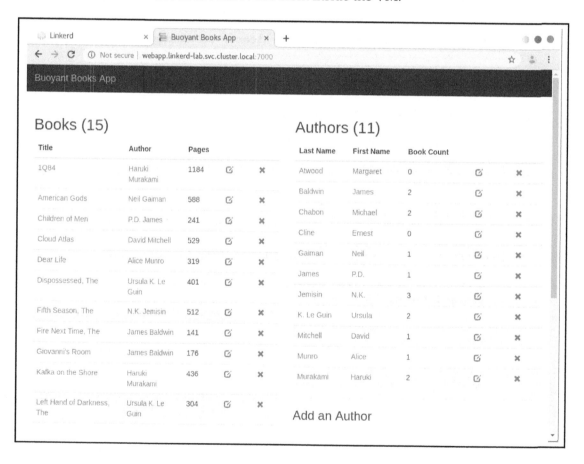

Let's check the current pod's status in the `linkerd-lab` namespace.

8. Check the pod status of `booksapp`:

```
$ kubectl -n linkerd-lab get pods
NAME                          READY   STATUS    RESTARTS   AGE
authors-84d65d4fb-5ppg6       2/2     Running   0          5m14s
books-5fbfb54988-844xg        2/2     Running   0          5m14s
traffic-66c7b9c4cc-cj7dn      2/2     Running   0          5m14s
webapp-579bfc8b44-6mmg7       2/2     Running   0          5m14s
webapp-579bfc8b44-b2m2p       2/2     Running   0          5m14s
webapp-579bfc8b44-fwjlx       2/2     Running   0          5m14s
```

Each pod has two containers, and one of them is the injected Linkerd sidecar proxy.

9. Describe one of the aforementioned pods to see its contents:

```
$ kubectl -n linkerd-lab describe pod -l app=authors
Name:          authors-84d65d4fb-5ppg6
Namespace:     linkerd-lab
...
IP:            192.168.230.232
Controlled By: ReplicaSet/authors-84d65d4fb
Init Containers:
  linkerd-init:
    ...
    Image:        gcr.io/linkerd-io/proxy-init:v1.0.0
    ...
Containers:
  service:
    ...
    Image:        buoyantio/booksapp:v0.0.3
    ...
  linkerd-proxy:
    Container ID:
docker://141f297daf74391099e6abcf0f275f5aa648e47ed53ab5d6817f64f3d9
62536d
    Image:        gcr.io/linkerd-io/proxy:stable-2.6.0
    ...
```

Note that the `linkerd-init` container sets the routing rules so that the inbound and outbound traffic is routed through the Linkerd proxy to the microservice:

```
Events:
  Type    Reason     Age     From                        ---
  ----    ------     ----    ----                        ---
  Normal  Scheduled  7m14s   default-scheduler           ---
```

```
Normal   Started    7m8s    kubelet, osc01.servicemesh.local   ---
Normal   Started    6m31s   kubelet, osc01.servicemesh.local   ---
Normal   Started    6m30s   kubelet, osc01.servicemesh.local   ---

---   Message
---   -------
---   Successfully assigned linkerd-lab/authors-84d65d4fb-jcpt6 to
         osc01.servicemesh.local
---   Started container linkerd-init
---   Started container service
---   Started container linkerd-proxy
```

The `linkerd-proxy` container was injected previously, and the events related to the pod show that the `linkerd-init`, `service`, and `linkerd-proxy` containers were started for the `authors` pod.

The `booksapp` web UI can be accessed in multiple ways. We will create a hostname and an Ingress rule to route the traffic.

10. Create the `booksapp.linked.local` entry in `/etc/hosts`:

```
$ sudo sed -i '/booksapp.linkerd.local/d' /etc/hosts

$ echo "$INGRESS_HOST booksapp.linkerd.local" | sudo tee -a /etc/hosts
```

You can access `http://booksapp.linkerd.local` from your localhost machine (outside of the VM) if you create an entry in your Windows/MacBook hosts file as you did in the VM.

11. Define the `booksapp` Ingress routing rule:

```
# Script : 04-create-booksapp-ingress.yaml

apiVersion: extensions/v1beta1
kind: Ingress
metadata:
  name: booksapp
  annotations:
    nginx.org/websocket-services: "webapp"
    ingress.kubernetes.io/rewrite-target: /
    nginx.ingress.kubernetes.io/configuration-snippet: |
      proxy_set_header l5d-dst-override
$service_name.$namespace.svc.cluster.local:7000;
      proxy_hide_header l5d-remote-ip;
      proxy_hide_header l5d-server-id;
spec:
```

```
rules:
- host: booksapp.linkerd.local
  http:
    paths:
    - backend:
        serviceName: webapp
        servicePort: 7000
      path: /
```

12. Create the `booksapp` Ingress rule:

```
$  kubectl -n linkerd-lab apply -f 04-create-booksapp-ingress.yaml
ingress.extensions/booksapp created
```

You can check Ingress access through the `curl -s -H "Host: booksapp.linkerd.local" http://$INGRESS_HOST | grep -i /title` command.

13. Access the `booksapp` web UI by opening `http://booksapp.linkerd.local` from your local browser or a browser in the VM:

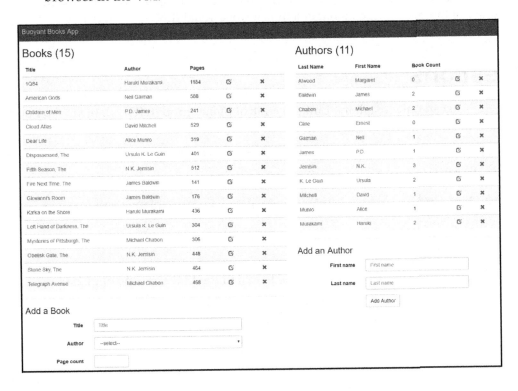

This is how Linkerd allows access to microservices through an Ingress controller. It is easy to define these rules through YAML deployment, as long as a service name and ports have been defined.

Summary

In this chapter, we looked at Linkerd, which provides a very smooth and easy install process. Linkerd is an attractive option in certain environments as a service mesh. Linkerd provides the Linkerd CLI, which runs on either Linux, Windows, or MacBook to offer an easy way for us to install its control plane if we only have `kubectl` access to the remote Kubernetes cluster.

Automatic sidecar injection through the admission webhook controller allows us to easily place all the already deployed applications into a service mesh data plane. The web dashboard of Linkerd provides instant insights into the control and data planes. Linkerd relies upon an external Ingress gateway.

In the next chapter, we will explore the traffic management capabilities of Linkerd. In the vocabulary of Linkerd, traffic management is termed reliability.

Questions

1. You can only install the Linkerd control plane through SSH to the master node of the Kubernetes cluster.

   A) True
   B) False

2. You need a `cluster-admin` role to install a control plane configuration.

   A) True
   B) False

3. You need a `cluster-admin` role to install the Linkerd control plane.

   A) True
   B) False

4. Linkerd allows us to automatically inject sidecars if we label our namespace with `linkerd.io/inject: enabled`.

   A) True
   B) False

5. If we want to exclude a pod so that it gets its own sidecar proxy, we can label the pod with `linkerd.io/inject: disabled`.

   A) True
   B) False

Further reading

- *Getting Started*, Linkerd, available at `https://linkerd.io/2/getting-started/`, accessed 5 May 2019

16
Exploring the Reliability Features of Linkerd

In this chapter, we will go through Linkerd's reliability features, such as automatic load balancing through dynamic requests routing, service profiles, retries, timeouts, and proactive error code hunting.

This chapter will explain the traffic management capabilities of a service mesh. Understanding this framework is necessary if you want to use networking resources that coordinate, restrict, and scale traffic throughout microservices.

We will be covering the following topics in this chapter:

- Load balancing traffic between services in the `booksapp` application
- Understanding and creating service profiles
- Routing traffic between the `booksapp` application for a newly created service profile
- Deploying service profiles for the `booksapp` application using Swagger specs
- Understanding aggregated routing for the `booksapp` application
- Enabling retries, retry budgets, and timeouts
- Troubleshooting the error code in the `emojivoto` application

Technical requirements

This chapter is dependent on Chapter 15, *Installing Linkerd*. You will need to complete the hands-on exercises of Chapter 15, *Installing Linkerd*, that deal with the following, in order to work through this chapter:

- Setting up Linkerd
- Installing a control plane
- Deploying the booksapp and emojivoto applications

Make sure that you are in the ~/linkerd/scripts directory for the exercises in this chapter:

```
$ cd ~/linkerd/scripts
```

Now, we're ready to begin!

Overview of the reliability of Linkerd

Reliability is a critical quality of any enterprise application. It is even more significant if the application is deployed in an ever-changing environment that meets business requirements through software innovation. **Ibryam** defines this concept as follows:

- **Fragile**: The system is unable to survive under stress.
- **Robust**: The system withstands stress to an extent, and then it breaks.
- **Resilient**: The system adapts to stress and failures before it reaches the breaking point.
- **Anti-fragile**: It feeds on stress and change and so it's much harder to create.

This is better understood with the help of the following diagram:

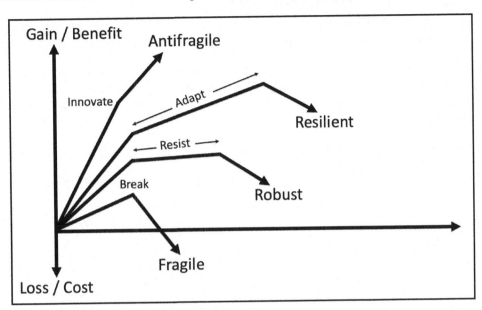

In parallel to reliability, a service mesh provides a resilient system through continuous improvement from sidecar proxies.

The use of specialized libraries such as Twitter's Finagle and Netflix's Hystrix help us build robust applications, but these libraries are language-specific. In a distributed computing environment, such as Kubernetes, such libraries evolved into language-agnostic implementations, for example, Linkerd or Envoy proxies.

To recap, the two most popular sidecar proxies that we have been discussing throughout this book are **Envoy** and **Linkerd**. An important purpose of a sidecar proxy is to provide application resiliency through load balancing, circuit breaking, outlier detection, and so on.

Let's begin by understanding Linkerd's load balancing features.

Configuring load balancing

We explained **load balancing** in Chapter 7, *Understanding the Istio Service Mesh*. Linkerd uses a smart load balancing mechanism, which is described by William Morgan as follows:

"Linkerd uses an exponentially weighted moving average of response latencies to send requests to the fastest pods automatically. If one pod slows down, even momentarily, Linkerd will shift traffic away from it. This intelligent load balancing can reduce end-to-end tail latencies."

Let's explore how load balancing is configured for the emojivoto application:

1. Validate the emojivoto microservice and the availability of its pods:

```
$ kubectl get pods -n emojivoto
NAME                         READY   STATUS    RESTARTS   AGE
emoji-697b575bd9-6487c       2/2     Running   0          29m
vote-bot-7bd97dfbdc-f8hfv    2/2     Running   0          29m
voting-6b4bf7494b-pxk5k      2/2     Running   0          29m
web-559684dbc5-9pmdf         2/2     Running   0          29m
```

2. Scale the voting and web deployments from 1 to 2 replicas. We can scale to any number, as long as enough CPU and memory is available:

```
$ kubectl -n emojivoto scale deploy voting --replicas=2
deployment.extensions/voting scaled

$ kubectl -n emojivoto scale deploy web --replicas=2
deployment.extensions/web scaled
```

To recap, the emojivoto application has an emoji-bot that continuously sends traffic to the application. The doughnut emoji has a built-in HTTP 404 error. The emoji-bot sends 15% of its traffic to this emoji, and it picks up other emojis at random. Later in this chapter, we will debug and determine the root cause of this issue.

3. Now, let's check the stats of deployment using the linkerd CLI:

```
$ linkerd -n emojivoto stat deployments
NAME       MESHED   SUCCESS      RPS   LATENCY_P50 ---
emoji        1/1    100.00%    2.0rps          1ms ---
vote-bot     1/1          -        -             - ---
voting       2/2     91.67%    1.0rps          1ms ---
web          2/2     95.76%    2.0rps          4ms ---

---   LATENCY_P95    LATENCY_P99     TCP_CONN
```

---	2ms	2ms	3
---	–	–	–
---	1ms	1ms	6
---	10ms	18ms	4

Notice the success rate, requests **rate per second (rps)**, and latency distribution percentile, as this is the aggregated information for deployment as a whole. The aggregated metrics are the values that Linkerd provides.

4. Check the aggregated information at the pod level for the web and voting pods:

```
$ linkerd -n emojivoto stat pods
NAME                          STATUS    MESHED    SUCCESS     RPS  ---
emoji-697b575bd9-6487c        Running    1/1      100.00%   2.0rps ---
vote-bot-7bd97dfbdc-f8hfv     Running    1/1         –        –    ---
voting-6b4bf7494b-8znt2       Running    1/1       64.29%   0.5rps ---
voting-6b4bf7494b-pxk5k       Running    1/1       81.25%   0.5rps ---
web-559684dbc5-9pmdf          Running    1/1       84.13%   1.1rps ---
web-559684dbc5-164dd          Running    1/1       90.91%   0.9rps ---
```

	LATENCY_P50	LATENCY_P95	LATENCY_P99	TCP_CONN
---	1ms	1ms	1ms	3
---	–	–	–	–
---	1ms	1ms	1ms	3
---	1ms	2ms	2ms	3
---	7ms	17ms	19ms	2
---	3ms	13ms	19ms	2

5. Browse to http://dashboard.linkerd.local in your VM.

6. Navigate to **Resources** | **Pods** | **All**. On the main console page, you will see HTTP metrics and TCP metrics.

7. Filter the HTTP metrics by clicking the three vertical bars on the top right corner and typing emojivoto.

8. Repeat the same for TCP metrics.

Initially, you may only see traffic on one web service, but if you wait for a few seconds, the traffic will balance automatically:

HTTP metrics

emojivoto ✕

Namespace ↑	Pod ↑	↑ Meshed	↑ Success Rate	↑ RPS	↑ P50 Latency	↑ P95 Latency	↑ P99 Latency	Grafana
emojivoto	emoji-6988d8b456-4p8t2	1/1	100.00% ●	2	1 ms	1 ms	1 ms	⊙
emojivoto	vote-bot-5cb9dc99db-kfnhs	1/1	—	—	—	—	—	⊙
emojivoto	voting-54944fb8f8-fxgp5	1/1	83.33% ●	0.4	1 ms	1 ms	1 ms	⊙
emojivoto	voting-54944fb8f8-vj6xx	1/1	81.58% ●	0.63	1 ms	1 ms	1 ms	⊙
emojivoto	web-58bd8f8c44-skhvw	1/1	92.63% ●	1.58	3 ms	6 ms	9 ms	⊙
emojivoto	web-58bd8f8c44-w7xpn	1/1	84.62% ●	0.43	3 ms	5 ms	5 ms	⊙

TCP metrics

emojivoto ✕

Namespace ↑	Pod ↑	↑ Meshed	↑ Connections	↑ Read Bytes / sec	↑ Write Bytes / sec	Grafana
emojivoto	emoji-6988d8b456-4p8t2	1/1	4	2.424kB/s	2.427kB/s	⊙
emojivoto	vote-bot-5cb9dc99db-kfnhs	1/1	—	—	—	⊙
emojivoto	voting-54944fb8f8-fxgp5	1/1	3	50.13B/s	54.72B/s	⊙
emojivoto	voting-54944fb8f8-vj6xx	1/1	3	78.63B/s	86.13B/s	⊙
emojivoto	web-58bd8f8c44-skhvw	1/1	2	3.853kB/s	3.957kB/s	⊙
emojivoto	web-58bd8f8c44-w7xpn	1/1	2	969.48B/s	997.22B/s	⊙

Notice that we didn't make any configuration changes to accomplish load balancing. This capability is offered out of the box.

Linkerd provides a mechanism for aggregating metrics through a service profile. This helps in obtaining better traffic assessments across services. We'll explore this further in the next section.

Setting up a service profile

A service profile in Linkerd is a way to aggregate information about routes. It collects route metrics for different dimensions, such as the success rate, the response latency for a designated source, and destination services. The service profile works off the host headers of the HTTP protocol. Linkerd's :authority refers to HTTP/2 headers, which is equivalent to HTTP/1.x's Host header. Let's create a service profile for the booksapp application we looked at in Chapter 15, *Installing Linkerd*.

booksapp is the demo application from Buoyant.io – the company behind Linkerd. This application consists of three microservices: webapp, authors, and books. The microservices are written in Ruby, and they use JSON over HTTP to communicate with other services.

Take the following example of the linkerd top command, which is a simple monitoring utility of Linkerd. It shows the metrics from the traffic to the webapp microservice in the linkerd-lab namespace:

```
$ linkerd top deployment/traffic --namespace linkerd-lab \
--to deployment/webapp --to-namespace linkerd-lab --path /books --hide-
sources
(press q to quit)
Destination            Method  Path                   Count  Best   Worst ---
webapp-57944-b2m2p     POST    /books                   12   13ms   48ms ---
webapp-57944-6mmg7     POST    /books                   12   14ms   55ms ---
webapp-57944-fwjlx     POST    /books                    9   12ms   51ms ---
webapp-57944-6mmg7     POST    /books/82489/edit         2   59ms   63ms ---
webapp-57944-6mmg7     GET     /books/82472              1   15ms   15ms ---
webapp-57944-6mmg7     GET     /books/82473              1   15ms   15ms ---
webapp-57944-b2m2p     POST    /books/82473/edit         1   57ms   57ms ---

--- Last   Success Rate
--- 20ms        58.33%
--- 15ms        58.33%
--- 51ms        55.56%
--- 63ms        50.00%
--- 15ms       100.00%
--- 15ms       100.00%
--- 57ms         0.00%
. . .
```

Notice that each /books path is unique and shows the top reports metrics for every unique path. Lots of these paths may overwhelm Prometheus since each path will be a separate time series. The unique path problem arises due to the parameters that are passed to the route.

It would be nice if metrics were reported on an aggregated path rather than similar-looking unique paths. Linkerd can aggregate metrics through service profiles. Implementing service profiles using a Kubernetes's Custom Resource Definition can be done in Linkerd's control plane namespace.

We can use a service profile to define a list of routes for a service. Here, we can use a regular expression for unique paths. These can be defined to aggregate metrics.

Through the service profile, it is possible for users to do the following:

- Define the paths that should be aggregated
- Aggregate paths to limit time series data for Prometheus
- Query Prometheus's backend for historical data

Now, let's set up a service profile:

1. First, validate if a service profile CRD has been deployed:

```
$ kubectl -n linkerd-lab get crd | grep -i linkerd
serviceprofiles.linkerd.io          2019-08-28T01:31:15Z
```

2. Let's look at the booksapp service:

```
$ kubectl -n linkerd-lab get svc
NAME      TYPE          CLUSTER-IP    EXTERNAL-IP        PORT(S)           AGE
authors   ClusterIP     None          <none>             7001/TCP          51d
books     ClusterIP     None          <none>             7002/TCP          51d
webapp    LoadBalancer  10.0.0.129    192.168.142.249    7000:30604/TCP    51d
```

3. Let's look at the routes that Linkerd discovered:

```
$ linkerd -n linkerd-lab routes services
==> service/authors <==
ROUTE        SERVICE   SUCCESS   RPS      LATENCY_P50   LATENCY_P95 ---
[DEFAULT]    authors   74.19%    6.7rps           5ms          26ms ---

--- LATENCY_P99
---          29ms

==> service/books <==
ROUTE        SERVICE   SUCCESS   RPS      LATENCY_P50   LATENCY_P95 ---
```

```
[DEFAULT]      books      78.38%   8.2rps          10ms            77ms ---

--- LATENCY_P99
---        95ms

==> service/webapp <==
ROUTE          SERVICE    SUCCESS    RPS   LATENCY_P50   LATENCY_P95 ---
[DEFAULT]      webapp     76.16%   7.2rps          26ms            83ms ---

--- LATENCY_P99
---        97ms
```

Here, you can see the aggregated live traffic that was reported at the route level for every service within `booksapp`.

4. Next, create a service profile template using the `linkerd profile` command:

```
$ linkerd profile --template webapp -n linkerd-lab > webapp.yaml
```

5. Edit the generated template so that it looks like this:

```
# Script : 05-create-service-profile-web.yaml

apiVersion: linkerd.io/v1alpha1
kind: ServiceProfile
metadata:
  name: webapp.linkerd-lab.svc.cluster.local
spec:
  routes:
  - name: '/books'
    condition:
      pathRegex: '/books'
      method: POST
  - name: '/books/{id}'
    condition:
      pathRegex: '/books/\d+'
      method: GET
```

The preceding `webapp` service profile defines two routes that the `webapp` service responds to: /books and /books<id>.

6. Deploy the preceding service profile for the `webapp` service:

```
$ kubectl -n linkerd-lab apply -f 05-create-service-profile-
web.yaml
serviceprofile.linkerd.io/webapp.linkerd-lab.svc.cluster.local
created
```

7. Next, let's see if the `linkerd route` command picks up the new additional routes:

```
$ linkerd -n linkerd-lab routes services/webapp
ROUTE           SERVICE   SUCCESS     RPS    LATENCY_P50   ---
/books          webapp    40.67%    2.5rps         24ms   ---
/books/{id}     webapp    100.00%   1.1rps         25ms   ---
[DEFAULT]       webapp    88.89%    4.7rps         28ms   ---

--- LATENCY_P95   LATENCY_P99
---        46ms          86ms
---        30ms          30ms
---       108ms         182ms
```

Notice the two additional routes that give a further breakdown of traffic for `/books` and `/books/{id}`.

A service profile can also be set up if Swagger specification for the service is available.

The Swagger specs for all three microservices are available at:

- https://run.linkerd.io/booksapp/webapp.swagger
- https://run.linkerd.io/booksapp/authors.swagger
- https://run.linkerd.io/booksapp/books.swagger

Optional: Use the following `linkerd profile` commands to see the generated profile across all three services:

```
$ linkerd -n linkerd-lab profile --open-api webapp.swagger webapp
```

```
$ linkerd -n linkerd-lab profile --open-api authors.swagger authors
```

```
$ linkerd -n linkerd-lab profile --open-api books.swagger books
```

The output from the preceding code can be saved in a file, and custom edits can be made before creating a custom resource definition.

8. Next, let's create Linkerd Kubernetes primitive service profiles for the `webapp`, `books`, and `authors` microservices using the Swagger specs:

```
$ linkerd -n linkerd-lab profile --open-api webapp.swagger webapp |
kubectl -n linkerd-lab apply -f -
serviceprofile.linkerd.io/webapp.linkerd-lab.svc.cluster.local
created

$ linkerd -n linkerd-lab profile --open-api books.swagger books|
kubectl -n linkerd-lab apply -f -
serviceprofile.linkerd.io/books.linkerd-lab.svc.cluster.local
created

$ linkerd -n linkerd-lab profile --open-api authors.swagger authors
| kubectl -n linkerd-lab apply -f -
serviceprofile.linkerd.io/authors.linkerd-lab.svc.cluster.local
created
```

9. Check out the service profile definition that was created in the `linkerd-lab` namespace:

```
$ kubectl -n linkerd-lab get serviceprofile
NAME                                        AGE
authors.linkerd-lab.svc.cluster.local       3m57s
books.linkerd-lab.svc.cluster.local         4m2s
webapp.linkerd-lab.svc.cluster.local        6m24s
```

10. Let's check the per route metrics that were accumulated from the `webapp` service:

```
$ linkerd -n linkerd-lab routes deploy/webapp
ROUTE                       SERVICE    SUCCESS     RPS ---
GET /                       webapp     100.00%     0.5rps ---
GET /authors/{id}           webapp     100.00%     0.5rps ---
GET /books/{id}             webapp     100.00%     1.0rps ---
POST /authors               webapp     100.00%     0.5rps ---
POST /authors/{id}/delete   webapp     100.00%     0.5rps ---
POST /authors/{id}/edit     webapp       0.00%     0.0rps ---
POST /books                 webapp      49.18%     2.0rps ---
POST /books/{id}/delete     webapp     100.00%     0.5rps ---
POST /books/{id}/edit       webapp      41.89%     1.2rps ---
[DEFAULT]                   webapp       0.00%     0.0rps ---

--- LATENCY_P50    LATENCY_P95    LATENCY_P99
---        38ms           49ms           50ms
---        30ms           47ms           49ms
---        25ms           39ms           40ms
---        22ms           29ms           30ms
---        35ms           93ms           99ms
```

```
   ---        0ms          0ms          0ms
   ---       31ms         46ms         49ms
   ---       15ms         29ms         30ms
   ---       80ms        170ms        194ms
   ---        0ms          0ms          0ms
```

11. Let's check the per route metrics that were accumulated from
    the authors service:

```
$ linkerd -n linkerd-lab routes deploy/authors
ROUTE                        SERVICE    SUCCESS     RPS     ---
DELETE /authors/{id}.json    authors    100.00%    0.5rps   ---
GET /authors.json            authors    100.00%    0.5rps   ---
GET /authors/{id}.json       authors    100.00%    1.6rps   ---
HEAD /authors/{id}.json      authors     43.78%    3.6rps   ---
POST /authors.json           authors    100.00%    0.5rps   ---
[DEFAULT]                    authors      0.00%    0.0rps   ---

--- LATENCY_P50    LATENCY_P95    LATENCY_P99
---        18ms          29ms          30ms
---         7ms          10ms          10ms
---         4ms          13ms          19ms
---         3ms           9ms          16ms
---         8ms          37ms          40ms
---         0ms           0ms           0ms
```

The preceding routes show aggregated metrics corresponding to requests for
different author IDs.

12. The following example shows traffic aggregation from the webapp service to the
    authors service. Notice that there are no instrumented errors embedded in the
    authors service. Here, we can see a 100% success rate:

```
$ linkerd -n linkerd-lab routes deploy/webapp --to svc/authors
ROUTE                        SERVICE    SUCCESS     RPS     ---
DELETE /authors/{id}.json    authors    100.00%    0.5rps   ---
GET /authors.json            authors    100.00%    0.5rps   ---
GET /authors/{id}.json       authors    100.00%    1.6rps   ---
HEAD /authors/{id}.json      authors      0.00%    0.0rps   ---
POST /authors.json           authors    100.00%    0.5rps   ---
[DEFAULT]                    authors      0.00%    0.0rps   ---

--- LATENCY_P50    LATENCY_P95    LATENCY_P99
---        25ms          37ms          39ms
---         9ms          19ms          20ms
---         4ms           9ms          10ms
---         0ms           0ms           0ms
```

---	12ms	19ms	20ms
---	0ms	0ms	0ms

13. The following example shows traffic from `webapp` to `books`. The `books` service has an instrumented error, and the following code shows a POST/PUT success rate of less than 100%:

```
$ linkerd -n linkerd-lab routes deploy/webapp --to svc/books
ROUTE                      SERVICE   SUCCESS      RPS    ---
DELETE /books/{id}.json     books    100.00%    0.5rps   ---
GET /books.json             books    100.00%    1.1rps   ---
GET /books/{id}.json        books    100.00%    2.2rps   ---
POST /books.json            books     47.14%    2.3rps   ---
PUT /books/{id}.json        books     43.66%    1.2rps   ---
[DEFAULT]                   books      0.00%    0.0rps   ---
```

	LATENCY_P50	LATENCY_P95	LATENCY_P99
---	8ms	17ms	19ms
---	5ms	18ms	20ms
---	5ms	18ms	20ms
---	16ms	30ms	38ms
---	67ms	97ms	99ms
---	0ms	0ms	0ms

A service profile is a nice way to get aggregated metrics per route, using regex when parameters are used, and report on success rates and different ranges for latency. These metrics provide immediate insight into performance bottlenecks and bugs. This is a great help to product development in terms of delivering resilient and performant systems. In comparison to Istio, this is a useful feature that's unique to Linkerd.

Next, we will explore traffic retries, budgets for the `booksapp` microservice, and how such enabled metrics are aggregated.

Retrying failed transactions

As we explained in Chapter 14, *Understanding the Linkerd Service Mesh,* a blind retry on failed transactions can lead to **retry storms**. At the time of writing, Linkerd attempts to address this issue by introducing the `retry` and `retry budget` configurations.

Before we attempt to retry the failed transactions, it is important to decide and know which request should be re-tried and how many times. To do this, follow these steps:

1. Run the `linkerd` routes from `books` to `authors` and view the metrics:

```
$ linkerd -n linkerd-lab routes deploy/books --to svc/authors
ROUTE                          SERVICE    SUCCESS      RPS    ---
DELETE /authors/{id}.json      authors     0.00%    0.0rps    ---
GET /authors.json              authors     0.00%    0.0rps    ---
GET /authors/{id}.json         authors     0.00%    0.0rps    ---
HEAD /authors/{id}.json        authors    53.77%    3.3rps    ---
POST /authors.json             authors     0.00%    0.0rps    ---
[DEFAULT]                      authors     0.00%    0.0rps    ---

--- LATENCY_P50    LATENCY_P95    LATENCY_P99
---        0ms            0ms            0ms
---        0ms            0ms            0ms
---        0ms            0ms            0ms
---        5ms           10ms           17ms
---        0ms            0ms            0ms
---        0ms            0ms            0ms
```

Notice that all the requests from `books` to `authors` are to the HEAD `/authors/{id}.json` route. Here, we can see that 50% of the requests are failing (which is intentional application design). Notice the latency for the HEAD route. We can expect it to increase if a retry is enforced.

Let's edit the `authors` service profile to add `isRetryable: true` for the HEAD `/authors/{id}.json` route.

2. The simplest way to do this is to run `kubectl -n linkerd-lab edit sp authors.linkerd-lab.svc.cluster.local` and add a line for the HEAD `/authors/{id}.json` route, like so:

```
apiVersion: linkerd.io/v1alpha1
kind: ServiceProfile
metadata:
  name: authors.linkerd-lab.svc.cluster.local
spec:
  routes:
  - condition:
      method: GET
      pathRegex: /authors\.json
    name: GET /authors.json
  - condition:
      method: POST
```

```
          pathRegex: /authors\.json
        name: POST /authors.json
    - condition:
          method: DELETE
          pathRegex: /authors/[^/]*\.json
        name: DELETE /authors/{id}.json
    - condition:
          method: GET
          pathRegex: /authors/[^/]*\.json
        name: GET /authors/{id}.json
    - condition:
          method: HEAD
          pathRegex: /authors/[^/]*\.json
        isRetryable: true
        name: HEAD /authors/{id}.json
```

Alternatively, we can patch the service profile. Count the correct position of the HEAD method (starting at base 0) and patch the service profile, like so:

```
$ kubectl -n linkerd-lab patch sp authors.linkerd-
lab.svc.cluster.local --type json --patch='[{"op": "add","path":
"/spec/routes/4/isRetryable","value": true}]'
serviceprofile.linkerd.io/authors.linkerd-lab.svc.cluster.local
patched
```

3. After adding isRetryable: true, Linkerd will begin the retry requests to this route automatically. Let's check this again by running the linkerd routes command:

```
$ linkerd -n linkerd-lab routes deploy/books --to svc/authors
ROUTE                          SERVICE    SUCCESS        RPS   ---
DELETE /authors/{id}.json      authors     0.00%     0.0rps   ---
GET /authors.json              authors     0.00%     0.0rps   ---
GET /authors/{id}.json         authors     0.00%     0.0rps   ---
HEAD /authors/{id}.json        authors   100.00%     2.2rps   ---
POST /authors.json             authors     0.00%     0.0rps   ---
[DEFAULT]                      authors     0.00%     0.0rps   ---

--- LATENCY_P50    LATENCY_P95    LATENCY_P99
---         0ms            0ms            0ms
---         0ms            0ms            0ms
---         0ms            0ms            0ms
---        12ms           25ms           29ms
---         0ms            0ms            0ms
---         0ms            0ms            0ms
```

As the retries are attempted, the failing request shows a `100%` success rate. However, note that the latency has increased due to the `retry`. Linkerd made this possible without us having to change the application logic and requires minimal configuration changes through the service profile.

Retries can be risky if we don't know the application logic. The domino effect of a retry storm can propagate to other services. We'll look at how to deal with this problem with the help of the *retry budget* in the next section.

Retry budgets

Linkerd implements *retry budgets*, which limit the number of retries against a service as a percentage. This prevents the retry logic from overwhelming the system or increasing the latency significantly.

Here is an example of a *retry* budget that can be specified at the service profile level:

```
...
spec:
  retryBudget:
    retryRatio: 0.2
    minRetriesPerSecond: 10
    ttl: 15s
...
```

The preceding specification is for a retry budget of 20% retries with a minimum of 20 retries per second. This retry attempt won't last for more than 15 seconds.

Next, we will define service-based timeouts and how these can be applied to a service profile.

Implementing timeouts

Linkerd allows a *timeout* definition that defines a wait time before failing (or rerouting) requests to another service. To demonstrate this, let's add a 25 ms timeout to the same spec route from the previous section. When this timeout limit is exhausted, the request will be canceled and will return a `504` HTTP code. By default, the timeout is set at 10 seconds. Let's get started:

1. Patch the service profile for `authors.linkerd-lab.svc.cluster.local` by adding `timeout: 25ms` to the `HEAD /authors/{id}.json` route. Note that we can either edit or patch the service profile:

```
$ kubectl -n linkerd-lab patch sp authors.linkerd-
lab.svc.cluster.local \
--type json --patch='[{"op": "add","path":
"/spec/routes/4/timeout","value": 25ms}]'
serviceprofile.linkerd.io/authors.linkerd-lab.svc.cluster.local
patched
```

2. Now, run the `linkerd route` command to see the effect of the timeout:

```
$ linkerd -n linkerd-lab routes deploy/books --to svc/authors
ROUTE                      SERVICE  SUCCESS     RPS ---
DELETE /authors/{id}.json  authors    0.00%  0.0rps ---
GET /authors.json          authors    0.00%  0.0rps ---
GET /authors/{id}.json     authors    0.00%  0.0rps ---
HEAD /authors/{id}.json    authors   98.50%  2.2rps ---
POST /authors.json         authors    0.00%  0.0rps ---
[DEFAULT]                  authors    0.00%  0.0rps ---

--- LATENCY_P50  LATENCY_P95  LATENCY_P99
---        0ms          0ms          0ms
---        0ms          0ms          0ms
---        0ms          0ms          0ms
---        8ms         24ms         29ms
---        0ms          0ms          0ms
---        0ms          0ms          0ms
```

After the timeout has been implemented, you will notice that the success rate is less than 100%.

Next, we will dive into the `emojivoto` application and debug the known `donut` error.

Troubleshooting error code

In this section, we will troubleshoot the error code that exists with the `donut` emoji (refer to `Chapter 15`, *Installing Linkerd*, for more information). Since the microservice is throwing an error, using Linkerd's dashboard, we will investigate the HTTP traffic routes across its service, deployment, and pods to debug this issue.

Switch to the `emojivoto` application in your browser by going
to `http://emojivoto.linkerd.local`. Vote for the doughnut emoji (third on the top
row) and notice the HTTP 404 error. Now, follow these steps:

1. Go to **Resources** | **Namespaces** | **All** in `http://dashboard.linkerd.local`.
   Notice that the success rate is less than 100% for the `emojivoto` namespace,
   which is due to the doughnut emoji error:

HTTP metrics

Namespace ↑	↑ Meshed	↑ Success Rate	↑ RPS	↑ P50 Latency	↑ P95 Latency	↑ P99 Latency	Grafana
cert-manager	0/1	—	—	—	—	—	
default	0/0	—	—	—	—	—	
emojivoto	6/6	94.61% ●	4.95	1 ms	5 ms	9 ms	⟲
istio-lab	0/6	—	—	—	—	—	
istio-system	0/12	—	—	—	—	—	
keepalived	0/2	—	—	.	—	—	
kube-public	0/0	—	—	—	—	—	
kube-system	0/37	—	—	—	—	—	
linkerd	7/7	100.00% ●	6.9	5 ms	87 ms	97 ms	⟲
linkerd-lab	6/6	76.22% ●	23.13	10 ms	83 ms	99 ms	⟲
platform	0/0	—	—	—	—	—	
services	0/0	—	—	—	—	—	
test-lab	1/1	—	—	—	—	—	⟲

2. Click on the **emojivoto** link under the **HTTP metrics** section to view the service discovery graph. This shows the dependency information of the emojivoto microservice application:

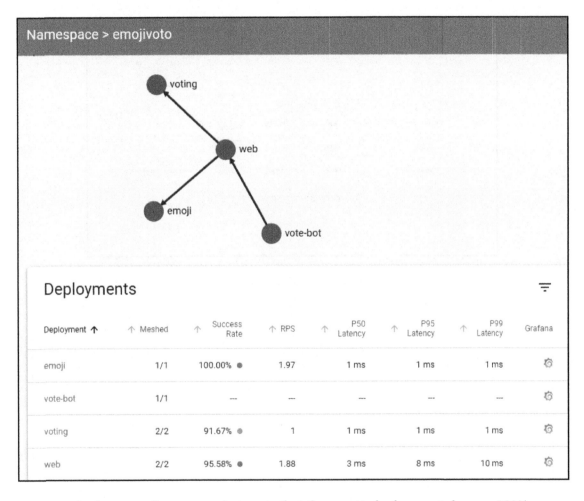

In the preceding screenshot, note that the emoji deployment shows a 100% success rate while voting, while web doesn't.

3. Click the `web` deployment. You will see a live traffic metrics visualization with indicators such as **success rate (SR)**, P99 latency, and **request per second (RPS)** for each microservice with a dependency relationship:

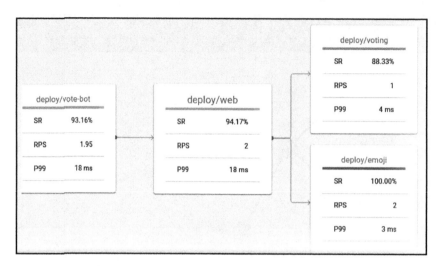

4. Scroll down to see a feed of **Live Calls** of requests. `vote-bot` generates continuous traffic to the application:

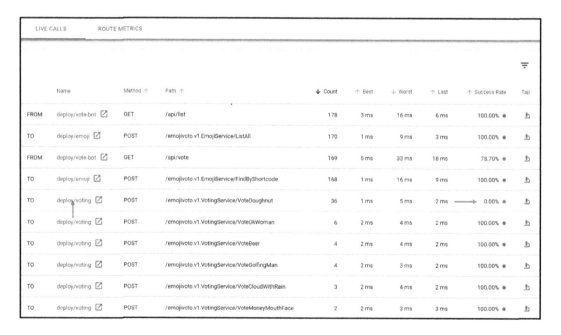

Notice the call to the `/emojivoto.v1.VotingService/VoteDoughnut` path, which results in a 0% success rate. Through Linkerd, by looking at the live feed of the data, we now know which REST API endpoint is failing.

5. On the far side of this line from the previous screenshot, click on the tap icon, which will only show the live list of requests from the endpoint.

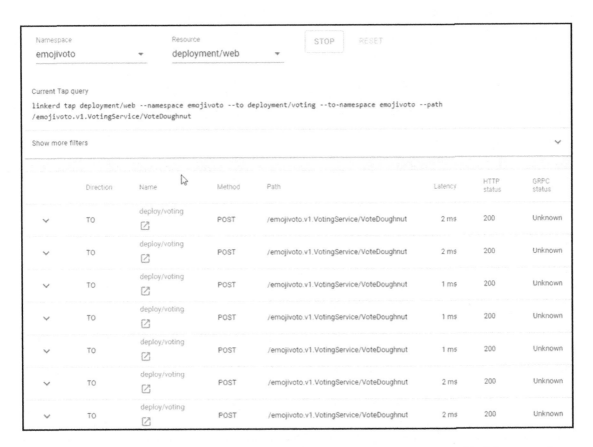

Notice that the gRPC status is **Unknown**. With this, we have drilled down to the exact REST API call, which is failing.

6. Linkerd shows a `tap` command line, along with an argument, which is very nice to watch without using the UI:

```
$ linkerd tap deployment/web --namespace emojivoto \
--to deployment/voting --to-namespace emojivoto \
--path /emojivoto.v1.VotingService/VoteDoughnut
```

After running the preceding command, press *Ctrl + C* after a few lines of output.

Now, let's switch to the booksapp application
called http://booksapp.linkerd.local. Booksapp comes with a traffic generator that
keeps on sending traffic to the application to explore service discovery capabilities.
Let's explore service discovery through Linkerd's dashboard:

1. Switch back to the Linkerd dashboard and click **Resources | Namespaces
   | All**. In the right pane, look for linkerd-lab and click on it to open the
   namespace:

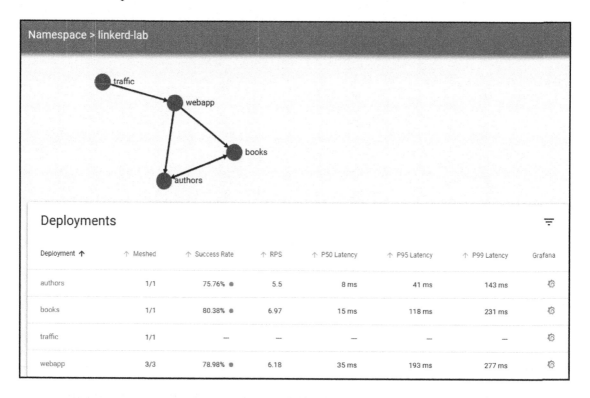

Notice that the service discovery *traffic* service is sending traffic
to the webapp service, which is sending traffic to both books and authors.
The books service communicates with the authors service.

Notice that the deployments and success rate is not 100%, indicating that
something is wrong. This is intentional and designed by the authors of the
application to show the built-in troubleshooting capabilities of Linkerd.

2. Switch to the tab running `http://booksapp.linkerd.local`, and scroll down to the **Add a Book** section. Here, write any title, select an author and page count, and hit **Add Book**:

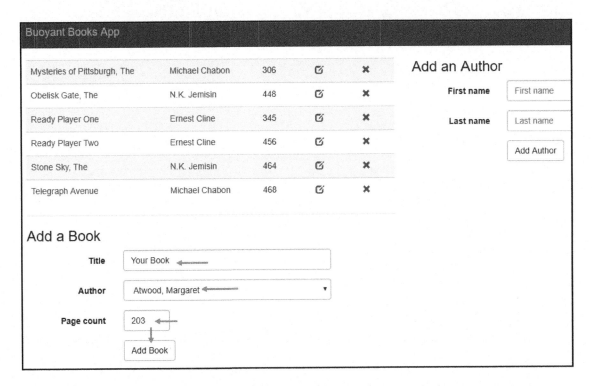

The book may be added, or you may receive an **Internal Server Error**. You may have to try a few times to add the book. Note that if you are unsuccessful in adding a book after a few attempts, continue to the next step for troubleshooting.

Now, let's go back to the dashboard to see if we can find the source of the problem.

3. Click on the `webapp` deployment to see more details:

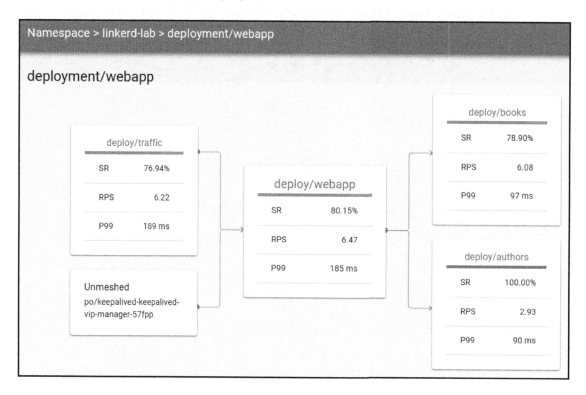

Notice that `deploy/authors` shows a 100% success rate – this service is working fine, but the `deploy/books` success rate is less than 100% and so are the success rates of `deploy/webapp` and `deploy/traffic`.

4. Scroll further down and view the live traffic feed for `webapp`:

	Name	Method ↑	Path ↑	↓ Count	↑ Best	↓ Worst	↑ Last	↑ Success Rate	Tap
FROM	deploy/traffic	POST	/books	529	18 ms	356 ms	90 ms	50.66% ●	🖹
TO	deploy/books ◄——	POST	/books.json	511	11 ms	127 ms	43 ms	50.88% ●	🖹
TO	deploy/books	GET	/books.json	263	6 ms	107 ms	8 ms	100.00% ●	🖹
FROM	deploy/traffic	POST	/authors	134	16 ms	144 ms	19 ms	100.00% ●	🖹
FROM	deploy/traffic	GET	/	134	27 ms	279 ms	31 ms	100.00% ●	🖹

Here, we can see that *deploy/traffic* (generator) is sending POST requests to `/books`.

5. Click the pop-out arrow next to `deploy/traffic` and check the name of the source and destination deployment microservices, which is from `deploy/traffic` to `deploy/webapp`.

   Similarly, check for `deploy/books`, which is from `deploy/webapp` to `deploy/books`. For operations, this information is crucial and needs to be communicated to developers.

6. Click the tap icon on the line showing `/books.json` to drill down and view only the live requests coming to `details/book`:

Notice: Some of the POST HTTP statuses show 500 for *Internal Server Error* and a few show *201 for Success*. It is easy to report this issue using the Linkerd dashboard.

Summary

Applications can switch from being robust to resilient through the use of Linkerd's sidecar proxy, which provides adaptive load balancing, easy to understand debugging capabilities, timeouts, and retries. We explored each of these capabilities in this chapter.

With the help of a service profile through Kubernetes' custom resource definition, you can define routes to report aggregated metrics on unique requests based on defined patterns. The service profile name is a fully qualified name that can match with HTTP/2 :authority or HTTP1.X hosts. Linkerd's load balancing implementation is at the L7 (application streams) level instead of the default Kubernetes L4 (TCP connection) level. You can implement retry budgets to prevent retry storms from overwhelming backends.

The Linkerd dashboard or the Linkerd CLI can be used to observe the live traffic arriving in the application.

In the next chapter, we'll delve into Linkerd's security capabilities, such as authentication, authorization, roles, and access control.

Questions

1. Kubernetes does load balancing at the connection level (L4).

   A) True
   B)False

2. Linkerd does load balancing at the application level (L7).

   A) True
   B)False

3. Linkerd load balancing is out of the box, and it requires no special configuration.

   A) True
   B)False

4. A Linkerd retry requires configuration.

    A) True
    B)False

5. Linkerd's service profile can be generated automatically, even if the Swagger API is not available for the service

    A) True
    B)False

6. The `retry budget` is about *done for adaptive retries* instead of a *fixed number of retries*.

    A) True
    B)False

7. The service profile is needed to provide aggregate route metrics, especially if a parameter is part of the route, which makes it difficult to group a route path.

    A) True
    B)False

Further reading

- *From Fragile To Antifragile Software – Red Hat Developer Blog*, Ibryam, Bilgin, Red Hat Developer Blog, 2019: `https://developers.redhat.com/blog/2016/07/20/from-fragile-to-antifragile-software/`
- *Linkerd v2: How Lessons from Production Adoption Resulted in a Rewrite of the Service Mesh*, Morgan, W. (2019), InfoQ, available at `https://www.infoq.com/articles/linkerd-v2-production-adoption`, accessed 5 May 2019
- *gRPC Load Balancing on Kubernetes without Tears*, Morgan, W. (2018), Linkerd.io, available at `https://linkerd.io/2018/11/14/grpc-load-balancing-on-kubernetes-without-tears/`, accessed 5 May 2019
- *What is L4-L7 Network Services? Definition and Related FAQs | Avi Networks*, Avi Networks, (2019), available at `https://avinetworks.com/glossary/l4-l7-network-services/`, accessed 6 May 2019

- *Linkerd 2.x With Network Policy,* Sim, I. (2019), available at `https://medium.com/@ihcsim/linkerd-2-x-with-network-policy-2657103333ca`, accessed 6 May 2019
- *Service Profiles for Per-Route Metrics - blog.linkerd,* Leong, A. (2018), blog.linkerd, available at `https://blog.linkerd.io/2018/12/07/service-profiles-for-per-route-metrics/`, accessed 7 May 2019
- *Retries and Timeouts,* Linkerd.io. (2018), available at `https://linkerd.io/2/features/retries-and-timeouts/`, accessed 7 May 2019

17
Exploring the Security Features of Linkerd

Linkerd provides mutual TLS for service-to-service communication. The securing of communication between services is an out-of-the-box capability and is enabled by default. In this chapter, we will explore Linkerd automatic encryption of TLS communication through sidecar proxies. It shows an important feature for which we do not have to write a single line of code in the application. Since we're running on Kubernetes, there are options for selecting an ingress controller. We will focus on the nginx controller because it is easy to set up, it secures the communication, and it allows certificate rotations.

In a nutshell, we will be learning about the following topics in this chapter:

- Understanding mTLS traffic checks for proxy-to-proxy communication
- Installing and deploying Smallstep for leaf certificates and key authority
- Setting up root and an intermediate certificate authority
- Redeploying the Linkerd control plane using a trusted certificate
- Enabling ingress and validating against TLS status
- Regenerating and increasing leaf certificate validity
- Setting up ingress for booksapp with the new leaf certificate
- Modifying ingress definition with TLS and verifying traffic routing

Technical requirements

This chapter has a dependency on Chapter 15, *Installing Linkerd*. You must complete the hands-on exercises of Chapter 15, *Installing Linkerd*, dealing with the following:

- Setting up Linkerd
- Installing a control plane
- Deploying the booksapp and emojivoto applications

Make sure that you are in the proper Linkerd scripts directory.

```
$ cd ~/ # Switch to home directory
$ cd linkerd/scripts
```

For a complete understanding of Linkerd, we also recommend you complete the hands-on exercises from Chapter 16, *Exploring the Reliability Features of Linkerd*.

Let's explore how mTLS in Linkerd can be used to authenticate and authorize communication for microservices.

Setting up mTLS on Linkerd

Refer to the *Enabling mutual TLS within the mesh* section of Chapter 11, *Exploring Istio's Security Features*, for a detailed discussion of mTLS.

Linkerd has made mTLS accessible and straightforward through the use of sidecar proxies by using ephemeral (short-lived) leaf certificates. It automatically uses mTLS across host boundaries to encrypt HTTP and gRPC communication between microservices that are using Linkerd as sidecar proxies. There is no need for any code at the microservice level to handle the TLS communication as the Linkerd control plane takes care of it automatically. Linkerd frees up developers' time for not having to secure communication between microservices.

Since the Linkerd sidecar proxy is attached to a container within the same pod, the existing microservice can have unencrypted (HTTP) communication. Between a service, sidecar proxy, and Linkerd, it provides mutual TLS across pod boundaries. Linkerd allows pre-service certificate setup, it generates a root CA certificate, and uses it to create and sign a leaf certificate (X.509 v3) for each service in the application.

Linkerd enables mTLS by default. We will validate this in this chapter and see how to use CA to integrate with Linkerd.

Validating mTLS on Linkerd

We will first verify whether mTLS is set up and enabled on Linkerd by inspecting the *identity* logs. This process is used to confirm proxy-to-proxy communication:

1. First, check the TLS status of traffic:

   ```
   $ linkerd tap deploy -n linkerd-lab
   ```

   You will see live traffic from all existing deployments.

2. Press *Ctrl + C* to break the output:

   ```
   rsp id=3:9 proxy=in src=10.1.230.253:39874 dst=10.1.230.238:7001
   tls=true :status=503 latency=3077µs
   end id=3:9 proxy=in src=10.1.230.253:39874 dst=10.1.230.238:7001
   tls=true duration=20µs response-length=0B
   req id=3:10 proxy=in src=10.1.230.253:39874 dst=10.1.230.238:7001
   tls=true :method=HEAD :authority=authors:7001
   :path=/authors/23955.json
   rsp id=3:10 proxy=in src=10.1.230.253:39874 dst=10.1.230.238:7001
   tls=true :status=503 latency=5351µs
   ```

   Notice that each line has `tls=true`, which is an indication that proxy-to-proxy communication is using mTLS.

3. Let's check the `linkerd` identity log:

   ```
   $ kubectl -n linkerd -c identity -l linkerd.io/control-plane-
   component=identity logs
   time="2019-08-09T16:32:19Z" level=info msg="certifying
   web.emojivoto.serviceaccount.identity.linkerd.cluster.local until
   2019-08-10 16:32:39 +0000 UTC
   ```

Notice the preceding message certifying `until <given time>` for the validity of keys. If generated internally, Linkerd will automatically re-provision certificates in 24 hours. If using CA, the rotation time is one year. The keys are generated locally in each pod (through the proxy), and then a **Certificate Signing Request (CSR)** is submitted with the pod's service account to re-validate the certificate. As long as a service account is valid, the pods will get new certificates automatically.

Next, we will explore Linkerd's certificate authority.

Using trusted certificates for the control plane

Linkerd comes with its own CA, and it generates its own self-signed root certificate for its control plane *identity* pod. The identity pod then uses this certificate to issue short (24 hours) certificates to the services that are running Linkerd proxy.

You can use a trusted certificate signed by a CA provider before installing the Linkerd control plane.

We will create our root and intermediate certificate and supply them to Linkerd install, assuming that they are from a trusted source. For this purpose, we will use an open source project, smallstep (`https://github.com/smallstep`). It is simple to use as it takes the complexity out of the certificate creation process. Let's understand this through an example.

Installing step certificates

To recap, we will be using the smallstep **Public Key Infrastructure** (PKI) to generate keys and certificates. The step CLI provides a helm chart for creating certificates:

1. First, let's add the helm repository to get the chart:

```
$ helm repo add smallstep https://smallstep.github.io/helm-charts/
"smallstep" has been added to your repositories
```

2. Now, check the helm repository list to view all recent charts:

```
$ helm repo list
NAME            URL
stable          https://kubernetes-charts.storage.googleapis.com
local           http://127.0.0.1:8879/charts
smallstep       https://smallstep.github.io/helm-charts/
nginx-stable    https://helm.nginx.com/stable
kaal            https://servicemeshbook.github.io/keepalived
```

3. Update the helm repository with the smallstep chart:

```
$ helm repo update
Hang tight while we grab the latest from your chart repositories...
...Skip local chart repository
...Successfully got an update from the "smallstep" chart repository
...Successfully got an update from the "kaal" chart repository
...Successfully got an update from the "nginx-stable" chart
repository
...Successfully got an update from the "stable" chart repository
Update Complete.
```

4. Install a smallstep certificate through the newly added helm chart:

```
$ helm install --name step --namespace step smallstep/step-
certificates \
--set fullnameOverride="step" --set ca.db.enabled=false
```

5. Finally, check the status of the step pods:

```
$ kubectl -n step get pods
NAME         READY   STATUS      RESTARTS   AGE
step-0       1/1     Running     0          2m17s
step-bdszd   0/1     Completed   0          2m17s
```

The smallstep certificate is now available.

Creating step root and intermediate certificates

We will now generate the root key and certificate and set up an intermediate certificate authority and validate its duration:

1. Create a root certificate:

```
$ kubectl -n step exec -t step-0 -- step certificate create --
profile root-ca "My Root CA" root-ca.crt root-ca.key --no-password
--insecure --force
Your certificate has been saved in root-ca.crt.
Your private key has been saved in root-ca.key.
```

 Note that, for simplicity, we are not providing a password to encrypt the key. In real life, you should use a password or let step generate one for you. Protecting the private key is very important for root and intermediate certificates.

2. Then, create an intermediate CA:

```
$ kubectl -n step exec -t step-0 -- step certificate create
identity.linkerd.cluster.local identity.crt identity.key --profile
intermediate-ca --ca ./root-ca.crt --ca-key ./root-ca.key --no-
password --insecure --force
Your certificate has been saved in identity.crt.
Your private key has been saved in identity.key.
```

3. Check the expiry date of the intermediate certificate:

```
$ kubectl -n step exec -t step-0 -- step certificate inspect
identity.crt --short
X.509v3 Intermediate CA Certificate (ECDSA P-256) [Serial:
7456...1790]
   Subject:     identity.linkerd.cluster.local
   Issuer:      My Root CA
   Valid from:  2019-08-11T14:27:14Z
           to:  2029-08-08T14:27:14Z
```

Notice that the preceding certificate is valid for 10 years, which is the default. It can cost a lot of money to get an intermediate certificate from a trusted CA, and generally, CA issues a leaf X.509 certificate, which has a much shorter life span.

4. Copy certificates from the pod as we did not use a persistent volume while creating the step helm chart:

```
$ kubectl -n step cp step-0:root-ca.crt /tmp/root-ca.crt
```

```
$ kubectl -n step cp step-0:identity.crt /tmp/identity.crt
```

```
$ kubectl -n step cp step-0:identity.key /tmp/identity.key
```

The preceding method using smallstep for creating certificates is simple and easy. However, we can obtain trusted certificates from commercial providers as well.

Redeploying control plane using certificates

You have to reinstall the Linkerd control plane to start using the root and intermediate certificates that you just generated using smallstep:

1. Delete the current installation of the Linkerd control plane:

```
$ linkerd install --ignore-cluster | kubectl delete -f -
```

The Linkerd control plane interacts with proxies to provide/rotate the leaf certificates, through a third-party provider such as smallstep. Service Mesh doesn't have in-depth capabilities to provision/rotate leaf certificates at this time without a reinstall.

2. Create a new Linkerd installation using trusted certificates:

```
$ linkerd install \
--identity-trust-anchors-file /tmp/root-ca.crt \
--identity-issuer-key-file /tmp/identity.key \
--identity-issuer-certificate-file /tmp/identity.crt \
--ignore-cluster | kubectl apply -f -
```

3. Now, perform a Linkerd check:

```
$ linkerd check
```

Since we dropped and recreated Linkerd install, we need to create the ingress definitions to access the dashboard.

4. Rerun the following commands:

```
$ cd ~/linkerd/scripts
$ kubectl -n linkerd apply -f 01-create-linkerd-ingress.yaml
ingress.extensions/linkerd created
```

5. Check the TLS status of the traffic:

```
$ linkerd tap deploy -n linkerd-lab
...
rsp id=5:24 proxy=out src=192.168.230.238:43774
dst=192.168.230.206:7000 tls=true :status=303 latency=10830µs
end id=5:24 proxy=out src=192.168.230.238:43774
dst=192.168.230.206:7000 tls=true duration=26µs response-length=0B
...
```

You should see tls=true for live traffic.

6. Press *Ctrl* + *C* to break the output.

In the preceding case, the certificate expiry time is 24 hours for the leaf certificates that the Linkerd identity CA generated for the Linkerd proxies running next to every microservice.

7. Verify that by looking at the Linkerd identity logs:

```
$ kubectl -n linkerd -c identity -l linkerd.io/control-plane-
component=identity logs
time="2019-08-10T15:35:45Z" level=info msg="certifying linkerd-
proxy-
injector.linkerd.serviceaccount.identity.linkerd.cluster.local
until 2019-08-11 15:36:05 +0000 UTC"
```

The output from the log shows when the leaf certificates will expire—which is 24 hours.

8. Next, validate the leaf certificate, and the `linkerd-identity-issuer` secret stores the key in the `linkerd` namespace:

```
$ kubectl -n linkerd get secret linkerd-identity-issuer -o
jsonpath='{.data.crt\.pem}' | base64 -d
```

9. The preceding output matches `/tmp/identity.crt`:

```
$ kubectl -n linkerd get secret linkerd-identity-issuer -o
jsonpath='{.data.key\.pem}' | base64 -d
```

The output from the preceding will match `/tmp/identity.key`. This `linkerd-identity-issuer` secret needs to be updated before the certificate expires.

Regenerating and rotating identity certificates for microservices

We show here the steps required to regenerate and rotate the identity certificates. This process uses the same root certificate created earlier. Note that updating of the root certificate requires a reinstall of the Linkerd control plane:

1. Re-generate the certificate:

```
$ kubectl -n step exec -t step-0 -- step certificate create
identity.linkerd.cluster.local identity.crt identity.key --profile
intermediate-ca --ca ./root-ca.crt --ca-key ./root-ca.key --no-
password --insecure --force

$ kubectl -n step cp step-0:identity.crt /tmp/identity.crt

$ kubectl -n step cp step-0:identity.key /tmp/identity.key
```

2. Delete the secret:

```
$ kubectl -n linkerd delete secret linkerd-identity-issuer
```

3. Recreate the secret with a new certificate:

```
$ kubectl -n linkerd create secret generic \ linkerd-identity-issuer \
  --from-file=crt.pem=/tmp/identity.crt \
  --from-file=key.pem=/tmp/identity.key
```

4. Restart the identity control plane deployments to pick up the new certificate:

```
$ kubectl -n linkerd rollout restart deploy linkerd-identity
```

5. Check Linkerd:

```
$ linkerd check
```

6. Check the leaf certificates issued to the control plane components by Linkerd:

```
$ kubectl -n linkerd -c identity -l linkerd.io/control-plane-
component=identity logs
```

The preceding process is the old-fashioned way to rotate a certificate before it expires. It would be ideal if this can be automated. This enhancement will likely appear in Istio as well as in Linkerd as the adoption of Service Mesh increases. However, there are open source solutions such as step autocert (`https://github.com/smallstep/autocert`) or cert-manager (`https://github.com/jetstack/cert-manager`), which can automatically rotate certificates before they expire. Cert-manager is especially useful for the ingress controller to use. Finally, let's encrypt for free (`https://letsencrypt.org`) provides trusted certificates for the application domain names.

Next, we will explore configuring ingress rules securely.

Securing the ingress gateway

Linkerd does not provide an out-of-the-box ingress gateway. Istio comes with its ingress and egress gateway resources. Linkerd depends on the following ingress gateways and others based on your Kubernetes provider. For example, OpenShift has its router. The following lists a few popular ingress controllers for Kubernetes:

- nginx ingress controller: `https://github.com/kubernetes/ingress-nginx` (community) and `https://github.com/nginxinc/kubernetes-ingress` (nginx)

- Traefik: `https://github.com/containous/traefik`
- HAProxy: `https://github.com/helm/charts/tree/master/incubator/haproxy-ingress`
- Ambassador: `https://github.com/datawire/ambassador`
- GLOO: `https://gloo.solo.io/installation/ingress/`

We set up an nginx ingress controller in the previous chapter. We created an ingress rule to route the `booksapp.linkerd.local` host to the `booksapp` microservice application.

TLS termination

Let's secure `booksapp.linkerd.local` with TLS termination at the nginx gateway:

1. Create a leaf certificate for `booksapp.linkerd.local`:

```
$ kubectl -n step exec -t step-0 -- \
step certificate create booksapp.linkerd.local booksapp.crt
booksapp.key \
--profile leaf --ca identity.crt --ca-key identity.key \
--no-password --insecure --force --kty=RSA --not-after=2160h
Your certificate has been saved in booksapp.crt.
Your private key has been saved in booksapp.key.

$ kubectl -n step cp step-0:booksapp.crt booksapp.crt

$ kubectl -n step cp step-0:booksapp.key booksapp.key
```

We need to pass the certificate chain along with the leaf certificate private key to the nginx ingress controller so that it can provide a secure TLS connection to the client.

2. Create a certificate chain of leaf and intermediate:

```
$ cat booksapp.crt /tmp/identity.crt > ca-bundle.crt
```

3. Create a Kubernetes TLS secret, `booksapp-keys`, using a certificate chain, `ca-bundle.crt`, for the leaf certificate with the **Computer Name (CN)** as `booksapp.linkerd.local` and the private key as `booksapp.key`:

```
$ kubectl -n linkerd-lab create secret tls booksapp-keys --key
booksapp.key --cert ca-bundle.crt
secret/booksapp-keys created
```

4. The nginx controller will pick up the Kubernetes TLS secret, `booksapp-keys`, when we create an ingress rule for an external domain name to associate it with an internal microservice name. The following shows the modified ingress definition that we created earlier to now include the TLS secret:

```
# Script : 07-create-booksapp-ingress-tls.yaml

apiVersion: extensions/v1beta1
kind: Ingress
...
spec:
  rules:
  - host: booksapp.linkerd.local
    http:
      paths:
      - backend:
          serviceName: webapp
          servicePort: 7000
        path: /
  tls:
  - hosts:
    - booksapp.linkerd.local
    secretName: booksapp-keys
```

5. Modify the ingress:

```
$ kubectl -n linkerd-lab apply -f 07-create-booksapp-ingress-tls.yaml
ingress.extensions/booksapp created
```

6. nginx watches for all endpoints generated in all namespaces. As soon as an endpoint is created or updated, nginx picks it up immediately. Find out the nginx pod name:

```
$ NGINX_POD=$(kubectl -n kube-system get pod -l app=nginx-controller -o jsonpath='{.items..metadata.name}') ; echo $NGINX_POD
nginx-controller-5dbfd77f4d-2plhd
```

7. List the configurations pushed:

```
$ kubectl -n kube-system exec -it $NGINX_POD -- ls -l /etc/nginx/conf.d
```

8. Check the newly updated configuration:

```
$ kubectl -n kube-system exec -it $NGINX_POD -- cat /etc/nginx/conf.d/linkerd-lab-booksapp.conf
```

9. List the TLS secrets:

```
$ kubectl -n kube-system exec -it $NGINX_POD -- ls -l
/etc/nginx/secrets
```

10. Check the updated secret—with certificate chain and private key:

```
$ kubectl -n kube-system exec -it $NGINX_POD -- cat
/etc/nginx/secrets/linkerd-lab-booksapp-keys
```

After TLS termination at the ingress gateway, we will now switch back to the browser in the VM to test it.

Testing the application in the browser

To test the application, follow these two simple steps:

1. Open the `http://booksapp.linkerd.local` URL in a new tab.

   You will notice that the URL is rewritten automatically from HTTP to the HTTPS protocol.

   In Chrome, you will receive a warning saying that **Your connection is not private**—which is normal since we have used a self-signed root certificate.

2. Now, click **Advanced** and then click **Proceed to booksapp.linkerd.local (unsafe)**.

Testing the application through curl

Let's check the same through curl by providing certificates. Run the following curl to check whether the nginx controller is routing the traffic well:

```
$ export INGRESS_PORT=$(kubectl -n kube-system get service nginx-controller
-o jsonpath='{.spec.ports[?(@.name=="https")].port}') ; echo $INGRESS_PORT
443

$ export INGRESS_HOST=$(kubectl -n kube-system get service nginx-controller
-o jsonpath='{.status.loadBalancer.ingress..ip}') ; echo $INGRESS_HOST
192.168.142.249

$ curl -Ls -HHost:booksapp.linkerd.local \
--resolve booksapp.linkerd.local:$INGRESS_HOST:$INGRESS_PORT \
--cacert root-ca.crt https://booksapp.linkerd.local
```

The IP address of the ingress gateway may change in your case. Note that we pass the root certificate to the `--cacert` flag and not the leaf certificate in the curl command. The server has the certificate chain comprising the leaf and intermediate certificates.

The booksapp opens using the HTTPS protocol—hence, you have secured your application through TLS termination at the nginx ingress gateway.

Linkerd enables mTLS automatically to secure microservice-to-microservice communication.

Summary

As we have seen in this chapter, the Linkerd control plane ships with a Certificate Authority (CA) called identity and sidecar proxies. Sidecars run alongside each microservice and receive certificates from the identity CA—which ties to a Kubernetes service account. The sidecar proxies automatically upgrade all communication between edges of the mesh to encrypted TLS connections.

Linkerd leaves it up to you to configure your ingress gateway to secure communications to the edge services of the applications in the Kubernetes cluster. There are choices of ingress controllers that you can use. In the examples of this chapter, we used the nginx ingress gateway to secure the communication and steps to rotate the certificates.

In the next chapter, we will explore the observability features in Linkerd. We will explain the process of metrics collection through sidecar proxies and different ways to visualize, query, and analyze the telemetry data.

Questions

1. The TLS between service-to-service communication is fully automated in Linkerd.

   A) True
   B) False

2. The TLS between the ingress gateway and edge service of the application is fully automated in Linkerd.

   A) True
   B) False

3. The `linkerd-identity` component of the control plane of Linkerd is the Certificate Authority (CA) for the data plane proxies.

   A) True
   B) False

4. `linkerd-identity` automatically rotates the certificates for `linkerd-proxy` in the data plane.

   A) True
   B) False

5. `linkerd-identity` automatically rotates the certificate for its own CA.

   A) True
   B) False

6. You can use trusted certificates of your own CA for `linkerd-identity` at the time of install only.

   A) True
   B) False

7. You can change the trusted certificate of the control plane at any time, but that requires reinstallation of the control plane.

   A) True
   B) False

Further reading

- Smallstep, GitHub, (2018), available at https://github.com/smallstep, accessed May 9, 2019
- Features, Linkerd.io, (2019), available at https://linkerd.io/2/features/, accessed May 9, 2019
- Automatic TLS, Linkerd.io, (2019), available at https://linkerd.io/2/features/automatic-tls/, accessed May 9, 2019
- Smallstep/autocert, Cano, Mariano, GitHub, 2019, available at https://github.com/smallstep/autocert/tree/master/examples/hello-mtls

18
Exploring the Observability Features of Linkerd

Visibility is critical for any service mesh. The visibility feature of Linkerd is simple and easy to use, as we will see in this chapter. Linkerd's service mesh is targeted mainly toward the **Site Reliability Engineering (SRE)** team or operators of enterprise customers.

In this chapter, we will gain an in-depth insight into the Linkerd service mesh. To do this, we will use three methods, including CLI, the GUI dashboard, and the Prometheus/Grafana dashboard. These dashboards show the **Key Performance Indicators (KPIs)**, which are easy to understand and provide us with the ability to determine issues/problems and potential bottlenecks besides the visual representation of aggregated data.

In a nutshell, we will cover the following topics:

- Gaining insight into the service mesh
- External Prometheus integration
- Cleaning up

Technical requirements

To complete this chapter, you will need to have completed the hands-on exercises of Chapter 15, *Installing Linkerd*, that deal with the following topics:

- Setting up Linkerd
- Installing a control plane
- Deploying the booksapp and emojivoto applications

For a complete understanding of Linkerd, we also recommend that you complete the hands-on exercises from `Chapter 16`, *Exploring the Reliability Features of Linkerd*, and `Chapter 17`, *Exploring the Security Features of Linkerd*.

Make sure that you are in the proper scripts directory for the hands-on exercises:

```
$ cd ~/ # Switch to home directory
$ cd linkerd/scripts
```

Gaining insight into the service mesh

Visibility into the service mesh with the help of proper tools is a necessity if you wish to resolve issues quickly. In the absence of appropriate tools, it becomes very time-consuming and expensive to find out the source of the problems. In `Chapter 16`, *Exploring the Reliability Features of Linkerd,* we used the Linkerd dashboard to debug a particular route, which showed a success rate of less than 100%. This information about a specific route is of great help and acts as a feedback loop for the developer so that they can fix issues.

The Linkerd dashboard (GUI) and the Linkerd CLI (command line) are two essential tools if we want to gain insight into the service mesh. These tools show key indicators such as live traffic, success rate, routes, latencies, and an overview of traffic flow from individual sources to different targets. These are important for the health and performance of any application from an HTTP or gRPC protocol standpoint. They help pinpoint issues much more quickly than having to go through the logs of different containers.

One of the salient features of Linkerd is to show P50, P95, and P99 latencies, as we explained in `Chapter 16`, *Exploring the Reliability Features of Linkerd*. It is possible to report such types of metrics due to aggregation that's done at the proxy level.

Linkerd also provides a pre-built Grafana dashboard for metrics that are scrapped through Prometheus, which stores data for up to 6 hours to give us a quick insight into the service mesh. For long-term history collection, we have to store the data in an external Prometheus backend.

In the next section, we will look at the aforementioned methods in more detail in order to gain insight into the service mesh. Let's begin with the Linkerd **command-line interface (CLI)**.

Insights using CLI

The Linkerd CLI has a top function, which works similarly to the `top` command. It shows the current top query for the number of executions, latency time, and success rate. To understand this better, let's look at an example of all the queries coming from deployments in the `emojivoto` namespace:

```
$ linkerd top deployment --namespace emojivoto --hide-sources
```

This results in the following output:

Destination	Method	Path	Count	Best	Worst	Last	Success Rate
emoji-6988d8b456-4p8t2	POST	/emojivoto.v1.EmojiService/ListAll	206	651µs	38ms	798µs	100.00%
emoji-6988d8b456-4p8t2	POST	/emojivoto.v1.EmojiService/FindByShortcode	193	630µs	37ms	2ms	100.00%
web-58bd8f8c44-w7xpn	GET	/api/list	134	4ms	58ms	4ms	100.00%
web-58bd8f8c44-w7xpn	GET	/api/vote	126	6ms	44ms	9ms	89.68%
web-58bd8f8c44-skhvw	GET	/api/list	72	4ms	58ms	5ms	100.00%
web-58bd8f8c44-skhvw	GET	/api/vote	65	6ms	88ms	15ms	87.69%
voting-54944fb8f8-vj6xx	POST	/emojivoto.v1.VotingService/VoteDoughnut	14	679µs	5ms	991µs	0.00%
voting-54944fb8f8-vj6xx	POST	/emojivoto.v1.VotingService/VotePrincess	8	829µs	2ms	2ms	100.00%
voting-54944fb8f8-fxgp5	POST	/emojivoto.v1.VotingService/VoteDoughnut	7	890µs	14ms	14ms	0.00%
voting-54944fb8f8-vj6xx	POST	/emojivoto.v1.VotingService/VotePoliceman	5	842µs	10ms	2ms	100.00%
voting-54944fb8f8-vj6xx	POST	/emojivoto.v1.VotingService/VoteFlightDeparture	4	829µs	5ms	5ms	100.00%
voting-54944fb8f8-vj6xx	POST	/emojivoto.v1.VotingService/VoteDog	4	1ms	4ms	2ms	100.00%
voting-54944fb8f8-fxgp5	POST	/emojivoto.v1.VotingService/VoteConstructionWorkerMan	4	2ms	6ms	6ms	100.00%
voting-54944fb8f8-vj6xx	POST	/emojivoto.v1.VotingService/VoteJackOLantern	4	784µs	3ms	2ms	100.00%
voting-54944fb8f8-vj6xx	POST	/emojivoto.v1.VotingService/VoteChampagne	4	906µs	7ms	2ms	100.00%
voting-54944fb8f8-fxgp5	POST	/emojivoto.v1.VotingService/VoteMan	4	1ms	5ms	1ms	100.00%
voting-54944fb8f8-fxgp5	POST	/emojivoto.v1.VotingService/VoteCloudWithRain	4	883µs	3ms	2ms	100.00%
voting-54944fb8f8-fxgp5	POST	/emojivoto.v1.VotingService/VoteJackOLantern	4	1ms	11ms	2ms	100.00%
voting-54944fb8f8-vj6xx	POST	/emojivoto.v1.VotingService/VoteGirl	4	882µs	3ms	882µs	100.00%
voting-54944fb8f8-vj6xx	POST	/emojivoto.v1.VotingService/VoteConstructionWorkerMan	4	996µs	6ms	2ms	100.00%
voting-54944fb8f8-vj6xx	POST	/emojivoto.v1.VotingService/VoteMan	4	697µs	2ms	2ms	100.00%
voting-54944fb8f8-vj6xx	POST	/emojivoto.v1.VotingService/VoteWoman	3	2ms	3ms	2ms	100.00%
voting-54944fb8f8-fxgp5	POST	/emojivoto.v1.VotingService/VoteTaco	2	1ms	2ms	2ms	100.00%
voting-54944fb8f8-vj6xx	POST	/emojivoto.v1.VotingService/VoteHeartEyesCat	2	933µs	2ms	2ms	100.00%
voting-54944fb8f8-fxgp5	POST	/emojivoto.v1.VotingService/VoteClap	2	823µs	2ms	823µs	100.00%
voting-54944fb8f8-fxgp5	POST	/emojivoto.v1.VotingService/VoteBurrito	2	4ms	5ms	5ms	100.00%
voting-54944fb8f8-vj6xx	POST	/emojivoto.v1.VotingService/VoteVulcanSalute	2	934µs	2ms	2ms	100.00%
voting-54944fb8f8-fxgp5	POST	/emojivoto.v1.VotingService/VoteRamen	2	910µs	2ms	910µs	100.00%
voting-54944fb8f8-fxgp5	POST	/emojivoto.v1.VotingService/VoteRocket	2	1ms	3ms	3ms	100.00%
voting-54944fb8f8-fxgp5	POST	/emojivoto.v1.VotingService/VoteMask	2	930µs	3ms	930µs	100.00%
voting-54944fb8f8-fxgp5	POST	/emojivoto.v1.VotingService/VoteCrystalBall	2	914µs	2ms	2ms	100.00%
voting-54944fb8f8-fxgp5	POST	/emojivoto.v1.VotingService/VoteCamping	2	924µs	2ms	2ms	100.00%
voting-54944fb8f8-fxgp5	POST	/emojivoto.v1.VotingService/VoteDancer	2	1ms	4ms	4ms	100.00%
voting-54944fb8f8-vj6xx	POST	/emojivoto.v1.VotingService/VoteBurrito	2	6ms	8ms	8ms	100.00%
voting-54944fb8f8-vj6xx	POST	/emojivoto.v1.VotingService/VoteRainbow	2	1ms	5ms	1ms	100.00%
voting-54944fb8f8-vj6xx	POST	/emojivoto.v1.VotingService/VoteInterrobang	2	915µs	2ms	2ms	100.00%

The preceding CLI gives us immediate insight into an application. Now, it is possible to focus on routes that show a success rate of less than 100%. The latency for the 50, 90, and 99 percentiles, coupled with the highest number of executions, helps you consider optimizations in your applications.

From the preceding output, we can choose a route that we want to look at in more detail. Let's take the `/api` path, showing only the `GET` methods for requests that have been filtered for the `web-svc.emojivoto` authority.

Run the following `tap` command:

```
$ linkerd tap deployment/vote-bot -n emojivoto --path /api --method=GET --
authority web-svc.emojivoto:80
req id=144:1 proxy=out src=10.1.230.223:52372 dst=10.1.230.213:80 tls=true
:method=GET
rsp id=144:1 proxy=out src=10.1.230.223:52372 dst=10.1.230.213:80 tls=true
:status=200 latency=3382µs
. . .
end id=144:7 proxy=out src=10.1.230.223:52556 dst=10.1.230.213:80 tls=true
duration=52µs
req id=144:8 proxy=out src=10.1.230.223:52556 dst=10.1.230.213:80 tls=true
:method=GET
rsp id=144:8 proxy=out src=10.1.230.223:52556 dst=10.1.230.213:80 tls=true
:status=500 latency=9922µs
end id=144:8 proxy=out src=10.1.230.223:52556 dst=10.1.230.213:80 tls=true
duration=22µs
```

There are a few things to note about the `tap` command:

- The mTLS between the edge of the services is in effect when you see `tls=true`.
- The status code of each request and response.
- The end-to-end response based on the duration.
- The latency of each request and response.

As we have seen, the `tap` command allows us to get the live feed from the system in a natural form that is easy to understand. Now, let's use the UI features of Prometheus for Linkerd data collection.

Insight using Prometheus

Prometheus is a backend time series data collection service that is configured by default in Linkerd. It only keeps data for 6 hours in order to limit the Linkerd telemetry footprint to an acceptable range without adversely affecting performance. Grafana is the frontend and contains Linkerd pre-built dashboards, as we will soon see.

We can access Prometheus from inside the VM or from outside if we define an ingress rule for it. Let's define the *Ingress* for Prometheus using `prometheus.linkerd.io` hostname, which resolves to the internal IP address of the VM through our simulated load balancer:

1. Let's define the Prometheus ingress so that we can direct external traffic to the Linkerd-Prometheus service:

```
# Script : 06-create-prometheus-ingress.yaml

apiVersion: extensions/v1beta1
kind: Ingress
metadata:
  name: prometheus
  annotations:
    nginx.org/websocket-services: "linkerd-prometheus"
    ingress.kubernetes.io/rewrite-target: /
    nginx.ingress.kubernetes.io/configuration-snippet: |
      proxy_set_header l5d-dst-override
$service_name.$namespace.svc.cluster.local:9090;
      proxy_hide_header l5d-remote-ip;
      proxy_hide_header l5d-server-id;
spec:
  rules:
  - host: prometheus.linkerd.local
    http:
      paths:
      - backend:
          serviceName: linkerd-prometheus
          servicePort: 9090
        path: /
```

2. Next, we need to create a Prometheus ingress:

```
$ kubectl -n linkerd apply -f 06-create-prometheus-ingress.yaml
ingress.extensions/prometheus created
```

3. Now, create an entry in `/etc/hosts` for the `prometheus.linkerd.local` host:

```
$ export INGRESS_HOST=$(kubectl -n kube-system get service nginx-
controller -o jsonpath='{.status.loadBalancer.ingress..ip}') ; echo
$INGRESS_HOST
192.168.142.249

$ sudo sed -i '/prometheus.linkerd.local/d' /etc/hosts

$ echo "$INGRESS_HOST prometheus.linkerd.local" | sudo tee -a
/etc/hosts
```

4. Run `http://prometheus.linkerd.local` from your browser. Select **Status |
Targets**:

Here, we can see the metrics for the endpoints for Grafana, Linkerd controllers,
Linkerd proxies, Prometheus, the status of the state, and the last scrapped
metrics.

You can check the Prometheus configuration by clicking on **Status
| Configuration**. The custom service discovery integration for Linkerd can be
viewed from **Status | Service Discovery**.

5. Click on **Prometheus** and type or select `process_cpu_seconds_total.` from
the drop-down menu.

6. Click **Execute** and select the **Graph** tab to see the time series graph:

Prometheus has some essential built-in graphing capabilities, but Grafana provides a better frontend GUI for the data that has been collected by the Prometheus pull model.

Prometheus is the data collector and contains basic GUI features, as we saw for the Linkerd data collection. Next, we will look at the data that's collected through the Grafana Web UI.

Insights using Grafana

We can access Grafana directly, or we can jump to context-based access from the Linkerd dashboard by clicking the Grafana icon. Switch back to the Linkerd dashboard and follow these steps:

1. Go to **Resources** | **Namespaces** | **Linkerd-Lab**:

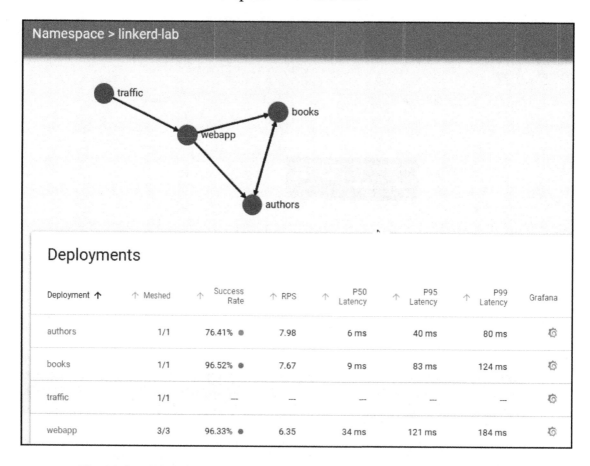

The Linkerd dashboard for the namespace shows the service dependency diagram and shows metrics based on deployment, pods, authorities, and TCP.

2. Click the Grafana icon under **Deployment/Authors**:

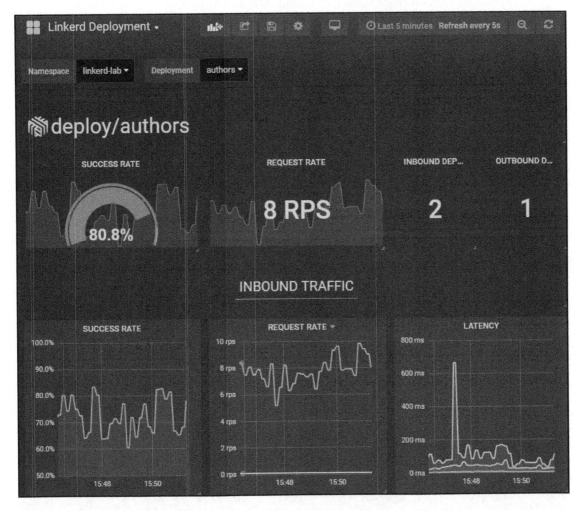

Notice the graphical view of the success rate, **request rate per second (RPS)**, inbound and outbound deployments, latency, and so on.

3. Scroll down to view the `deploy/books` in the Grafana dashboard. Alternatively, you can select it from Linkerd's dashboard dropdown:

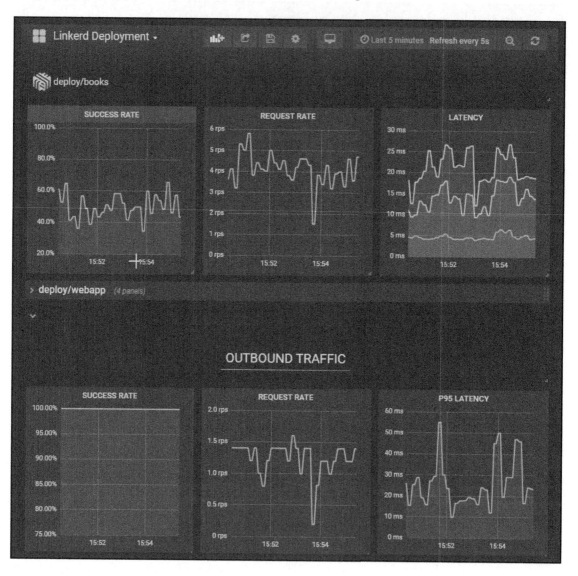

4. From the left sidebar, click on the dashboard (the four-square icon) and click
   Home.

   This panel shows the metrics for several namespaces that Linkerd is managing,
   along with the total number of deployments and the overall success rate. The
   global latency metrics are useful for drilling down into latency issues
   downstream:

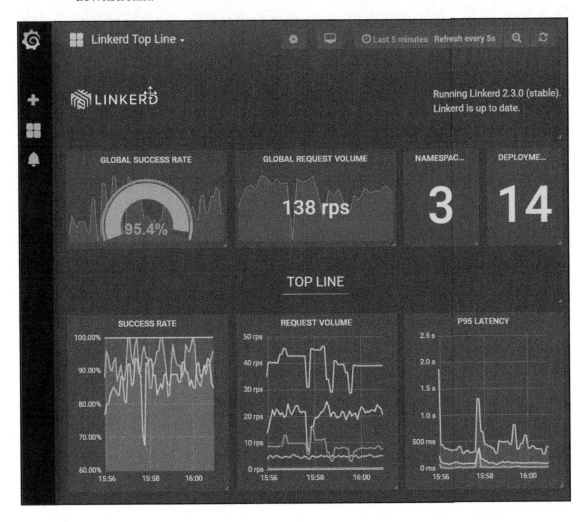

5. Scroll down and check for `emojivoto` and the Linkerd control plane at the namespace level:

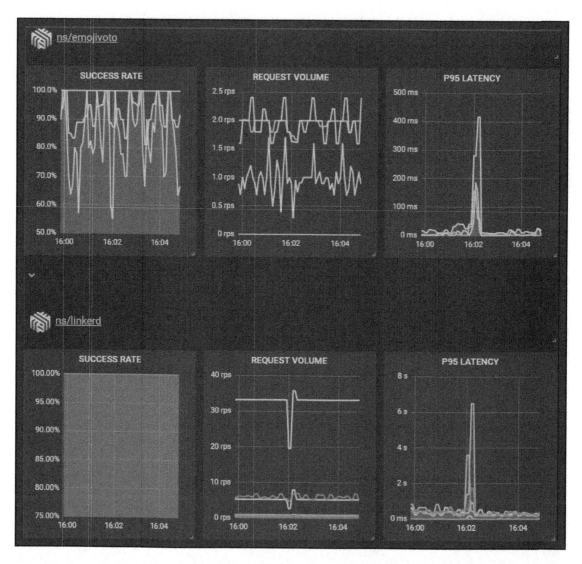

6. Scroll down to the `linkerd-lab booksapp` namespace. This shows you the overall metrics at the namespace level:

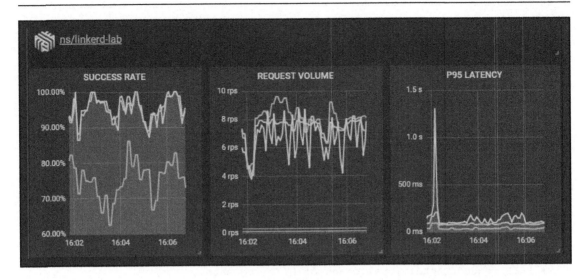

If you click `ns/linkerd-lab`, then you can drill down to the deployment and pod level to look at the metrics. The visualization of metrics in Grafana is collected through Prometheus, which puts observability into the service mesh and makes things easier in terms of operational purposes. The visual representation of the success rate helps us close the feedback loop with the development team so that they can improve upon the issues that were detected through observability.

Linkerd only provides 6 hours of data collection in order to keep the footprint small. To deal with this and maintain the long-term storage of data, we need to look at external Prometheus integration. We'll do this in the next section.

External Prometheus integration

To export data from Prometheus to another full-fledged metrics backend, you can either pull data directly from Linkerd proxies or federate data to a dedicated Prometheus cluster. You can also use Prometheus APIs to extract data from the local Prometheus store to your dedicated Prometheus data store. Let's get started:

1. For example, call the federation API directly:

```
$ curl -G --data-urlencode 'match[]={job="linkerd-proxy"}' --data-urlencode
'match[]={job="linkerd-controller"}'
http://prometheus.linkerd.local/federate

response_latency_ms_bucket{authority="webapp.linkerd-
lab.svc.cluster.local:7000",control_plane_ns="linkerd",deployment="traffic"
```

```
,direction="outbound",dst_control_plane_ns="linkerd",dst_deployment="webapp
",dst_namespace="linkerd-lab",dst_pod="webapp-64668f866c-
qhnmz",dst_pod_template_hash="64668f866c",dst_service="webapp",dst_servicea
ccount="default",instance="10.1.230.199:4191",job="linkerd-
proxy",le="20",namespace="linkerd-lab",pod="traffic-
f5b9987bd-9jjrk",server_id="default.linkerd-
lab.serviceaccount.identity.linkerd.cluster.local",status_code="500",tls="t
rue"} 0 1557454168022
```

2. Gather data directly from the Linkerd proxies:

```
$ export AUTHORS_PODIP=$(kubectl -n linkerd-lab get pods -l app=authors -o
jsonpath='{.items[0].status.podIP}') ; echo $AUTHORS_PODIP
192.168.230.238
```

```
$ curl -s http://$AUTHORS_PODIP:4191/metrics
```

```
# HELP request_total Total count of HTTP requests.
# TYPE request_total counter
request_total{direction="inbound",tls="no_identity",no_tls_reason="not_prov
ided_by_remote"} 10559
request_total{authority="authors.linkerd-
lab.svc.cluster.local:7001",direction="inbound",tls="true",client_id="defau
lt.linkerd-lab.serviceaccount.identity.linkerd.cluster.local"} 911614
```

In Linkerd, Prometheus keeps resource consumption small by storing only 6 hours of data. To keep data for an extended period of time, we can use the Prometheus metrics collection, which can be fed to a dedicated backend server.

The Prometheus federation API, or ServiceMonitors, can be used to copy data using the /federate path from Linkerd Prometheus to the dedicated Prometheus store.

Alternatively, you can call the federation API directly so that it can be ingested by a Kafka stream, which can then dump it to an ELK stack:

```
$ curl -G \
  --data-urlencode 'match[]={job="linkerd-proxy"}' \
  --data-urlencode 'match[]={job="linkerd-controller"}' \
  http://linkerd-prometheus.linkerd.svc.cluster.local:9090/federate
```

Now, it's time to clean up so that we can start learning about the Consul service mesh in the next chapter.

Cleaning up

Run the following commands:

1. Remove the Linkerd control plane:

   ```
   $ linkerd install --ignore-cluster | kubectl delete -f -
   ```

2. Remove the `booksapp` and `emojivoto` applications:

   ```
   $ kubectl delete ns linkerd-lab
   namespace "linkerd-lab" deleted

   $ kubectl delete ns emojivoto
   namespace "emojivoto" deleted
   ```

Remember that by the time you read this book, new versions of Linkerd may be available with new features and functions. You can visit `https://github.com/servicemeshbook/linkerd` for updated Linkerd scripts.

Summary

As we have seen in this chapter, the Linkerd observability feature is simple and out of the box, which means it doesn't need any special configuration. It presents the key performance indicators for the deployment, pod, and route levels through both the CLI and the dashboard. Its integration with Prometheus through a built-in panel for Grafana is an easy way to drill down from a higher level to a lower level, as shown in the exercises in this chapter.

One of the interesting and useful features of Linkerd is that it can aggregate and show **Key Performance Indicators (KPI)** such as RPS, P50, P95, P99, and **Success Rate (SR)**. These KPIs can be very helpful to SRE team members when they need to investigate problems.

With this chapter, we have explored the various features of the Linkerd service mesh. In the next chapter, we will go through the third service mesh – Consul, which also has its unique and useful features.

Questions

1. Linkerd only stores data for 6 hours, and this can be configured so that we can increase or decrease the time limit.

   A) True
   B) False

2. Linkerd provides distributed tracing, which can be seen from the dashboard as well as through the CLI's `tap` command.

   A) True
   B) False

3. Linkerd integration with external Prometheus is the user's responsibility.

   A) True
   B) False

4. Linkerd Prometheus uses the Pull model to collect the data from service proxies.

   A) True
   B) False

Further reading

- *Dashboard and Grafana*, Linkerd.io, (2018), available at `https://linkerd.io/2/features/dashboard/`, accessed May 9, 2019
- *Exporting Metrics*, Linkerd.io, (2018), available at `https://linkerd.io/2/tasks/exporting-metrics/`, accessed May 9, 2019
- *Now with Extra Prometheus*, Andrew Seigner, Buoyant and Frederic Branczyk, CoreOS, Seigner, A., and Branczyk, F. (2019), Linkerd 2.0, YouTube, available at `https://www.youtube.com/watch?v=bnDWApsH36Yt=954s`, accessed May 10, 2019

6
Section 6: Learning about Consul through Examples

In this section, you will learn about the Consul service mesh through hands-on exercises. Consul is unique due to its ability to run in Kubernetes, VMs, and bare-metal environments.

This section contains the following chapters:

- Chapter 19, *Understanding the Consul Service Mesh*
- Chapter 20, *Installing Consul*
- Chapter 21, *Exploring Consul's Service Discovery Features*
- Chapter 22, *Exploring Consul's Traffic Management Capabilities*

19
Understanding the Consul Service Mesh

In previous sections in this book, we discussed Istio and Linkerd. Now, we will move on to Consul, another service mesh. Consul, an open source project, was started by HashiCorp (`https://github.com/hashicorp/consul`), and it has 17,000+ stars and nearly 30,000 forks at the time of writing. This is a testament to the vibrant community around it.

Consul supports both VM and as well as Kubernetes. In this chapter, we will cover mostly Consul Connect, which is the Consul service mesh implementation of the Kubernetes environment. First, we will understand the Consul architecture and the concepts of control and data planes. Then, we will look at Consul Connect's traffic management features, monitoring, and visualization.

In a nutshell, we will cover the following topics in this chapter:

- Introducing the Consul service mesh
- The Consul architecture
- Consul's control and data planes
- Monitoring and virtualization
- Traffic management

Technical requirements

You'll need the VM that you used to learn about Linkerd. Make sure that you performed the cleanup procedure at the end of the previous chapter to free up resources so that you can use the same VM and the Kubernetes environment to try out the Consul service mesh.

You can find the code files for Consul at: `https://github.com/servicemeshbook/consul`.

Introducing the Consul service mesh

Consul started in 2014 when Kubernetes was also entering the market. It is a first-class citizen for configuring and discovering services, especially when the infrastructure (Compute, Storage, and Network) is dynamic, which is a combination of Kubernetes clusters and VMs in multiple data centers.

The following table will give you a clear picture of the traditional and dynamic infrastructures:

	Traditional infrastructure	Dynamic infrastructure
What is it?	In a traditional infrastructure, there is static connectivity in an insecure flat network protected by firewall rules.	In a dynamic infrastructure, ephemeral workloads with dynamic IP addresses can run on any machine in a zero-trust network.
How does it handle network traffic?	Traffic is routed through a hardware or software load balancer across multiple applications (horizontal scalability), which is why it is sometimes known as North-South traffic.	The load balancer sits just before the Ingress gateway, and then traffic is distributed dynamically to different service endpoints. This is why it is sometimes known as East-West traffic.
Examples	Multiple federated Kubernetes clusters can be viewed as serving North-South traffic.	A single Kubernetes cluster can be viewed as serving East-West traffic.

Consul can be viewed as serving both North-South (WAN Gossip Protocol) and East-West (LAN Gossip Protocol) traffic:

- **North-South traffic**: The traffic travels between outside and inside of a k8s cluster; that is, the traffic goes through the Ingress controller.
- **East-West traffic**: The traffic travels between the services inside a k8s cluster.

One of the benefits of Consul is that it can run in heterogeneous environments such as Kubernetes and VMs or directly on a bare-metal machine. It provides functionality for service catalogs, configuration, TLS certificates, authorization, and so on.

Consul is a single Go binary that runs as an agent on each node in a cluster, and it manages/monitors all services on that node. Consul agents (clients) hold service registration and health check data.

The Consul cluster is made up of members, collections of Consul agents and Consul servers. A typical production environment comprises an odd number of servers (3 and 5 maximum) to ensure that the majority of the quorum is met in the event of failures.

Consul is a distributed system where agent nodes communicate with server nodes:

- Consul servers are responsible for maintaining the state of the cluster.
- Consul Client (agent) is responsible for performing a health check of a node and the services running on that node.

Consul provides the following features:

- **Multi-data center deployment**: One of the main features of Consul is its support for multiple data centers using the gossip protocol to register members leaving and joining the cluster and to check the health status of members and services.
- **Service discovery**: When applications are broken down into microservices, they are no longer available through a memory call to a public function. However, these microservices can reside on any machine in a data center, and the call is done through the network. The IP address can change any time the pod is rescheduled. Service registration is automatic in the Kubernetes environment. In a VM or bare-metal environment, applications can register to a centralized Consul service discovery, which is maintained as a key-value store.
- **Configuration**: Monolithic applications have a centralized configuration, but when microservices are built there is a need for a centralized configuration that provides a consistent view of all the services. Consul, through its key-value store, provides a central place in which configurations can be stored as a name/value pair, which can be pushed down dynamically to the microservices.
- **Key-value store**: This is a hierarchical key-value store for configuration data.
- **Network segmentation**: For microservices, Consul provides network segmentation to allow services to communicate securely in a flat zero-trust network.

A Consul service mesh provides a very good integration of traditional and dynamic infrastructures by way of service discovery, secure communication, network segmentation, and a multi-data center approach.

Next, we will go through the Consul architecture to understand the core components that will help us use Consul from an implementation standpoint.

The Consul architecture

Cloud-native applications require their workloads to be dynamically provisioned, so network modifications cannot be made manually for one service (say, the frontend) to connect to other services (say, the backend). The Consul architecture evolved differently compared to Kubernetes service discovery. Kubernetes uses iptables to point service IP addresses to the dynamic IP addresses of the pod, whereas Consul uses DNS for service discovery. Consul's service discovery can work with Kubernetes by injecting its DNS as an upstream server to the Kubernetes DNS. This architecture is mainly influenced by the modern gossip protocol, which works across multiple data centers.

The architecture of Consul supports loose coupling of data centers so that connectivity failures in a data center do not affect the availability of Consul in other data centers. With a dedicated group of servers, each data center runs independently using a private LAN gossip pool. Multiple data centers are connected with others using a WAN gossip pool. This can be seen in the following diagram:

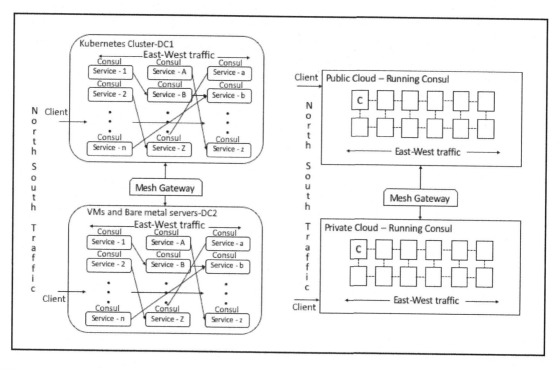

The key components that define the architecture for Consul are as follows:

- Data center

- Client/server
- Protocol management

We will take a look at each of these individually in upcoming sections.

Data center

Each machine in a data center should have a Consul agent running, which is a single Go program that acts like a client and a server. Each data center should ideally have 3 or 5 Consul servers, but clients can number tens of thousands. Consul servers participate in read and write operations using the consensus protocol, so their sizing is very important. Read operations are limited by the number of cores, while write operations are limited by the IOPS of the storage. For example, you may need 2 to 8 cores and 8 to 64 GB of RAM per server, depending on the number of read and write operations you wish to perform.

Client/server

Consul agents take part in failure detection and consensus to agree that a failure has occurred. Failure detection is done through periodic random probing. If a Consul agent in a failed node does not provide an acknowledgment, the other Consul agents are asked to probe the failed node. If no acknowledgment is received, the node is marked as **suspicious**, but still remains a member of the cluster. The node is assumed dead if the suspicious node does not dispute its status within a configurable time period. Once a node is assumed dead, its status is gossiped to the entire cluster. HashiCorp has implemented modifications to the failure detection protocol and has achieved 20% faster failure detection with a 20 times reduction in false positives.

Consul servers maintain the cluster state through a distributed key-value store. Each data center has a minimum of three servers, which form a RAFT peer set; one of the servers is elected as a leader and writes to the key-value store. The other servers can only read, and they delegate write operations to the leader. Transactions are also replicated to other peer servers. All the agents take part in the LAN gossip pool within a data center.

Consul servers are the only ones that take part in the WAN gossip pool across multiple data centers. The WAN gossip protocol is designed to work in a high-latency environment. Any random server in a data center can receive requests from the different data centers, but it forwards those requests to the local leader. The data is not replicated across Consul data centers; instead, the information is exchanged through a request/response between Consul servers across data centers.

Protocols

Consul uses modern protocols to quickly detect failures and significantly reduce false positives. To achieve these objectives, it uses the following protocols:

- RAFT protocol to elect a leader
- Consensus protocol to replicate data from a leader server to its peers
- Gossip protocol for failure detection

Let's go through these protocols to understand how the Consul cluster works.

RAFT

The RAFT protocol was designed by *Diego Ongaro* and *John Ousterhout* from *Standford University in 2014 – In Search of an Understandable Consensus Algorithm*. It is a fairly new protocol. The *etcd* (`https://etcd.io`) protocol that's used in Kubernetes and *CockroachDB* (`https://github.com/cockroachdb`) is a good example of RAFT implementation along with HashiCorp's *Consul*.

The RAFT protocol in Consul is used to elect a leader from three or five servers that run in a data center. Every node using RAFT can have three states: leader, follower, and candidate. Here, the following steps are taken:

1. Each node starts with a *follower* state with no leader.
2. After a timeout period, a node elevates itself to a *candidate* state and asks for votes.
3. The node that gets the majority votes promotes itself to be the *leader* with a message to all the other nodes.
4. Once a leader has been elected, all changes to the state of the cluster go through the leader, which is responsible for state management.

Only Consul servers in a data center participate in RAFT and are part of a **peer set**. A majority quorum within a peer set is required to agree to a committed state. The ideal number of Consul servers is either 3 or 5. New servers can get added to the peer set to increase the quorum size. When servers start for the first time, Consul adopts a practice called *bootstrap* mode in which the first server elects itself as a leader. The other servers are added to the peer set.

Consensus protocol

Consul uses a consensus protocol to provide consistency of transactions, as defined by the **Consistency, Availability, and Partition (CAP)** tolerance theorem. The CAP theorem states that in a distributed system, we can achieve any two of the following qualities, but not all three:

- **Consistency (C)**: Provides a single up-to-date copy of the data
- **Availability (A)**: High availability of data for updates
- **Partition (P)**: Tolerance to network partitions

 Eric Brewer of the University of California presented CAP as a theory in 2000; it was proved by Seth Gilbert and Nancy Lynch of MIT in 2002.

Consul provides CP tolerance. Please refer to `https://www.consul.io/intro/vs/serf.html` for more information.

The basic steps involved in transaction processing using CAP are as follows:

1. The **Remote Procedure Call (RPC)** of the reading query type is returned by the leader.
2. When a log entry (or event) is received by a leader, it sends the log entry to its followers (each server has one of three states: leader, follower, and candidate).
3. The followers send an `OK` message as an acknowledgment of a successful write.
4. The leader writes its entry and sends the commit state to followers while asking to change their state to commit.
5. When it receives `OK` messages from followers, the leader changes its state to commit.

Through consensus, the log entries are committed, and the Consistency part of the CAP theorem is achieved. Consensus is fault-tolerant as long as a quorum is available.

Consul follows the bootstrap for each data center to reduce network latency. A local data center server leader maintains separate peer sets to allow data to be partitioned by the data center. This way, every server leader of a data center is responsible for maintaining the state of its own data center. If a request is received for a remote data center, that request will be forwarded to the correct leader. This framework is designed for higher performance, low-latency transactions, and high availability of servers.

Gossip protocol

In Consul, the gossip protocol is used to manage client and server communication through message broadcasting between multiple data centers and within the same data center.

The gossip protocol in Consul is based on the **Scalable Weakly-consistent Infection-style Process Group Membership (SWIM)** protocol that was developed by Cornell University. Its implementation is done through a tool called **Serf** (`https://www.serf.io/docs/internals/gossip.html`), which is based on a modified SWIM protocol that has been enhanced by Hashicorp. This protocol is used to provide communication membership, failure detection, and event broadcasting.

Gossip protocol communicates over UDP to build a membership list and to converge it as soon as possible. TCP is used to exchange full details about nodes.

Consul uses two gossip protocols:

- LAN gossip protocol
- WAN gossip protocol

Within a data center, Consul agents enable the LAN gossip protocol across all servers and clients. Its primary functions are as follows:

- Allowing clients to discover servers automatically.
- Distributing failure detection communication across the entire cluster
- Enabling reliable and fast broadcasting for events such as the election of a new leader

The WAN gossip protocol is deployed across all data centers. Only servers can take part in WAN gossip, regardless of which data center it has been configured in. When all the servers have been identified, the WAN gossip protocol does the following:

- Allows servers to communicate with other servers across other data centers
- Integrates failure detection, allowing the Consul agents to decommission servers or isolate data centers
- Uses embedded libraries in Consul

 The purpose of this book is not to delve into the intricate working of the RAFT, CAP and Gossip protocols. You can refer to the *Further reading* section for more information.

In this section, we have gone through the Consul tenants of a data center and client/server, as well as the protocols that are used in Consul. In the next section, we will go through the control and data plane concepts for the purpose of showing how Consul implements the service mesh.

Consul's control and data planes

Consul is easy to understand and use. It is highly available and dynamically distributed. This section will detail how Consul works as a service mesh and its architecture components for the control plane and data plane.

Consul is configured as a control plane that provides four main functionalities: service discovery, secure communication, resource configuration, and network segmentation. These components are managed by a cluster manager (Consul server) to provide a robust service mesh.

Consul provides a data plane through the use of a proxy and native integration model with microservices. It is shipped with the popular sidecar Envoy (built by *Lyft*) proxy. This can be seen in the following diagram:

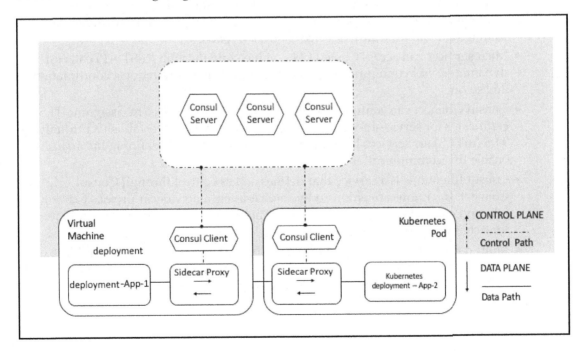

The preceding diagram shows the Consul control and data planes. Some primary features of Consul's control plane are as follows:

- Consul can discover and register services by enabling service discovery through API or database calls. Consul also enables service tracking through DNS or HTTP protocols to identify application dependency. Users can also leverage Consul to discover microservice providers and their end-to-end deployment definitions.

- The Consul server (leader) writes to a key-value store to record the states of the services, agents, clients, and servers. It can also hold configuration parameters for individual services through the use of name-value pairs. The central configuration can be pushed down to services dynamically, providing a consistent view of all services as opposed to individual configurations for each service.

- Consul provides network segmentation, thereby allowing certain services to communicate securely in a flat network.

- Consul can conduct health checks for running services, validate whether the server or client of the service side is routing traffic, and discover how many network requests are being transmitted and received. Consul collects physical node metrics to track CPU and memory utilization, along with other monitoring data. This data is used to monitor overall applications, platforms, infrastructure health, and performance. These metrics can also enable load balancing and traffic routing to avoid unhealthy service containers/pods.

- Microservices can access Consul's key-value store through REST API calls for dynamic service configurations, feature flagging, network request coordination, and so on.

- Consul Connect can configure secure connections to services by assigning TLS certificates for service-to-service communication. This will establish a **mutual TLS (mTLS)** for services by assigning sidecar proxies and defining *Intentions* to enable this communication.

- Consul Intentions is a service that defines access control through Consul Connect. Intentions are enforced by service-integrated sidecar proxies for inbound connections. It can also manage network segmentation and apply real-time changes to services.

- Multi-data center are provided out of the box, and Consul supports multiple data centers. This capability allows services and the Consul mesh to be scaled without us having to define additional abstraction layers on the network.

When IP addresses change in a dynamic infrastructure environment, connecting to a service through its IP address is no longer a reliable method unless DNS or iptables are used to update endpoints dynamically. Consul provides service discovery within an infrastructure in which applications can discover available services through the Consul agent running on the node, which then forwards queries to Consul server in a data center. Since Consul servers from one data center are connected to Consul servers in all the other data centers through the WAN gossip protocol, local Consul servers can forward the discovery request to the appropriate remote data centers.

Now, let's explore Consul's agent configuration.

Configuring agents

When Consul is installed, the very first task we need to perform is configuring the Consul agent. All the nodes within a Kubernetes cluster manager that have containerized services will deploy the Consul agent. The agent performs health checks and gathers metrics for the infrastructure, platform, and overall services running within Kubernetes. The Consul agent is not used for service discovery or to gather key-value data.

If there are multiple Kubernetes clusters, the Consul agent can be enabled to communicate with multiple Consul servers as long as the agent is installed across all Kubernetes clusters. The Consul server is where all the data is stored, and a primary server is defined to serve as a master server.

The Consul agent is Consul's core feature and is used to maintain server/client membership, service registry, health checks, address queries, and many more capabilities. The Consul agent is installed on every node within a cluster or data center for all the servers and clients. These nodes take part in the RAFT and Serf protocols.

It's good practice to deploy server nodes on dedicated machines to avoid high latencies and slow response times. The reason for this is that servers have higher resource workloads than client nodes. As we mentioned earlier, there are a lot more client nodes than servers because client nodes are lightweight and only interact with the server.

We can use Consul CLI commands using configuration files either in the **HashiCorp Configuration Language (HCL)** or the **JavaScript Object Notation (JSON)** format to spin up a server or client node.

Take a look at the following example of a Consul configuration file, which has been taken from `https://www.consul.io/docs/agent/options.html#configuration-files`:

```
{
  "datacenter": "remote-location",
  "data_dir": "/opt/consul",
  "log_level": "INFO",
  "node_name": "server1",
  "addresses": {
  "https": "0.0.0.0"
  },
  "ports": {
  "https": 8501
  },
  "key_file": "/etc/pki/tls/private/my.key",
  "cert_file": "/etc/pki/tls/certs/my.crt",
  "ca_file": "/etc/pki/tls/certs/ca-bundle.crt"
}
```

From the preceding JSON, we can see that a Consul server has been defined using TLS, the address, ports, and key certificate files.

The `consul agent` command is used to manage nodes, run server checks, announce services, apply queries, and much more.

The following is some sample output after executing the `consul agent`:

```
$ consul agent -data-dir=/opt/consul
==> Starting Consul agent...
==> Consul agent running!
 Node name: 'MyLaptop'
 Datacenter: 'dc1'
 Server: false (bootstrap: false)
 Client Addr: 127.0.0.1 (HTTP: 8500, DNS: 8600)
 Cluster Addr: 192.168.108.141 (LAN: 8301, WAN: 8302)
==> Log data will now stream in as it occurs:
 [INFO] serf: EventMemberJoin: MyLaptop.local 192.168.108.141
 ...
```

The five main messages that the preceding Consul agent command displays are as follows:

- **Node name**: This is the hostname of the machine where the Consul agent was executed.
- **Data center**: This tags where the Consul agent is configured to run. Consul can support multiple data centers, but each node is configured to a specific data center. The data center parameter is used to define that value. In the preceding example, the Consul agent is running in a single node environment, so by default, it assigns dc1 as the data center.
- **Server**: Value determines whether the Consul agent is running in either client or server mode. If the value is true, it is running in server mode. If it's false, then it is running in client mode. A server can be running in bootstrap mode. Since client nodes are stateless and rely on server nodes for state information, the bootstrap process allows the initial server nodes to be tied to a cluster.
- **Client Addr**: This is the localhost address that's used by the Consul agent for client interfaces. It includes HTTP and DNS ports, where the address and port can be changed as long as the -http-addr property is defined.
- **Cluster Addr**: This is the cluster IP address and provides a defined list of ports for the LAN and WAN protocols to enable communication between other Consul agents. It is good practice to define unique ports for all the Consul agents.

Running the Consul agent in a cluster provides a life cycle of interactions among its nodes. It's imperative to understand such interactions to see how a cluster manages its nodes. When a Consul agent is first enabled, that agent isn't aware of any other nodes and their interactions within the cluster. Node discovery, getting added to the cluster through the join command, or enabling auto-join configuration enables such interactions. The first interaction is a *gossip*, which notifies all the nodes within the cluster that a new node has been added.

If a node is removed from a cluster, the cluster will define that node as *left* and update the service catalog accordingly as not registered. If the Consul agent is a server, it will halt all replications. The process of keeping the Consul service catalog up to date with only active and running nodes and removing all failed and left nodes is called *reaping*. The reaping process is configured at 72 hours and it is recommended to factor any cluster outages, downtime, and so on.

Now that the Consul agents (client/servers) have been configured either through CLI options or through JSON configuration files, we can look at the service discovery process and the service catalog.

Service discovery and definitions

A service catalog contains all available nodes and their services running in a cluster. The Consul agent registers the service definition details, availability, and health metrics using the catalog.

Service configuration definitions are enabled by setting the `-config-file` option for the Consul agent as either an `HCL` or `JSON` extension. Definitions can be updated through the agent, and dynamic service registrations are made through REST API calls.

The following example configuration is a service definition that highlights high-level fields:

```
{
  "service": {
    "id": "redisuniquevalue",
    "name": "redis",
    "tags": ["primary"],
    "address": "",
    "meta": {
      "meta": "for my service"
    },
    "port": 8000,
    "enable_tag_override": false,
    "checks": [
      {
        "args": ["/usr/local/bin/check_redis.py"],
        "interval": "10s"
      }
    ],
    "kind": "connect-proxy",
  ...
```

The service definition configs must include a `name` and the following properties:

- `id`: If a name is not provided, the `id` is set as the name. It is a recommended best practice to define a unique ID for all the services within a node. This way, if any names conflict with other services, the unique ID is exclusive to that service.
- `tags`: These are values that are used to define node details, including primary or secondary, node versions, service labels, and many other attributes.
- `address`: This is the consul agent IP address that generates the service definition. This property is optional and doesn't need to be specified.
- `meta`: This is an ASCII semantic that can contain a maximum of 64 keys or value characters with no special characters. If security or performance is enabled, keys can be 128 chars, and values can be up to 512 chars.

- `port`: Along with the IP address, this can facilitate service discovery.
- `enable_tag_override`: This is an optional property that can be used to enable or disable other Consul agents outside the service to update the service catalog and definition tags. If the property is `false`, override is disabled.
- `checks`: This is the health check property that's used to identify any failed or left nodes. The use of this property is highly recommended and should be enabled with the health check scripts.
- `kind`: This property is optional, and its value will be a connect proxy. If the service instance is a non-proxy, then this field is removed altogether.
- `connect`: This property enables connected capabilities for the service.
- `native`: This is either `true` or `false` and states whether connection parameters are native.
- `sidecar_service`: This property is the sidecar proxy service definition and registration service. This property should not be defined if `native` is true.
- `weights`: This is an optional property that is specific to a service weight for DNS responses. If no values are defined, the default value for passing is `1`, and the warning is `1` if a service definition is critical or if there are warning checks.

HashiCorp also allows us to integrate Consul with Kubernetes. We will discuss this in the next section.

Consul integration

Hashicorp's collection of tools, such as Terraform (provisioning), Vault (Security), Consul (networking), and Nomad (Development), are alternatives to the Kubernetes orchestration. Consul can work natively using these Hashicorp tools.

Consul has provided a service sync-up between the Kubernetes Service Catalog and Consul since September 2018 to provide a cross-platform service discovery. It also migrates service workloads in and out of Kubernetes with Consul. The service sync-up feature can be enabled either through configuration files or through the Helm chart for Consul installation in a Kubernetes environment. Once enabled, the Consul catalog will sync with microservices deployed on Kubernetes, and it doesn't require any changes to be made to its resource definitions. This process can confirm that the Consul catalog will have the latest state of the Kubernetes cluster for its service definitions.

This concludes a brief introduction to the Consul control and data planes. Please refer to `https://consul.io/docs` for up-to-date and detailed information.

A service mesh is incomplete without observability features. We need these due to the challenges of the distributed microservices architecture, especially for testing and debugging. Next, we will cover monitoring and visualization support in Consul.

Monitoring and visualization

In Consul, metrics collection is available in different file formats. These metrics are used to monitor and visualize the health and stability of services, servers, clients, and communication protocols within a data center for every cluster and its designated nodes.

In this section, we will explore the monitoring and log collection method using Telegraf and then visualize the data using Grafana.

Telegraf

Using the *StatsD* protocol, a plugin called Telegraf enables monitoring and metrics collection in Consul. *StatsD* (https://github.com/statsd/statsd) is a daemon that summarizes and aggregates key application metrics.

Telegraf collects metrics about the specific host where the Consul agent is deployed and running. The key attributes to collect are: CPU, memory, disk I/O, networking, and process status.

To enable Telegraf's metrics collection, within the Consul agent configuration file the following code needs to be added and enabled:

```
{
  "telemetry": {
    "dogstatsd_addr": "localhost:8125",
    "disable_hostname": true
  }
}
```

Note that, when Consul is deployed using a Helm chart in a Kubernetes environment, the same feature can be enabled in `values.yaml` for the Consul connect section, as shown in the following code:

```
connectInject:
  enabled: true
  default: true
  centralConfig:
    enabled: true
```

```
defaultProtocol: "http"
proxyDefaults: |
{
  "envoy_dogstatsd_url": "udp://127.0.0.1:9125"
}
```

`dogstatsd_addr` or `envoy_dogstatsd_url` is the host IP address and port name for the `statsd` daemon. This property sends tags for each metric that can be leveraged by Grafana to visualize, filter, and derive data insights on its dashboard.

Grafana

To visualize data, we can use Grafana. Go to `https://grafana.com/grafana/dashboards/2351` to create a Grafana dashboard for Consul.

Now that we've looked at the visualization and monitoring features of Consul, we will look at the native traffic management features that are implemented in Consul to provide an out-of-band centrally managed configuration that can be executed through an Envoy proxy in a Kubernetes environment.

Traffic management

The traffic management feature of Console was introduced with Consul 1.6.x in August 2019. This feature is brand new and evolving rapidly. Consul Connect version 1.6 or higher provides traffic management features through L7 global configuration.

The basic components of traffic management are as follows:

- **Traffic Routing**: Accomplished through service-router
- **Traffic Shifting**: Accomplished through service-splitter and service-resolver

To provide seamless coordination of traffic management between VM (traditional) environments and Kubernetes (modern - cloud-native) environments, Consul has introduced the following four primitives akin to Kubernetes **Custom Resource Definitions (CRDs)**:

- `service-defaults` and `proxy-defaults`
- `service-router`
- `service-splitter`
- `service-resolver`

Service defaults

Take a look at the following configuration, which is used to define protocol and gateway defaults for an existing service. These are identified through `Name`:

```
Kind = "service-defaults"
Name = "web"

Protocol = "http"

MeshGateway = {
  mode = "local"
}
```

The preceding configuration is valid for both Kubernetes and non-Kubernetes environments. It is created automatically through the `consul-connect-inject-init` init-container when a Consul sidecar Envoy proxy is injected when a deployment is created. The following is an example of this:

```
Init Containers:
  consul-connect-inject-init:

...

        # Create the central config's service registration
        cat <<EOF >/consul/connect-inject/central-config.hcl
        kind = "service-defaults"
        name = "web"
        protocol = "http"
        MeshGateway = {
          mode = "local"
        }
        EOF
        /bin/consul config write -cas -modify-index 0 \
            /consul/connect-inject/central-config.hcl || true
...
```

However, for services running in a non-Kubernetes environment, `service-defaults` needs to be created manually or needs to be part of some automation. One of the interesting features of `service-defaults` is the use of the mesh gateway, which provides configuration so that individual services to failover from one data center to another or provide distributed services to act together through mutual TLS to provide a mesh of services that can span multiple zones/regions and hybrid configurations.

`proxy-defaults` is used to provide defaults at the global level to enable the gateways for all Consul services. This can be seen in the following code:

```
Kind = "proxy-defaults"
Name = "global"
MeshGateway {
    Mode = "local"
}
```

Remember that service defaults are configured automatically in a Kubernetes environment, as shown through `init-containers` while deploying a sidecar proxy. However, `service-defaults` need to be created manually for services in the VM environment.

Traffic routing

The following diagram shows how traffic routing works in Consul:

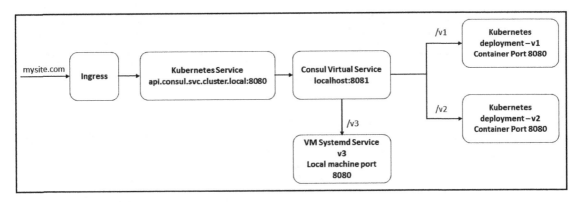

Let's assume that **mysite.com** hits the Ingress controller from outside and that the Ingress rule forwards this traffic to the Kubernetes `api.consul.svc.cluster.local` service at container port `8080`. Through the use of proper annotation for Consul at the Kubernetes deployment level, a virtual Consul service is created that will route traffic based upon the path. If the path begins with **/v1**, the traffic is routed to the **v1** deployment, and the **/v2** path directs the traffic to the **v2** deployment. However, there could be a Consul service that points to a Linux systemd service that runs in a VM running an external service and can receive the traffic if the path starts with **/v3**.

An example of traffic routing for path `/v1` using `service-router` is as follows:

```
kind = "service-router"
name = "api"
```

```
routes = [
  {
    match {
      http {
        path_prefix = "/v1"
      }
    }
    destination {
      service = "api-v1"
    }
  },
```

We will cover the implementation details of `service-routing` in `Chapter 22`, *Exploring Traffic Management in Consul*. Now, let's move on to traffic splitting.

Traffic split

Traffic splitting or traffic shifting in Consul is accomplished through **service-resolver** and **service-splitter**. This can be seen in the following diagram:

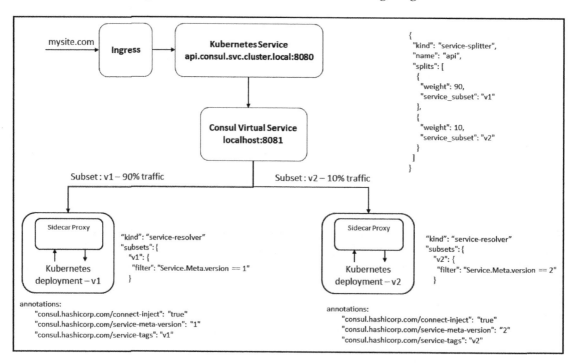

service-resolver defines the subset based upon the metadata filter, which is defined in the Kubernetes deployment through the use of annotations. **service-splitter** provides a configuration that is weight-based to shift the traffic from the Consul virtual service to the actual deployments, which are **v1** and **v2** in this case.

Implementing of these will be covered in detail in `Chapter 22`, *Exploring Traffic Management in Consul*. Now, let's move on to the mesh gateway.

Mesh gateway

The role of the mesh gateway or cross-cluster gateway is very important as it provides a flat network that we can use to connect multiple Consul clusters, regardless of their location in a zero-trust network environment through mutual TLS.

This can be seen in the following diagram:

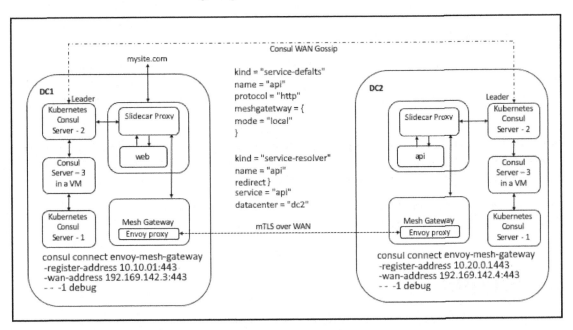

Two Consul servers are running in a Kubernetes environment and one Consul server is running in a VM. **server-2** is the leader in both data centers.

The mesh gateway works as follows:

1. The Consul **web** service receives traffic through the Ingress gateway from the internet.
2. **service-defaults** for the **api** Consul service (residing on **DC2**) is defined using the local mode of the mesh gateway.
3. **service-resolver** for **api** redirects the traffic to **DC2**.
4. When the web application invokes the **api** service, it goes through the mesh gateway of DC1, and the service resolves to the **api** service on DC2.
5. The traffic is **mTLS** between two configured gateways and between services and the mesh gateway.
6. The mesh gateway does not decrypt network traffic.

This concludes the mesh gateway, which is used to securely connect Consul clusters.

Summary

We started this chapter by understanding the Consul architecture and how it operates using the WAN and LAN protocols between and within data centers. The control plane of Consul comprises Consul servers and clients. Then, we explained automatic mTLS for service discovery and encrypted communication between services.

Next, we looked at the Consul data plane, which uses Envoy sidecar proxies. The concepts of traffic routing and shifting were explained. The Consul data plane, in conjunction with the control plane, defines the Consul service mesh.

Now that we have looked at the fundamentals of Consul, in the next chapter we will install Consul so that we can perform some hands-on exercises.

Questions

1. Consul does not have a centralized control plane.
   A. True
   B. False

2. The Consul agent must run on all Kubernetes nodes.
   A. True
   B. False

3. Consul services can be viewed as North-South network traffic, whereas Ingress gateways to multiple Kubernetes clusters can be treated as East-West network traffic.
   A. True
   B. False

4. A mesh gateway decrypts network traffic between two gateways to determine the destination service.
   A. True
   B. False

5. Consul service discovery is automatic in a Kubernetes environment.
   A. True
   B. False

6. Consul supports multiple data centers out of the box.
   A. True
   B. False

Further reading

- Hashicorp/Consul, GitHub, 2019: https://github.com/hashicorp/consul
- Gossip Protocol - Serf By Hashicorp, 2019: https://www.serf.io/docs/internals/gossip.html
- *Consul Architecture - Consul By Hashicorp*, Consul By Hashicorp, 2019: https://www.consul.io/docs/internals/architecture.html
- *Consul Reference Architecture | Consul - Hashicorp Learn*, Hashicorp Learn, 2019: https://learn.hashicorp.com/consul/datacenter-deploy/reference-architecture
- *Consensus Protocol - Consul By Hashicorp*, Consul By Hashicorp, 2019: https://www.consul.io/docs/internals/consensus.html
- *Gossip Protocol - Consul By Hashicorp*, Consul By Hashicorp, 2019: https://www.consul.io/docs/internals/gossip.html
- Cs.Cornell.Edu, Das Abhinandan et al. 2019: https://www.cs.cornell.edu/projects/Quicksilver/public_pdfs/SWIM.pdf
- Web.Stanford.Edu, Ongaro Diego, and John Ousterhout, 2019: https://web.stanford.edu/~ouster/cgi-bin/papers/raft-atc14, accessed 19 Aug 2019

- *Perspectives on the CAP Theorem*, Gilbert Seth, and Lynch Nancy: `https://groups. csail.mit.edu/tds/papers/Gilbert/Brewer2.pdf`, accessed 3 Oct 2019
- *Monitoring Consul With Telegraf | Consul - Hashicorp Learn*, Hashicorp Learn, 2019: `https://learn.hashicorp.com/consul/integrations/telegraf`

20
Installing Consul

Consul is very simple to install. It is a single Go binary that acts as a client and as well as a server. You can include Consul by provisioning VMs or bare metal servers. We will use the Consul Helm chart to show the installation process in a Kubernetes environment.

In this chapter, you will learn how to install the Consul agent in a VM and look at the Consul installation procedure in a Kubernetes cluster. The Consul service mesh is very easy to form in a Kubernetes environment using the Consul Connect feature, which enables automatic injection of the sidecar proxy for existing and new applications. However, it is slightly more complex to build the service mesh in a VM or bare-metal environments for Consul.

In a nutshell, in this chapter, we will cover the following topics:

- Installing Consul in a VM
- Installing Consul in Kubernetes

Technical requirements

To complete the exercises in this chapter, you will need a VM and the Kubernetes environment. We will continue to use the same environment that we used to learn about Istio and Linkerd.

Check if the `keepalived` pods are showing `READY 1/1` and that their `STATUS` is `Running`:

```
$ kubectl -n keepalived get pods
```

 The keepalived load balancer was installed in `Chapter 9`, *Installing Istio*.

To follow the examples in this chapter, you need to clone the scripts from GitHub:

```
$ cd ~/ # Switch to home directory
$ git clone https://github.com/servicemeshbook/consul.git
$ cd consul
$ git checkout 1.6.1
$ cd scripts
```

 Consul is open source and is maintained at https://github.com/ hashicorp/consul. Its home page is https://www.consul.io and is supported by Hashicorp.

Installing Consul in a VM

First, we will download and install Consul on the VM and then install it in Kubernetes. To install Consul in a VM, follow these steps:

1. Visit the download site for Consul: https://www.consul.io/downloads.html.
2. To be consistent with the exercises in this book, download the v1.6.1. package for Linux AMD64:

   ```
   $ wget
   https://releases.hashicorp.com/consul/1.6.1/consul_1.6.1_linux_amd6
   4.zip
   ```

 Note: Consul maintains its releases at https://releases.hashicorp.com/ consul, where you can pick a particular version to work with. For this book, we'll be using version 1.6.1.

3. Extract consul from the .zip archive and move it to a directory that's on PATH:

   ```
   $ unzip consul_1.6.1_linux_amd64.zip
   $ sudo mv consul /bin
   ```

   This completes the installation.

4. Check the version of Consul that's been installed:

```
$ consul version
Consul v1.6.1
Protocol 2 spoken by default, understands 2 to 3 (agent will
automatically use protocol >2 when speaking to compatible agents)
```

One of the best characteristics of Consul is that it can run in a heterogeneous environment that spans multiple data centers. For example, if a data center is running hundreds of VMs for service legacy applications, Consul can run as an agent on each VM to monitor their health and the services running on the nodes.

 Consul is available as a VM as well as in Kubernetes environments. The Consul version we're using is 1.6.1. The same version of Consul is available in the Kubernetes environment, but with a different version number. For example, Consul Helm chart 0.9.1 is equivalent to Consul 1.6.1. Hashicorp may integrate both as a single release in the future, but they are released separately as of now and can be updated independently of each other.

Now, we have installed Consul in a VM. Since we are running Kubernetes in the same VM, we will install Consul in Kubernetes.

Installing Consul in Kubernetes

Consul can run in each Kubernetes cluster as a server, a client, or both. If a data center has combinations of applications in VMs and in Kubernetes, it is possible to place Consul servers in a VM as well as in the Kubernetes environment. Similarly, the Consul agent should run on every VM and on each Kubernetes node as a daemon set. Consul forms a cluster automatically in a heterogeneous environment consisting of bare-metal machines, VMs, and Kubernetes.

To install Consul in Kubernetes, we'll need persistent volumes so that Consul can store cluster data in its key/value store. Let's create these first.

Creating persistent volumes

The following steps are a prerequisite to creating the persistent volume manually since we are not using an enterprise storage provisioner such as IBM Spectrum Scale, NetApp, Dell EMC, RedHat Ceph, or Portworx, which will create the persistent volume automatically when a persistent volume claim is made. To create a persistent volume, follow these steps:

1. Create a Consul persistent volumes directory:

```
$ sudo mkdir -p /var/lib/consul{0,1,2}
```

2. Create a consul namespace:

```
$ kubectl create ns consul
namespace/consul created
```

3. Grant cluster_admin to the consul namespace:

```
$ kubectl create clusterrolebinding consul-role-binding --
clusterrole=cluster-admin --group=system:serviceaccounts:consul
clusterrolebinding.rbac.authorization.k8s.io/consul-role-binding
created
```

The following are the definitions of the no-provisioner storage class and the persistent volumes that are provided by the 01-create-pv-consul.yaml script:

```
apiVersion: storage.k8s.io/v1
kind: StorageClass
metadata:
  name: consul-storage
provisioner: kubernetes.io/no-provisioner
reclaimPolicy: Delete
volumeBindingMode: WaitForFirstConsumer
```

4. Define the first physical volume:

```
apiVersion: v1
kind: PersistentVolume
metadata:
  name: consul-data-0
spec:
 accessModes:
 - ReadWriteOnce
 capacity:
 storage: 2Gi
 claimRef:
 apiVersion: v1
```

```
kind: PersistentVolumeClaim
name: data-consul-consul-consul-server-0
namespace: consul
 local:
   path: /var/lib/consul0
```

The following portion of the `01-create-pv-consul.yaml` script specifies the node that the persistent volume will be created on:

```
nodeAffinity:
    required:
      nodeSelectorTerms:
      - matchExpressions:
        - key: kubernetes.io/hostname
          operator: In
          values:
          - osc01.servicemesh.local
   persistentVolumeReclaimPolicy: Retain
   storageClassName: consul-storage
   ---
```

This is an example of a persistent volume claim. We'll do the same for the second and third ones in the same script, that is, `01-create-pv-consul.yaml`.

5. Create a storage class and three persistent volumes:

```
$ kubectl -n consul apply -f 01-create-pv-consul.yaml
storageclass.storage.k8s.io/consul-storage created
persistentvolume/consul-data-0 created
persistentvolume/consul-data-1 created
persistentvolume/consul-data-2 created
```

Now that we've created the persistent volumes, we can go ahead and download the Consul Helm chart for installing Consul. We'll learn how to do this in the next section.

Downloading the Consul Helm chart

Hashicorp recommends installing Consul in Kubernetes through a Helm chart. Note that this may change in the future as Kubernetes Operators are being used to install and maintain the life cycle of the Kubernetes resources. To install Consul Helm for Kubernetes, follow these steps:

1. Find the available versions of the Consul Helm for Kubernetes:

   ```
   $ curl -L -s
   https://api.github.com/repos/hashicorp/consul-helm/tags | grep
   "name"
   ```

2. Here, we're going to use version 0.11.0. You should download this version so that everything is consistent with the exercises in this chapter:

   ```
   $ cd # switch to home dir
   $ export CONSUL_HELM_VERSION=0.11.0
   $ curl -LOs
   https://github.com/hashicorp/consul-helm/archive/v${CONSUL_HELM_VER
   SION}.tar.gz
   $ tar xfz v${CONSUL_HELM_VERSION}.tar.gz
   ```

3. In the Helm chart for Consul, we need to modify the `failureThreshold` and `initialDelaySeconds` parameters. Change the default values of 2 and 5 seconds to 30 and 60 seconds, respectively. This was necessary for the VMs since we are in a resource-constrained environment:

   ```
   $ sed -i 's/failureThreshold:.*/failureThreshold: 30/g' \
   ~/consul-helm-${CONSUL_HELM_VERSION}/templates/server-
   statefulset.yaml
   ```

   ```
   $ sed -i 's/initialDelaySeconds:.*/initialDelaySeconds: 60/g' \
   ~/consul-helm-${CONSUL_HELM_VERSION}/templates/server-
   statefulset.yaml
   ```

After making these changes, we can install Helm for Consul in Kubernetes.

Installing Consul

To install Consul, follow these steps:

1. Switch to the scripts directory for this chapter:

   ```
   $ cd ~/consul/scripts # Switch to scripts for this exercise
   ```

2. Create a new Consul cluster.

We will run three consul servers in our Kubernetes environment, even though we only have one node. Define the input parameters for the Consul Helm chart to be able to run three servers using a single node:

```
# Script : 02-consul-values.yaml

global:
  datacenter: dc1
  image: "consul:1.6.1"
  imageK8S: "hashicorp/consul-k8s:0.9.1"

server:
  enabled: true
  replicas: 3
  bootstrapExpect: 0
  affinity: ''
  storage: 2Gi
  disruptionBudget:
    enabled: true
    maxUnavailable: 0

client:
  enabled: true
  grpc: true

dns:
  enabled: true

ui:
  enabled: true
```

The following portion of the `02-consul-values.yaml` script specifies the parameters for the Consul Connect sidecar proxy install:

```
connectInject:
  enabled: true
  imageEnvoy: "envoyproxy/envoy:v1.10.0"
  default: true
  centralConfig:
  enabled: true
  defaultProtocol: "http"
  proxyDefaults: |
  {
  "envoy_dogstatsd_url": "udp://127.0.0.1:9125"
  }
```

If we need to sync services between Kubernetes and Consul, we could define an additional parameter, syncCatalog, in the preceding values.yaml file:

```
# Sync Kubernetes and Consul services
syncCatalog:
    enabled: true
```

Note that a data center should only have three or five Consul servers, but there can be hundreds of Consul agents. Using the preceding values.yaml file, we are defining three Consul servers. An actual Kubernetes environment may have hundreds of nodes, but only three or five of them will host Consul servers, and the other nodes will be running Consul clients.

We are setting connectInject.enabled to true so that the Envoy proxy sidecar is injected into each service when they are created.

3. Run the following helm install command to create the Consul cluster by installing Consul servers, clients, and a Consul Connect injector service. The Consul injector will be used to inject sidecar proxies into the pods:

```
$ helm install ~/consul-helm-${CONSUL_HELM_VERSION}/ --name consul \
--namespace consul --set fullnameOverride=consul -f ./02-consul-
values.yaml
```

4. Make sure that the persistent volume claims are bound to the persistent volume that you created previously:

```
$ kubectl -n consul get pvc
NAME                          STATUS   VOLUME          ---
data-consul-consul-server-0   Bound    consul-data-0   ---
data-consul-consul-server-1   Bound    consul-data-1   ---
data-consul-consul-server-2   Bound    consul-data-2   ---

--- CAPACITY   ACCESS MODES   STORAGECLASS   AGE
--- 2Gi        RWO                           105s
--- 2Gi        RWO                           104s
--- 2Gi        RWO                           103s
```

Since we are running a single node VM, it is difficult to run three replicas of Kubernetes StatefulSet. In a production Kubernetes cluster, each replica will run in a separate node. We have simulated the same by running three replicas in a single VM by using setting the `affinity` variable to `null` in the helm `values.yaml` file. We created three persistent volumes ahead of time by using the filesystem through no provisioner storage class that was introduced in Kubernetes 1.14. In an actual production Kubernetes environment, you would use cloud-native storage for your storage providers, such as `portworx.io`, `robin.io`, or `rook.io`, or any other storage vendor that allows a **Container Storage Interface (CSI)** enabled driver to connect to their dedicated storage.

5. Also, make sure that all Consul servers are in the READY 1/1 state and have a status of Running:

```
$ kubectl -n consul get pods
NAME                                                                  READY ---
consul-6frhx                                                          1/1   ---
consul-connect-injector-webhook-deployment-699976587d-wrzcw          1/1   ---
consul-server-0                                                       1/1   ---
consul-server-1                                                       1/1   ---
consul-server-2                                                       1/1   ---

--- STATUS    RESTARTS    AGE
--- Running   0           19m
--- Running   0           19m
--- Running   0           19m
--- Running   0           19m
--- Running   0           19m
```

Now, you have deployed Consul in a Kubernetes environment that's simulating three consul servers in a single VM.

Both the Consul server and the client have been installed in your Kubernetes environment. Let's check their deployments. The Consul servers are deployed through `StatefulSet`, like so:

```
$ kubectl -n consul get sts
NAME            READY   AGE
consul-server   3/3     4h43m
```

Note that the Consul server replicas were set to three in `values.yaml`, and hence three consul servers are running. The persistent volumes were created at the start of the install process.

Check `ls -l /var/lib/consul?` to verify the data that was generated by each Consul server.

Each Consul server node ID is persisted in a `node-id` file. This won't cause an issue, even if that server is rescheduled on another node and gets a new IP address. The Consul servers are normally created with an anti-affinity rule so that they are placed on different nodes. However, for this demonstration VM environment, we disabled the anti-affinity rule by setting `server.affinity` to null in `values.yaml` so that we can create all the three Consul servers on the same Kubernetes node.

1. Check the version of the Consul running in Kubernetes like so:

   ```
   $ kubectl -n consul exec -it consul-server-0 -- consul version
   Consul v1.6.1
   Protocol 2 spoken by default, understands 2 to 3 (agent will
   automatically use protocol >2 when speaking to compatible agents)
   ```

2. Out of the three Consul servers, go through the server log of any one of them to ascertain which server is the leader:

   ```
   $ kubectl -n consul logs consul-server-0 | grep -i leader
   2019/08/26 15:50:52 [INFO] raft: Node at 192.168.230.233:8300
   [Follower] entering Follower state (Leader: "")
   2019/08/26 15:51:00 [ERR] agent: failed to sync remote state: No
   cluster leader
   2019/08/26 15:51:09 [INFO] consul: New leader elected: consul-
   server-1
   ```

3. The Consul clients are installed as a `DaemonSet` so that they execute on every Kubernetes node, like so:

```
$ kubectl -n consul get ds
NAME    DESIRED  CURRENT  READY  UP-TO-DATE  AVAILABLE  NODE SELECTOR  AGE
consul 1        1        1      1           1          <none>         4h59m
```

This shows the Consul client on the sole node of our demonstration environment.

If we set `global.enabled` to `false` and `client.enabled` to `true` in the preceding `values.yaml` file, only the client components will be installed in Kubernetes. It joins the existing cluster by setting the join property. While installing this, it is also possible to join an existing Consul cluster. Then, we can extend each Kubernetes node so that it joins the existing Consul cluster by creating the `value.yaml` file like so:

```
global:
enabled: false
client:
enabled: true
join:
- "provider=my-cloud config=val ..."
```

Now, let's connect the Consul DNS server to Kubernetes.

Connecting Consul DNS to Kubernetes

Since Consul uses its own DNS, we will link the Consul DNS server as an upstream server to the Kubernetes `coredns` server. Follow these steps:

1. Consul runs its own DNS for service discovery. Let's check it out:

```
$ kubectl -n consul get svc
NAME                           TYPE        CLUSTER-IP       ---
consul-connect-injector-svc    ClusterIP   10.111.4.98      ---
consul-dns                     ClusterIP   10.99.221.20     ---
consul-server                  ClusterIP   None             ---
consul-ui                      ClusterIP   10.110.177.68    ---

--- EXTERNAL-IP    PORT(S)                                      AGE
--- <none>         443/TCP                                      22m
--- <none>         53/TCP,53/UDP                                22m
--- <none>         8500/TCP,8301/TCP,8301/UDP,8302/TCP,8302/UDP,
                   8300/TCP,8600/TCP,8600/UDP                   22m
--- <none>         80/TCP                                       22m
```

We need to connect the `consul-dns` service to the Kubernetes DNS.

Let's take a look at the `03-create-coredns-configmap.sh` script, which modifies the original `coredns` config map by adding the IP address of `consul-dns` as a reverse proxy so that Kubernetes; `coredns` server adds the Consul DNS server to its configuration:

```
#!/bin/bash

echo create coredns config map to integrate consul dns with ICP
coredns

cat << EOF | kubectl apply -f -
apiVersion: v1
kind: ConfigMap
metadata:
  labels:
    addonmanager.kubernetes.io/mode: EnsureExists
  name: coredns
  namespace: kube-system
data:
  Corefile: |
  ...
    consul {
      errors
      cache 30
      proxy . $(kubectl -n consul get svc consul-dns -o
jsonpath='{.spec.clusterIP}')
    }
EOF
```

 By using Consul discovery through its own DNS server, the Kubernetes environment is also modified to use the Consul DNS server. This is an integration point in which Kubernetes also has visibility to the services running outside its own cluster through the Consul service discovery.

2. Run the `03-create-coredns-configmap.sh` script:

```
$ chmod +x 03-create-coredns-configmap.sh

$ ./03-create-coredns-configmap.sh
create coredns config map to integrate consul dns with ICP coredns
configmap/coredns created
```

By executing the preceding script, we have modified the `coredns` of Kubernetes to include Consul DNS for service discovery. You can check the consul DNS server that we added to the `coredns` config map by running `kubectl -n kube-system get cm coredns -o yaml`.

Consul server in a VM

One of the beneficial features of Consul is that you can have a hybrid service mesh that can span multiple data centers, Kubernetes clusters, VMs, or just bare-metal servers.

Though it does not serve any useful purpose in a single node, we will use consul at the VM level and join the Kubernetes cluster, which is running three servers, just as a demonstration to show the Consul method of service discovery and spanning multiple heterogeneous environments. In our demonstration environment, which is running on a single VM node, we'll simulate a VM and a Kubernetes cluster running three Consul servers. Let's get started:

1. Find out the endpoints for `consul-server`:

```
$ kubectl -n consul get ep
NAME                          ENDPOINTS                          AGE
consul-connect-injector-svc   192.168.230.218:8080               47m
consul-dns                    192.168.230.219:8600,
                              192.168.230.237:8600,
                              192.168.230.245:8600 + 5 more...   47m
consul-server                 192.168.230.219:8301,
                              192.168.230.237:8301,
                              192.168.230.245:8301 + 21 more...  47m
consul-ui                     192.168.230.219:8500,
                              192.168.230.237:8500,
                              192.168.230.245:8500               47m
```

Note that *+ 5 more* or *21 more* in the preceding output is an indication of the additional output that we can see by using the `kubectl -n consul describe ep consul-server` command. The endpoint IP addresses may be different in your case.

The Kubernetes `consul-server` service points to three Consul pods. Kubernetes will do the load balancing for us. The Fully Qualified Domain Name of this service name is `consul-server.consul.svc.cluster.local`. The preceding service name should resolve to the cluster pod addresses in a round-robin fashion.

Note that the request for the read and write for the Consul server can be routed to any server in a round-robin fashion. The `AnyConsul` server can fulfill the read operation, but all writes are forwarded to the leader server. The leader writes the information in a distributed key-value store to maintain the state of the cluster.

Let's assume that you have VMs running on other machines and you want to join those VMs to the Consul cluster. To do this, you need to create an ingress rule that will forward an external domain name (say, consul.example.com) to the `consul-server.consul.svc.cluster.local` service. At the VM level, you can run a command such as a consul join `<name of the consul server>`. The Consul server can run in VMs, bare-metal servers or, as in our example, in the Kubernetes clusters.

2. Now, query the node names using the REST API:

```
$ curl -s localhost:8500/v1/catalog/nodes | json_reformat
[
  {
  "ID": "1a36a121-9810-887f-78e0-30721fab90c5",
  "Node": "consul-server-0",
  "Address": "192.168.230.219",
  "Datacenter": "dc1",
  "TaggedAddresses": {
  "lan": "192.168.230.219",
  "wan": "192.168.230.219"
  },
  "Meta": {
  "consul-network-segment": ""
  },
  "CreateIndex": 12,
  "ModifyIndex": 14
  },
  ...
```

3. Check the members of the Consul cluster from inside one of the Kubernetes Consul pods:

```
$ kubectl -n consul exec -it consul-server-0 -- consul members
Node                     Address                   Status   Type      ---
consul-server-0          192.168.230.219:8301      alive    server ---
consul-server-1          192.168.230.245:8301      alive    server ---
consul-server-2          192.168.230.237:8301      alive    server ---
osc01.servicemesh.local  192.168.230.249:8301      alive    client ---

--- Build  Protocol  DC    Segment
--- 1.6.1  2         dc1   <all>
--- 1.6.1  2         dc1   <all>
--- 1.6.1  2         dc1   <all>
--- 1.6.1  2         dc1   <default>
```

4. Check the same from the VM:

```
$ consul members
Node                      Address                 Status   Type     ---
consul-server-0           192.168.230.219:8301    alive    server   ---
consul-server-1           192.168.230.245:8301    alive    server   ---
consul-server-2           192.168.230.237:8301    alive    server   ---
osc01.servicemesh.local   192.168.230.249:8301    alive    client   ---

--- Build  Protocol  DC   Segment
--- 1.6.1  2         dc1  <all>
--- 1.6.1  2         dc1  <all>
--- 1.6.1  2         dc1  <all>
--- 1.6.1  2         dc1  <default>
```

Note that the list of Consul members includes Kubernetes nodes as well as the VMs that are running the Consul agent.

5. Use the `consul info` command to find out about the configuration information of the Consul cluster from inside one of the Consul servers in the Kubernetes environment:

```
$ kubectl -n consul exec -it consul-server-0 -- consul info
agent:
        check_monitors = 0
        check_ttls = 0
        checks = 0
        services = 0
build:
        prerelease =
        revision = 34eff659
        version = 1.6.1
consul:
        acl = disabled
        bootstrap = false
        known_datacenters = 1
        leader = false
        leader_addr = 10.1.230.238:8300
        server = true
raft:
        applied_index = 8267
        commit_index = 8267
        fsm_pending = 0
        last_contact = 85.424007ms
        last_log_index = 8267
        last_log_term = 403
        last_snapshot_index = 0
    ...
```

The preceding output shows information about various Consul server components, such as their LAN, WAN gossip, and raft protocol, as well as their metrics. The `consul info` command can also be executed from the VM and will produce the same output.

> Consul provides an HTTP API for the `consul info` command and other commands. Please refer to `https://www.consul.io/api` for details about HTTP APIs.

Summary

In this chapter, we explored how to install Consul in a heterogeneous environment such as a VM (or bare metal) and Kubernetes clusters. You also discovered that the Consul install can be done from GitHub for VMs and use the Helm chart for Kubernetes. Consul integration with VMs and legacy systems make it easy to have a hybrid service mesh spanning multiple Kubernetes clusters, VMs, bare-metal machines, and even data centers.

The Consul way of discovering services not only in the Kubernetes cluster but from other heterogeneous environments as well, was integrated by registering the Consul DNS server as one of the servers in the Kubernetes CoreDNS for the discovery of the services from outside of the Kubernetes cluster. Now, you should feel comfortable with applying the knowledge you gained in this chapter in order to build a Consul cluster consisting of a heterogeneous environment. Using this, you can build a Consul service mesh for new and existing Kubernetes cloud-native applications.

In the next chapter, we will explore the capabilities of the Consul service mesh by going through the service discovery process.

Questions

1. The Consul service mesh works across heterogeneous environments and data centers across different regions.

   A) True
   B) False

2. In a Consul cluster, the Consul servers can be in Kubernetes or in VMs.

   A) True
   B) False

3. Consul members can't join the existing Consul cluster from a VM or Kubernetes.

   A) True
   B) False

4. Consul servers can span multiple data centers.

   A) True
   B) False

5. Kubernetes can send write requests to any Consul server, but only the lead Consul server writes that information to the distributed key-value store.

   A) True
   B) False

6. Consul extends Kubernetes' key-value database store, etcd, to maintain the state of Consul clusters.

   A) True
   B) False

Further reading

- *Consul Curriculum – HashiCorp Learn*, HashiCorp Learn, (2018), available at https://learn.hashicorp.com/consul/, accessed May 11, 2019.
- *Introduction to HashiCorp Consul Connect with Kubernetes*, Huysmans, C. (2019), available at https://medium.com/hashicorp-engineering/introduction-to-hashicorp-consul-connect-with-kubernetes-d7393f798e9d, accessed May 12, 2019.

21
Exploring the Service Discovery Features of Consul

One of the most powerful features of Consul is that you can build a service mesh using a heterogeneous environment spanning multiple data centers. In this chapter, we will cover Consul Connect and use this method to form a service registration process with sidecar proxy injection in a Kubernetes environment. Consul also allows us to perform this in a non-Kubernetes environment, such as a workload running in a VM. However, since we are only focusing on cloud-native workloads in a Kubernetes environment, it is outside the scope of this book to cover Consul's service mesh extension for legacy workloads.

First, we will install a demo application and then perform some hands-on exercises in order to explore the features of Consul Connect from a service discovery standpoint.

To understand Consul's service discovery features, we will focus on the following topics in this chapter:

- Installing a Consul demo application
- Discovering the native Consul dashboard
- Learning about service discovery and its intentions
- Implementing mutual TLS
- Exploring the Consul key-value store
- Securing Consul with ACL
- Monitoring and metrics
- Registering external services

Technical requirements

In order to complete the exercises in this chapter, you need to install Consul on your VM and Kubernetes environment, as detailed in the previous chapter. Once you have installed Consul, you can follow the exercises in this chapter.

 We are only focusing on running Consul in a Kubernetes environment. Refer to https://github.com/hashicorp/demo-consul-101 to get hands-on with Consul Connect while using non-Kubernetes workloads.

Installing a Consul demo application

To explore the service mesh capabilities of Consul through a Kubernetes environment, we will install a demo application that is available from Hashicorp. This demo uses two simple services: a counting service and a frontend web UI service (connects to the counting service to show the results). Let's get started:

1. Let's take a look at the counting pod definition, which shows counting and a counting-init container:

```
# Counting pod

apiVersion: v1
kind: Pod
metadata:
  name: counting
  annotations:
    "consul.hashicorp.com/connect-inject": "true"
spec:
  containers:
  - name: counting
    image: hashicorp/counting-service:0.0.2
    ports:
    - containerPort: 9001
      name: http
  initContainers:
  - name: counting-init
    image: hashicorp/counting-init:0.0.9
    env:
    - name: POD_IP
      valueFrom:
        fieldRef:
          fieldPath: status.podIP
```

```
    - name: HOST_IP
      valueFrom:
        fieldRef:
          fieldPath: status.hostIP
```

The `consul.hashicorp.com/connect-inject` annotation, when set to `true`, will inject a sidecar proxy into the pod through the admission webhook controller. The counting service endpoint's REST URL is at port 9001.

2. Now, let's take a look at the front end dashboard service using a dashboard container and its init container:

```
# Dashboard pod

apiVersion: v1
kind: Pod
metadata:
  name: dashboard
  labels:
    app: dashboard
  annotations:
    "consul.hashicorp.com/connect-inject": "true"
    "consul.hashicorp.com/connect-service-upstreams":
"counting:9001"
spec:
  containers:
  - name: dashboard
    image: hashicorp/dashboard-service:0.0.4
    ports:
    - containerPort: 9002
      name: http
    env:
    - name: COUNTING_SERVICE_URL
      value: "http://localhost:9001"
```

The preceding code is for the frontend dashboard pod. The following snippet shows the `init` container:

```
initContainers:
- name: dashboard-init
  image: hashicorp/dashboard-init:0.0.4
  env:
  - name: POD_IP
    valueFrom:
      fieldRef:
        fieldPath: status.podIP
  - name: HOST_IP
```

```
valueFrom:
  fieldRef:
    fieldPath: status.hostIP
```

The `consul.hashicorp.com/connect-inject` annotation, when set to true, will inject a sidecar proxy into this frontend GUI. The new annotation, `consul.hashicorp.com/connect-service-upstreams`, in the dashboard pod defines the upstream counting microservice that provides a REST API endpoint at port `9001`. For the dashboard service to connect to `counting`, it is necessary for the Consul DNS to be connected to the Kubernetes DNS.

The dashboard service provides a hook for the counting service through the `COUNTING_SERVICE_URL` environment variable. The dashboard service web UI is exposed at port `9002`.

3. The following Kubernetes service will provide an endpoint to the dashboard microservice at its internal port, that is, `9002`:

```
# Define service

apiVersion: v1
kind: Service
metadata:
  name: dashboard-service
  labels:
    app: dashboard
spec:
  ports:
  - protocol: "TCP"
    port: 80
    targetPort: 9002
  selector:
    app: dashboard
  type: NodePort
```

4. Let's create backend counting and frontend dashboard services:

```
$ kubectl -n consul apply -f 04-counting-demo.yaml
pod/counting created
pod/dashboard created
service/dashboard-service created
```

5. Check the `counting` and dashboard pods and take a look at the injected sidecar proxies in them:

```
$ kubectl -n consul get pods
NAME                                                          READY  ---
consul-9tkg9                                                  1/1    ---
consul-connect-injector-webhook-deployment-699976587d-n9qmp  1/1    ---
consul-server-0                                               1/1    ---
consul-server-1                                               1/1    ---
consul-server-2                                               1/1    ---
consul-sync-catalog-8444f97fc6-ptfwg                         1/1    ---
counting                                                      2/2    ---
dashboard                                                     2/2    ---


---  STATUS    RESTARTS    AGE
---  Running   1           19m
---  Running   0           19m
---  Running   0           19m
---  Running   0           19m
---  Running   0           19m
---  Running   1           19m
---  Running   0           10s
---  Running   0           10s
```

6. Describe one of the microservices and check the injected sidecar proxy:

```
$ kubectl -n consul describe pod counting
    ...
Containers:
  counting:
    ...
    Image:          hashicorp/counting-service:0.0.2
    ...
    Port:           9001/TCP
    Host Port:      0/TCP
    State:          Running
      Started:      Mon, 26 Aug 2019 10:21:40 -0400
    Ready:          True
    Restart Count:  0
    Environment:    <none>
    Mounts:
      /var/run/secrets/kubernetes.io/serviceaccount from default-
  token-bq5xd (ro)
  consul-connect-envoy-sidecar:
    ...
    Image:          envoyproxy/envoy-alpine:v1.9.1
    ...
    Port:           <none>
```

```
Host Port:       <none>
Command:
  envoy
  --config-path
  /consul/connect-inject/envoy-bootstrap.yaml
State:           Running
  Started:       Mon, 26 Aug 2019 10:21:40 -0400
Ready:           True
Restart Count:   0
Environment:
  HOST_IP:       (v1:status.hostIP)
...
```

By doing this, we have deployed the `counting` and `dashboard` services from HashiCorp to explain the service discovery features of Consul. Next, we will create an Ingress entry so that we can access the Consul dashboard.

Defining Ingress for the Consul dashboard

Even without using Ingress, it is possible to use `NodePort` to access the dashboard from within the VM. However, we will create an optional Ingress entry for the Consul dashboard so that this can be accessed from outside the Kubernetes cluster. Follow these steps:

1. Add an entry in `/etc/hosts` in the VM for the Consul Web UI called `webconsole.consul.local` that points to the Nginx Ingress controller:

```
$ export INGRESS_HOST=$(kubectl -n kube-system get service nginx-
controller \
-o jsonpath='{.status.loadBalancer.ingress..ip}') ; echo $INGRESS_HOST
192.168.142.249

$ sudo sed -i '/webconsole.consul.local/d' /etc/hosts

$ echo "$INGRESS_HOST webconsole.consul.local" | sudo tee -a /etc/hosts
```

The following is the definition of the Ingress entry for
the `webconsole.consul.local` hostname so that it points to `consul-ui`:

```
# Script : 05-create-ingress.yaml

apiVersion: extensions/v1beta1
kind: Ingress
metadata:
  name: webconsole
  namespace: consul
  annotations:
    ingress.kubernetes.io/rewrite-target: /
spec:
  rules:
  - host: webconsole.consul.local
    http:
      paths:
      - backend:
          serviceName: consul-ui
          servicePort: 80
        path: /
```

2. Create Ingress definitions for the service:

```
$ kubectl apply -f 05-create-ingress.yaml
ingress.extensions/webconsole created
```

The preceding Ingress definitions will route traffic coming from the external
`webconsole.consul.local` host to the internal `consul-ui` service at port 80 running in
the Consul namespace to provide access to the Consul control plane web UI.

So far, we have installed the demo application, which is comprised of two
services: `counting` and `dashboard`. Then, we used Ingress to allow external traffic to be
routed to the demo application. Next, we will go through the service discovery features of
Consul.

Service discovery

The service discovery process in Consul is integrated with health checks, DNS, and HTTP
interfaces. The Consul agent registers the service by adding an entry to the key-value store.
When service discovery information is available in the Consul key-value store, that service
can be discovered by other services.

In Consul, the process of service discovery uses a registry to keep a real-time list of services, their health, and their location information. It has the ability to find the location of upstream services so that the connection to it is transparent without a need for an external load balancer. However, a load balancer may be required for Ingress traffic coming to the service mesh from outside.

Consul has two approaches to service discovery, as follows:

- **Sidecar proxy**: Consul connects services to each other by using sidecar proxies to form a service mesh to automatically establish TLS for inbound and outbound connections. Due to its ability to connect services to each other, it is also referred to as Consul Connect. The use of Envoy sidecar proxies makes this feature language-agnostic.
- **Native integration**: Consul allows non-Kubernetes applications to integrate with the help of the Connect API to establish TLS for inbound and outbound connections without the overhead of a sidecar proxy. This process involves acquiring proper TLS certificates and authorizing inbound connections with the use of the Consul HTTP API, which allows us to get proper certificates and verify connections.

At the time of writing, the native integration feature is only available for the Go programming language (please refer to `https://www.consul.io/api` for more information). Due to this, we'll be looking at the sidecar proxy approach:

1. Find out the node port for the demo application's `dashboard-service`:

```
$ kubectl -n consul get svc dashboard-service
NAME                TYPE       CLUSTER-IP       EXTERNAL-IP   PORT(S)        AGE
dashboard-service   NodePort   10.111.225.214   <none>        80:30144/TCP   5h28m
```

2. Take note of the node port number from the preceding command. It is `30144`. Use this to open `http://192.168.142.101:30144` in the first tab of the browser. Note that the port number of `dashboard-service` may be different in your VM environment.
3. The counting dashboard will show an increasing counter being returned from the backend counting service. If the backend service is in a disconnected state, it will show `-1`:

We just demonstrated a simple web application that is successfully calling an upstream service. Next, we will look at the various aspects of the Consul service from the Consul web console.

Using the Consul web console

The Consul web console is the GUI representation of Consul primitives such as services, nodes, and intentions. Let's take a look at it:

1. Open a tab in your browser and open `http://webconsole.consul.local` to get a view of the services that have been discovered by Consul. You will see the total number of services that have been discovered and their health statuses:

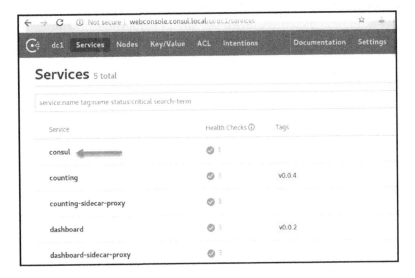

Note that the Consul dashboard displays sidecar proxies as separate services, even for a Kubernetes environment.

2. Click on the **consul** service. The Consul dashboard will show the status of the three consul servers running in a Kubernetes cluster:

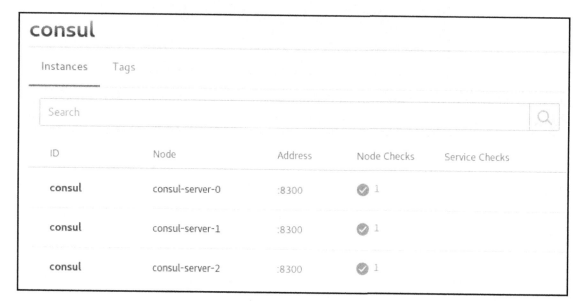

3. Click **Nodes**. The Consul dashboard shows four healthy nodes. `consul-server-0|1|2` which are Consul servers in Kubernetes, while `osc01.servicemesh.local` is the VM. Now, click on `osc01.servicemesh.local`:

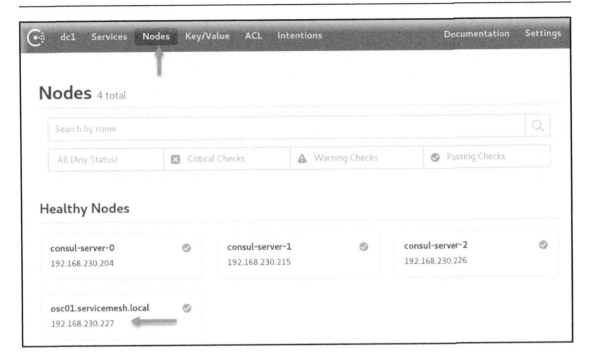

Here, we can see the REST endpoint result for the service health status.

4. Click **Round Trip Time**:

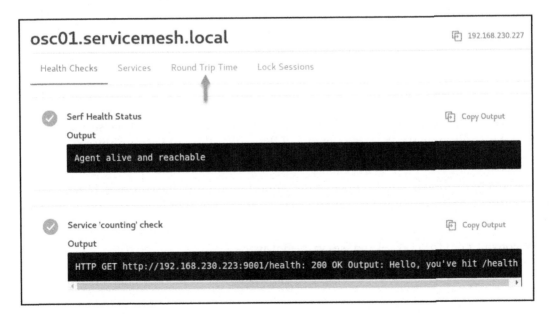

5. Notice the minimum, median, and maximum round trip time for the services as a whole. These metrics are captured by Consul:

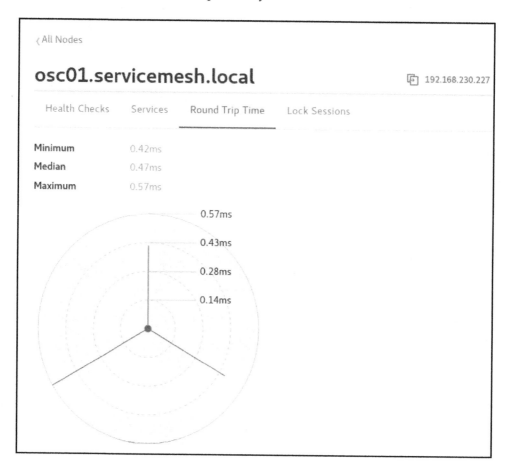

The Consul dashboard is a simple GUI that we can use to take a look at the services in Kubernetes environments, the health status of the nodes, the services running in nodes, and so on.

The discovered and registered services can be queried through the command line, as well. For example, run the following command to list the services that have been registered with Consul:

```
$ consul config list -kind service-defaults
counting
dashboard
```

So far in this chapter, we've used the Consul web dashboard and command line to discover the services that are running in the Kubernetes cluster. Since we installed the demo application, which is comprised of two services (`counting` and `dashboard`), the health status and details could be viewed through the Consul dashboard. Next, we will go through the mutual TLS implementation between services.

Implementing mutual TLS

The communication between services is encrypted through sidecar proxies using mutual TLS. Each service is provided an identity through the SPIFFE X.509 certificate (please refer to `Chapter 5`, *Service Mesh Interface and SPIFFE*, for a discussion on SPIFFE). Since the services are not tied to fixed IP addresses, the SPIFFE-based identity can be used to connect and accept requests between SPIFFE-compliant services.

Consul has a built-in Certificate Authority, through which it assigns leaf certificates to sidecar proxies. These sidecar proxies can be configured for upstream configuration to specify alternate data centers that services can access for high availability. The CA federation can be enabled between multiple data centers. The CA federation helps the alternate data center to continue issuing leaf SPIFFE X509 certificates in the case of WAN disruptions. The root key rotation and the signing of CSR for an intermediate certificate can be performed by any data center. Mutual TLS provides security in a zero-trust network through in-transit encryption and authorization.

In this section, we will explore the mutual TLS implementation that happens automatically through the Consul Connect service mesh. Developers do not have to write a single line of code to enable encrypted communication between services. This allows services to run securely in a zero-trust network environment without the use of a dedicated VPN. To implement mTLS, follow these steps:

1. Check the log of the sidecar proxy for TLS. By doing this, you will see `tls` shown against every communication:

```
$ kubectl -n consul logs counting -c consul-connect-envoy-sidecar |
grep tls
[2019-12-23 16:29:53.442][1][info][main]
[source/server/server.cc:215] filters.listener:
envoy.listener.original_dst,envoy.listener.original_src,envoy.liste
ner.proxy_protocol,envoy.listener.tls_inspector
[2019-12-23 16:29:53.442][1][info][main]
[source/server/server.cc:225] transport_sockets.downstream:
envoy.transport_sockets.alts,envoy.transport_sockets.tap,raw_buffer
,tls
```

```
[2019-12-23 16:29:53.442][1][info][main]
[source/server/server.cc:228] transport_sockets.upstream:
envoy.transport_sockets.alts,envoy.transport_sockets.tap,raw_buffer
,tls
```

2. By default, the time to live of the leaf certificates is 72 hours:

```
$ curl -s
http://consul-server.consul.svc.cluster.local:8500/v1/connect/ca/co
nfiguration | json_reformat
{
    "Config": {
        "LeafCertTTL": "72h",
        "RotationPeriod": "2160h"
    },
    "CreateIndex": 6,
    "ModifyIndex": 6,
    "Provider": "consul"
}
```

Consul automatically rotates the root certificate. Please refer to https://www.consul.io/docs/connect/ca.html for more details about root certificate rotations. The /connect/ca REST API endpoints can be used to manage Consul Connect certificate authorities such as updating CA configuration, changing CA provider, and bootstrapping with your own private CA for key and root certificates.

3. The root certificates can be viewed using the following REST API call:

```
$ curl -s
http://consul-server.consul.svc.cluster.local:8500/v1/connect/ca/ro
ots | json_reformat
{
    "ActiveRootID":
"1f:9a:35:33:2f:c0:fe:d3:c1:10:f0:16:2d:88:b6:69:2d:33:9d:4a",
    "Roots": [
        {
            "Active": true,
            "CreateIndex": 9,
            "ExternalTrustDomain": "2e672591-
fd0d-2538-9eb5-13763ebaf74a",
            "ID":
"1f:9a:35:33:2f:c0:fe:d3:c1:10:f0:16:2d:88:b6:69:2d:33:9d:4a",
            "IntermediateCerts": null,
            "ModifyIndex": 9,
            "Name": "Consul CA Root Cert",
            "NotAfter": "2029-08-27T01:00:28Z",
```

```
"NotBefore": "2019-08-27T01:00:28Z",
"PrivateKeyBits": 0,
"PrivateKeyType": "",
```

. . .

From this, it should be clear that nothing needs to be done to enable mutual TLS between services in Consul, since the process is fully automated. Consul uses SPIFFE-based X.509 leaf certificates, which makes it simple to connect to a remote service through a strong identity. However, we should be aware that it is the responsibility of the user to enable encryption from the Ingress controller (on the edge of the service mesh) to the first service connected to another service. Also, it is the responsibility of the user to enable TLS termination at the Ingress gateway for the external traffic. The preceding discussion points out the capability of the Consul Connect service mesh to enable mTLS for polyglot microservices using Envoy sidecar proxies.

Envoy sidecar proxy configuration is not trivial. Service meshes such as Istio and Consul hide this complexity and automatically configure the sidecar proxies for the Kubernetes environments. It is important to note that Consul allows the same for non-Kubernetes workloads. Note that this capability is only available for Go applications at the time of writing this book.

Next, we will explore the authorization features of Consul and how they are implemented to control access to services.

Exploring intentions

Intentions are access controls in Consul that are used to define accessibility to various services. Intentions can be defined either through a UI, CLI, or through REST API calls. Once the intentions have been defined, they are enforced by the sidecar proxies to allow or disallow connections between services. For example, you may want to restrict access to the database backend services, but only for the services that have legitimate access requirements. This prevents unauthorized access to a service.

Intentions, once defined, can be replicated across data centers, and they are cached locally so that inbound connections can be allowed if there is a disruption in a service that stops reaching the Consul service.

Let's learn how to create an intention so that we can allow connections from the `dashboard` to the `counting` service:

1. Click **Intentions** on the top menu bar of the Consul dashboard. Click **Create** to define rules for the connections:

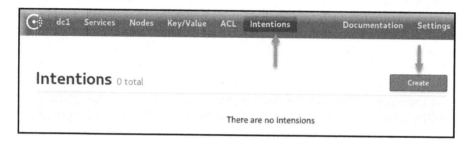

2. We will create a deny rule for all the source and destination services. Select **All Services** for the source and destination, check **Deny**, and click **Save**:

3. It may take a few seconds for a new rule to propagate. Switch to the demo application tab. The dashboard of the demo application should show **Counting Service is Unreachable**:

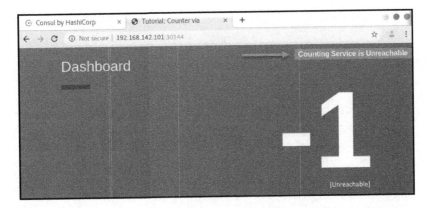

4. After switching to the Consul dashboard tab, click **Create** for an allow rule for the dashboard service to connect to the counting service, as shown in the following screenshot:

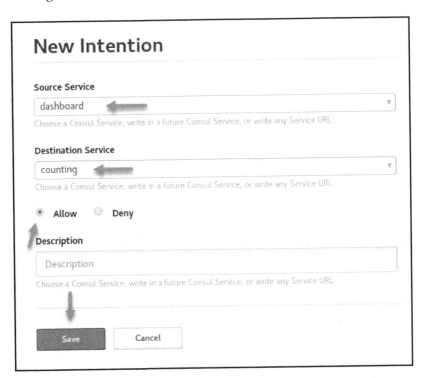

5. Switch to the dashboard of the demo application tab. The counting service should now be available for the dashboard, but it should remain unavailable for any other service. Note that this is accomplished without writing any code:

We just saw the use of **intentions** to provide access control to services. Now, we will delete the intentions rules that we created previously.

6. Switch back to the Consul dashboard (`webconsole.consul.local`). Navigate to **Intentions** and delete both rules.
7. Click the three horizontal dots against each intention and delete both services.

The purpose of intentions is to create a blacklist and whitelist of the services. Note that it is good practice to deny access from all and then allow access by whitelisting the required services, as shown in this section. From a security standpoint, this is an important feature for blocking access to services that a user does not have any legitimate need to access.

Next, we'll learn about Consul's key/value store, which stores the service mesh configuration.

Exploring the Consul key-value store

Consul's key-value store is a persistent layer that allows users to store configuration parameters and the metadata of services within a data center. The Consul Replicate (`https://github.com/hashicorp/consul-replicate`) tool can be used to perform cross-data center K/V asynchronous replication.

Consul's `kv` command is used to interact with the Consul K/V store via the command line to insert, update, and delete operations. The K/V store is also accessible through the HTTP API. The key-value can be monitored through watches, which can invoke handlers to take a specific action.

Let's go through an example of how to store key-values:

1. We need to use a command-line tool to store values in a key-value store. Note that the keys are stored by separating its `path` components with a forward slash. This represents a tree structure, which can be queried using a REST API:

```
$ consul kv put redis/config/minconns 1
Success! Data written to: redis/config/minconns

$ consul kv put redis/config/maxconns 25
Success! Data written to: redis/config/maxconns

$ consul kv put redis/config/users/admin password
Success! Data written to: redis/config/users/admin
```

2. Extract the key from the store, along with any other metadata:

```
$ consul kv get --detailed redis/config/minconns
CreateIndex      7904
Flags            0
Key              redis/config/minconns
LockIndex        0
ModifyIndex      7904
Session          -
Value            1
```

3. Get all the values from the key-value store recursively:

```
$ consul kv get -recurse
redis/config/maxconns:25
redis/config/minconns:1
redis/config/users/admin:password
```

4. The keys can also be obtained using the REST API. Note that the value is base64 encoded:

```
$ curl -s http://localhost:8500/v1/kv/redis/config/minconns |
json_reformat
[
    {
        "LockIndex": 0,
        "Key": "redis/config/minconns",
        "Flags": 0,
        "Value": "MQ==",
        "CreateIndex": 1923,
        "ModifyIndex": 1923
    }
]
```

Consul also provides atomic key updates using check-in set operations and many other capabilities. Please refer to the Consul documentation for more information: https://www.consul.io/api/kv.html.

The key-value store is a centralized database that's used internally by Consul to store the service mesh configuration for services running in Kubernetes, VMs, or bare-metal servers. It can be accessed through a variety of methods, such as the CLI, utilities, and REST APIs. The other important feature of the key-value store is that the values can be JSON objects, which are validated by Consul before they are inserted.

Next, we will explore how Consul helps enforce ACL at the service level to protect them.

Securing Consul services with ACL

By default, **Access Controls Lists** (ACLs) are disabled in the Kubernetes Helm chart, and they need to be enabled explicitly. Please refer to https://learn.hashicorp.com/consul/security-networking/production-acls to learn how to enable ACL.

ACLs are used to secure the servers, clients, services, DNS, Consul key-values, and UIs. ACLs operate by grouping rules into policies, then associating one or more policies with a token. To manage ACL, you can use the consul acl command. Alternatively, ACLs can be managed through HTTP APIs. Please refer to https://www.consul.io/api/acl/acl.html for more information.

Next, we'll learn how to monitor Consul and collect metrics.

Monitoring and metrics

Monitoring and collecting metrics play a very important role in keeping the system healthy and up and running. Consul can be monitored using the `consul monitor` command. Let's take a look:

1. Run the `consul monitor` command:

    ```
    $ consul monitor
    2019/08/27 02:24:12 [INFO] agent: Synced service "counting-
    counting-sidecar-proxy"
    2019/08/27 02:24:12 [INFO] agent: Synced service "dashboard-
    dashboard-sidecar-proxy"
    2019/08/27 02:25:24 [INFO] agent: Synced service "counting-
    counting-sidecar-proxy"
    2019/08/27 02:25:24 [INFO] agent: Synced service "dashboard-
    dashboard-sidecar-proxy"
    2019/08/27 02:26:29 [INFO] agent: Synced service "counting-
    counting-sidecar-proxy"
    2019/08/27 02:26:29 [INFO] agent: Synced service "dashboard-
    dashboard-sidecar-proxy"
    ```

2. Press *Ctrl* + *C* to exit from the preceding `consul monitor` command.

3. You can watch for changes for any data view, such as nodes and services, using the `consul watch` command:

    ```
    $ consul watch -type=service -service=consul
    [
        {
            "Node": {
                "ID": "081722b1-4d2d-479e-1f5b-daf6c22dcfb7",
                "Node": "consul-consul-server-0",
                "Address": "10.1.230.253",
                "Datacenter": "dc1",
                "TaggedAddresses": {
                    "lan": "10.1.230.253",
                    "wan": "10.1.230.253"
                },
    ...
            "Checks": [
                {
                    "Node": "consul-consul-server-2",
                    "CheckID": "serfHealth",
    ```

```
        "Name": "Serf Health Status",
        "Status": "passing",
        "Notes": "",
        "Output": "Agent alive and reachable",
. . .
        }
    ]
}
]
```

Note that the monitoring features are also available in the Consul dashboard web UI.

Now, let's move on to Consul metrics collection. Consul server metrics for Prometheus can be exported using a Consul exporter (https://github.com/prometheus/consul_exporter). Consul server metrics can be collected through REST APIs in a Prometheus-enabled format that can be scrapped by a Prometheus collector:

```
$ curl -s http://localhost:8500/v1/agent/metrics | json_reformat
{
    "Counters": [
        {
            "Count": 25,
            "Labels": {},
            "Max": 152,
            "Mean": 93.72,
            "Min": 39,
            "Name": "consul.memberlist.udp.received",
            "Rate": 234.3,
            "Stddev": 57.16170046455931,
            "Sum": 2343
        },
        {
. . .
        }
}
```

Consul can be configured to send telemetry data to remote monitoring systems so that we can monitor the health of the systems over time, spot trends, and more. At the time of writing, Consul supports Circonus, DataDog, and StasD.

As an example, in the Helm chart that we used to deploy Consul, the Envoy sidecar proxy is configured to send metrics to udp://127.0.0.1:9125 for DataDog. If we deploy DataDog, it can receive metrics from each sidecar proxy, like so:

```
connectInject:
    enabled: true
    default: true
```

```
centralConfig:
  enabled: true
  defaultProtocol: "http"
  proxyDefaults: |
    {
      "envoy_dogstatsd_url": "udp://127.0.0.1:9125"
    }
```

Next, we will learn how an external service can be registered with Consul.

Registering an external service

We can register an external service with a built-in /health REST endpoint. The Consul dashboard or the Consul monitor command can invoke the /health endpoint to monitor the health of the external service. This feature makes Consul useful for integration purposes.

Let's understand this through an example.

In this section, we will extract a go binary from the counting microservice and run it on the VM host as a systemd service. Copy the counting-service Go binary from the counting pod's /app directory to the host's home directory and then make it executable. Now, follow these steps:

1. Extract the counting service binary and copy it to the VM:

```
$ kubectl -n consul -c counting cp counting:counting-service
~/counting-service
$ chmod +x ~/counting-service
$ sudo cp ~/counting-service /bin
```

2. Define a systemd service in the local VM in order to run the counting service:

```
# Script : 06-create-systemd-service.sh

#!/bin/bash

# Use absolute path for the go bonary
cat << EOF | tee /etc/systemd/system/external-counting.service
  [Unit]
  Description = "External Counting Service"
  [Service]
  KillSignal=INT
  Environment="PORT=10001"
  ExecStart=/bin/counting-service
```

```
      Restart=always
      [Install]
      WantedBy=multi-user.target
   EOF
```

3. Create a `systemd` service for the external counting service:

```
$ chmod +x 06-create-systemd-service.sh
$ sudo ./06-create-systemd-service.sh
```

4. Enable and start the `external-counting` service:

```
$ sudo systemctl enable external-counting
$ sudo systemctl start external-counting
$ sudo systemctl status external-counting
```

```
● external-counting.service – "External Counting Service"
   Loaded: loaded (/etc/systemd/system/external-counting.service;
enabled;
            vendor preset: disabled)
   Active: active (running) since Mon 2019-08-26 22:52:38 EDT; 4s
ago
 Main PID: 12283 (counting-servic)
    Tasks: 5
   Memory: 844.0K
   CGroup: /system.slice/external-counting.service
           └─12283 /bin/counting-service

Aug 26 22:52:38 osc01.servicemesh.local systemd[1]: Started
"External Counting Service".
Aug 26 22:52:38 osc01.servicemesh.local counting-service[12283]:
Serving at http://localhost:10001
Aug 26 22:52:38 osc01.servicemesh.local counting-service[12283]:
(Pass as PORT environment variable)
```

5. Test the `external-counting` service:

```
$ curl http://localhost:10001/health
Hello, you've hit /health
```

Now that we have our `external-counting` service up and running, we will register this service with the Consul agent. To do this, follow these steps:

1. Create a JSON file to register the external service:

```
# Script : 07-define-external-service-json.sh

cat <<EOF > external-counting.json
```

```
{
  "Name": "external-counting",
  "Tags": [
    "v0.0.4"
  ],
  "Address": "$(hostname -i)",
  "Port": 10001,
  "Check": {
    "Method": "GET",
    "HTTP": "http://$(hostname -i):10001/health",
    "Interval": "1s"
  }
}
EOF
```

2. Create a JSON definition of the service:

```
$ chmod +x 07-define-external-service-json.sh
$ ./07-define-external-service-json.sh
{
  "Name": "external-counting",
  "Tags": [
  "v0.0.4"
  ],
  "Address": "192.168.142.101",
  "Port": 10001,
  "Check": {
  "Method": "GET",
  "HTTP": "http://192.168.142.101:10001/health",
  "Interval": "1s"
  }
}
```

3. Register the external-counting service with the Consul agent:

```
$ curl -X PUT -d @external-counting.json
http://localhost:8500/v1/agent/service/register
```

 Note: To deregister the service, use `curl -X PUT`
`http://localhost:8500/v1/agent/service/deregister/externa`
`l-counting`.

4. Note that the `external-counting` service appears on the Consul web dashboard, as shown in the following screenshot:

5. Click on `external-counting` and click the same again on the next page to see the status of the service:

With this, you now know how to register an external service in Consul so that it is visible and can be monitored.

Summary

In this chapter, we covered Consul in a Kubernetes environment. We covered service discovery, intentions, mTLS, key-value stores, and external services registration. It is important to note that Consul works in heterogeneous environments spanning multiple data centers. This makes it a very good candidate for service discovery and for providing mTLS out of the box while covering both Kubernetes as well as non-Kubernetes environments.

You can use this service discovery knowledge process to build a catalog of enterprise services so that your cloud-native applications can discover and use them.

In the next chapter, we will go through the traffic management capabilities of Consul Connect in the Kubernetes environment. You will learn how easy it is to shift and route traffic between different versions of the same service.

Questions

1. Consul Connect is the service mesh for Kubernetes.

   A) True
   B) False)

2. Consul Connect uses sidecar proxies for services either through native app integration or automatic injection.

   A) True
   B) False

3. Consul intentions are authorizations for services.

   A) True
   B) False

4. Consul's K/V store is replicated across data centers automatically.

   A) True
   B) False

5. Consul mTLS from a sidecar proxy to another sidecar proxy is fully automatic.

   A) True
   B) False

6. Consul comes with its own Certificate Authority so that it can issue certificates to sidecar proxies.

   A) True
   B) False

7. Consul integration with Kubernetes for service discovery is done by defining a Consul DNS server as an upstream DNS in the Kubernetes CoreDNS configuration.

   A) True
   B) False

Further reading

- *Hashicorp/Demo-Consul-101*. GitHub, 2019: https://github.com/hashicorp/demo-consul-101/tree/master/k8s
- *Introduction to HashiCorp Consul Connect with Kubernetes*, Huysmans, C. (2019), available at https://medium.com/hashicorp-engineering/introduction-to-hashicorp-consul-connect-with-kubernetes-d7393f798e9d, accessed 12 May 2019
- *Nicholasjackson/Demo-Consul-Service-Mesh*, GitHub, 2019: https://github.com/nicholasjackson/demo-consul-service-mesh
- *Hashicorp/Consul-Demo-Traffic-Splitting*, GitHub, 2019: https://github.com/hashicorp/consul-demo-traffic-splitting

22
Exploring Traffic Management in Consul

In this final chapter, we will go through Consul's native traffic management capabilities in a Kubernetes environment. Through Consul, we can implement configuration-driven traffic management without making any application code changes. Like Istio and Linkerd, configuration-driven traffic management is also done by sidecar proxies.

To demonstrate the various traffic management capabilities of Consul, we will install a demo application and then use some sample code that you should be able to run and practice with in the Kubernetes environment that we built in Chapter 6, *Building Your Own Kubernetes Environment*.

In a nutshell, we will cover the following topics in this chapter:

- Traffic management implementation in a Kubernetes environment
- Installing a demo application to show traffic management
- Demonstrating a canary deployment and traffic shifting
- Path-based traffic routing
- Mesh gateways

Technical requirements

This chapter consists of hands-on exercises and is dependent on the previous chapter. You must have gone through the previous chapter and complete the following exercises:

- *Installing a demo application*
- *Consul dashboard*

Make sure that you are in the `~/consul/scripts` directory so that you can use scripts:

```
$ cd ~/consul/scripts
```

Now, we will walk through the native integration of traffic management through Kubernetes.

Overview of traffic management in Consul

Consul integration with Kubernetes is done through a separate project called `consul-k8s`, which is maintained at `https://github.com/hashicorp/consul-k8s`.

In `Chapter 20`, *Installing Consul*, we installed the Consul CLI (a single Go binary that serves as a server and a client) in our VM. We also installed a Helm chart for the `consul-k8s` project in order to integrate Consul with Kubernetes.

Previously, Consul operated at Levels 3 and 4 of the network traffic. However, Consul version 1.6.0+ provided support for the OSI Layer 7's (application layer) traffic management features so that we can divide the traffic between different subsets of services through the use of sidecar proxies. The Consul service mesh can now provide HTTP traffic routing, traffic shaping, failover, and rerouting capabilities. The following are key dynamic routing features at the application layer that support various deployment strategies:

- **Traffic shifting**: Weight-based routing for canary testing, round-robin testing, and permanent traffic shifting through Consul configurations, all of which can be implemented and realized via sidecar proxies
- **HTTP path-based routing**: Traffic routing to different upstream services based on the HTTP request path
- **Mesh gateways**: Using the mesh gateway to route traffic securely across different network environments

Traffic management in Consul is done in three stages: routing, splitting, and resolution. This is done to manage upstream Connect proxies. L7 traffic management at the application layer is outside the application code and is managed by Consul at every stage so it can be dynamically configured using Consul primitives such as the following:

- **service-router**: Routes L7 traffic based on the HTTP route
- **service-splitter**: Divides traffic based on the percentage defined (Canary testing, and so on)
- **service-resolver**: Filters options based on subsets that have been defined in the service catalog metadata

- **service-defaults**: Configures defaults for all the service instances
- **proxy-defaults**: Modifies proxy configuration defaults

Consider the aforementioned primitives as equivalent to Kubernetes Custom Resource Definitions, which provide extensions for Consul Connect in Kubernetes using config maps through Kubernetes jobs. The preceding primitives can also be defined for VMs using JSON-formatted files, which can be loaded either through the Consul CLI or through PUT requests to an API using the JSON file.

The implementation of the preceding Consul primitives is done at the L7 network traffic layer. Now, we'll look at Consul's configuration implementation so that we can use the preceding primitives.

Implementing L7 configuration

Consul Connect's core strength is its service mesh, which spans and covers both Kubernetes and VMs. Consul traffic management is available for services that might run in VMs and/or in Kubernetes environments. The Consul configuration can be pushed through the Consul CLI or API, or by using Kubernetes jobs. Let's take a look:

1. Define an instance of `service-defaults` for the `web` service that will use the `http` protocol:

   ```
   # Script: 08-service-defaults-web.hcl

   kind = "service-defaults"
   name = "web"
   protocol = "http"
   ```

Here, an example of the Consul CLI demonstrates creating Consul primitive service-defaults for the web service. Notice that the web service does not exist yet – we will create that later on.

We can load the L7 configuration using one of the following three methods:

- Via the Consul CLI, using a *consul config write* for **Hashicorp Command Language (HCL)** or JSON files.
- Through PUT requests to the API for JSON files
- Through a Kubernetes job

For simplicity, we will be using either HCL or JSON files using the Consul CLI.

2. The Consul CLI can apply the preceding definition as follows:

```
$ consul config write 08-service-defaults-web.hcl
```

3. Now, list all the service-defaults registered in Consul:

```
$ consul config list -kind service-defaults
counting
dashboard
web
```

4. Next, read the web service-defaults configuration entry that we just created:

```
$ consul config read -kind service-defaults -name web
{
    "Kind": "service-defaults",
    "Name": "web",
    "Protocol": "http",
    "MeshGateway": {},
    "CreateIndex": 5384,
    "ModifyIndex": 5384
}
```

Next, we will use an API to create a service-defaults configuration. Refer to https://www.consul.io/api/ for detailed documentation on using APIs to manage and configure Consul. We will use the /config path to create service-defaults for the api service.

5. Define a JSON configuration to set up an http protocol for the web service:

```
# Script: 09-service-defaults-api.json

{
  "Kind": "service-defaults",
  "Name": "api",
  "Protocol": "http"
}
```

6. Create service-defaults for the web service so that it can use the http protocol using the Consul REST API:

```
$ curl -XPUT --data @09-service-defaults-api.json
http://localhost:8500/v1/config ; echo
true
```

7. List the web `service-defaults` that we just created:

```
$ curl -s http://localhost:8500/v1/config/service-defaults/api |
json_reformat
{
    "Kind": "service-defaults",
    "Name": "api",
    "Protocol": "http",
    "MeshGateway": {

    },
    "CreateIndex": 5616,
    "ModifyIndex": 5619
}
```

The preceding examples showed us how to define `service-defaults` using the Consul CLI and Consul REST APIs. Using the same approach, we will demonstrate the three stages of Consul L7 traffic management for services running in any VM in any data center in any region. These three steps are as follows:

1. Routing (`service-router`)
2. Splitting (`service-splitter`)
3. Resolution (`service-resolver`)

Let's assume that we have two versions of a service `api` for which a Consul primitive called `service-resolver` has been defined using two subsets, `v1` and `v2`. These subsets will resolve to the respective version of the `api` service based upon the annotations that have been defined for the Kubernetes service. We will create these later in this chapter.

8. The following is an example of a `service-resolver` for subsets based on the service catalog metadata:

```
# Script : 10-service-resolver-api.hcl

kind = "service-resolver"
name = "api"

default_subset = "v1"

subsets = {
  v1 = {
    filter = "Service.Meta.version == 1"
  }
```

```
        v2 = {
          filter = "Service.Meta.version == 2"
        }
      }
```

9. Create a Consul primitive called `service-resolver` for the `api` service in order to define subsets `v1` and `v2`:

   ```
   $ consul config write 10-service-resolver-api.hcl

   $ consul config list -kind service-resolver
   api
   ```

10. Note that the `sevice-resolver` API has been created.

By now, you should have a clear picture of the advantages that Consul provides through its support for the L7 configuration. Next, we will deploy a demo application to demonstrate Consul's traffic splitting and shifting features.

Deploying a demo application

Sample microservices for the `web` and `api` deployments are maintained at `https://github.com/servicemeshbook/hello-echo` the `main.go` is the web microservice, that calls the upstream API microservice through the use of the `UPSTREAM_SERVICE` environment variable.

Review the pod and service definition in the `11-web-deployment.yaml` script:

```
...
  template:
    metadata:
      labels:
        app: web
      annotations:
        "consul.hashicorp.com/connect-inject": "true"
        "consul.hashicorp.com/connect-service-upstreams": "api:8081"
...
        env:
...
        - name: UPSTREAM_SERVICE
          value: "http://localhost:8081"
```

Note the `consul.hashicorp.com/connect-service-upstreams` annotation in the preceding definition, which points to the Consul `service-defaults` primitive `api` with the `http` protocol using port `8081`, which we created previously. The web microservice calls an upstream microservice through the use of the `UPSTREAM_SERVICE` environment variable, which we point to the same `8081` port on the localhost. The Consul agent is responsible for connecting the web microservice at port `8081` to the Consul `service-defaults` API, which in turn will connect to a subset defined through the Consul `service-resolver` primitive we created in the previous steps. We will see how a subset connects to a proper API pod when we define the `api` deployment later.

First, we deploy a web microservice. Perform the following steps to do so:

1. Create a Kubernetes deployment and the service for the web:

   ```
   $ kubectl -n consul apply -f 11-web-deployment.yaml
   service/web created
   deployment.apps/web created
   ```

   The Kubernetes service web endpoint is a web pod.

2. Now, check the web pod and web service:

   ```
   $ kubectl -n consul get pods -l app=web
   NAME                     READY   STATUS    RESTARTS   AGE
   web-7dc47f6678-fcnzv     2/2     Running   0          40s

   $ kubectl -n consul get svc web
   NAME   TYPE       CLUSTER-IP      EXTERNAL-IP   PORT(S)          AGE
   web    NodePort   10.111.32.161   <none>        8080:30145/TCP   43s
   ```

   Note that the Kubernetes principle as followed, links the web service to the web pod. For the `api` deployment, which is the upstream service for the web, the Consul agent calls the `api` service through the use of the `UPSTREAM_SERVICE` environment variable.

   Next, we'll deploy two versions of the `api` microservice. Note that both versions are identical. The purpose here is to illustrate Consul's traffic shifting concepts.

3. Review the `12-api-v1-deployment.yaml` script for the annotation description that links the Consul `api` service to the Kubernetes `api-deployment`:

```
# Script: 12-api-v1-deployment.yaml

...
template:
    metadata:
      labels:
        app: api-v1
      annotations:
        "consul.hashicorp.com/connect-inject": "true"
        "consul.hashicorp.com/service-meta-version": "1"
        "consul.hashicorp.com/service-tags": "v1"
...
```

4. Review the `13-api-v2-deployment.yaml` script to link the Consul `api` service to the Kubernetes `api-deployment`:

```
# Script: 13-api-v2-deployment.yaml

...
template:
    metadata:
      labels:
        app: api-v1
      annotations:
        "consul.hashicorp.com/connect-inject": "true"
        "consul.hashicorp.com/service-meta-version": "2"
        "consul.hashicorp.com/service-tags": "v2"
...
```

5. Compare the scripts in *step 3* and *step 4*.

   Note that the `consul.hashicorp.com/service-meta-version` annotation is set to 1 and 2, while `consul.hashicorp.com/service-tags` is set to v1 and v2, respectively. Refer to the Consul primitive `service-resolver` API we created in the previous step (`10-service-resolver-api.hcl`):

```
subsets = {
  v1 = {
    filter = "Service.Meta.version == 1"
  }
  v2 = {
    filter = "Service.Meta.version == 2"
  }
}
```

We can see that the `v1` subset is linked to the
`consul.hashicorp.com/service-tags` annotation we defined in the API
deployment. Service-Meta-version is linked to the
`consul.hashicorp.com/service-meta-version` annotation.

6. Create the `api-v1` and `api-v2` services and deployments:

```
$ kubectl -n consul apply -f 12-api-v1-deployment.yaml
service/api-v1 created
deployment.apps/api-v1 created

$ kubectl -n consul apply -f 13-api-v2-deployment.yaml
service/api-v2 created
deployment.apps/api-v2 created
```

With this, we have created the `api-v1` and `api-v2` Kubernetes deployments.

7. Check the `api-v1` service at node port `30146`:

```
$ curl http://localhost:30146
=================================================
Request time : 2019-09-23 14:33:12.92445239 +0000 UTC
Requested path : /
Host IP : 192.168.142.101
Pod IP : 192.168.230.246
Pod Name : api-v1-7fcf5d98d4-tgqrk
Pod Namespace : consul
Host : localhost:30146
RemoteAddr : 192.168.142.101:44900
=================================================
```

8. Similarly, check the `api-v2` service at node port `30147`:

```
$ curl http://localhost:30147
=================================================
Request time : 2019-09-23 14:33:15.979164994 +0000 UTC
Requested path : /
Host IP : 192.168.142.101
Pod IP : 192.168.230.205
Pod Name : api-v2-5d64d5f8ff-zlcp6
Pod Namespace : consul
Host : localhost:30147
RemoteAddr : 192.168.142.101:40690
=================================================
```

Note that the `api-v1` and `api-v2` Kubernetes services are not used by Consul for traffic management. Actually, the Consul service `api` is used for that purpose – please refer to the `consul.hashicorp.com/connect-service-upstreams` annotation defined in `11-web-deployment.yaml` for more information.

The sample microservice that we have just deployed will help us understand the various traffic management features of Consul. We will explore these features one by one in the next section.

Traffic management in Consul

Consul's native traffic management features are implemented for both cloud-native as well as traditional VM applications. We will go through the features of traffic shifting and traffic routing in this section.

Directing traffic to a default subset

Consul's traffic shifting feature allows us to direct traffic to a default subset. Follow these steps to learn how to do so:

1. The `web` node port is `30145`. Run `curl -s http://localhost:30145` and check the output:

```
$ curl -s http://localhost:30145
==================================================
Request time    : 2019-09-21 01:25:29.844609478 +0000 UTC
Requested path : /
Host IP         : 192.168.142.101
Pod IP          : 192.168.230.202
Pod Name        : web-7dc47f6678-fcnzv
Pod Namespace   : consul
Host            : localhost:30145
RemoteAddr      : 192.168.142.101:47332
.. continued ...
```

Notice that, when we call the service web at node port `30145`, it calls the web microservice using familiar Kubernetes principles.

2. The upstream Consul service `api` at port `8081` is invoked by Consul like so:

```
==================================================
Request time : 2019-09-23 14:11:06.091295669 +0000 UTC
```

```
Requested path : /
Host IP : 192.168.142.101
Pod IP : 192.168.230.205
Pod Name : api-v1-5d64d5f8ff-zlcp6
Pod Namespace : consul
Host : localhost:8081
RemoteAddr : 127.0.0.1:57152
======================================================
```

3. Repeat the same `curl` command 10 times. You will notice that the traffic is
   always shifted to the `api-deployment-v1` pod:

```
$ curl -s http://localhost:30145?[1-10] | grep "Pod Name.*api"
Pod Name : api-v1-5d64d5f8ff-zlcp6
Pod Name : api-v1-5d64d5f8ff-zlcp6
Pod Name : api-v1-5d64d5f8ff-zlcp6
Pod Name : api-v1-5d64d5f8ff-zlcp6
Pod Name : api-v1-5d64d5f8ff-zlcp6
Pod Name : api-v1-5d64d5f8ff-zlcp6
Pod Name : api-v1-5d64d5f8ff-zlcp6
Pod Name : api-v1-5d64d5f8ff-zlcp6
Pod Name : api-v1-5d64d5f8ff-zlcp6
Pod Name : api-v1-5d64d5f8ff-zlcp6
```

This is due to the fact that we haven't defined traffic split criteria yet. Please refer to the
`service-resolver` API, in which the default subset is set to `v1` (`10-service-resolver-api.hcl`).

Now, we will apply this traffic shifting concept to a canary deployment.

Canary deployment

Canary deployment is related to dark launches or friends-and-family testing, in which only
a few people are given access to new features without their knowledge. Let's apply the
principle of traffic shifting to a canary deployment:

1. You can configure a percentage of traffic for each subset using
   Consul's `service-splitter` primitive. An example of a `service-splitter` can be seen in the following code, in which 99% of the traffic is routed
   to subset `v1`, while the other 1% of the traffic is routed to subset `v2`:

```
# Script: 14-service-splitter-canary.hcl

kind = "service-splitter",
name = "api"
```

```
splits = [
  {
    weight = 99,
    service_subset = "v1"
  },
  {
    weight = 1,
    service_subset = "v2"
  }
]
```

2. Create `service-splitter` for the Consul service `api` using the Consul CLI:

```
$ consul config write 14-service-splitter-canary.hcl

$ consul config list -kind service-splitter
api
```

3. Repeat the same `curl` command 200 times. You will notice that `api-v2` is only called 1% of the time:

```
$ curl -s http://localhost:30145?[1-200] | grep "Pod Name.*api-v1"
$ curl -s http://localhost:30145?[1-200] | grep "Pod Name.*api-v2"
...

Pod Name : api-v1-7fcf5d98d4-tgqrk
Pod Name : api-v1-7fcf5d98d4-tgqrk
Pod Name : api-v2-5d64d5f8ff-zlcp6
Pod Name : api-v1-7fcf5d98d4-tgqrk

...
```

The preceding code is an example of a canary deployment in which a very small percentage of traffic is shifted to v2 of the service. Next, we will learn how to split traffic in a round-robin fashion.

Round-robin traffic

Traffic can be split in a round-robin fashion by specifying a 50-50 weight for both services, as follows:

```
# Script: 15-service-splitter-round-robin.hcl

...

splits = [
```

```
{
  weight = 50,
  service_subset = "v1"
},
{
  weight = 50
  service_subset = "v2"
}
]
```

1. Create `service-splitter` for `api` by assigning a 50-50 weight to each subset using `15-service-splitter-round-robin.hcl`:

   ```
   $ consul config write 15-service-splitter-round-robin.hcl

   $ consul config list -kind service-splitter
   api
   ```

2. Repeat the same `curl` command 10 times. You will notice that the traffic is split equally between the `api-v1` and `api-v2` pods:

   ```
   $ curl -s http://localhost:30145?[1-10] | grep "Pod Name.*api"
   Pod Name : api-v1-7fcf5d98d4-tgqrk
   Pod Name : api-v1-7fcf5d98d4-tgqrk
   Pod Name : api-v2-5d64d5f8ff-zlcp6
   Pod Name : api-v1-7fcf5d98d4-tgqrk
   Pod Name : api-v1-7fcf5d98d4-tgqrk
   Pod Name : api-v2-5d64d5f8ff-zlcp6
   Pod Name : api-v2-5d64d5f8ff-zlcp6
   Pod Name : api-v1-7fcf5d98d4-tgqrk
   Pod Name : api-v1-7fcf5d98d4-tgqrk
   Pod Name : api-v2-5d64d5f8ff-zlcp6
   ```

Here, we can see that the traffic is equally split between the two services. Next, we will explore how to shift the entire traffic to subset `v2`.

Shifting traffic permanently

If it has been determined that 100% of the traffic should now be shifted to `v2` of `api` after testing it successfully, the weight can be defined as 100% to subset `v2`. This can be done with the following code:

```
# Script: 16-service-splitter-100-shift.hcl

. . .
```

```
splits = [
  {
    weight = 0,
    service_subset = "v1"
  },
  {
    weight = 100
    service_subset = "v2"
  }
]
```

1. Create `service-splitter` for the Consul service `api` using the Consul CLI using `16-service-splitter-100-shift.hcl`:

   ```
   $ consul config write 16-service-splitter-100-shift.hcl

   $ consul config list -kind service-splitter
   api
   ```

2. Repeat the same `curl` command 10 times, like so:

   ```
   $ curl -s http://localhost:30145?[1-10] | grep "Pod Name.*api"
   Pod Name : api-v2-5d64d5f8ff-zlcp6
   Pod Name : api-v2-5d64d5f8ff-zlcp6
   Pod Name : api-v2-5d64d5f8ff-zlcp6
   Pod Name : api-v2-5d64d5f8ff-zlcp6
   Pod Name : api-v2-5d64d5f8ff-zlcp6
   Pod Name : api-v2-5d64d5f8ff-zlcp6
   Pod Name : api-v2-5d64d5f8ff-zlcp6
   Pod Name : api-v2-5d64d5f8ff-zlcp6
   Pod Name : api-v2-5d64d5f8ff-zlcp6
   Pod Name : api-v2-5d64d5f8ff-zlcp6
   ```

From the preceding command, you can see that the entire traffic has been permanently shifted to the `api-v2` pod.

Refer to the following keynote address by Nick Jackson on using traffic management. It covers non-Kubernetes environments: `https://www.hashicorp.com/resources/consul-1-6-layer-7-traffic-management-mesh-gateways`.

Next, we will go through path-based traffic routing in a Kubernetes environment.

Path-based traffic routing

In the following example, we'll show you how to use HTTP path-based routing to direct traffic between two versions of a service. For example, /v1 will route traffic to the A service, while /v2 will route traffic to the B service. Let's get started:

1. Delete the previous deployments of web and api:

   ```
   $ kubectl -n consul delete -f 11-web-deployment.yaml

   $ kubectl -n consul delete -f 12-api-v1-deployment.yaml

   $ kubectl -n consul delete -f 13-api-v2-deployment.yaml
   ```

2. We created service-defaults for web and api in the *L7 configuration management* section. Check the service-defaults list:

   ```
   $ consul config list -kind service-defaults
   api
   counting
   dashboard
   web
   ```

3. Read the web configuration:

   ```
   $ consul config read -kind service-defaults -name web
   {
       "Kind": "service-defaults",
       "Name": "web",
       "Protocol": "http",
       "MeshGateway": {
           "Mode": "local"
       },
       "CreateIndex": 186,
       "ModifyIndex": 1750
   }
   ```

4. Read the api configuration:

   ```
   $ consul config read -kind service-defaults -name api
   {
       "Kind": "service-defaults",
       "Name": "api",
       "Protocol": "http",
       "MeshGateway": {
           "Mode": "local"
       },
   ```

```
            "CreateIndex": 218,
            "ModifyIndex": 218
    }
```

5. Define a `service-router` for the `api`, which will allow us to accomplish path-based routing to a specific service:

```
# Script: 17-service-router.hcl

. . .
    match {
      http {
        path_prefix="/v1"
      }
    }
    destination {
      service = "api"
      service_subset = "v1"
    }
. . .
```

6. Create an `api` called `service-router`:

```
$ consul config write 17-service-router.hcl
```

7. Create a Kubernetes web service and deployment:

```
$ kubectl apply -f 18-web-deployment.yaml
service/web created
deployment.apps/web created
```

8. Create an `api-v1` service and deployment:

```
$ kubectl apply -f 19-api-v1-deployment.yaml
service/api-v1 created
deployment.apps/api-v1 created
```

9. Similarly, create an `api-v2` service and deployment:

```
$ kubectl apply -f 20-api-v2-deployment.yaml
service/api-v2 created
deployment.apps/api-v2 created

# Check status of pods. Must show Ready 2/2
$ kubectl -n consul get pods -l 'app in (web, api-v1, api-v2)'
```

Nicholas Jackson of Hashicorp formulated the path-based example. You can find out more at https://github.com/nicholasjackson/demo-consul-service-mesh/tree/master/kubernetes/traffic_routing.

Through the preceding example, we have created a frontend web service that receives traffic from the internet through an Ingress definition. There are two upstream deployments, api-v1 and api-v2, that we call through a virtual upstream service defined in the 18-web-deployment.yaml web development script, as shown in the following code:

```
annotations:
  "consul.hashicorp.com/connect-inject": "true"
  "consul.hashicorp.com/connect-service-upstreams": "api:8081"
...
  - name: "LISTEN_ADDR"
    value: "0.0.0.0:8080"
  - name: "UPSTREAM_URIS"
    value: "http://localhost:8091"
```

10. We can run the web service using curl at node port 30145 without using any path. Notice that it will always call the api-v2 upstream service since we shifted 100% traffic to this service in the *Shifting traffic permanently* section:

```
$ curl -s http://localhost:30145
{
  "name": "web",
...
  "body": "Hello World",
  "upstream_calls": [
    {
      "name": "api-v2",
      "uri": "http://localhost:8081",
...
      "body": "Response from API v2",
      "code": 200
    }
  ],
  "code": 200
}
```

11. Run the same `curl` command by using the /v1 path. Note that traffic shifts to the api-v1 service due to the `service-router` implementation:

```
$ curl -s http://localhost:30145/v1
{
  "name": "web",
  ...
  "body": "Hello World",
  "upstream_calls": [
    {
      "name": "api-v1",
      "uri": "http://localhost:8081",
  ...
      "body": "Response from API v1",
      "code": 200
    }
  ],
  "code": 200
}
```

Though not shown in the preceding code, traffic routing can also be based upon headers, query parameters, and so on. The following example shows that, if the x-debug header is set to 1, the traffic will be routed to another service web using the `service-resolver` canary:

```
match {
  http {
    header = [
      {
        name = "x-debug"
        exact = "1"
      },
    ]
  }
}
destination {
  service = "web"
  service_subset = "canary"
}
```

Next, we will use the Consul dashboard to check services and explore, sidecar proxies and upstream services.

Checking Consul services

We will use the Consul-provided dashboard to monitor services, nodes, and other features. Let's take a look:

1. Switch back to the browser tab of the Consul dashboard (`http://webconsole.consul.local`) and check the services that have been registered with Consul. We created the `api` and `web` services in the preceding traffic management examples:

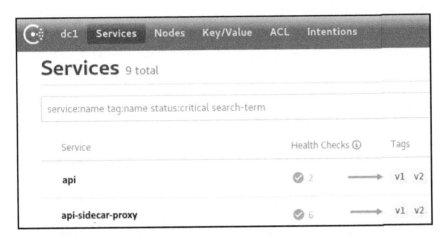

Notice that the `v1` and `v2` tags against `api` and `api-sidecar-proxy` were defined using the Consul `service-resolver` primitive for the `v1` and `v2` subsets. The connection between Consul's `v1` and `v2` tags and the `api` deployment was made through annotations. These are as follows, and have been taken from the `12-api-v1-deployment.yaml` script:

```
template:
  metadata:
    labels:
      app: api-v1
    annotations:
      "consul.hashicorp.com/connect-inject": "true"
      "consul.hashicorp.com/service-meta-version": "1"
      "consul.hashicorp.com/service-tags": "v1"
```

2. Click the Consul service `api`. Note that it has two instances of `api-v1` and `api-v2`. Click **Tags** and notice that it has the following tags of: v1 and v2:

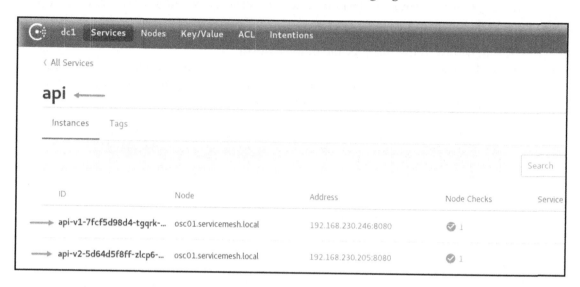

3. Click **Services** and click on `web-sidecar-proxy`. Then, click `web-xxx-xxx`:

4. Click **Upstreams**:

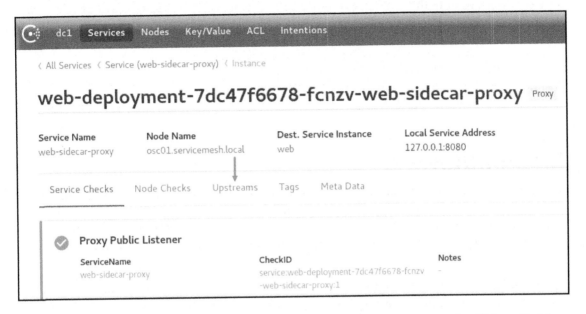

5. Note that the upstream service `api` is running at port `8081` and will be called by the `web-sidecar-proxy`:

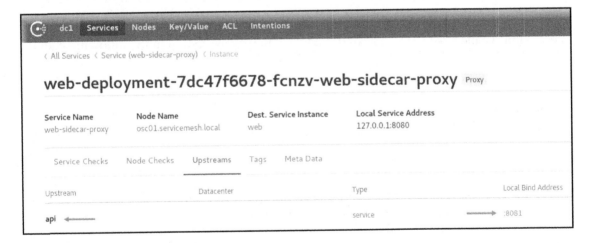

The upstream `api` service was defined through an annotation when we deployed the web service. Please refer to the `"consul.hashicorp.com/connect-service-upstreams"`: `"api:8081"` annotation defined in the `11-web-deployment.yaml` script for more information.

Now that we've looked at the traffic management features natively built into Consul, we will go through the mesh gateway, a very important Consul's feature that allows seamless integration between different Consul clusters running in heterogeneous environments.

Mesh gateway

Mesh gateway, or multi-cluster gateways, is the Consul primitive that allows you to bridge traffic between two or more completely separate Consul service meshes securely and transparently across different network environments. The configuration for the service mesh needs to be written only in one location, and it gets federated and copied automatically to the other locations.

The gateway acts as a bridge between two locations: if one service wants to communicate to another service in another location, it does so through lightweight Envoy proxies. These proxies have no way of decrypting traffic, so the traffic between the services in two locations is done through the mTLS flowing through two gateways. Consul uses SNI headers inside HTTPS requests so the gateway can determine where to send the traffic.

To enable a service so that it can use the mesh gateway, the `service-defaults` primitive uses a stanza called `meshgateway` to define the gateway, as shown in the following code:

```
kind = "service-defaults"
name = "web"
protocol = "http"
meshgateway = {
  mode = "local"
}
```

The mode has three values: local, remote, and none. Let's go over these now:

- With **local** mode, the service will communicate with the local gateway first, and the local gateway communicates with other cluster gateways, which then communicates to the upstream service.
- In **remote** mode, the local gateway is bypassed. It is like Egress, where we are able to communicate directly to the remote cluster gateways and then forward traffic to the destination service.

- In **none** mode, no gateway is used, and the outbound connection is made directly to the destination service.

In this chapter, we used the Consul web and api services to show you how traffic splitting and routing works. Let's assume that the Consul service web is running in one data center, dc1, and that the api service is running in another data center, dc2. We can use the Consul service-resolver primitive to route traffic between web and api through a virtual resolver, as shown here:

```
kind = "service-resolver"
name = "api"

redirect {
  service = "api"
  datacenter = "dc2"
}
```

Once we have defined this, the traffic will flow through the gateway between two data centers.

With the use of the Consul service-resolver primitive, it is possible to perform a service failover from one data center to another seamlessly. A mesh gateway provides a flat network without users having to worry about network routing rules. The Envoy proxy acts as a gateway so that it can route Consul Connect traffic across data centers using SNI headers.

As an example, let's assume the dc1 data center has web and api services but that data center dc2 has only the api service. Cross-cluster and cross-cloud service failover can be provided through service-resolver. If the api service is not available in dc1, the failover will happen seamlessly and automatically in the api service in the dc2 data center:

```
kind = "service-resolver"
name = "api"

failover = {
  "*"= {
    datacenter = ["dc2"]
  }
}
```

It should be noted that multiple data centers can also be defined in the datacenter field of the failover stanza in order to provide a robust high availability for the desired services in the service-resolver for the api service.

Summary

In this chapter, we explored Consul Connect's traffic management features that are configured at the application layer. L7 configuration is achieved through centrally managed Consul primitives that can be replicated to other data centers, thereby providing service resiliency and redundancy through mesh gateways.

We explained `service-resolver` by defining subsets of services that can be used to split traffic through `service-splitter` for canary deployments and traffic shifting. We also explained using path-based routing to shift traffic to different services.

This brings us to the end of our studies and our hands-on exercises for the three popular service meshes in the industry today. The service mesh, which started in 2015, is a fairly new technology and continues to evolve. It remains to be seen whether it continues in its present form. We anticipate consolidation and interoperability through service mesh interface specifications and the convergence of features and functions among different service mesh architectures.

Questions

1. Consul traffic management is done at Layer 7 of **Open System Interconnection (OSI)**.

   A) True
   B) False

2. The `service-resolver` definition is used to declare subsets based upon filters on the metadata of the services. In Kubernetes deployments, such metadata is picked up automatically by Kubernetes through its integration with Consul.

   A) True
   B) False

3. Mesh gateway's remote mode is akin to the Egress gateway.

   A) True
   B) False

4. If `service-defaults` defines a mesh gateway mode to local, each call is made to the mesh gateway to determine the upstream service.

   A) True
   B) False

5. Traffic routing using a `service-router` can only be used for path-based routing.

   A) True
   B) False

6. `service-resolver` can be used to provide a service failover from one data center to another.

   A) True
   B) False

Further reading

- *Consul Curriculum – HashiCorp Learn*, HashiCorp Learn (2018), available at `https://learn.hashicorp.com/consul/`, accessed 11 May 2019
- *Datawire – Resilient Microservices on Kubernetes*, Datawire.io (2019), available at `https://www.datawire.io`, accessed 13 May 2019
- *Introduction to HashiCorp Consul Connect with Kubernetes*, Huysmans, C. (2019), available at `https://medium.com/hashicorp-engineering/introduction-to-hashicorp-consul-connect-with-kubernetes-d7393f798e9d`, accessed 12 May 2019
- *Layer 7 Traffic Management and Mesh Gateways*, Jackson, N. (2019), Hashicorp, available at `https://www.hashicorp.com/resources/consul-1-6-layer-7-traffic-management-mesh-gateways`

Assessment

Chapter 1: Monolithic versus Microservices

1. True – Microservices are difficult to test due to their distributed nature.
2. False – Monolithic applications belong to static infrastructures, while microservices belong to dynamic infrastructures.
3. True – When a monolithic application becomes too big, its benefits start to disappear.
4. True – Debugging becomes difficult due to its distributed nature.
5. True – Due to tight interdependencies, monolithic applications are difficult to maintain and patch in the long-term.

Chapter 2: Cloud-Native Applications

1. True – Kubernetes allows different runtimes for containers.
2. False – Due to the independent size of microservices, cloud-native applications are simpler than monolithic applications but difficult to test.
3. True – Without tools, it is difficult to diagnose cloud-native applications.
4. True – Apache Mesos does much more than Kubernetes, but Kubernetes excels in container orchestration compared to Mesos.
5. True – Due to its large community and support for a variety of features, Kubernetes has become the de-facto container orchestration system.

Chapter 3: Service Mesh Architecture

1. True – The service mesh is an abstract layer on top of applications.
2. False – Sidecar proxies live next to a microservice, mainly in the data plane. However, system components in a control plane may also have associated sidecars.

3. True – The service mesh is like an abstract application layer on top of the application stack and provide a L7 traffic management, security, and observability.

Chapter 4: Service Mesh Providers

1. True – At the time of writing, Istio and Linkerd are available in Kubernetes. Istioctl can run in a VM environment for integration but it doesn't have good adoption rates.
2. False – Linkerd developed its own sidecar proxy written in Rust, whereas Istio and Consul use the Envoy sidecar, which is developed by Lyft.
3. False – The non-availability of a control plane will not stop sidecar-enabled microservices from functioning, though some capabilities may not be available.

Chapter 5: Service Mesh Interface and SPIFFE

1. True – SPIFFE is a specification and not a toolset, similar to Kubernetes' **Container Network Interface (CNI)**, **Container Storage Interface (CSI)**, and **Container Runtime Interface (CRI)**.
2. False – The service mesh interface is a specification that service mesh providers can use to provide interoperability.
3. True – At the time of writing, Istio and Consul use SPIFFE.
4. True – Istio developers produced their own SPIFFE implementation instead of using SPIRE.

Chapter 6: Building Your Own Kubernetes Environment

1. A). Apache Mesos is not a Kubernetes platform.
2. False – Kubernetes can be deployed in many environments, including a simple VM.
3. True – A Kubernetes cluster is meant for container-based applications.

4. True – Kubernetes services can be used to register a monolithic application to provide integration between cloud-native applications hosted in Kubernetes and monolithic applications outside Kubernetes.

5. False – It is simple to build your own Kubernetes cluster.

Chapter 7: Understanding the Istio Service Mesh

1. Layer 7 – This is the network layer that the service mesh works on.

2. All of the above.

3. False – The Istio control plane is not a single point of failure since applications can continue to run without a control plane,

4. True – A true service mesh is formed through a data plane where there's an Envoy sidecar proxy next to each microservice, which helps achieve service mesh functions.

5. False – Istio can span multiple Kubernetes clusters through a replicated control plane, a shared control plane using a single network and a shared control plane using a multi-network.

6. True – At the time of writing, Istio service discovery integration with Consul is in its alpha phase.

7. False – This should be the other way around. Pilot pushes configuration to Envoy, which manages traffic.

8. False – Istio primitives are **Custom Resource Definitions (CRD)** and can be managed by `kubectl`, as well as `istioctl`.

9. True – Istio's mTLS implementation comes as a self-service model since it is out of the box and controlled through a parameter.

10. True – Kiali (originally developed at RedHat) is used to observe the service mesh for connectivity and traffic patterns.

Chapter 8: Installing a Demo Application

1. True – Kubernetes provides its own DNS server.

2. Polyglot application – Each microservice can use its own language.

3. True – The service mesh architecture is only for microservice applications.

4. False – A pod's IP address can change when it is redeployed/rescheduled.

5. True – For the duration of the service, its IP address is immutable.

6. True – The service's IP address is linked to the pod's IP address through Kubernetes endpoints.

Chapter 9: Installing Istio

1. True – At the time of writing, Istio can only be used in a Kubernetes environment, though integration with VMs is being planned.

2. False – The Istio sidecar can be enabled for new applications if the namespace is annotated with the `istio-injection=enabled` label. The sidecar can be enabled through the `istioctl` command.

3. True – Istio has more than 57 CRDs.

4. True – It is necessary to install CRDs to extend Kubernetes so that it can use Istio's features.

5. True – The existing application needs to be taken down first and then you need to enable sidecar proxy injection, either by annotating the namespace with a label or by using `istioctl kube-inject` to modify the existing application's manifest.

6. False – It is possible to disable the sidecar for a microservice by setting the pod annotation to `sidecar.istio.io/inject: "false"`, even when a namespace has already been annotated with the `istio-injection=enabled` label.

7. False – Istio custom resources can be managed through the `istioctl` command, as well as through the `kubectl` command.

Chapter 10: Exploring Istio Traffic Management Capabilities

1. True – Traffic routing is a feature of Envoy, which receives its configuration from Pilot.

2. True – Istio can work in a zero-trust network and still provide enterprise-grade security.

3. True – You can enable a reverse firewall in Istio through an Egress gateway, which will block outbound access from microservices.

4. True – Dark launches/Family-and-Friend Testing is used to route traffic to select groups of users without their knowledge.
5. True – An Istio gateway can have multiple virtual services that can be used by different application owners.
6. True – Istio's virtual service is a superset of a Kubernetes service since it provides more features and functions than its native service.
7. True – The destination rule defines the configuration, but it has no role in traffic routing since the subsets that it defines are used in virtual services.
8. True – Load balancing at the Envoy level is done at the L7 networking layer and not at L3/L4.
9. True – You don't get the response back from the mirrored service.

Chapter 11: Exploring Istio Security Features

1. True – It is the end user's responsibility to rotate certificates and keys that have been defined for the Ingress gateway in order to secure traffic from external clients and send it to the edge microservice. Note that Istio's Citadel rotates certificates for microservices.
2. True – There can only be one `MeshPolicy` (with `name` as the default) that will apply mTLS mesh-wide.
3. True – Mutual TLS can be as granular as possible from the namespace level to the service level by defining a policy.
4. True – Mutual TLS can be enabled through destination rules or by using MeshPolicy.
5. True – Istio is capable of shielding modern microservices applications from running in a zero-trust network without any changes needing to be made to the application code.
6. True – Istio makes VPNs and firewalls redundant if security has been implemented properly.
7. True – It is the responsibility of the edge microservice to manage JWT for authorizations.
8. True – Istio's Secret Discovery Service mounts secrets in pods automatically.
9. True – Istio's Citadel will rotate certificates and keys every 90 days by default.

10. True – The Envoy sidecar checks the TTL of the certificates. The Istio node agent, if enabled, can request a new certificate from Citadel. It is Citadel that pushes certificates to Envoy, not the node agent.

Chapter 12: Enabling Istio Policy Controls

1. False – Quota assignment to services is enforced through Mixer.
2. True – Rate limits to services are pushed down to the Envoy proxy through Mixer.
3. True – A list checker handler is assigned a list of source IPs to create a list. A source IP instance list entry is created to check the IP address that was found at the Ingress gateway. A rule can be created to enforce a blacklist or whitelist for IP addresses that can connect to the service.
4. True – To enable policy enforcement, you can edit the Istio config map and set `disablePolicyChecks=true`.

Chapter 13: Exploring Istio Telemetry Features

1. True – A sidecar proxy sends asynchronous telemetry data to backend services.
2. False – Observability and monitoring a system are two different things.
3. True – The recommended web UIs for Istio's monitoring and observability features are Grafana, Prometheus, Kiali, and Jaegar.
4. False – Port forwarding is not the only way to access different web UI components. Ingress rules and node port mechanisms can also be used to access a web UI.
5. True – Istio reports multiple spans within a microservice chain.
6. True – Prometheus is a web UI tool that can visualize collected data or metrics.
7. True – Custom dashboards in Grafana provide details for inbound and outbound workloads.
8. True – All mis-configurations are highlighted in red under the YAML viewer in Kiali.

Chapter 14: Understanding the Linkerd Service Mesh

1. True – Linkerd has an automatic protocol and TCP connection detection.
2. False – Linkerd does not provide its own ingress controller.
3. False – The Linkerd proxy is written in Rust, while control plane components are written in Go.
4. True – The control and data planes can be in a single namespace if we want them to be. Note that admin privileges are required to create CRDs.
5. True – When a Linkerd proxy is injected into a running pod using the `linkerd inject` command, the pod is restarted automatically.
6. False – The pod will be recreated if we want to add a debug sidecar.
7. True – The retry budget helps us avoid a retry storm. We don't need to configure Linkerd to achieve this.
8. True – For automatic sidecar injection, Istio needs a namespace to be labeled with `istio-injection=enabled` and also needs a namespace to be annotated as `linkerd.io/inject: Enabled`.

Chapter 15: Installing Linkerd

1. False – You do not need SSH access to the master node to create the Linkerd control plane.
2. True – You require a `cluster-admin` role to install control plane configuration.
3. False – You do not require a `cluster-admin` role to install the control plane.
4. False – You need to annotate a namespace, not a label, with `linkerd.io/inject: enabled`.
5. False – You need to annotate the pod with `linkerd.io/inject: disabled` to exclude it from getting the sidecar proxy.

Chapter 16: Exploring the Reliability Features of Linkerd

1. True – Kubernetes does load balancing at the connection level (L4).
2. True – Linkerd does load balancing at the application level (L7).
3. True – Linkerd's load balancing is out of the box and requires zero configuration.
4. True – Retrying Linkerd requires a configuration-patch service profile with `isRetryable: true`.
5. True – A Linkerd service profile can be generated automatically, even if the Swagger API isn't available for the service through the Linkerd profile command.
6. True – The retry budget is about adaptive retries instead of a fixed number of retries.
7. True – The service profile is needed to provide aggregated route metrics.

Chapter 17: Exploring the Security Features of Linkerd

1. True – The TLS between service-to-service communication is fully automatic in Linkerd.
2. False – The TLS between the Ingress gateway and the edge service of the application is the application user's responsibility.
3. True – The `linkerd-identity` component of Linkerd's control plane is the **Certificate Authority (CA)** for the data plane proxies.
4. True – The `linkerd-identity` component automatically rotates the certificates for `linkerd-proxy` in the data plane.
5. False – The `linkerd-identity` component doesn't automatically rotate certificate for its own CA.
6. True – You can use trusted certificates from your own CA for `linkerd-identity`, but only at the time of install.
7. True – You can change the trusted certificate of the control plane at any time, but it requires reinstalling the control plane.

Chapter 18: Exploring the Observability Features of Linkerd

1. True – Linkerd only stores data for 6 hours. This can be configured so that we can increase or decrease the time limit.
2. True – Linkerd provides distributed tracing, which can be seen from the dashboard as well as through the CLI `tap` command.
3. True – Linkerd integration with the external Prometheus is the user's responsibility.
4. True – Linkerd's Prometheus uses the Pull model to collect data from service proxies.

Chapter 19: Understanding the Consul Service Mesh

1. False – Consul is a distributed control plane.
2. True – The Consul agent must run on all Kubernetes nodes.
3. True – Consul services can be viewed as North-South network traffic, whereas Ingress gateways to multiple Kubernetes clusters can be treated as East-West network traffic.
4. False – The Mesh gateway does not decrypt network traffic between two gateways to determine the destination service.
5. True – Consul service discovery in a Kubernetes environment is automatic.
6. True – Consul supports multiple data centers out of the box.

Chapter 20: Installing Consul

1. True – Consul's service mesh works across heterogeneous environments and data centers across different regions.
2. True – In a Consul cluster, the Consul servers can be in Kubernetes or in VMs.
3. False –The Consul members can join an existing Consul cluster from a VM or Kubernetes.

4. False – Consul servers remain within the same data centers but they can communicate with other data center. Consul servers use the WAN protocol.

5. True – Kubernetes can send write requests to any Consul servers, but only the leader Consul server writes that information to the distributed key-value store.

6. False – Consul uses its own key-value database store to maintain the state of Consul clusters. It doesn't use Kubernetes etcd.

Chapter 21: Exploring the Service Discovery Features of Consul

1. False – Consul Connect is the service mesh for Kubernetes, as well as VMs.

2. False – Consul Connect uses sidecar proxies for services in a Kubernetes environment.

3. True – Consul Intentions are authorizations for services.

4. True – Consul's K/V store is replicated across data centers automatically.

5. True – Consul mTLS from a sidecar proxy to another sidecar proxy is fully automatic.

6. True – Consul comes with its own Certificate Authority so that it can issue certificates to sidecar proxies.

7. True – Consul integration with Kubernetes for service discovery is done by defining a Consul DNS server as an upstream DNS in the Kubernetes CoreDNS configuration.

Chapter 22: Exploring Traffic Management in Consul

1. True – Consul traffic management is done at Layer 7 of the **Open System Interconnection (OSI)**.

2. True – The service-resolver definition that's used to declare subsets is based on filters that are used on the metadata of the services. In Kubernetes deployments, such metadata is picked up automatically by Kubernetes through its integration to Consul.

3. True – The Mesh gateway mode is akin to the Egress gateway.

4. True – If service-defaults defines a Mesh gateway mode as being local, each call is made to the Mesh gateway to determine the upstream service.

5. True – Traffic routing using a service-router can only be used for path-based routing.

6. True – Service-resolver can be used to provide a service failover from one data center to another.

Other Books You May Enjoy

If you enjoyed this book, you may be interested in these other books by Packt:

Hands-On Serverless Computing with Google Cloud
Richard Rose

ISBN: 978-1-83882-799-1

- Explore the various options for deploying serverless workloads on Google Cloud
- Determine the appropriate serverless product for your application use case
- Integrate multiple lightweight functions to build scalable and resilient services
- Increase productivity through build process automation
- Understand how to secure serverless workloads using service accounts
- Build a scalable architecture with Google Cloud Functions and Cloud Run

Mastering Azure Serverless Computing

Lorenzo Barbieri, Massimo Bonanni

ISBN: 978-1-78995-122-6

- Create and deploy advanced Azure Functions
- Learn to extend the runtime of Azure Functions
- Orchestrate your logic through code or a visual workflow
- Add caching, security, routing, and filtering to your APIs
- Use serverless technologies in real-world scenarios
- Understand how to apply DevOps and automation to your working environment

Leave a review - let other readers know what you think

Please share your thoughts on this book with others by leaving a review on the site that you bought it from. If you purchased the book from Amazon, please leave us an honest review on this book's Amazon page. This is vital so that other potential readers can see and use your unbiased opinion to make purchasing decisions, we can understand what our customers think about our products, and our authors can see your feedback on the title that they have worked with Packt to create. It will only take a few minutes of your time, but is valuable to other potential customers, our authors, and Packt. Thank you!

Index